D1035405

TOWARD A NEW ORDER OF SEA POWER, 1918-1922

Toward a New Order of Sea Power

AMERICAN NAVAL POLICY

AND THE WORLD SCENE, 1918-1922

By

HAROLD AND MARGARET SPROUT

GREENWOOD PRESS, PUBLISHERS

NEW YORK

The Library of Congress cataloged this book as follows:

Sprout, Harold Hance, 1901–

Toward a new order of sea power; American naval policy and the world scene, 1918–1922, by Harold and Margaret Sprout. New York, Greenwood Press [1969, °1943]

xii, 336 p. illus., maps. 24 cm.

Continuation of the authors' The rise of American naval power.
Bibliographical footnotes.

1. U. S. Navy—History. 2. U. S.—History, Naval—20th century. 3. Sea-power. I. Sprout, Margaret (Tuttle) 1903– joint author. II. Title.

E182.S79 1969 359'.009 69–14092
MARC

Library of Congress [3]

Originally published in 1943 by Princeton University Press, London

Reprinted with the permission of Princeton University Press

Reprinted by Greenwood Press, Inc.

First Greenwood reprinting 1969
Second Greenwood reprinting 1974
Third Greenwood reprinting 1975
Fourth Greenwood reprinting 1976

Library of Congress Catalog Card Number 69-14092

ISBN 0-8371-1168-4

Printed in the United States of America

Foreword to the Second Edition

NEARLY three years have elapsed since the initial publication of this book. At that time, German planes and submarines were hammering at the citadels of British sea power in the Atlantic and Mediterranean. A year later, Japan struck at the bases of British and American sea power in the Pacific. Today the United Nations are carrying the war to the Axis. Tomorrow, as in 1918, we shall have to build a new world order upon the ruins of the old. Discussion and study of this problem returns again and again to the Versailles Treaty and to the Washington Conference.

In this connection one recalls the pre-Washington Conference discussions of the future rôle of airplanes in control of the seas. In retrospect one is amazed both at the foresight of a few and at the blind conservatism which prevented so many from grasping the inevitable implications of revolutionary advances in aviation and in other branches of military technology.

We have expanded the section of chapter one which deals with the foundations of England's global sea power in the nineteenth century. This analysis, it is hoped, will help to focus more clearly certain elements of potential stability upon which a more durable peace may be constructed in the future.

We have also amplified the passage in chapter two relating to the discussion of 1898 over the fate of Spain's Caroline and Marianas Islands in the Western Pacific. Japan's seizure of these islands in 1914 had strategical implications for the United States which were not finally hammered home until the tragic winter of 1941-42. But some Americans, both inside and outside government circles, foresaw in 1918 the danger of leaving Japan astride our military road to the Philippines. Since the first appearance of this book the State Department has made public an important document on this question. This document, paraphrased in chapter six of this new edition, is a memorandum prepared within the State Department for the use of the American Peace Commission of 1919. It states in unequivocal terms the consequences of leaving Japan in possession of the Western Pacific Islands.

Elsewhere in the book we have made numerous minor revisions, in some instances to correct errors of interpretation, in others to clarify possibly ambiguous passages. In making these changes we have had deeply appreciated assistance from Dr. A. C. Davidonis of Princeton University, author of an important forthcoming book on the naval settlement following the last war.

H. S.
M. S.

Princeton, May 20, 1943.

Contents

Maps, Tables, and Illustrations

☆ ☆ ☆ ☆ ☆ ☆ ☆ ☆ ☆ ☆ ☆ ☆ ☆ ☆ ☆ ☆ ☆ ☆ ☆ ☆

Chart and Compass

THE central theme of this book is the changing rôle of sea power, especially American sea power, both in the crumbling world order which crashed to ruin in August 1914, and during the years of political chaos and uncertainty which followed the armistice of November 1918.

Our point of departure is 1890, the year in which appeared the first of Captain Alfred Thayer Mahan's books on sea power—books which were to recast naval thought and give impetus and direction to naval development the world over. By 1890, moreover, Great Britain, whose virtually global command of the seas had been Mahan's chief inspiration, had definitely reached the zenith of a rise to world dominion and influence without precedent in political annals.

This Pax Britannica, which had fostered and was then still supporting a world economy that approached the dimensions of political sovereignty and a world order, had evolved from a unique combination of geographical and other factors. But by 1890 there were perceptible signs of impending change in that historic order of sea power. Developments even then upon the horizon—strategic, technological, economic, and political—were destined steadily to undermine and weaken, and finally to destroy, the edifice of Pax Britannica which had seemed at one time as enduring as the Rock of Gibraltar itself.

The war of 1914 brought crashing down in ruins the whole structure of world order. For reasons to be analyzed later in these pages, British sea power, despite its phenomenal wartime development and the overwhelming victory of the Allies, was unable after the war to reassert that stabilizing world influence which had formerly been the essence of Pax Britannica. And for reasons likewise manifest to readers of this volume, no other single Power in 1918 could step into England's historic rôle.

The United States, it is true, was at that time widely hailed as England's destined successor to the trident of Neptune. The American Government had well advanced plans for raising the United States to first rank upon the sea. But there were grounds for doubting whether the American Navy, under conditions then prevailing, could translate nominal primacy into a Pax Americana which could be enforced in distant seas. And statesmen, furthermore, could not safely ignore the possibility that any determined attempt thus to extend the sway of American naval power into distant seas might well embroil the United States with Great Britain and Japan, and even conceivably result in renewed conflict which would postpone indefinitely the task of economic and political reconstruction.

In brief, the world naval problem of 1918 was to fashion some new order of sea power along lines which would head off the impending struggle for control of the seas and which would at the same time provide that steadying global influence that British sea power alone had formerly provided, but could no longer provide.

The efforts of statesmen and of their peoples to envisage this problem, and their uncertain steps toward its solution—from the armistice of 1918, through the Peace Conference of 1919, through the fateful struggle over the League of Nations, and on through the Washington Conference for the Limitation of Armament—these are some of the events with which this study is fundamentally concerned.

This concern, however, arises from no mere historical curiosity. During the years herein covered, the defense problem of the United States was critically reexamined in the light both of World War experience and of rapid developments in war technology; and many of the contentions then put forward are today, after twenty years of procrastination and delay, obtaining belated acceptance under the stress of another grave national emergency.

Indeed, it would be difficult to select a period more instructive with regard to so many aspects of the fatefully interrelated problems of national defense and world order. During the years following 1918, for example, some of the most widely accepted doctrines of sea power were fearlessly challenged with arguments destined to be tested twenty years later in the crash and roar of battle. In the historic League of Nations debate of 1919-1920, to cite another example, the necessary rôle of American sea power in any enduring world order was repeatedly asserted with contentions which may yet have to prevail if even a remnant of western civilization is to survive. The events which preceded the Washington Conference emphasized the dangers of Anglo-American antagonism. The Conference itself dramatically emphasized the potentialities of Anglo-American cooperation. And the Washington Treaties sketched in outline a new order of sea power which, with a little more of imagination and of courage, might have guarded the world's peace for generations still to come.

That opportunity was wasted; but another opportunity, one fervently hopes, may yet come again. If it does, we shall need all the wisdom we can derive from past experience. And it is with the hope that it may contribute something at least to the solution of these national and world problems, that we offer this chapter in the annals of sea power and world politics.

ACKNOWLEDGMENTS

A large number of institutions and individuals have assisted in varying degrees and ways in the execution of this study. Broadly speaking, this assistance has included the location of basic materials, access to new sources of information, helpful criticism, and financial support. Without such help and cooperation, the book would have been indefinitely delayed, if indeed it could have been completed at all.

We have received invaluable aid from a number of men who participated actively in the grand attempt to establish a new order of sea power after the war of 1914-1918. Through the good offices of President Harold Willis Dodds of Princeton University, our work was brought to the favorable attention of Mr. Chief Justice Charles Evans Hughes and Colonel Theodore Roosevelt. These two men, together with Admiral William Veazie Pratt, played leading rôles in the naval phase of the Washington Conference for the Limitation of Armament.

We are particularly indebted to Mr. Hughes who read our entire manuscript and offered much invaluable criticism, together with additional information nowhere else available.

We are similarly indebted to Colonel Roosevelt and to Admiral Pratt. The former generously allowed us unrestricted access to his voluminous day-by-day diary of the Washington Conference. The latter very kindly supplied vitally essential information derived from his own extremely important rôle in that political drama.

From beginning to end we have had most cordial support and cooperation from members of the Navy Department. We owe a great deal to Captain Dudley W. Knox, Chief of the Office of Naval Records and Library, and to many other gentlemen, for repeated consultations and for their untiring assistance in finding fugitive materials and information. The Department of State has likewise extended to us every possible courtesy.

We are also indebted to the Library of Congress, particularly to the Division of Manuscripts. Through the courtesy of Dr. St. George L. Sioussat, chief of that division, we were given access to the unpublished diary of the late Honorable Chandler P. Anderson who served in an important capacity on the American legal staff at the Washington Conference.

We acknowledge a steadily accumulating indebtedness to the staff of the Princeton University Library, in particular to Mr. Malcolm O. Young, chief of the reference section. And for more general though not less helpful cooperation, we desire to thank the staff of the New York Public Library.

Adequate financial aid has inestimably expedited the execution of our project. The Benjamin D. Shreve research fellowship, awarded by Princeton University, and a Penfield travelling fellowship from the University of Pennsylvania made possible a year's release from University duties while collecting materials in the field and while preparing the manuscript for publication.

We acknowledge with deep appreciation our indebtedness to the scholars who read our manuscript in whole or in part, and whose criticism has improved every page. Among these friends are Professors Robert G. Albion, William S. Carpenter, Edward S. Corwin, Charles P. Stacey, and Walter L. Whittlesey, all of Princeton University; Professor Edward M. Earle, Dr. Alfred Vagts, and Dr. Herbert Rosinski, all of the Institute for

Advanced Study; Professor Thomas A. Bailey of Stanford University; and Dr. Tyler Dennett, formerly of the Department of State. We desire also to acknowledge the many helpful criticisms and suggestions offered by members of Professor Earle's seminar at the Institute for Advanced Study, in which several of these chapters were read and discussed during the winter of 1939-1940. While we have benefited inestimably from the help and criticism which so many have thus generously given, we alone of course are responsible for all facts and conclusions presented in this volume.

Further, we acknowledge the kind permission granted us by the following publishers to make extensive quotations from copyrighted materials: to Doubleday, Doran & Company, for quotations from Mr. R. S. Baker's *Woodrow Wilson and World Settlement* (vol. 3, copyright, 1922); to the same publisher for quotations from Mr. Mark Sullivan's *The Great Adventure at Washington* (1922); to Houghton Mifflin Company for quotations from Mr. Hector Bywater's *Sea Power in the Pacific* (1921); to the same publisher for quotations from Dr. Charles Seymour's *Intimate Papers of Colonel House* (vol. 4, 1928); to the American Society of International Law for quotations from Admiral H. S. Knapp's address, "The Limitation of Armament at the Conference of Washington," published in the *Proceedings* of that Society (1922); to the *Army and Navy Journal* for quotations from Captain D. W. Knox's *The Eclipse of American Sea Power* (1922); to *Current History Magazine* for quotations from Admiral B. A. Fiske's article, "The Strongest Navy (July 1922); to *The Fortnightly Review* for quotations from Sir Archibald Hurd's article, "The British Fleet 'Dips Its Ensign' " (March 1922); to *The Nineteenth Century & After* for quotations from Admiral Wester-Wemyss's article, "Washington: and After" (March 1922); and to *The North American Review* for quotations from Admiral W. V. Pratt's article, "Naval Policy and the Naval Treaty" (May 1922).

Finally, to the officers of the Princeton University Press we acknowledge sincere appreciation for constant aid and advice, and for an association which grows more cordial year by year.

H. S.
M. S.

Princeton, October 1, 1940.

TOWARD A NEW ORDER OF SEA POWER, 1918-1922

CHAPTER ONE

☆ ☆ ☆ ☆ ☆ ☆ ☆ ☆ ☆ ☆ ☆ ☆ ☆ ☆ ☆ ☆ ☆ ☆ ☆ ☆

The Old Order of Sea Power: Pax Britannica

IN the summer of 1884 the U.S.S. *Wachusett* was cruising on the west coast of South America. This old wooden man-of-war, dating from the early 'sixties, was a fair representative of the sea power of the United States a generation after the Civil War. The *Wachusett's* displacement of 1,600 tons was about that of a modern destroyer. She had a steam engine, but it was obsolete and out of repair. Her chief motive power was wind and sail. Her tall masts, maze of rigging, and spread of canvas differed in detail, but not in principle or in general appearance from those of the historic frigate *Constitution* built almost ninety years before, at the end of the eighteenth century. And the *Wachusett's* outmoded smooth-bore guns, except for their larger size, were not essentially unlike those which had blazed defiance at Great Britain in the War of 1812.

This old ship would soon pass on to the junk heap, along with many another veteran of the old wooden navy. Their places would soon be taken by the steel ships of a new American navy. But the old *Wachusett* would never quite pass from memory. For it was from her quarterdeck that Captain Alfred Thayer Mahan stepped in the autumn of 1884, to begin a career which would lead to fame, and affect the course of world history for generations to come.

Mahan's extraordinary rise to fame commenced with his acceptance, while serving on the Pacific Station, of an invitation to lecture on naval history and tactics at the newly founded Naval War College at Newport, Rhode Island. Mahan was at that time a middle-aged officer of solid reputation within the Service, but practically unknown outside the Navy. He had previously shown some talent for scholarship and literary expression. Freed from the drag of routine duties, this talent underwent rapid development. And in 1890, his War College lectures culminated in a book which not only carried all the leading admiralties by storm but also recast civilian thinking and national policies the world over.

This book, *The Influence of Sea Power upon History, 1660-1783*, appeared at a critical juncture in naval development and world politics. Naval art and science were at that time passing through the later stages of a sweeping technological revolution. The old *Wachusett* more closely resembled the frigates of the preceding century than the steel cruisers which in 1890 constituted the nucleus of the New American Navy. The long struggle between sails and steam was drawing to a close, with the forces of reaction everywhere in retreat. Smooth-bore, muzzle-loading guns had given way to breech-loading rifles. If naval gunnery was still an uncertain art, the invention of range-finders and other precision instruments was soon to give it some of the attributes of a science.

Wooden walls had become, by 1890, as obsolete as sails and smooth-bores. Only steel could support the ever increasing weight and thrust of ordnance and engines. Only armored decks and sides could hope to withstand the shattering impact of explosive shells. The practical impossibility of combining maximum speed, gun power, and armor protection in a single ship of any given displacement had already brought about far greater differentiation of types than had ever developed in the era of sails.

These naval types ranged downward in size from the battleship, direct descendant of the eighteenth century ship-of-the-line. The battleship (a term which the layman too often associates with any and all types of warships) embodied a combination of features that distinguished it from other naval craft. These included a battery of the largest guns housed in revolving turrets; heavy armor plating on these gun houses as well as on waterline, decks, control tower, and other vital parts of the ship; and engines capable of driving the vessel at a moderate rate of speed. The exact ratio between these three elements—gun power, armor protection, and speed—varied from time to time, and from one navy to another. Persistent efforts, under the spur of international competition, to secure as much as possible of all three qualities, were already reflected in the increasing size and cost of battleships, a trend which was eventually to produce the huge hundred million dollar super-dreadnought of the present day.

The armored cruiser was just emerging as a distinct type in 1890. In this type, gun power and defensive strength were partially sacrificed so as to allow a higher proportion of total weight for propelling machinery, with a resultant increase in speed. The armored cruiser also was destined to evolve into an ever larger and costlier ship, culminating in the 40,000 to 50,000-ton battle cruiser. And these two types—battleships and battle cruisers—together comprise the category known as capital ships.

A third type which had taken form by 1890 was the so-called protected cruiser. This was a smaller ship, with greater speed, lighter guns, an armored deck, and perhaps a little protection at a few other vital spots. This type was the modern counterpart of the eighteenth century frigates and war sloops. Designed mainly as a commerce raider, the chief requisites of a protected cruiser were sufficient speed to overhaul merchantmen and to escape the enemy's heavy ships; and a battery adequate to overwhelm its prey, and if necessary to fight hostile cruisers sent in pursuit. The protected cruiser was destined to evolve into a number of subtypes—light cruisers, heavy cruisers, etc.—with a variety of functions which included fleet reconnaissance and commerce protection as well as commerce destruction.

A fourth type, just taking form in 1890, was the sea-going torpedo boat. Invention of the automotive torpedo had created a need for small craft which could discharge these fairly short-range self-propelling projectiles close to enemy ships, and then escape quickly from the storm of shell fire that would be directed at them. The resulting need of protection for the larger ships was soon to give rise to the so-called torpedo boat destroyer—really a bigger and faster torpedo boat equipped with guns as well as torpedo tubes. And the destroyer was to become not only a formidable offensive craft, but also (especially after the advent of the submarine) the special protector of all surface shipping against the menace of hostile torpedo attack.

Other developments in war technology were just over the 1890 horizon. The marine mine was a well known, though inadequately appreciated weapon. The "submarine torpedo boat" was an experimental toy which a handful of dreamers predicted would one day revolutionize naval warfare. And only slightly more distant was the airplane whose rapid rise was within a generation to shake the foundations of naval doctrine and theory.[1]

Advances in naval architecture and technology already achieved, to say nothing of those still to come, had far reaching strategic implications. Of these none was more important than the steadily narrowing radius of large-scale naval operations in war. None, moreover, was to be so persistently ignored by the civilian public. Again and again, public opinion, especially in America, was to grow hysterical over the menace of dangers so remote as to be virtually nonexistent, and in the same breath to expect its own armed forces to perform miracles without precedent in the annals of modern war.

This propensity, it must be admitted, was not infrequently fostered by alarms emanating from the armed Services and from other groups interested in armament expansion. But it is also true that Mahan, acknowledged dean of modern naval strategy, did not hesitate to deplore this tendency of the lay mind to exaggerate the mobility of mechanically powered warships, and to ignore the limiting factor of distance in modern naval warfare.

Early in his literary career, Mahan lamented that "scientific advances" blinded the public to the "qualifying conditions" of technological progress. "Men's imaginations," he observed, "have developed abnormal agility" for drawing "mental pictures . . . in which fleets get about as though by magic," whereas the "movements of modern fleets are in fact extremely hampered, and their scope restricted, by the very elements to which they owe much of their power." Steam conferred "ease of movements both in time and direction" never known in the era of sails. But the fuel, ammunition, and other supplies required to keep modern warships in operation limited their movements in "duration of time" far more rigidly than had the "corresponding

[1] Another popular weapon of 1890 was the ram, a steel shoe fitted to the prow of naval craft. The ram, which at one time was widely hailed with enthusiasm, became useless as the development of more powerful ordnance steadily lengthened gunnery ranges. And it became a positive encumbrance as the demands for higher speed necessitated radical changes in bow design.

factors" essential to the operations of the eighteenth century frigate or ship-of-the-line.[2]

Passing from technology to naval doctrine and theory, the outstanding fact of 1890 was the prevailing conservatism of naval thought, nowhere more so than in the United States. For nearly a century the framers of American naval policy had proceeded on the assumption that commerce raiding and passive coast defense were the Navy's two basic functions in war.

The second envisaged sea power merely as an adjunct of land power. The aim was to stop the enemy at the water's edge; and the method was to reenforce stationary fortifications and mobile land forces with various kinds of defensive war craft—floating batteries, torpedo boats, etc.—distributed among the principal harbors and other strategic points along the seaboard.

Commerce raiding, technically known as a *guerre de course*, was a hit-and-run guerilla warfare, akin to piracy. It was carried on with solitary roving cruisers and privateers. And its object was to disrupt the sea-borne commerce, and hence the economic life and military power of the enemy country.

Both commerce raiding and local coast defense unquestionably entered into any comprehensive system of naval strategy. But past experience seemed to show that neither was in itself adequate to cope with certain war situations in which a maritime country might find itself involved. Commerce raiding had crippled neither Great Britain in the Anglo-American War of 1812, nor the North in the American Civil War. Dispersion of naval forces along the seaboard had not saved the United States from invasion in the earlier conflict, nor the Southern Confederacy in the later. Observers had repeatedly criticized the strategic dispersion of naval forces, whether along the coast or upon the high sea, as contrary to the first principle of military art and science. But they had been voices crying in the wilderness. And in 1890 the strategic doctrine and theory of the United States still envisaged local coast defense and a *guerre de course* as the Navy's two functions in war.

Turning from strategic theory to the world of affairs, the outstanding fact of 1890 was the political importance of sea power in general, and in particular the world-wide naval dominance of

[2] "Blockade in Relation to Naval Strategy," *Proc. of U.S. Nav. Inst.*, Vol. 21, Nov. 1895, pp. 851, 863.

Great Britain. This situation was the result of a long revolutionary as well as evolutionary process. From earliest recorded times, mankind had utilized the seas as highways of communication and commerce. Empire builders had repeatedly fought for control of these marine highways. Pirates and privateers had roamed the seas in search of loot and plunder. The sea was a factor in the military defense of every country with a maritime frontier. Depending on conditions and circumstances, it might be either a barrier against attack or an avenue of approach for blockade and invasion. On the struggle for the world's sea routes had depended the outcome of many wars and the fate of nations.

Armed force upon the seas had played a rôle of considerable importance in the political economy of ancient and medieval times. Its importance had grown with the discoveries and explorations of the fifteenth and sixteenth centuries. Sea power was a large if incommensurable factor in the mercantilistic expansion of the seventeenth and eighteenth centuries. Ability to seize, hold, and exploit oversea colonies turned in one way or another on a country's armed forces upon the seas. The successes and failures of British and other empire builders in those restless times were closely related to the relative strength and efficiency of their respective navies, and to their consequent ability or inability to dominate the water routes between western Europe on the one hand, and Africa, Asia, and the Americas on the other.

Sea power, especially British sea power, played a still larger rôle in the world economy which arose from the industrial revolution. For various reasons, the application of mechanical power to manufacturing and the accumulation of investment capital commenced earlier and proceeded more rapidily in England than in other countries. British imports of food and raw materials, and exports of manufactures, came in the nineteenth century to comprise a considerable portion of the world's seaborne commerce. London became the business and financial center of an economic community which eventually embraced not only the British Empire but also many politically independent countries in several continents. The British Navy, exercising a virtually world-wide command of the seas, gave to the members of this world community, as well as to the components of the British Empire, a fair assurance of uninterrupted trade as long as Great Britain chose to remain at peace with them. And the combined power of fleets and finance enabled British statesmen to wield an influence abroad which approached, though it never quite attained, the dimensions of sovereignty and a world order.

The Sea-Power Interpretation of History

When Mahan embarked in 1884 upon his momentous voyage of historical discovery and exploration, he was an avowed anti-imperialist, sternly opposed to oversea expansion and to the military trappings of imperialism.[3] As fate would have it, his studies gradually focused on the commerce, politics, and wars of the seventeenth and eighteenth centuries. Reading and reflection on that era of mercantilism in the Old World, and of colonial exploitation in the New, wrought a profound transformation in Mahan's thinking and outlook. *The Influence of Sea Power upon History*, published in 1890, revealed him as a thoroughgoing expansionist and a crusader for a brand of imperialism which bore the unmistakable imprint of eighteenth century mercantilism.[4]

According to the Mahan of 1890, history taught the ineluctable lesson that nations may rise or decline but never stand still. Expansion—political, economic, cultural—was the essence of national greatness. To support a program of expansion, a government must have access to accumulated wealth. A large and flourishing foreign commerce was the surest means of accumulating wealth. But a vigorous and growing foreign commerce was not to be had merely for the asking. To compete successfully in the world-wide struggle for markets, a country must maintain a large merchant marine. In addition, such a marine would itself contribute materially to a nation's wealth, by sharing in a carrying trade that would otherwise go to the ships of competing nations.[5]

[3] Captain W. D. Puleston, *The Life and Works of Captain Alfred Thayer Mahan* (1939), Chap. 11.

[4] Mahan frankly admitted his conversion to imperialism. See, for example, his "The Growth of our National Feeling," *World's Work*, Vol. 3, Feb. 1902, pp. 1763, 1764.

[5] According to the theory of eighteenth century mercantilism, national power, security, and prosperity, all depended upon a country's ability to accumulate large and ever increasing stocks of the precious metals used in coinage. One way to secure these was to increase exports and reduce imports of merchandise. An excess of

These valuable assets all required protection. To provide its merchantmen with secure havens on their outward as well as on their homeward voyages, a country must have oversea colonies. To guard these vessels upon the high seas, a strong navy was indispensable. Such a navy was likewise essential to defend the sea approaches to the mother country and to its oversea colonies. And the colonies, in turn, provided sites for bases and stations to support the navy overseas.

While a strong navy was necessary to guarantee security to a country's shipping, a prosperous merchant marine was, at the same time, the backbone of its naval power. Such a marine fostered seafaring and maritime industries. Merchant shipping, a seafaring class, and strong maritime industries provided a "shield of defensive power behind which" a people could gain time in an emergency to "develop its reserve of strength." And in countries with a representative form of government, such maritime interests could be depended upon, in turn, to exert the political pressure and influence necessary to keep the navy at a high standard of strength and excellence.[6]

Foundations of British Sea Power

Mahan's mercantilistic and imperialistic interpretation of history was largely and more or less admittedly rationalized and generalized from the simultaneous rise of the British Navy and the British Empire. The principal sea routes of the world had become the internal communications of that Empire. The security of those communications which radiated in every direction from the British Isles, crossing and criss-crossing all the oceans and larger seas, depended ultimately upon armed force. And that force was supplied in the main by the British Navy which had come to exercise virtually a world-wide command of the seas.

exports—a so-called favorable balance of trade—would cause bullion to flow into a country. To prevent an outflow of money for freight charges and seamen's wages, a government should restrict the ocean carrying trade to its own nationals. Colonies were desirable assets, to be likewise administered for the benefit of home industries. And to this end, foreign goods as well as ships should be excluded as far as possible from a country's home and colonial markets.

[6] The foregoing summary is based exclusively on Mahan's first book. See especially Chap. 1, and pp. 225-6.

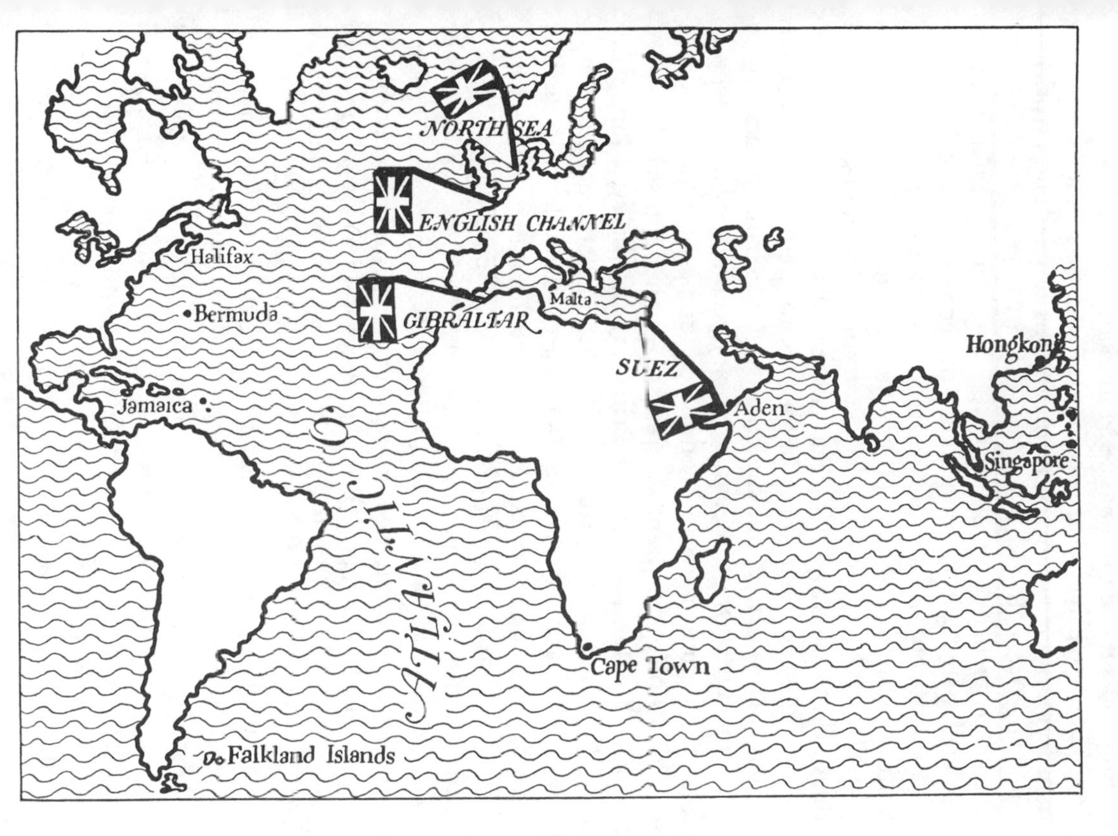

Geography and British Sea Power

England's naval dominance Mahan attributed largely, though not quite exclusively, to certain strategic dispositions and tactical formations which, after generations of trial and error, had come to govern British naval operations in war. England's remarkable security, he pointed out, had not been achieved by dispersing the British Navy along the coasts of the British Isles or by distributing its ships among the oversea colonies. The British Admiralty in time of war had not guarded the Empire's global sea communications by scattering its men-of-war around the world by ones and twos. Such operations were sometimes useful; but they were distinctly secondary to the primary objective which was to search out the enemy's forces, and to destroy or drive them from the seas, as a necessary preliminary to the wholesale destruction of enemy commerce, and to the protection of England's own merchant shipping upon the high seas.[7]

From his interpretation of British naval history, Mahan deduced a fundamental principle: the doctrine of concentration of power; in its applied form, the doctrine of battle-fleet supremacy. This doctrine he endorsed and supported with reasoning which ran somewhat as follows: Local floating defenses might supplement land forces in repelling an invader; but these could neither prevent nor break up sea blockades. Solitary roving cruisers might raid the enemy's coast and commerce, and conceivably do a great deal of damage. But commerce raiding could never in itself yield decisive results. And it could not even seriously harass the enemy unless one's cruisers could restock and refit at ports conveniently near to the heavily traveled lanes of enemy commerce.

History, as Mahan read it, taught the inescapable lesson that this kind of hit-and-run guerilla warfare, while often a useful supplement to, was not an effective substitute for, command of the sea by a massed fleet of line-of-battle ships capable of destroying the enemy's armed forces or of driving them to cover; of blockading their seaports and thereby disrupting their oversea communications at the source; and of supporting one's own

[7] For Mahan's analysis of the development of British naval strategy, see, for example, *The Influence of Sea Power upon History*, pp. 296, 525, 534; *The Influence of Sea Power upon the French Revolution and Empire* (1892), Vol. 2, pp. 61-2, 106; *Naval Strategy* (1911), p. 68.

cruisers patrolling the sea routes and escorting one's own merchant shipping through zones of special danger.[8]

It is important to remember, however, though all too frequently forgotten or ignored, that British sea power rested upon a number of things besides a big navy and a particular strategic doctrine. England owed its global command of the seas also and quite as much to a remarkable and unique concurrence of conditions—geographical, technological, economic, and political—which began to take shape in the seventeenth century and lasted down to the close of the nineteenth century. Without this favorable setting a vastly greater expenditure of military effort would have been required to achieve the same preponderance of power, if indeed it could have been achieved at all.

The first requisite of military power is a secure primary base. Countries vary widely in the natural strength of their frontiers, and hence in the proportion of their national effort that must be devoted to purely defensive purposes. England was most favorably situated in this respect. England alone among the European Powers enjoyed the decisive advantage of insularity. The British Isles provided a national military base of great natural strength, one that could be made secure without the continuous and heavy outlays that were necessary for the defense of European land frontiers.

There was never any doubt in the mind of Mahan that England's insularity had played a vital rôle in the spectacular rise of British sea power. He repeatedly stressed this point in his historical accounts of England's successive and successful struggles with the sea power of Spain, Holland, and France. In one of his most emphatic utterances, Mahan declared: "History has conclusively demonstrated the inability of a state with even a single continental frontier to compete in naval development with one that is insular, although of smaller population and resources."[9]

British fleets also enjoyed secure havens overseas. Through a remarkable combination of muddling and foresight, England gradually acquired during the eighteenth and nineteenth centu-

[8] See, for example, *Influence of Sea Power upon French Revolution*, Vol. 2, pp. 207*ff.*, 222-3, 227-8, 343.

[9] "Considerations Governing the Disposition of Navies," *National Review*, Vol. 39, July 1902, pp. 701-11; and see also "The Persian Gulf and International Relations," *ibid.*, Vol. 40, Sept. 1902, pp. 27, 43; *Influence of Sea Power upon History*, pp. 140-1, 170; *Influence of Sea Power upon French Revolution*, Vol. 2, p. 17.

ries a world-wide network of advanced naval bases. Almost without exception these outlying stations resembled the British Isles in their natural defensive strength under conditions then prevailing. One of the earliest to pass into British hands was the Rock of Gibraltar, wrested from Spain in 1704. Connected with the mainland by only a narrow isthmus, this massive natural fortress had all the advantages of complete insularity. Malta, occupied during the Napoleonic Wars, was an island in the central narrows of the Mediterranean. The port of Alexandria, eventually to become the main citadel of British power in the eastern Mediterranean, lay on the Nile delta flanked by formidable deserts.

The Cape of Good Hope, which passed into British hands in 1805, had no overland communication whatever with the European world. Aden, occupied in 1839, was set upon a desert coast at the foot of the Red Sea, with land access only across the forbidding waterless waste of southern Arabia. Ceylon, on which another British depot developed, was an island off the tip of India. The British position in India itself was protected by the lofty Himalayan cordillera which stood athwart the land approaches from central Asia. A long chain of British island possessions extended southeastward from Singapore to Australia and New Zealand. And British shipping had, in the island of Hongkong, a secure haven off the great port of Canton in the China Sea.

In American waters the situation was much the same. Bermuda, several West Indian stations, and the Falkland Islands provided England easily defended bases at safe distances from the mainland. Halifax in Nova Scotia was England's only continental American base easily accessible from the hinterland. Thus, from Canada to Cape Horn, and from the British Isles to the China coast, British warships and merchantmen were always within reach of a haven of refuge and supply. These protected ports, of which there were many more besides those specifically mentioned, were with very few exceptions invulnerable to attack from the rear; and as long as British fleets held sway upon the oceans, they were reasonably secure against attack by sea.

This global network of British naval stations possessed not only great defensive strength but incomparable offensive value as well. Admiral Lord Fisher once declared that England held the "five keys" which "lock up the world"—Dover, Gibraltar, Alexandria, the Cape of Good Hope, and Singapore.[10] This figure of speech aptly summed up both the nature and the geographical extent of the influence wielded by the British Navy at the apex of its power.

The British Isles were the master key to this whole structure of power. England and Scotland lay between northern Europe and the Atlantic Ocean. This forced the deep-sea commerce of all northern Europe, from the farthest reaches of the Baltic, to pass through the narrow Strait of Dover under the guns of the British Navy. The only alternative was to make the long and difficult detour around to the north of Scotland with no assurance even then of escaping British cruisers patrolling those northern waters. British squadrons from a central position within easy reach of their home dockyards could blockade the Atlantic and Channel ports of France, close the Dover Strait, patrol the North Sea, and even make sweeps into the Baltic. By concentrating superior force in these narrow seas, England could prevent the junction of hostile forces from northern and from western Europe, and pretty thoroughly disrupt the flow of seaborne commerce to and from the Continent all the way from St. Petersburg to Brest. And the same British forces which denied Continental access to the Atlantic, simultaneously provided a strong shield against counterattack either on the British Isles or on British merchant shipping in the Atlantic.

The Rock of Gibraltar dominated even more completely the narrow strait which provided the only marine exit from the Mediterranean prior to the construction of the Suez Canal. All seaborne commerce to and from eastern Spain, southern France, the whole of Italy, the Balkan peninsula, the Levant, and the Black Sea hinterland had to pass through this bottleneck. The Rock also constituted a formidable military barrier between the Atlantic and Mediterranean coasts of France and of Spain. The British fortress of Malta constituted a similar barrier dominating the flow of commerce between the eastern and western basins of the Mediterranean.[11]

The opening of the Suez Canal in 1869 placed a heavier burden on British sea power but in no sense weakened England's

[10] Quoted in A. J. Marder, *The Anatomy of British Sea Power* (1940), p. 473.

[11] See, for example, *Influence of Sea Power upon History*, pp. 30, 328; *Influence of Sea Power upon the French Revolution*, Vol. 1, p. 110; *The Interest of America in Sea Power*, p. 129; "Disposition of Navies," *National Review*, Vol. 39, July 1902, pp. 709*ff*.

grip on the ports of southern Europe. The British Admiralty already possessed a naval station at Aden near the Red Sea exit into the Indian Ocean. Alexandria was later developed into a strong base near the northern terminus of the Canal. These positions, together with Malta and Gibraltar, commanded every narrow strait along this short-cut to India and the Far East, which, though legally an international thoroughfare, was actually in a military sense a British waterway under the domination of British sea power.

Thus through its hold on four narrow seas—the Suez Canal, the Mediterranean, the English Channel, and the North Sea—Great Britain could virtually dictate the terms of Europe's access to the "outer world." Under conditions prevailing until near the end of the nineteenth century, control of these four narrow seas had political and military effects felt around the globe. As long as no important center of naval power existed outside Europe, England's grip on the ocean portals of that Continent constituted in effect a global command of the seas.[12]

Mahan eventually grasped the unique character of this Pax Britannica, but only after it had begun seriously to crumble under the impact of changing conditions. In 1910 he pointed out, with reference to German naval expansion and its menace to Great Britain, that England defended its scattered dominions and colonies "not indeed by local superiorities in their several waters, an object at once unattainable and needless, but by concentrated superiority of naval force in Europe, which as yet remains the base, at once of defense and of attack, as far as other quarters of the world are concerned."[13] The following year he observed that "so long as the British fleet can maintain and assert superiority in the North Sea and around the British Isles, the entire imperial system stands secure."[14]

This incomparable position *vis-à-vis* Europe was, as we have already emphasized, the key to England's global sea power. Because of its hold on the ocean portals of Europe, the British Admiralty rarely had to station especially strong squadrons in the more distant seas. But the bases were there when needed. British

[12] For early allusions to this unique position of Great Britain, see *Influence of Sea Power upon History*, pp. 31-2; *Influence of Sea Power upon French Revolution*, Vol. 1, p. 10.

[13] *Interest of America in International Conditions* (1910), p. 61.

[14] *Naval Strategy*, p. 177; and see *ibid.*, pp. 73-4, 128-9.

detachments operating from Halifax, Bermuda, and the West Indies maintained a tight blockade of United States ports in the War of 1812. From the Falkland Islands and from the Cape of Good Hope, British naval power dominated the older sea routes to India and the Far East. From other positions already described, British sea power held every passage leading into the Indian Ocean, and penetrated into the farthest reaches of the Pacific.

There were some exceptions and qualifications of course. Britain's command of the seas approached, but never quite attained, the point of incontestability. No blockade was ever completely effective. The British Navy passed through periods of decay and mismanagement. There was always a possibility, usually a fairly remote one, that the Continental Powers would successfully combine against England. A momentary loss of command in the Atlantic contributed materially to the winning of American independence. Certain marine areas were never brought permanently under British domination. And other qualifying details might be added. But such details, even in the aggregate, detract but little from a totality of power and a leverage on world politics without precedent in naval annals; a position which, for geographical reasons, no other Power could even approach; and a position which even Great Britain itself could not sustain after the rise of modern fleets in the Western Hemisphere and the Far East, and after the rise of submarine and air power in the opening decades of the twentieth century.

CHAPTER TWO

☆ ☆ ☆ ☆ ☆ ☆ ☆ ☆ ☆ ☆ ☆ ☆ ☆ ☆ ☆ ☆ ☆ ☆ ☆ ☆

The Changing Order of Sea Power, 1890-1914

MAHAN'S master work on sea power, and the subsequent books and essays that streamed from his hurrying pen, had world-wide repercussions on naval development and world politics. Mahan's interpretation of history excited expansionist forces already stirring in Europe, in America, and in the Far East. His strategic ideas, derived largely from the history of British naval policy and operations, were accepted as precepts of universal application and utility, without qualification as to time or place. And the impact of these ideas was widely felt in accelerated naval development which, inside of two decades, was profoundly to alter the balance of naval power, with political repercussions on every ocean and continent.

This changing order of sea power was but one of many shifts in international power relations which followed the spread of the industrial revolution. For more than a century, British manufacturing and related industries had dominated the world economy. But similar industries had gradually taken root elsewhere, often with the direct aid of English capital. And these came in time to be serious rivals of the mines and factories of Great Britain.

The growth of mutually competitive industrial economies on the European Continent, in America, and in other lands, inaugurated a new era of imperialism which in certain respects closely resembled the mercantilistic expansion of the eighteenth century. This neo-mercantilistic imperialism received in the 1890's a tremendous stimulus from the vision of power, glory, profit, and moral destiny, set forth with crusading zeal in

Mahan's prolific writings. These as well as the trend of political and economic events, stimulated the growth of navies which supported and at the same time fostered the new imperialism. The rising wave of imperialism further accelerated the pace of naval expansion the world over. And this in turn undermined the historic world-wide naval dominance of Great Britain.

That dominance rested not only upon the greater material strength and the peculiar strategic doctrine of the British Navy, but also upon the incomparable geographic position of the British Isles and upon the configuration of the narrow seas. Battle-fleet supremacy in the North Sea, in the English Channel, in the Mediterranean, and in the adjacent waters of the eastern Atlantic, gave naval dominance over the Powers of Continental Europe. As long as these Continental Powers were the only ones possessing strong navies, this local primacy gave England a virtually world-wide command of the seas.

The rise of Japanese naval power undermined England's strategic dominance, and hence political influence, in the Far East. Through one of the ironies of history, Englishmen themselves contributed materially to this result. British shipyards in the 1880's and 1890's built one warship after another for Japan. And British naval officers were loaned to the Mikado's Government to teach the elements of naval science and administration.

It could be argued of course, that someone else would have built the ships and given the advice if England had refused. It could also be argued that Great Britain needed a counterpoise to Russian imperialism which was at that time encroaching on British preserves in Asia. But all that does not alter the fact that a modern Japanese fleet in Asiatic waters fundamentally altered the strategic situation to the disadvantage of Great Britain; that British squadrons guarding the English Channel, the North Sea, and the Mediterranean no longer *ipso facto* dominated the sea communications of the Far East.

Meanwhile, parallel developments were taking place in the Western Hemisphere. Prior to the Civil War, the United States had both a navy and a naval policy. But neither affected the main currents of world politics in any large or continuing manner. Even within the Western Hemisphere, England rather than the United States was the dominant naval Power. After a brief war-induced growth, the American Navy passed into a prolonged eclipse. Reconstruction commenced in the early 'eighties, and by 1890 was acquiring some momentum. Mahan's writings, in conjunction with other influences, accelerated the pace and changed the direction of American naval development. And by 1898, the Navy of the United States had evolved from a handful of commerce-raiding cruisers into a rapidly growing fleet of first-class battleships. Control of Europe's narrow seas no longer assured naval dominance in the New World.

Only by progressively strengthening its oversea squadrons could the British Admiralty have preserved even a semblance of its former primacy in American and Far Eastern waters. And whatever the desires and inclinations of British naval authorities, developments nearer home soon rendered such a course practically impossible.

Acceleration of the naval building pace in Europe, especially the very rapid growth of the German Navy after 1900, threatened England's historic dominance in European waters. So instead of strengthening its oversea squadrons, the British Government had progressively to deplete them in order to maintain a safe margin of superiority in the narrow seas and eastern Atlantic.[1]

Great Britain's growing commitments in Europe and shrinking power overseas profoundly affected international politics in the Far East. Security for British interests in Asia was sought through a multilateral equipoise stable enough to support the status quo in that remote sector. Englishmen encouraged our annexation of the Philippine Islands in 1898, regarding the United States as a friendly steadying influence in the Far East. When they failed to secure a formal alliance with the United States, they entered into a military partnership with Japan, directed first against Russia, later against Germany. And in various other ways they labored to fashion a political substitute for their former naval dominance in the Far East.

In the Western Hemisphere Great Britain followed a radically different course. Here the materials were lacking for a political equipoise, or balance of power. British statesmen had either to resist or to accept the naval primacy of the United States. Necessarily they chose the latter. British dreams of controlling, or at

[1] See, for example, Mahan, *The Interest of America in International Conditions* (1910), pp. 61*ff*., 195*ff*.; *Naval Strategy* (1911), pp. 69, 73.

least of sharing in the control of, the projected isthmian canal were abandoned. A continuing and generally successful effort was made to liquidate outstanding disputes and to cultivate friendly relations with the United States in order that British statesmen and naval authorities might safely strike this country from their list of possible enemies, and perhaps even fall back upon the great American republic for support in case of emergency in Europe or in the Far East.

The implications of all this are clearer in retrospect, of course, than they were in prospect. With increasing difficulty the British Government did manage to keep a margin of naval superiority that seemed to assure its hold on the sea approaches to Europe. There was a fair presumption that Great Britain could still cut off its Continental enemies from their oversea colonies and from the foodstuffs and raw materials of the Western Hemisphere and the Far East. However, the ability to maintain such a blockade would thereafter depend not only on Britain's naval dominance in European waters but also on the attitude and policy of the transoceanic naval Powers, Japan and the United States.

British statesmen could still exercise a large, often a decisive, influence on world events, through commerce, finance, diplomacy, and propaganda. But they had irretrievably lost the ultimate sanction of superior force in the Western Hemisphere and in the Far East. Great Britain's world-wide command of the seas had vanished, and with it the historic balance wheel of the vast, intricate, and swiftly moving machinery of that advantageous world economic community and quasi-political order which British sea power had fostered and supported during the preceding century.

America's Continental Fortress

The changing order of sea power improved the already strong defensive position of the continental United States. From the standpoint of resistance to external aggression, Continental America, then as today, bore a superficial, often remarked, and very much overstressed resemblance to the British Isles.[2] Bodies of water separated both countries from other centers of military power. In both, as a result, sea power had traditionally played

[2] See, for example, Mahan, *Interest of America in Sea Power* (1897), pp. 110-11.

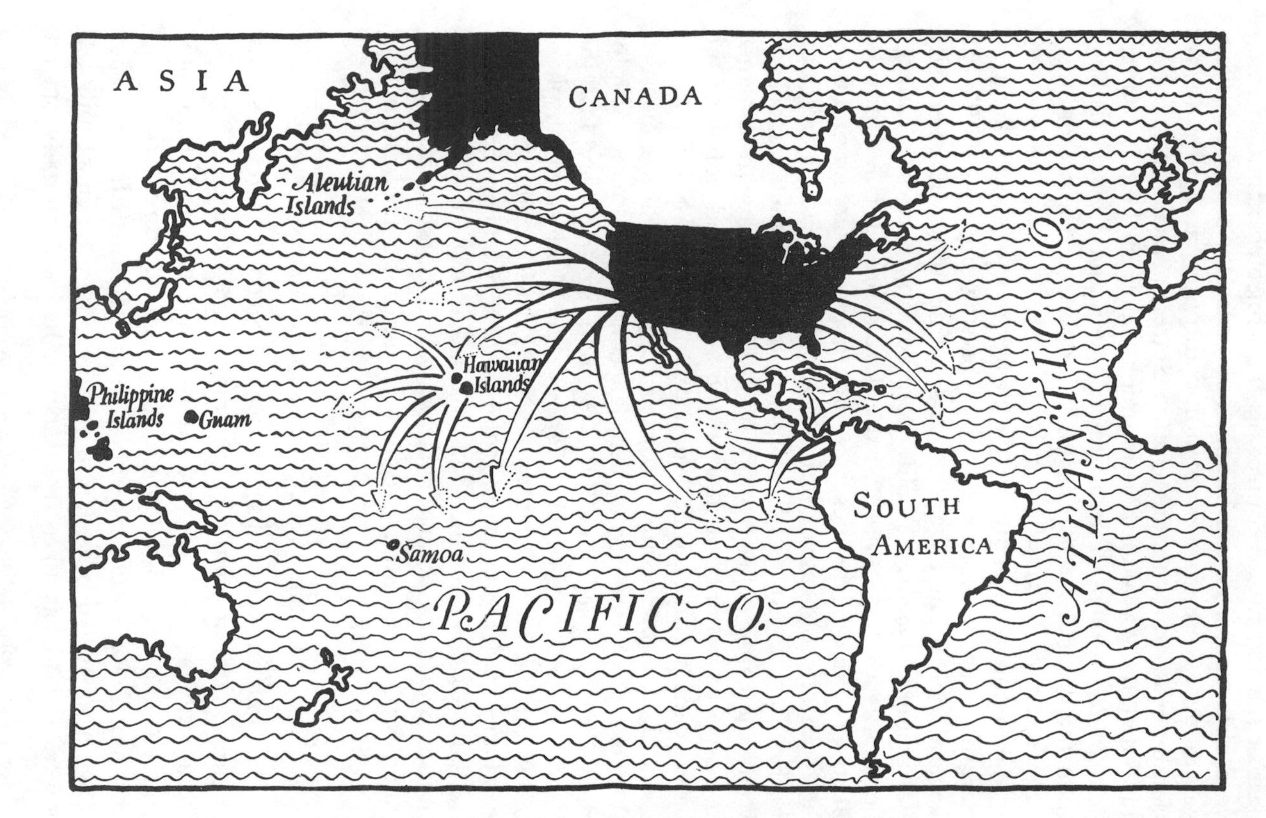

Geography and American Sea Power, 1898-1922

a larger rôle than land power in the conception and practice of statecraft. But there the similarity ended.

Owing to the immense width of the oceans, as well as to the inherent military weakness of all other countries in the Western Hemisphere, the American position was immeasurably stronger than England's for purposes of defense against armed aggression from overseas. Distance, as Mahan once put it, was a "factor equivalent to a certain number of ships."[3] And for this reason the minimum naval requirements for the defense of the continental United States were proportionately smaller.[4]

From the standpoint of world politics, and for purposes of waging war offensively in distant seas, however, the American position was infinitely weaker than England's. As was explained and emphasized in the preceding chapter, the geographical location of the British Isles, the early seizure of Gibraltar, and the possession of a superior navy had given Great Britain an invincible grip on the ocean portals of Europe. British squadrons guarding the North Sea, the English Channel, and the Mediterranean could disrupt the transoceanic commerce and military communications of their European enemies, while simultaneously covering the communications between the British Isles and the scattered colonies and distant outposts of the British Empire. And in consequence, the fact of British sea power exercised a continuous, if fluctuating, influence on European diplomacy in peace as well as in war.

For geographical reasons, obvious though too often ignored by empire-minded Americans, no exercise of sea power within the Western Hemisphere could possibly produce world results in any way comparable to those which flowed from England's historic command of Europe's narrow seas. There were no commercial bottlenecks in the New World comparable to the English Channel and the Strait of Gibraltar.

Naval strategists frequently drew an analogy between the Caribbean and the Mediterranean Seas. Mahan and others confidently prophesied that the opening of an isthmian canal would transform the Caribbean into a thoroughfare of world commerce, rivaling Suez and the Mediterranean as a short-cut

[3] "Considerations Governing the Disposition of Navies," *National Review*, Vol. 39, July 1902, p. 710.

[4] See, for example, Mahan, *The Problem of Asia* (1900), pp. 197-9.

to the Far East. But they failed to appreciate, or at least neglected to state, that it would be a thoroughfare politically and strategically vital to no Great Power except the United States.

Military control of the Caribbean, as well as of the Atlantic and Pacific approaches to the United States, might be imperatively necessary to render the continental homeland of the American people invulnerable to external pressure and armed aggression. That idea in one form or another was historically one of the foundation stones of American diplomacy. It was the very essence of the Monroe Doctrine. American statesmen and their naval advisers might, and did, conclude under the tutelage of Mahan that military control of these waters required building a fleet of capital ships and adopting England's strategic doctrine. But it was difficult to see, Mahan and his disciples to the contrary notwithstanding, how any fleet, however strong, or any strategic doctrine, however sound, could give the United States Government a leverage on world politics even remotely approaching that exercised by Great Britain down to the end of the nineteenth century.[5]

The contrasts between the strategic position of Great Britain and that of the United States tended on the whole to increase with the passage of time. The growing complexity of war technology, resulting from the introduction of steam, from the development of new weapons, and from other advances, steadily narrowed the range of major fleet operations and raised up new obstacles in the way of landing and maintaining large expeditionary forces on distant hostile shores.[6] The revolutionary rise of submarine and air power in particular, while progressively undermining the security of England's island base just off the coast of Europe, actually strengthened the defenses of our continental base three thousand miles from Europe and farther still from Asia.[7]

[5] Overdrawing political and strategic analogies was always one of Mahan's propensities. Failure to appreciate that the Caribbean was politically and strategically vital to no Great Power except the United States was one instance of this propensity. See, for example, his *Influence of Sea Power upon History* (1890), p. 33; *Interest of America in Sea Power*, pp. 12-13, 104, 276-7; and *Interest of America in International Conditions*, p. 193.

[6] See Mahan, "Blockade in Relation to Naval Strategy" in *Proc. U.S. Nav. Inst.*, Vol. 21, Nov. 1895, p. 863; *Naval Strategy*, pp. 118-19, 381.

[7] Mahan late in his career showed some appreciation of the defensive potentialities of submarines. *Naval Strategy*, pp. 2-3.

Continental expansion and internal development likewise improved this already strong defensive position. By the end of the last century, the United States had evolved into an immense, compact, united country with varied and abundant resources, accumulated wealth, diversified industries, superior technology, and excellent internal communications. These all contributed to making the United States virtually proof against sea-blockade, even if there had existed anywhere in the world a Power with the naval forces and freedom of action necessary to undertake so herculean a task. In this respect also, the United States stood in marked and advantageous contrast to Great Britain whose scattered empire, highly specialized internal economy, and consequent dependence upon oversea commerce became sources of increasing weakness as military and naval developments in Europe, America, and Asia progressively undermined Great Britain's global command of the seas.[8]

The United States derived additional security from England's naval dominance in European waters and from Europe's historic balance of power. Political rivalries in the Old World contributed measurably to the achievement and maintenance of American independence. Those rivalries indirectly, and quite incidentally, safeguarded the early life of our republic.[9] For several generations it served British interests to support the nominal independence of the Latin American countries. And on more than one occasion British naval power stood between Latin America and potential aggressors from overseas.

At the same time, Great Britain's recurrent preoccupation with balance-of-power politics in the Old World, quite as much as any opposition or resistance on the part of the United States, repeatedly frustrated England's own imperial ambitions in this hemisphere. Especially after 1900, as previously noted, circumstances compelled the British Government to begin concentrating its forces in European waters and to cultivate friendly rela-

[8] This was perfectly obvious to Mahan who, in 1900, justified Great Britain's naval primacy saying: "To Great Britain the navy she maintains is indispensable to national safety, to the British Islands as such, and to the integrity of the widely dispersed British Empire." The United States in contrast "need not to fear vital injury by an external blow to our communications with the world. . . . We have no distant possessions vital to our mere existence, however useful they may be to our external development and influence." *Problem of Asia*, pp. 197-8.

[9] See Mahan, *Interest of America in Sea Power*, p. 104.

tions with the United States. And there was never a time from then until the World War of 1914, when either Great Britain or any other European country enjoyed the political freedom of action necessary to challenge in this hemisphere the rapidly rising naval power of the United States.

This point was repeatedly stressed in the writings of Mahan. In 1890, he held that a "careful determination of the force that Great Britain or France [then the first and second sea Powers of Europe] could probably spare for operations against our coasts, if the latter were suitably defended, without weakening their European position or unduly exposing their colonies and commerce, is the starting-point from which to calculate the strength of our own navy."[10] In 1897, Mahan was reminding his countrymen that the great European naval Powers which had "interests in the Western Hemisphere," had "elsewhere yet wider and more onerous demands upon their attention."[11] And in 1910, after Germany had displaced France as the second naval Power in the Old World, Mahan again stressed the mutual antagonism which chained the two strongest fleets to European waters "in peace as well as in war."[12]

The defensive position of the United States was still further strengthened, down to 1898, by a truly remarkable dearth of oversea commitments and responsibilities. After the Civil War the American foreign-trade merchant marine all but disappeared from the seas. We had no detached possessions except Alaska which then lay beyond the grasp of any potential aggressor. Non-intervention, neutrality, and no "entangling alliances" were the guiding principles of America's relations with Europe. And though the foundation was already laid for a more assertive Far Eastern policy, that policy did not begin to assume a definitely interventionist cast until after our war with Spain.

The naval implications of all this were clear to Mahan. As he frankly admitted in 1890, for a country situated as the United States then was, the primary object of naval policy was neither to defend a scattered empire nor to support a program of expansion overseas, but rather to insure to merchant shipping safe

[10] *ibid.*, p. 16, and also pp. 54-5. [11] *ibid.*, p. 182.

[12] *Interest of America in International Conditions*, pp. 195-7, and *passim.*

and uninterrupted access to its home ports in war as well as in peace.[13]

To realize this objective, Mahan continued, there was needed a navy capable of driving any hostile forces from the sea approaches to the continental United States. It was not sufficient merely to provide local harbor defenses and land forces to stop the enemy at the coastline. Hostile fleets hovering well beyond sight of land, might conceivably disrupt the flow of commerce into and out of our principal seaports. Nor was it safe to rely wholly on the smaller and cheaper types of seagoing ships, such as cruisers, though these were essential for various secondary operations. Only a fighting fleet could drive off hostile blockading squadrons. And that fleet, in Mahan's judgment, must include battleships, as powerfully armed and as stoutly armored as any capital ships in existence.

While Mahan fervently hoped in 1890, that the time was not far distant when the United States would embark upon oversea expansion which in turn would necessitate a still greater navy, he recognized that American requirements were for the time being comparatively modest. Defense of our continental position and of the sea approaches thereto did not require a navy strong enough to seize command of distant waters such as, for example, the English Channel, the Indian Ocean, or the China Sea. What was needed, and this was easily within reach, was a fleet strong enough to overpower any hostile force that might attempt to penetrate a broad zone of open sea extending outward from our continental coastline. And owing to the wide oceans, to the rigid fuel and service requirements of modern warships, as well as to the political situation overseas, no Old World Power could detach all, or anywhere near all, of its armed forces for an attack in the Western Hemisphere.

Our position in this hemisphere was still further buttressed by the insular accessions which resulted directly and indirectly from the war with Spain. Conquest of Spain's West Indian islands, and provision for a naval base in a nominally independent Cuba, insured American dominance in the Caribbean. Annexation of the Hawaiian Islands in 1898, and partition of the Samoan archipelago the following year, foreshadowed a similar primacy throughout a vast triangle in the eastern Pacific.

[13] See *Influence of Sea Power upon History*, pp. 26, 83-8.

The far side of this triangle lay roughly along the International Date Line (180th meridian) about 1,200 nautical miles west of Honolulu, from the Aleutian Islands to American Samoa, and thence east 5,000 miles to the coast of Peru. Pearl Harbor near Honolulu flanked every line of approach from the west and northwest. And Samoa, 2,200 miles to the south, covered the more roundabout and much less vulnerable approach through the South Seas.

Completion of the Panama Canal in 1914 transformed the Caribbean into a world thoroughfare as Mahan and others had foreseen; but a thoroughfare under the exclusive, undisputed, and indisputable control of the American Navy. The gradual development of a strongly fortified fleet base at Pearl Harbor assured equally exclusive control of the eastern Pacific. And the Canal, the security of which was thus insured, cleared the way for the ultimate concentration of American naval forces into a single fighting fleet whose command of the American seas no Power or likely combination of Powers could challenge with any hope of success.

America's "Achilles Heel" in the Western Pacific

The war with Spain resulted also in the annexation of Guam and the Philippine Islands. The latter lay in the far western Pacific, nearly 5,000 nautical miles beyond Hawaii, more than two weeks continuous steaming for the fastest ships then in service. And as a glance at the political and military geography of the western Pacific readily shows, these accessions radically altered and unbelievably complicated the hitherto relatively simple defense problem of the United States.

The configuration of the western Pacific, like that of the eastern, may be said to be roughly triangular. The base of this western triangle, some 5,000 nautical miles in length, lies north and south between the Aleutian Islands and New Zealand on about the 180th meridian which, it will be recalled, also forms the western boundary of the eastern strategic triangle. From the Aleutian Islands and New Zealand, the western triangle converges to a point on the coast of central China, the north side skirting the Kamchatka Peninsula, the Kurile Islands, and Japan; the south side, the Philippines, East Indies, and Australia. Within this vast triangle, and on its periphery, lie thousands of islands large and small, the majority of which are grouped into clusters or archipelagoes within twenty degrees of the equator.

By 1898 European empire builders had staked out claims covering practically all the islands of the western Pacific and the adjoining mainland of southeastern Asia. The lion's share was divided among Great Britain, France, and The Netherlands. Germany's holdings included part of the large island of New Guinea; the nearby Bismarck Archipelago; and the scattered group of coral atolls known as the Marshall Islands, 2,000 miles southwest of Hawaii.

Spain's empire in the Pacific comprised the Philippine, Caroline, and Marianas archipelagoes. The largest in area and importance was the Philippine group which with Borneo formed the eastern littoral of the South China Sea. East of the Philippines lay the Carolines, scattered through 1,500 miles of tropical ocean just north of the equator. One of these, distant about 1,000 miles east of the southern Philippines, was the island of Yap, only a few square miles in area, but destined to become the cable center and communications focus of the western Pacific. Some 500 miles northeast of Yap lay the island of Guam, southernmost of the Marianas archipelago which reached northward several hundred miles toward the main islands of Japan.

The strategic location of Guam in the western Pacific triangle resembled that of Hawaii in the eastern. From Port Apra, Guam, to Yokohama the distance was approximately 1,300 nautical miles; to Shanghai, 1,700; to Hongkong and Canton, 1,800; to Manila, 1,500; and a comparable distance to the northeastern periphery of the East Indies. All these points lay within striking range of a modern fleet based on Guam. Pearl Harbor, though 3,300 miles away, was still within supporting distance, certainly if a subsidiary fueling station were set up on Wake, 1,300 miles east of Guam, a tiny islet to which the United States laid claim in 1899.

Under conditions prevailing down to 1914, possession of Wake, Guam, and the Philippines gave the United States a position of some potential military strength in the western Pacific. Development of a properly equipped and adequately fortified base, probably in Guam, would have transformed this position from one of potential into one of actual strength.[14] Such an establishment, together with a subsidiary base somewhere in the vicinity of Manila, would have enabled the American fleet to operate over an immense area in the far western Pacific. And this, for better or for worse, would have given the United States, on the critical eve of the World War, a considerably greater leverage on international developments in the Far East.

Actually, very little was done to improve our strategic position in either Guam or the Philippines. Experts disagreed as to the proper location of dockyards and defensive works. There was considerable popular opposition in America to any action which seemed to envisage our permanent occupation of those distant islands. Members of Congress, with their eyes on patronage, the pork barrel, and the next election, were chiefly interested in public works nearer home. As a result, our military road across the Pacific faded out a thousand miles or so west of Hawaii. American diplomacy in the Far East lacked the support of readily available superior force. And American insular possessions in the western Pacific remained a remote and indefensible salient, virtually a hostage to Japan, or, as Theodore Roosevelt aptly said of the Philippines, the "Achilles heel" of the United States.

It is difficult to reconcile this inaction with the trend of American political commitments in eastern Asia. Since before the middle of the nineteenth century, American statesmen had stood for equality of commercial opportunity in the Far East. But they had rarely shown any disposition to back this up with anything stronger than words. Following the war with Spain, however, the United States Government, with verbal encouragement and support from London, assumed the leadership and a degree of responsibility for maintaining this open-door principle as against Japan and the Continental European Powers which were moving in from all directions on the moribund Chinese Empire. This undertaking, springing partly from expectations of pecuniary gain, and partly from conceptions of moral duty, entailed large risks and paid dividends chiefly in ill will. The trend toward conflict in the Pacific was accentuated by recurring difficulties aris-

[14] See, for example, Hector Bywater, *Sea Power in the Pacific* (1921), Chap. 9; and *Bibliography of the Island of Guam* (edited by C. F. Reid, 1939), pp. 87*ff*.

ing from the entry and settlement of Japanese subjects in the United States. And at no time after 1905 could American statesmen entirely ignore either the possibility of war with Japan or the certain repercussions in the Far East of a general war in Europe.

The possibility of the latter was especially disquieting, or should have been, because of a fateful strategic decision embodied in the peace settlement of 1898 with Spain. Whether it was wise for the United States to retain any of the Spanish islands in the western Pacific is certainly a debatable question. But it is clear in retrospect at least, that it was a strategic mistake to take only Guam and the Philippines, leaving the rest to fall into the hands of some other first-class Power.

Throughout a distance of approximately fifteen hundred miles, these islands—the Caroline and Marianas groups—crowded the southern flank of the sea route to the Philippines and Far East by way of Hawaii and Guam. In Spanish hands these islands presented no serious threat, for Spain was no longer a power with which to reckon. But their cession from Spain to one of the Great Powers would inevitably alter the strategical situation, and might, under readily conceivable circumstances, undermine the entire military position of the United States in the western Pacific.

This possibility was explicitly brought to the attention of the American commissioners sent to Paris in the autumn of 1898 to fix the terms of peace with Spain. A spokesman for the United States Navy forcefully urged the commissioners to insist on Spain's ceding to the United States not only the entire Philippine archipelago and Guam, but also "the Carolines, including the Pelews, and the [rest of the] Ladrones [subsequently called the Marianas]." These island groups, he pointed out, contained many sheltered anchorages suitable for naval stations. With the whole chain in American hands, the United States would hold a secure route and a dominating position through the western Pacific. "In the hands of an enemy they would offer a serious menace to the line of communications between the Pacific coast [of the United States] and the Philippines."[15]

The disposition to be made of these western Pacific islands was

[15] Statement of Commander R. B. Bradford before the American Peace Commissioners, Paris, Oct. 14, 1898. 55 Cong. 3 Sess., *Sen. Doc.* No. 62, pt. 1, p. 472*ff*.

also extensively discussed within the United States during the summer and autumn of 1898. The religious press urged their annexation as a means of fostering missionary enterprise. Others emphasized their value in connection with various trans-Pacific cable projects. Here and there someone grasped their geomilitary bearing on American plans and policies in the Far East. But the military argument seems to have made but little impression either on the public mind or on national policy. The Caroline Islands were discussed at the peace conference, but the question was not pressed in the face of Spanish resistance. The American commissioners demanded and secured the Philippines and Guam. The remainder were left in Spanish hands. Perhaps the general feeling was best summed up by the journalist who observed that "many Americans familiar with the question think that the Philippines and Guam furnish all the coaling bases necessary in the Pacific."[16]

Early in 1899, the Spanish Crown liquidated the last remnant of its shattered Pacific empire by ceding the Caroline and Marianas Islands to Germany which already held the Marshall group still farther to the east. Years afterward, Mahan recalled that "when the Caroline and Ladrone Islands were about to be ceded to Germany by Spain . . . I received more than one letter urging me to use any influence I could exert to induce our government to resist the step. My reply was that, besides having no influence, I saw no sufficient reason for our opposition."[17] This was also the official view, and German forces took possession with the full acquiescence of the United States.

Under conditions prevailing in 1899, this doubtless seemed to be a safe enough national policy. Germany was a strong and rapidly growing Power. But Germany's European entanglements and England's command of the European seas precluded any concentration of German naval strength in the Pacific Ocean. What this complacent view ignored was the possibility of a further transfer at some later date from Germany to Japan. Such a

[16] *New York Herald*, Dec. 4, 1898, p. 10. For discussion of the Caroline and Marianas Islands during the peace negotiations, see the privately published "Official Verbatim Report" of the Paris Conference, circulated by the *New York Journal*, pp. 170, 180, 204. For views of the American commissioners, see 56 Cong. 2 Sess., *Sen. Doc.* No. 148, pp. 39, 45*ff*., 50. In general, see J. W. Pratt, *Expansionists of 1898* (1936), pp. 274, 290, 302, 303, 304, 340-4.

[17] *Armaments and Arbitration* (1912), p. 80.

transfer would instantly alter the strategical situation to the serious disadvantage of the United States. It would jeopardize the security of American insular possessions in the western Pacific and weaken American influence throughout the Far East, since Japanese imperialists had large ambitions in that region and the steadily growing naval power of Japan was and would remain concentrated in the Pacific.

The possibility that the Marshall, Caroline, and Marianas Islands might eventually pass into the hands of Japan began to take shape after the formation in 1902 of the Anglo-Japanese Alliance.

That possibility markedly increased when Germany succeeded Russia as the primary object against which that Alliance was directed. And the dangers inherent in that possibility grew steadily larger as Japan advanced step by step in Asia, as Japan's Navy rose in strength and prestige, as Japanese-American relations surmounted one diplomatic crisis after another, and as the European Powers hurried on to war and disaster.

What lay in the future, no one could wholly foresee. The rise of American naval power, together with the conception of national security embodied in the Monroe Doctrine, seemed to assure a fair degree of international stability within the Western Hemisphere, *come what might in Europe*. But a combination of conditions, circumstances, and events had thus far prevented any single Power from succeeding to Great Britain's former primacy in the Far East. And it required no prophetic gift to foresee that war in Europe might well lead to chaos in Asia, with the United States drifting toward armed conflict with a militant expanding Japan, bent on establishing political hegemony in the Far East, and naval dominance in the western Pacific.

CHAPTER THREE

Sea Power and World Crisis, 1914-1918

THE World War of 1914-1918 destroyed the last vestiges of the strategic unity which the world had all but achieved under the Pax Britannica of the preceding century. That conflict shattered the politico-naval equipoise which had governed the disposition and movements of European fleets since early in the twentieth century. It swept away the frail dikes which had held at least partially in check the tide of Japanese imperialism in the Far East. And it gave a tremendous and portentous impetus and momentum to militarism and navalism the world over.

In short, the war to end all war sowed in every continent the seeds of future strife; and not the least among the disruptive consequences that followed in its wake, was a condition of international chaos and anarchy which threatened to project the American people into a bitter and futile naval race with Great Britain, and into a struggle with Japan for control of the far western Pacific and of the future destiny of eastern Asia.

The War's Legacy in the Pacific

Especially sinister were the potentialities for trouble in the Pacific. The war crisis of 1914 had inevitably produced immediate and disturbing repercussions in that region. The principal European belligerents all held territories, concessions, and other interests in the Far East. Great Britain was joined in a military alliance with Japan. And it was only to be expected that Japanese imperialists would seize this opportunity to further their long-standing ambition to establish an hegemony over eastern Asia.

Under these circumstances, any move to exclude the European struggle from the Pacific and Far East would have confronted great difficulties. Yet it was undeniably in the ultimate interest of every Western Power to make the effort. Above all, it was in Great Britain's interest to conserve the status quo in the Pacific as well as on the mainland of Asia. England no longer wielded the military power necessary to defend its scattered empire in the Pacific and its huge economic stake in China against the encroaching advance of Japan. With a desperate European war on their hands, British statesmen were more than ever dependent on the United States for support in the Far East. The ability of the United States to make a strong stand on behalf of Western interests depended on the American Navy's power and prestige in the western Pacific. And that in turn rested in very large measure on the strength and inviolability of our long military road to Asia by way of Hawaii, Guam, and the Philippines.

Actually, short-sighted expediency took precedence over long term interest at this critical juncture. Germany at the outbreak of war had a strong cruiser squadron in the Far East. The mere presence of this force partially paralyzed British commerce in the Pacific. It would have taken some time to concentrate a British force strong enough to cope with these German cruisers. Japan, however, possessed sufficient naval forces immediately available. The Anglo-Japanese Alliance was accordingly invoked, and Japan was invited to aid in clearing German naval forces from the Pacific.

British statesmen seem to have fully appreciated the danger inherent in this course. Japan might easily get out of hand. It was no part of British war strategy to substitute Japan for Germany in Shantung, or to encourage Japanese occupation of Germany's Pacific Islands. And it was clearly anticipated in London that the United States Government might raise strong objections to Japan occupying those island groups which flanked our military road across the Pacific.

These anticipations proved well founded. The prospect of Japan's entry into the war immediately aroused American apprehensions. A belated effort was made to neutralize the entire

Pacific and Far East. British statesmen were willing to exclude the war from eastern Asia, but not from the Pacific. The most that they would do was to issue assurances that Japanese military action would not extend "beyond the China Seas," except insofar as might be "necessary to protect Japanese shipping lanes." And though Japanese naval forces took possession of the Marshall, Caroline, and Marianas archipelagoes early in October 1914, it was still pretended both in London and in Tokio that this occupation was purely temporary, and that Japan entertained no intention of holding these islands beyond the duration of the war.

One can only speculate whether the United States could have prevented this occupation which was to stretch on into permanence. It is possible that the Wilson Administration could have done so, even without the support of Great Britain. That no serious effort was made to that end, seems now to be fairly well established.[1] And this inaction was to have lasting consequences, comparable to McKinley's annexation of a part (instead of all or none) of Spain's Pacific empire, and comparable also to the failure of McKinley's successors to develop even one well fortified naval base in the islands that were taken. For as we have already emphasized, the islands which in 1914 passed into the hands of Japan flanked through a distance of more than a thousand miles our line of military communications from Hawaii to Guam, and thence to the Philippines and to the China coast.

The destruction of German power in the Pacific and Far East, accompanied by the all but complete withdrawal of Russian, French, and British forces from eastern Asia, left only the United States in any position whatever to guard Occidental interests in that region. But the United States, lacking modern naval bases in the western Pacific, outflanked as a result of Japan's early occupation of the German islands, and involved in serious difficulties with revolutionary Mexico, in recurrent crises with the European belligerents, and finally as a belligerent partner in the desperate struggle in the Old World, was after 1914 in no position to retrieve past mistakes or even to make a very strong stand in the Far East.

[1] See *For. Rels. 1914, Supplement*, pp. 161*ff.*

Japanese imperialists were not slow to exploit this providential opportunity. Early in 1915, they followed up their successful assault on Germany's foothold in Shantung, by presenting the notorious "twenty-one demands" on China, which if fully carried out would have reduced that country to a helpless protectorate of Japan. By 1917, Japan had driven diplomatic bargains with the principal European Allies, which confirmed that Power's succession to all German rights and possessions in the Pacific and Far East north of the equator. Meanwhile, Japanese arms, diplomacy, and finance were busy consolidating and extending their position in Shantung, and in tightening their grip on southern Manchuria. Following the Bolshevist Revolution of 1917, Japanese forces moved into the Russian sphere of influence in northern Manchuria. And in 1918 the Japanese Government carried out a series of moves which looked to the outside world very much like a deliberate enterprise for conquering and detaching the maritime province of Siberia.

These developments did not pass unnoticed in the United States. American newspapers denounced Japanese imperialism. The State Department protested against the Japanese aggressions. The "Japanese menace" was cited as one of the reasons justifying further expansion of the American Navy. And the possibility of our entering the war by way of the Far East was frequently discussed during 1915 and 1916.

Events, however, did not unfold in accordance with such a pattern. Japanese-American relations improved temporarily following our entrance into the European struggle in April 1917. Shortly thereafter, the visit of Japan's Foreign Minister, Viscount Ishii, to the United States resulted in a famous diplomatic understanding, known as the Lansing-Ishii Agreement of 1917, which further disarmed suspicion and secured some recognition of Japan's claims in Asia. And the year closed with the tension much relieved, but with the two Powers no nearer agreement on the future disposition of the German islands which Japan, it now transpired, had secretly agreed to divide with the British Empire on a line following the equator.

Clouds again darkened the Pacific early in 1918. As one means of breaking the stranglehold which Japanese finance was tightening on China, the Wilson Administration revived a scheme, inaugurated under President Taft, for international subscription and control of loans to that distracted country. Several thousand American troops were dispatched for the real, if unstated, purpose of blocking Japan's advance into eastern Siberia. And the European war drew to a close in the autumn of 1918 with fresh war clouds gathering over the western Pacific, and with American statesmen and their army and navy advisers compelled to envisage the possibility of an early conflict fought under enormous technical difficulties, thousands of miles overseas, in virtually the home waters of Japan whose rapidly expanding navy seemed at that time to be approaching, if indeed it had not already established, unassailable command in the western Pacific.

The War's Legacy in the Atlantic

Only slightly less ominous was the World War's politico-naval legacy in the Atlantic. The defeat of Germany, followed by surrender and subsequent self-destruction of the German fleet, removed the menace which had previously chained British sea power to European waters. Defeat also destroyed the secondary, but not wholly negligible sea power of Austria. The struggle on land had consumed the energies of France and Italy, with consequent deterioration in their forces upon the sea. And revolutionary upheaval had at least temporarily disorganized the naval power of Russia.

Great Britain, on the other hand, emerged from the war stronger upon the sea than ever before. The British Navy had undergone tremendous expansion, and numbered at the Armistice over 1,300 combatant vessels of all classes, including forty-two first-line capital ships.[2] Its total displacement exceeded three million tons. Not since the close of the Napoleonic Wars had the British Admiralty wielded such overwhelmingly superior power in European waters.[3] With no formidable European "enemy" in sight, the statesmen and naval authorities of Great Britain were free once again to take a large view of sea

[2] Henry Newbolt, *Naval Operations* (1931), Vol. 5, p. 430. Several hundred of these were small or improvised craft which were soon scrapped or otherwise disposed of. On January 1, 1920, our Navy Department reported the British Navy as including 812 combatant ships. *Navy Yearbook, 1919*, p. 782.

[3] Archibald Hurd, "Shall We Suffer Eclipse by Sea? American Progress," *Fortnightly Review*, Vol. 113, June 1920, pp. 849, 851.

power in relation to empire defense, national policy, and world politics.

As fate would have it, England's strategic emancipation coincided with an upward surge of navalism in the United States. The war overseas had early stimulated an American "preparedness" movement. This movement had culminated in several legislative enactments designed to strengthen the armed forces of the United States. One of these, the Naval Act of 1916, embodied a widely avowed purpose of providing as soon as possible a navy "second to none" in all the world. And to that end it had authorized the construction of 156 new men-of-war, including ten super-dreadnought battleships and six giant battle cruisers.[4]

Official and popular discussion leading to this legislation was conspicuous neither for clarity of thought nor for unity of purpose. The arguments advanced in its support showed the influence both of pre-war stereotypes and of wartime panic and hysteria. From about 1901, the standard of American naval power, implicit in legislation, and explicit in numerous public utterances, had been a fleet second only to England's. This had really been a veiled way of saying a fleet superior to that of Germany which, contrary to the plain and inescapable import of conditions and events overseas, as well as of the ineluctable facts of war technology, American leaders had persisted in officially regarding as a probable future aggressor in the Western Hemisphere.[5] This alarming assumption was consistent with the view prevalent in the United States by 1916, that Germany was waging an imperialistic war for world domination. And it was widely proclaimed that the United States must have a navy second to none, to insure against future aggressions that might follow a German victory in Europe, which in 1916 seemed well within the bounds of possibility.

The entrance of the United States into the war in 1917 delayed execution of this unprecedented building program, and

[4] For fuller descriptions of the wartime surge of navalism in the United States, see our *Rise of American Naval Power* (1939), Chap. 18; and G. T. Davis, *A Navy Second to None* (1940), Chap. 10.

[5] See Alfred Vagts, "Hopes and Fears of an American-German War, 1870-1915," *Political Science Quarterly*, Vol. 54, Dec. 1939, pp. 514*ff*., and Vol. 55, March 1940, pp. 53*ff*.

at the same time insured the defeat of Germany against whom that program had been mainly directed. This last event made necessary some reorientation of American naval objectives. According to one view, the destruction of German sea power removed the only conceivable threat of European aggression in this hemisphere. According to another, however, Great Britain's newly recovered strategic freedom itself carried a threat of trouble for the United States. British statesmen, it was once more recalled, as the European conflict drew to a close in the autumn of 1918, had arrogantly ignored or parried American protests against repeated violations of what we had claimed as neutral rights during the early years of the war. And it was further emphasized that England was still joined in a formal military alliance with Japan, America's potential enemy in the Pacific.

On the other side of the Atlantic, the surge of navalism in America was viewed with anxiety verging on alarm. Had England destroyed the sea power of Germany, only to raise up a new menace across the Atlantic? It could be pointed out, of course, that British statesmen and naval authorities had long since recognized American naval dominance in the Western Hemisphere. It was arguable that American naval primacy in the western Pacific would in the long run benefit Great Britain as much as the United States. It was also arguable that the great North American republic was in no sense a potential enemy of Great Britain. And it required only the most elementary strategic knowledge and insight to perceive that there was little or no danger of the United States, whatever its naval program, ever becoming even a theoretical menace to England's supply lines in the narrow seas and eastern Atlantic.

There was, however, another side to the question. The successful blockade of Germany from the outbreak of the war, was possible partly because the British fleet controlled the narrow seas through which alone the Central Powers had access to the oceans. But naval superiority and geographical advantage might have been wholly insufficient, save for the belligerent assistance of Japan, and above all the benevolent neutrality (and subsequent belligerency) of the United States.

Had the United States assumed a hostile posture at the outset, countering the Allied blockade with threats of reprisal, the strategic weakness of the Allies could scarcely have been concealed. When one also recalls England's absolute dependence on oversea supplies of food and raw materials, drawn from the Western as well as from the Eastern Hemisphere, it is difficult to resist the conclusion reached by one of England's foremost wartime statesmen, that the Allies' highly successful command of the seas had come to be exercised in some degree at least on the sufferance of the United States.[6] And when one reflects on the tremendous if still largely unexploited leverage on Great Britain, which commerce and finance, backed up by the threat of sea power, thus placed in the hands of the United States, it is not difficult to understand why many Englishmen viewed with considerable alarm the prospect of the United States forging ahead after the war to first place upon the sea.

While the problem in 1918 was incipient rather than acute, there was no ignoring its potentialities for future trouble. The British Navy's war-induced inflation, together with its strategic emancipation through the defeat of Germany, provided telling arguments for continuing the American program of naval expansion originally directed in the main against Germany. Such a course would sooner or later provoke counter naval measures on the part of Great Britain. The result might well be cut-throat competition for a statistical primacy upon the sea. And such a naval race, fostered by annual war scares and jingoistic propaganda, would almost certainly have political repercussions and consequences that would postpone the gigantic task of world reconstruction, if indeed it did not set the stage for another world conflagration that might finally and irretrievably consume the crumbling remnants of western civilization.

A New Order of Sea Power: Signs and Portents

The political and strategic outlook was further colored, and to an extent far greater than was generally appreciated in 1918,

[6] In his memoirs, Viscount Grey of Fallodon (the Sir Edward Grey of the war years) stated: ". . . blockade of Germany was essential to the victory of the Allies, but the ill will of the United States meant their certain defeat. . . . Germany and Austria were self-supporting in the huge supply of munitions. The Allies soon became dependent for an adequate supply on the United States. If we quarrelled with the United States we could not get that supply. It was better therefore to carry on the war without blockade, if need be, than to incur a break with the United States. . . . The object of diplomacy therefore was to secure the maximum of blockade

by the startling advances in military and industrial technology which had taken place during the war.

For over four years, Europe lived in a state of siege. The flow of goods back and forth across land frontiers and across the oceans either stopped altogether or was modified to suit the requirements of the war makers. Every country experienced critical shortages of essential raw materials and manufactured products. These shortages were most acute in Central Europe, but they existed everywhere. And in varying degrees, in belligerent and neutral countries alike, the effect was to stimulate research and invention, and to foster the development of new industries to overcome, either by duplication or by substitution, the merchandise deficiencies resulting from the war.

This universal trend toward industrial diversification (which incidentally was merely the acceleration of a trend perceptible long before 1914) had profound strategic implications. The potency of blockade as a method of naval warfare varied with the blockaded country's degree of dependence upon external supplies of food or war material. Had the American people possessed in 1812 the highly developed internal communications and diversified industrial system which they acquired by the end of the nineteenth century, they might have held out indefinitely against the British sea blockade. Had the Southern States in 1861 been less dependent upon European and Northern manufactures, the Confederacy would have been decidedly less vulnerable to the Union Navy's ever tightening blockade. And if the Central Powers had been somewhat more self-sustaining in 1914, the British Navy's grip on the narrow seas might have produced merely secondary strategic results.

Actually, as events demonstrated, the Central Powers were very far from self-sustaining. But the war did reveal the amazing ability of modern science to circumvent the limitations of nature. Though there was every prospect that war technology would grow more rather than less complex in the future, there were also indications that research and invention would forge ahead still more rapidly in the quest for national autarchy, and hence security, against siege by land and blockade by sea. And to a degree nowhere appreciated in 1918, the projection of these

that could be enforced without a rupture with the United States." *Twenty-Five Years* (1925), Vol. 2, p. 107.

trends into the post-war world was destined to affect the actual (as distinguished from the formal or theoretical) balance of military power on land, in the air, and upon the sea.

A more immediate and tangible effect of the war's stimulus to technology was the rapid development of new weapons and methods of warfare. Despite the introduction of steam, and the development of high explosives, protective armor, armor piercing shells, precision gunnery instruments, and many other technical devices, it was rather generally assumed in 1914, that this war in its naval phase would unfold according to the pattern of earlier conflicts, as analyzed and formalized in Mahan's literary classics.

For a time events seemed in the main to bear out this assumption. As in earlier wars, England's enemies found their fleets driven to cover, most of their roving cruisers run down and destroyed, their merchant shipping swept from the seas, and their internal strength and military power sapped by an ever tightening sea blockade. Once more Great Britain's control of Europe's narrow seas gave assurance of comparative safety to Allied and neutral merchantmen ploughing the Atlantic, the Pacific, and the Indian Oceans.

Presently, however, despite the Central Powers' grave handicap of having access to the oceans only through the narrow seas, England's naval dominance was all but successfully challenged in a wholly unprecedented and quite unexpected manner. The marine mine, the automotive torpedo, and the submarine all antedated the war. But few students of naval warfare had appreciated the immense potentialities for attack latent in these new and largely unproved weapons. Early in the struggle, submarines armed with torpedoes were used with such deadly effect against combatant surface craft that the British fleet was temporarily driven from the North Sea. By providing submarines with mine-laying equipment, it became possible for the blockaded Central Powers to plant mine fields at the enemy's portals, thereby presenting a serious hazard to warships and merchant vessels alike. And in 1915, the U-boat itself assumed the ancient rôle of roving commerce destroyer.

This new form of *guerre de course* gradually developed into a virtual counter-blockade of the British Isles. By 1917 German submarines, sinking neutral as well as belligerent merchantmen at sight, were threatening Great Britain with starvation, despite the British Navy's overwhelming command on the ocean's surface. Timely reenforcements from the United States, together with strenuous defensive efforts including revival and adaptation of the ancient principle of convoy, barely saved the Allies from irretrievable disaster. The war closed in 1918 with the situation at least partially under control. But only incurable optimists and hopeless reactionaries believed that the submarine peril had been laid to final rest.

The rise of air power likewise challenged the conventional theory and practice of naval warfare. Aircraft like mines and submarines also antedated the war. But students of naval strategy had paid even less attention to the potentialities of aerial warfare. Events demonstrated the folly of their neglect. And though hostilities ceased with military aviation still in its infancy, experience gained during the last months of the struggle left no shadow of doubt that aircraft would play a rôle, possibly a decisive rôle, in future wars for control of the sea.

These developments shook the established foundations of sea power. Devotees of the newer weapons confidently predicted that submarines and aircraft could sink any warship in existence, and even, under favorable conditions, the most heavily armored dreadnought that human ingenuity and modern science could devise. And while one might discount such predictions, there was no ignoring certain strategic ramifications of recent developments in war technology.

It was widely accepted that the newer weapons added measurably to the difficulties and perils which would thereafter confront a fighting fleet operating far from its nearest fortified haven. Hostile submarines and aircraft might levy terrible toll on such a fleet accompanied by a vulnerable train of transports and supply ships, as might be the case, for example, in a war between the United States and Japan.

It was also agreed that the new weapons raised all but insuperable obstacles to the invasion of a hostile seaboard, or even to the blockade of an open coastline. High-standing authorities even expressed doubts as to whether a surface fleet organized around a nucleus of capital ships, would be able in the future even to maintain itself within, much less to dominate, narrow seas infested by minefields and submarines, and menaced by shore-based aircraft.

Conversely, the developments which tended thus to circumscribe conventional fleet operations, measurably enlarged the potentialities of the *guerre de course*. The Germans had demonstrated that submarine commerce raiding could assume the dimensions of a counter-blockade. There had arisen a considerable body of expert opinion to the effect that fast cruisers, with great fuel endurance, heavy batteries, and aircraft for reconnaissance and attack, could range far and wide with possibly devastating effects on enemy commerce in the vast stretches of open ocean.

Large submarines with powerful armament and long cruising radius, it was further contended, could seriously harass, and possibly even disrupt, enemy communications in distant seas. The naval aircraft carrier, supported by heavily armed battle cruisers, was frequently suggested as a means of breaking up merchant convoys such as finally defied the submarine during the last months of the late war.

In short, submarines and aircraft, both alone and in various combinations with surface craft, gave promise of restoring the strategic initiative far beyond the narrowing boundaries of a traditional command of the sea. Indeed, the question was squarely raised whether such a "streamlined" *guerre de course* might not ultimately supersede Mahan's classic doctrine of battle-fleet supremacy so far as long-range operations upon the open sea were concerned.

Doubts as to the battle fleet's future utility either in narrow seas or for distant transoceanic operations, raised still more disturbing questions. That the newer techniques of commerce raiding offered at least theoretical solutions to certain strategic problems hitherto regarded as virtually insoluble, admitted of no argument. Whether the potentialities of a streamlined *guerre de course* also invalidated the older and all but universally accepted doctrine of battle-fleet supremacy, was a subject of heated and continuing debate. Was the capital ship still the backbone of sea power? Did the concentration of these massive floating forts into a fighting fleet any longer provide the necessary cover and protection for the manifold secondary operations involved in guarding a country's sea approaches and vital communications, and in closing those of the enemy? Were submarines and aircraft destined to drive the capital ship from the sea, or to so circumscribe its movements as virtually to destroy its strategic utility and value?

These questions, doubts, and speculations all had a direct or indirect bearing on the naval problem of the United States. There was little disagreement that submarine and air power buttressed the defensive position of the continental United States, separated by thousands of miles from Europe and Asia. If invasion from overseas would have been difficult before, it would be more so in the future. And it was a question whether all the navies in the world combined could blockade our continental coastline in the face of incessant counter-attacks below and above as well as upon the ocean's surface. In short, there was little room for doubt that developments in war technology immeasurably strengthened the remote continental base upon which American sea power ultimately depended.

These developments, however, had no such salutary effect on the strategic position of Great Britain. There was no denying that mines and torpedoes had pushed England to the verge of disaster. There were uneasy forebodings in certain quarters that further advances in submarine and air power might progressively undermine the security of the island base which supported the sea power of Great Britain. And there were contemporary observers here and there who sensed that time and technology might further weaken and possibly even break England's historic grip on the ocean portals of Europe.

American statesmen and naval authorities could not entirely ignore these possibilities, however remote they might appear. England's control of the narrow seas and eastern Atlantic had been a stabilizing influence of undeniable value to the United States. American naval plans had long assumed the permanence and incontestability of that control, the highly publicized prewar bogey of German aggression to the contrary notwithstanding. How would a serious weakening of England's European position affect the world relations of the United States, in peace as well as in war? And conversely, what bearing did this have on the incipient bogey of a war-inflated British Navy itself becoming a menace to the United States?

Turning to the Pacific, one confronted a still more confusing situation. If recent advances in war technology laid to final rest the specter of a Japanese attack in force anywhere in the Western Hemisphere, these advances placed just as strict a limitation on the United States in the western Pacific. Yet there were certain other possibilities to be considered. What bearing, for example, did the rise of submarine and air power have on the defense of remote island possessions? What, if anything, did recent advances in the technique of commerce raiding suggest as to the possible course and outcome of a war with Japan? And what bearing, if any, did these considerations have on the future of international relations in the Pacific and Far East?

On the answers which statesmen and their military advisers should give to these and similar questions, would depend the direction, and to some extent the tempo, of future naval development in Europe, America, and the Far East. And on these answers, in some degree, would depend also the pattern of American foreign policy and the drift of world politics in the years to come.

Sea Power and World Reconstruction: The Problem of 1918

The destruction of German sea power, the advance of Japan in the Pacific and Far East, the wartime surge of navalism in Great Britain, the United States, and Japan, and the astounding development of military and industrial technology, all set the stage for the next act in the drama of sea power and world politics.

Great Britain's dominance in European waters was reaffirmed at least temporarily by the defeat of Germany. But neither England's triumph nor the vast increase in naval power through which it was brought about, could restore that global command of the seas which had supported the Pax Britannica of the preceding century. Nor could any other Power assume that historic rôle of Great Britain.

The American Navy wielded overwhelming force throughout the western Atlantic and eastern Pacific. And the war had incalculably strengthened the strategic position of Japan in the western Pacific. But for obvious geographical reasons, neither of these Powers, despite the yearnings of super-patriots, could transmute, save at prohibitive cost, its inherently regional command of the sea into a world dominance, as England had done before the rise of modern fleets in America and the Far East.

Nevertheless, all three leading naval Powers either held territories or claimed important interests within the strategic sphere of one or both of the others. The United States had widely scattered possessions in the Pacific. The British Empire stretched around the globe. Japan's Asiatic program challenged the policies and threatened the real and speculative interests of both Western Powers. The status of Japanese subjects in America was still in dispute. And there were definite and disquieting indications that the United States might be slipping into Germany's fateful rôle as the chief commercial rival of Great Britain.

Any attempt on the part of these Powers to reach a purely military solution could result only in armament competition trending toward bankruptcy or war, or both. Any move to reassert British sea power in the Western Hemisphere or in the Pacific would inevitably provoke counter moves by the United States and Japan. Further expansion of the Japanese Navy would be taken as a threat to Western interests and possessions in the Pacific and Far East. An American fleet strong enough to wage war in virtually the home waters of Japan, would be regarded in that country as a menace to be countered at any cost. Armament competition between any two Powers, as past experience had abundantly shown, would stimulate navalism everywhere. And when to these and other ramifications were added the imponderable, but ever present factors of national tradition, national pride, and national prestige, it was clear that no purely military solution could hope to assure even a semblance of order and international stability in the years ahead.

The appalling costs and futilities of such an approach were more generally appreciated immediately following the war than they had been earlier, or were to be later on when time should have dimmed somewhat the horrors of the recent conflict. These were the considerations, among others, which impelled men toward the gospel of internationalism, as specifically embodied in President Wilson's prospectus of a league of nations. Only by pooling their weapons, both military and economic, it was believed, could the nations establish a foundation upon which to build a new world order. Only thus, it was insisted, could they escape from another circle of armament competition which offered little but the promise of future anarchy and world conflict.

CHAPTER FOUR

American Sea Power in a New World

SEA power entered prominently and basically into plans for some new world order to be set up after the war. The problem as it was widely discussed during 1918 was to devise ways and means to overawe, or if necessary to overpower, any country contemplating or perpetrating acts of aggression against another member of the society of nations. The crux of the problem was to frame a system of collective sanctions, or coercive measures, military as well as economic and moral, that would deter or halt aggressors, great and small alike. And for geographical and other reasons, sea blockade was generally deemed the most economical, the least dangerous, and altogether the most useful military sanction that could be devised.

The great majority of countries were more or less dependent upon oversea commerce. Of the four Great Powers in Continental Europe, all, with the possible exception of Russia, were vulnerable in varying degrees to sea blockade. So was Great Britain whose war-inflated navy outweighed all other European navies combined. It was accepted as inevitable that the British Navy, through its grip on the ocean gateways of Europe, would necessarily have to play a large part in any system of collective sanctions or world police. But it was intolerable to many Americans that the proposed league of nations should become merely an instrument of British policy, to be used or ignored as might suit the interests of British diplomacy and politics. To avoid this, it was held indispensable that the league have at its command armed force sufficient to counterbalance and even to restrain the historic guardian of Europe's narrow seas.

Reasoning such as this led easily to the conclusion that the naval police power of the proposed league of nations must be headed by two national components of approximately equal strength. Great Britain, it was admitted, would obviously have to provide one of these; and the United States necessarily the other. Only the United States possessed the financial and industrial resources to match the dominant sea power of Great Britain. And for this reason, if for no other, it was contended, the American people could not escape the moral obligation to attain naval parity with Great Britain at the earliest possible moment.

This argument provided an excellent rationalization to justify the war-induced American aim to possess a navy second to none in all the world. But this was not the only argument invoked for that purpose. As we shall show more fully in a later chapter, navalism in America received a strong impetus from the deepening crisis in the Far East. The wartime revival and presumptive post-war survival of the American foreign-trade merchant marine was cited as another reason for uninterrupted naval expansion. And the ambition to possess a navy second to none was further buttressed by the argument that only the threat of American naval supremacy would bring the ruling group in England to accept other features of President Wilson's peace program which, as originally conceived, included general recognition of the liberal standard of neutral rights symbolized by the historic slogan, freedom of the seas, and also a universal reduction of all armaments to the lowest level consistent with domestic safety.

America's Naval Program, 1918-1919

At the close of the World War, the American Navy ranked second only to that of Great Britain. In capital ships ready for service, England had a considerable superiority. Sixteen dreadnought-type battleships[1] with a total displacement exceeding 400,000 tons, and a total main armament of eighty 12-inch and

[1] The term dreadnought was derived from the British battleship of that name completed in 1906, in which was introduced the all-big-gun main battery, a marked departure from earlier battleships which mounted not more than four guns of the largest caliber. See our previous work, *The Rise of American Naval Power*, pp. 263*ff*.

UNITED STATES NAVY FIRST-LINE CAPITAL SHIPS BUILT, BUILDING, AND AUTHORIZED, JANUARY 1, 1919

SHIPS BUILT	*displacement [tons]*	*main battery [guns]*	*attained speed [knots]*	*cost, approximate [dollars]*	*authorized [year]*	*completed [year]*
BATTLESHIPS:						
Michigan	16,000	8 12-in.	19.0–	6,655,773	1905	1910
South Carolina	16,000	8 12-in.	19.0–	6,671,886	1905	1910
Delaware	20,000	10 12-in.	21.5+	8,235,917	1906	1910
North Dakota	20,000	10 12-in.	21.0+	8,551,481	1907	1910
Utah	21,825	10 12-in.	21.5–	8,504,492	1908	1911
Florida	21,825	10 12-in.	21.0–	10,359,979	1908	1911
Arkansas	26,000	12 12-in.	21.0+	10,061,453	1909	1912
Wyoming	26,000	12 12-in.	21.0+	11,077,118	1909	1912
Texas	27,000	10 14-in.	21.0+	10,971,524	1910	1914
New York	27,000	10 14-in.	21.5–	11,323,130	1910	1914
Nevada	27,500	10 14-in.	20.5	11,401,073	1911	1916
Oklahoma	27,500	10 14-in.	20.5	11,548,573	1911	1916
Pennsylvania	31,400	12 14-in.	21.0+	13,393,681	1912	1916
Arizona	31,400	12 14-in.	21.0	12,593,531	1913	1916
Mississippi	32,000	12 14-in.	21.0	13,556,324	1914	1917
New Mexico	32,000	12 14-in.	21.0	12,705,750	1914	1918

SHIPS BUILDING OR AUTHORIZED	*displacement [tons]*	*main battery [guns]*	*designed speed [knots]*	*authorized [year]*	*per cent completed Feb.1919*
BATTLESHIPS:					
Idaho	32,000	12 14-in.	21.0	1914	99.1
Tennessee	32,300	12 14-in.	21.0	1915	60.7
California	32,300	12 14-in.	21.0	1915	53.6
Maryland	32,600	8 16-in.	21.0	1916	39.9
West Virginia	32,600	8 16-in.	21.0	1916	19.0
Colorado	32,600	8 16-in.	21.0	1916	6.8
Washington	32,600	8 16-in.	21.0	1916	4.3
South Dakota	43,200	12 16-in.	23.0	1916	00.0
No. 50 [unnamed]	43,200	12 16-in.	23.0	1916	00.0
Montana	43,200	12 16-in.	23.0	1916	00.0
North Carolina	43,200	12 16-in.	23.0	1916	00.0
No. 53 [unnamed]	43,200	12 16-in.	23.0	1916	00.0
No. 54 [unnamed]	43,200	12 16-in.	23.0	1916	00.0
BATTLE CRUISERS:					
Lexington	43,500	8 16-in.	33.0+	1916	00.0
Constellation	43,500	8 16-in.	33.0+	1916	00.0
Saratoga	43,500	8 16-in.	33.0+	1916	00.0
Ranger	43,500	8 16-in.	33.0+	1916	00.0
Constitution	43,500	8 16-in.	33.0+	1916	00.0
No. 6 [unnamed]	43,500	8 16-in.	33.0+	1916	00.0

eighty-eight 14-inch guns, constituted the American battle line late in 1918. This force compared with Great Britain's forty-two first-line capital ships—thirty-three battleships and nine battle cruisers—whose aggregate displacement approached a million tons, and whose total main armament consisted of 136 12-inch, 144 13.5-inch, and ninety-six 15-inch guns.

In addition to ships ready for service, however, the United States had, under construction or authorized, three more dreadnoughts, ten so-called super-dreadnoughts,[2] and six battle cruisers, which would increase the American battle line by nearly 750,000 tons, with the addition of thirty-six 14-inch and 152 16-inch guns. Early completion of these ships would give the United States a battle line superior in almost every respect to that of Great Britain which at the end of 1918 had but four capital ships building, only one of which, the battle cruiser *Hood*, was destined to be finished.

In modern light cruisers—fleet scouts, commerce raiders, etc. —the United States Navy still suffered from a long standing deficiency, with none in service, and only ten authorized or in early stages of construction. The wartime demand for anti-submarine craft had resulted in an extraordinary destroyer-building program. By the end of 1918 the United States had nearly 100 destroyers in service, and more than 200 still under construction. The war had also stimulated a demand for submarines with which to ambush enemy U-boats, the number built and building reaching a total of 167 at the time of the armistice.

Altogether, excluding minesweepers, patrol boats, and other craft smaller than submarines and destroyers, the United States had in service, at the beginning of 1919, nearly 250 combatant ships with a total displacement exceeding 900,000 tons; and 350 more ships building or authorized, with a displacement of 1,100,000 tons. In contrast, Great Britain at that time had in service some 700 comparable ships aggregating 2,400,000 tons, but less than 500,000 tons under construction.

Because post-armistice demobilization was proceeding at different rates in the two countries, it is impossible to make

[2] The term super-dreadnought was more or less loosely employed. It usually designated a battleship embodying the lessons deduced from experience in the Battle of Jutland, May 31, 1916, the only major fleet action in the World War.

precise personnel comparisons. But one may safely assume, in the light of World War experience, that in quality American naval personnel was at least equal, man for man, to that of any other Power. And American naval authorities were laying plans for a peace establishment large enough to man the great fleet of ships still under construction.

The import of all this is clear. As matters stood in the winter of 1918-1919, the United States had ready for service a navy quantitatively inferior to England's. But the American Navy was forging ahead while England's was virtually standing still. And work in hand, if pushed to completion on schedule, would raise the former within five or six years at the latest to substantial statistical parity with, and probably actual superiority over, the historic mistress of the seas.

Meanwhile, in addition to this unprecedented total of ships in hand or awaiting construction, the Navy Department had drawn plans during the summer of 1918 for a still greater development. These plans called for authorization of over 1,000 additional combatant vessels to be constructed over a period of six years. And at the head of this list stood twelve more battleships and sixteen more battle cruisers.[3]

This tremendous building program was expressly predicated on continuance of war for at least another year. But its capital-ship provisions just as certainly looked far beyond the existing conflict. Great Britain's Grand Fleet, reenforced by one squadron of American battleships, was proving fully adequate to immobilize Germany's High Sea Fleet within the North Sea. The Navy Department had therefore slowed or temporarily suspended work on thirteen battleships and six battle cruisers previously authorized. And by the late summer of 1918, there was no longer room for doubt that the war would come to an end long before American shipyards could even lay down any additional capital ships that might thereafter be authorized.

All this was implicitly recognized by the General Board of the Navy, chief architect of the proposed building program. In a supporting memorandum, dated September 10, 1918, this body explained that its aim was to give the United States, at a

[3] 65 Cong. 3 Sess. House Naval Committee, *Hearings on Naval Estimates for 1919*, p. 495.

date not later than 1925, a navy at least the equal of any other in the world—an unmistakable, if veiled, reference to the greatly expanded Navy of Great Britain. And it was further stated that naval construction on the scale recommended, was necessary not only to "render us reasonably secure for the future," but also to sustain our own war-inflated shipbuilding industry.[4]

The Navy Department's building plans underwent downward revision as the war hurried on to its victorious climax. At the instance of the Administration, the number of additional battleships projected was reduced to ten; battle cruisers to six; and the total of all classes to 156.[5] In this form, the proposed building program duplicated in all essential particulars the one previously authorized in the Naval Act of 1916.[6]

As in the earlier program, it was proposed to lay down within three years the total number of ships authorized. But unlike the specific list of ships detailed in the 1916 Act, this 1919 program introduced the radical innovation of listing only the sixteen capital ships, leaving it to the executive to determine the types and specifications of the remaining 140 vessels, depending on developments abroad, and on conclusions to be reached after further study of World War experience.

Enactment and execution of this program, on top of its 1916 prototype, would increase the American Navy to approximately 800 modern combatant units. And it would give the United States a fighting fleet of thirty-nine first-line battleships and twelve battle cruisers—a force not even approached at the peak of the British fleet's extraordinary wartime development.[7]

This second three-year building program—presented to Congress in December 1918, and kept before that body until May 1919—became the storm center of heated debate which disclosed the desires of the naval authorities, the objectives of the Administration, and the tone and temper of American public opinion during the months following the Armistice.[8]

[4] *loc. cit.*

[5] Navy Department, *Annual Reports, 1918*, pp. 32*ff*.; *New York Times*, Oct. 23, 1918, p. 1; *Hearings, 1919*, p. 495.

[6] See our *Rise of American Naval Power*, pp. 339*ff*.

[7] See *New York Times*, Nov. 23, 1918, p. 5; Dec. 9, p. 4.

[8] For a discussion of public opinion, see Chap. 7, "The Popular Revolt Against Navalism in America."

The position of the naval authorities was laid before Congress in a memorandum read to the House Naval Committee by Admiral Charles J. Badger, spokesman for the General Board. It was that body's mature professional judgment that "under present world conditions and the conditions likely to obtain in the future, the United States Navy should steadily continue to increase." The three-year version of the Board's original six-year program represented the irreducible minimum if the Navy was to fulfill its mission. This mission, he explained, was by no means limited to defending our coasts from "actual invasion." The Navy must also be ready to "protect our sea-borne commerce and [to] drive that of the enemy from the sea." The best way to accomplish both these objects was "to find and defeat the hostile fleet or any of its detachments at a distance from our coast sufficiently great to prevent interruption of our normal course of national life."

In words reminiscent of Mahan, Badger elaborated still larger aspects of the Navy's mission. The United States, he noted, was "building a great merchant marine," and was at last, it seemed, "about to compete for a fair share of the carrying trade of the world." It was the Navy's responsibility to "keep the trade routes open to our shipping." Sea power was also a "factor of vast importance in international relations." In particular, the efficacy of the proposed league of nations would ultimately depend in large measure upon naval power. And Badger anticipated that the United States, "from its wealth, influence, and power," would find itself "called upon to contribute a very large share of the international police force to render such a league effective."

In view of these large responsibilities, a navy "of the size recommended" by the General Board "in previous years" could "no longer be considered adequate" either "to give due weight to the diplomatic remonstrances of the United States in peace" or to "enforce its policies in war." And while that body had recommended a considerably greater building program, the one which the Administration had placed before Congress "would appear to meet immediate necessities."[9]

Admiral Henry T. Mayo, commander in chief of the Atlantic Fleet, translated these sentiments into more picturesque and

[9] *Hearings, 1919*, pp. 494, 495.

forcible language. He openly favored building the greatest navy in the world. Frankly anticipating that this would bring on a naval race with England, he advocated forging ahead as rapidly as possible before the European Powers had time to recover from the recent war. He envisaged a future dominated by brute force, and had very little faith in the proposed league of nations. Such an organization, he predicted, would be "just a little sewing circle" without any coercive force whatever. Even if one assumed that the Powers could "agree upon an international police force," there was no excuse or justification for halting naval construction, because our fleet was not yet strong enough to have in such an enterprise "a full share" which the prestige and safety of the United States required.[10]

Whether these statements faithfully reflected the general drift of American Service opinion at this juncture, it would be impossible of course to say. The *Scientific American*, long a strong advocate of naval expansion, declared in January 1919 that "with the exception, possibly, of a few officers with whom" the Secretary of the Navy had "surrounded" himself in Washington, "we find that there is practically unanimous conviction that the strength of the British Navy is warranted by her island position and the scattered condition of the British Empire, and that it is sufficient that we should be a powerful second."[11]

The *Army and Navy Journal*, however, reported that the current was running in just the opposite direction. Late in December 1918, while hearings were in progress before the House Naval Committee, this conservative organ of Service opinion declared that "Navy officers of many years' experience are quite of one mind . . . that a league of nations on the idealistic lines laid down by its advocates will never be formed." All that "these Navy experts" anticipated was "simply an understanding" among the victorious Powers "as to future concert of action." Therefore, "the Navy," was "unalterably opposed to any policy which would put the United States, the greatest nation in the world, in the position of second to any other nation as to sea power for offensive and defensive purposes. . . . To adopt a policy other than that of attaining by 1925 an equality on the sea with Great Britain is, in the mature opinion of the Navy, an

[10] *ibid.*, pp. 1124, 1147; *New York Times*, Dec. 4, 1918, p. 5; Jan. 31, 1919, p. 1.
[11] Vol. 120, Jan. 18, 1919, p. 48.

admission that the United States, a nation second to none in its resources and the greatness of its people, is ready to lean upon others for support and henceforth to occupy the second position and all that such a position entails."[12]

As already intimated, the proposed building program, duplicating the one enacted in 1916, also had Administration approval and support. President Wilson gave it blanket endorsement in his annual message to Congress in December 1918. Secretary of the Navy Josephus Daniels strongly recommended it in his annual report. And he warmly defended it as the Administration's own program in two appearances before the Naval Committee of the House of Representatives.[13]

It was the desire of the Administration, Daniels blandly informed the Committee, to resume without delay the progressive enlargement of the Navy initiated under the Act of 1916 and interrupted by the exigencies of emergency wartime construction. The projected league of nations, he contended, would need a "tremendous police power" to enforce its decisions. National safety, dignity, and prestige, all required that the United States be able to contribute to such a police force as much as any other Power. And it was felt that the proposed supplement to the 1916 program was necessary to bring up the American Navy to the desired standard.

If the Administration's hopes for a new world order were realized, it was expected that a general agreement for the reduction of all national armaments would follow. To this end, it was proposed that the bill for 1919 include the escape clause first embodied in the Act of 1916.[14] Such a clause would show the Administration's real desire for disarmament, and would leave the President a free hand to suspend or execute the building

[12] Vol. 56, p. 616.

[13] Navy Dept., *Ann. Repts. 1918*, pp. 32*ff*.; *Hearings, 1919*, pp. 820*ff*.; *New York Times*, Nov. 21, 1918, p. 13; Dec. 31, p. 1.

[14] This clause provided: "If at any time before the construction authorized by this Act shall have been contracted for, there shall have been established, with the cooperation of the United States of America, an international tribunal or tribunals competent to secure peaceful determination of all international disputes, and which shall render unnecessary the maintenance of competitive armaments, then and in that case such naval expenditures as may be inconsistent with the engagements made in the establishment of such tribunal or tribunals may be suspended, when so ordered by the President of the United States."

program, depending on the outcome of his plans for a new world order and a general limitation of armaments.

If, however, the forthcoming peace conference should fail "to put an end to competitive naval building on the part of all the nations," it was the Administration's view that the United States then "must bend her will . . . energies . . . men, and . . . money to the task of the creation of incomparably the greatest navy in the world."

In no event, Daniels insisted, could anyone legitimately accuse or even suspect the United States of aggressive intentions. The American people coveted neither the territory nor the trade of any other nation. But they were "pledged to the support of the Monroe Doctrine" and "to the protection of the weak wherever they may suffer threats." If we were to fulfill our "destiny as a leader of democratic impulse" and to play our part "in the protection of small nations, the preservation of freedom of the seas, and for the world at large," we "must be incomparably strong in defense against aggressors and in offense against evil-doers."[15]

Freedom of the Seas—or a Naval Race

While American naval authorities in 1918 generally favored progressive naval expansion as a settled policy after the war, the Wilson Administration sponsored the proposed building program with a somewhat different end in view. The Administration's purpose, as intimated in Secretary Daniels's statements before the House Naval Committee, was primarily to fashion a club to hold over the European Allies in general, and over Great Britain in particular, pending their adherence to President Wilson's comprehensive plans for reduction of armaments and creation of a new world order.

One essential of such a new order as the President and some of his associates envisaged during the year 1918, was a redefinition of the rules of maritime warfare. Neutrals in the future must have assurance against repetition of the lawless belligerent aggressions which had characterized every stage of this desperate

[15] *Hearings, 1919*, pp. 820*ff.*; *New York Times*, Dec. 31, 1918, p. 1. *The Times* of London reported Secretary Daniels as saying that "if Great Britain . . . insists that Britannia rules the waves, the United States will lay two keels to every one Britain does, or five to one if necessary. . . ." Dec. 9, p. 9.

struggle for command of the sea. In January 1918 Wilson had included that aim as one of his "fourteen points" of a just and enduring peace. There must be "absolute freedom of navigation upon the seas outside territorial waters, alike in peace and in war, except as the seas may be closed in whole or in part by international action for the enforcement of international covenants."

Adoption of this sweeping proposal would drastically curtail the historic belligerent rights, not only to blockade enemy seaports, but also to seize neutral goods destined even indirectly for the enemy country. It would transfer from the British Government to an international body as yet non-existent, the right to enforce the kind of blockade which had sapped the strength of Germany in the late war. Indeed, it would virtually prohibit offensive use of British sea power altogether, and would largely nullify the advantages of England's incomparable strategic position *vis-à-vis* the Continent of Europe.

"Freedom of the seas" was therefore utterly abhorrent to British naval authorities and to the majority of British statesmen. And in the autumn of 1918, as the Allied armies pounded away at the crumbling frontier of Germany, British and American statesmen behind the lines were locked in seemingly hopeless disagreement over Wilson's insistence on peace terms which embodied the historic American principle.

Colonel House, the President's personal representative in London, left no doubt as to the possible consequences of continued intransigence on the part of Great Britain. He "did not believe the United States and other countries would willingly submit to Great Britain's complete domination of the seas any more than to Germany's domination of the land, and the sooner the English recognized this fact, the better it would be for them; furthermore, that our people, if challenged, would build a navy and maintain an army greater than theirs. We had more money . . . men, and . . . natural resources. . . . Such a programme would be popular in America and, should England give the incentive, the people would demand the rest."[16]

President Wilson was equally frank. On October 30, with the pre-armistice deadlock still unbroken, he cabled House that we were "pledged to fight not only Prussian militarism but

[16] Charles Seymour, *The Intimate Papers of Colonel House* (1928), Vol. 4, p. 160.

militarism everywhere." He could "not consent to take part in the negotiations of a peace" which failed to include both freedom of the seas and a league of nations. And he hoped he would not be "obliged to make this decision public."[17]

In short, if the European Allies would not accept all of the "fourteen points," Wilson would have publicly to seek congressional advice, with the possibility of the United States making a separate peace with Germany. If Great Britain would not at least discuss freedom of the seas, the United States would have no alternative but to build up its navy to a point where it could enforce American interpretations of neutral rights in future wars.[18]

The reaction in Great Britain was one of alarm and moral indignation. Englishmen had immemorially taken for granted their primacy upon the seas. At enormous cost in men and treasure, they had destroyed the rising sea power of Germany, only to find themselves confronted with another possible rival across the Atlantic. Sea power was the ultimate sanction of British diplomacy. The essence of British sea power was blockade, or the threat of blockade—using that term in the broadest nontechnical sense. The more successful the blockade, the greater the injury not only to the enemy but to neutral bystanders as well. And the greater the relative power of the neutral countries, the more serious to Great Britain was the danger of reprisals.

While the leverage of a neutral United States on a belligerent Great Britain would depend, in the future as in the past, on the relative strength of economic as well as of military weapons, experience seemed to indicate that resolution to use the commercial and financial weapon, as well as ability to do so with impunity, would turn in no small degree on the balance of naval power. And it could perhaps be argued that a progressive inclination of that balance in favor of the United States would not only imperil Britain's position in future wars, but also seriously weaken the latter's peacetime influence on events in Europe and overseas.

All this and more was implicit in the British outcry, popular as well as diplomatic, that greeted American insistence on freedom of the seas and the simultaneous announcement of a huge post-war building program in the late autumn of 1918. While

[17] *ibid.*, p. 168. [18] *ibid.*, pp. 164-5.

British diplomatists labored to modify Wilson's peace terms, leading English spokesmen reiterated that Great Britain would never yield the trident to any Power on earth.

"Great Britain would spend her last guinea," Prime Minister Lloyd George told Colonel House, "to keep a navy superior to that of the United States or any other Power, and . . . no Cabinet official could continue in the Government in England who took a different position."[19] Especially outspoken was Winston Churchill, Minister of Munitions and former First Lord of the Admiralty. In a series of public speeches in November and December, he repeatedly asserted that no league of nations would provide an adequate substitute for the "supremacy of the British fleet." And he defiantly informed the United States that "we enter the peace conference with the absolute determination" to accept "no limitation" on "our naval defense." "We do not intend," he warned, "no matter what arguments . . . are addressed to us, to lend ourselves in any way to any fettering restrictions which will prevent the British Navy maintaining its well-tried and well-deserved supremacy."[20]

"The Naval Battle of Paris"

The Anglo-American impasse over freedom of the seas dissolved in President Wilson's broadening conception of a league of nations in which there would be no neutral Powers, and hence no controversies over neutral rights. But that episode had thoroughly alarmed British statesmen and naval authorities who tended to interpret the huge building program now before Congress, as a threat to the independence and security of the British Empire. Englishmen, as one American journalist reported from Europe, simply could "not conceive" that the "maritime and oversea interests" of the United States required "the greatest fleet in the world." And they just as firmly believed that their own "imperial interests" did require such a fleet.[21] But there were urgent reasons for avoiding a naval building contest with the United States.

[19] *ibid.*, p. 180.

[20] *New York Times*, Nov. 27, 1918, p. 2; Dec. 6, p. 1; Dec. 10, p. 1. And see R. S. Baker, *Woodrow Wilson and World Settlement* (1922), Vol. 1, p. 381; and R. A. Chaput, *Disarmament in British Foreign Policy* (1935), pp. 70, 72.

[21] Arthur Sweetser, "Naval Policy and the Peace Conference" in *Sea Power*, Vol. 6, Feb. 1919, pp. 77, 78.

British naval constructors and architects wanted time to analyze and to digest the technical lessons of the war before charting a course of future development. British statesmen and strategists needed time to examine the ramifications of their post-war situation, and to formulate a defense policy commensurate with their probable future commitments and acceptable to the self-governing Dominions. Furthermore, Great Britain faced a desperate and worsening fiscal crisis, with a national debt approaching £8,000,000,000.[22] And there could be no doubt as to the ultimate outcome of an Anglo-American contest to the bitter end for a theoretical or mathematical primacy upon the seas. Under these conditions the task confronting British statesmanship was to find some way to halt American naval expansion without giving important naval concessions in return.

A flood of publicity, official and unofficial, prepared the way for this undertaking. While one group in England hurled verbal defiance across the Atlantic, another dwelt on the long friendship, common heritage, and parallel interests of the English-speaking peoples; deplored the growing estrangement which imperilled the Anglo-American solidarity so recently welded in the heat of battle; stressed the vital importance of sea power to the scattered elements of the British Empire; and pleaded for sympathetic understanding and recognition of the special needs and difficulties of imperial defense.

Simultaneously, British naval authorities were taking practical steps to safeguard their interests at the forthcoming Peace Conference. In November 1918, they had imperiously demanded outright surrender of the German fleet as one prerequisite to an armistice. Only with reluctance had they accepted internment pending the final peace settlement, as a compromise. And contrary to the spirit, if not the letter, of that compromise, they had promptly engineered the delivery and virtual surrender of that fleet into British hands.[23]

With the German ships securely imprisoned in Scapa Flow, British statesmen held a strong hand with which to bargain. Actually, they preferred destruction to distribution among the victorious Powers. But British intentions were clouded in verbal

[22] Chaput, *op. cit.*, pp. 80-92.

[23] Seymour, *House Papers*, Vol. 4, pp. 127*ff*.

ambiguities. And the possibility that some of the enemy ships might further augment the world's strongest navy was subtly exploited in an attempt to maneuver the United States into an agreement to reduce and stabilize armaments in the ratio of the existing strength of the British and American navies.[24]

This skirmishing developed into a frontal assault on the American position, afterwards referred to as the "naval battle of Paris."[25] That assault which threatened momentarily to disrupt the Peace Conference opened immediately after Secretary of the Navy Josephus Daniels arrived in Paris for a brief stop late in March 1919. With scant regard for the amenities of diplomatic etiquette, Admiral Sir Rosslyn Wester-Wemyss, First Sea Lord of the Admiralty, called without appointment on the American Secretary, demanded to know why the United States was so intent on further increasing its fleet, and bluntly asserted that Great Britain needed the "largest navy afloat."

This was followed by a properly arranged conference in which Admiral Wemyss met Secretary Daniels accompanied by Admiral W. S. Benson, head of the American naval staff in Paris. Once more he asserted England's case for maintaining the "largest navy afloat." His was an "island nation, with colonies all over the globe, making the greatest navy essential to Great Britain's existence."

The United States, replied Admiral Benson, would "never agree to any nation having the supremacy of the seas or the biggest navy in the world." The responsibilities of the American Navy extended "from the Philippines to the Virgin Islands; from Alaska to the . . . farthest portion of South America, because the Monroe Doctrine imposes a duty upon us we must always be ready to perform." For these reasons, "equality with the British

[24] Baker, *World Settlement*, Vol. 1, pp. 386*ff.*

[25] The chief sources of information regarding this important, and much too neglected, episode are as follows: an article by Josephus Daniels, published in the Hearst newspapers on Jan. 23, 1927; a confidential memorandum by Admiral W. S. Benson, dated May 16, 1921, a verified copy of which, in the files of the Navy Department, confirms a text published without citation in G. H. Payne's *England, Her Treatment of America* (1931), pp. 214*ff.*; a memorandum dated April 7, 1919, and published in R. S. Baker's *Woodrow Wilson and World Settlement* (1922), Vol. 3, pp. 206*ff.*; certain passages in Charles Seymour's *Intimate Papers of Colonel House* (1928), Vol. 4, pp. 417*ff.*; and journal entries and documents quoted in D. H. Miller, *My Diary at the Conference of Paris* (1924), Vols. 1 and 8.

Navy" was the minimum standard acceptable to the United States.

A further conference between Secretary Daniels and Walter Long, First Lord of the Admiralty, with Admirals Benson and Wemyss in attendance, likewise ended in deadlock. The British Government, Long stated, "was alarmed lest the program of construction by the United States, then under way, would reduce the British navy to second place." He was also apprehensive regarding the rapid increase of the American merchant marine. It was intolerable that Great Britain should have to suffer "tremendous losses . . . in men, money, and ships, and in addition become a second-rate sea power commercially or otherwise."[26]

The United States had "no ambition to acquire supremacy," Daniels assured Long. There was "no purpose in any naval program to replace Britain as 'mistress of the seas.'" But the Administration did believe that "the peace of the world demanded equality of naval strength" between England and America.

That argument made no impression, however. Long said "his country could neither contemplate nor discuss the completion of the American naval construction program." If President Wilson would not agree to suspend work under that program, his Prime Minister, Mr. Lloyd George, could "not support the League of Nations."

This thrust was aimed at the weakest point in Wilson's armor. He was irrevocably committed, by political necessity as well as by personal conviction, to his program for a league of nations. But that program was encountering difficulties both at home and abroad. And without British support at the Peace Conference, he could make no headway at all.

In a subsequent interview, Lloyd George denied that cessation of American naval construction was a "condition precedent to his support and the support of his country to a league of nations." But he was no less insistent than his Navy Minister

[26] In 1918, the Departmental Committee on Shipping and Shipbuilding of the British Government Board of Trade brought in an extended report in which it was emphatically reiterated that "the maritime ascendancy of the Empire must be maintained at all costs" after the war, and that the United States was destined to become England's most dangerous competitor for the world's carrying trade.

that the United States come to an agreement with Great Britain on the question of relative naval strength. The proposed "league of nations would be a mere piece of rhetoric," he contended, "if we continue to build dreadnoughts."

There could be no naval agreement, Daniels reiterated, as long as the league issue remained unsettled. With the league of nations "a going concern," the United States would gladly collaborate in a "large reduction" of armaments—on the basis of naval parity with Great Britain. But Daniels would "not consent to recommend any agreement in advance of a league of nations to preserve the peace of the world." And this position was expressly confirmed a few days later when President Wilson stated that he could "not make any sort of agreement as to armaments" until he saw what was to be the outcome of the peace negotiations.

These statements furnish the key to the Administration's naval policy at this juncture. Wilson and Daniels were skilfully playing the British game, but in reverse. Their objective, as previously noted, was to force Great Britain to support the league-of-nations project and then to collaborate in a general reduction of armaments on the basis of naval equality with the United States. And while it was repeatedly denied that the Administration was sponsoring the proposed building program for purposes of diplomatic bargaining, the evidence to the contrary is voluminous and convincing.

Daniels, for example, reported the President as saying, on the latter's departure for Europe in December 1918, that "nothing would so aid him in the Peace Conference as Congress's authorization of a big navy."[27] In February while still abroad, Wilson threw the full weight of his presidential office into an effort to force the naval bill out of committee and through the lower house. It was widely reported, and not very convincingly denied, that he had cabled in substance that failure to pass the bill would be "fatal" to his negotiations.[28]

Whatever the exact words cabled from Paris, that was undeniably the sense in which the message was understood in Washington. A favorable report was rushed through the Naval Com-

[27] *New York Times*, Dec. 31, 1918, p. 1.

[28] *ibid.*, Feb 1, 1919, p. 1; Feb. 5, p. 3; *New York Herald*, Feb. 5, sec. 2, p. 5; *New York Sun*, Feb. 4, p. 1; and 65 Cong. 3 Sess., *Cong. Rec.* (Vol. 57), pp. 2682*ff*.

mittee so that the American delegation in Paris could "lay its cards on the table in respect to competitive armaments."[29] The belief persisted among members of the committee, that this program would "never be carried out"; and that the President merely desired "to have the United States on record" so that everyone could "see what was proposed in the way of a naval establishment if the Peace Conference" reached no agreement as to "limitation of armament."[30]

American journalists covering the Peace Conference drew the same conclusion from facts available to them in Paris. One of them learned from an "authoritative source" that the American delegation would "adhere to a big navy program" until there was positive assurance that "the nations of the world will reduce armaments."[31] And another summarized the President's strategy as one of "offering the debt torn nations of Europe the alternative of international cooperation with proportional disarmament or national competition with crushing naval armaments, the rate of increase . . . to be dictated by the untouched wealth of America."[32]

This strategy was likewise implicit, indeed all but explicit, in Secretary Daniels's repeated iterations that the Administration, while urging a great building program, was ready and anxious to collaborate in any feasible scheme for insuring world peace and reducing national armaments.[33] It was further implicit in

[29] *New York Sun*, Feb. 1, 1919, p. 1. According to the *New York Herald*, Feb. 1, sec. 2, p. 3, this action was taken to confer upon the President "the authority to present the [armament] matter squarely to the peace conference." The *New York Times*, Feb. 1, p. 1, used language less explicit, but to substantially the same effect.

[30] *New York Times*, Feb. 10, 1919, p. 12; *New York Tribune*, May 28, pp. 1, 8.

[31] R. V. Oulahan, *New York Times*, Feb. 9, 1919, p. 2.

[32] Arthur Sweetser, "Why President Wilson Wants a Big Navy," *Sea Power*, Vol. 6, March 1919, pp. 169-70, 216.

[33] The following are typical examples of many interchanges that took place in the Hearings before the House Naval Committee in Dec., 1918:

Rep. Kelley: ". . . You want us to state to the House that three years ago [1916] we actually adopted a policy which in a reasonable time would make us the first naval Power in the world, unless some agreement for the reduction of armaments should be made?"

Sec. Daniels: "Yes."

Rep. Kelley: "And you think that the best thing to do is to boldly state that we are now pursuing a policy which will make us the first naval Power as soon as our building facilities can produce it?"

Sec. Daniels: "Unless we come to an international agreement." *Hearings, 1919*, pp. 864, 865; and see *ibid.*, pp. 820*ff.*, 836, 837, 839-41, 886; also Navy Dept., *Ann. Repts. 1918*, pp. 144, 386*ff.*

the House Committee's stipulation that no work on the new ships should start before February 1, 1920—when the Peace Conference would presumably have completed its labors. And such was also the purport of the escape clause, previously mentioned, which left discretion in the Executive to suspend the building program in the event of successful negotiations for a league of nations and for a general reduction of armaments.[34]

While it is thus fairly clear that the Administration viewed the building program as an instrument of high policy to be carried out, modified, or even abandoned, depending on the turn of events in Paris, the naval advisers of the American delegation, like the naval authorities in Washington, were adamant in opposing any concessions that would leave Great Britain with even a theoretical primacy upon the sea. This view, which was shared to some extent by prominent civilian members of the American Peace Commission,[35] was trenchantly stated in two memoranda prepared by the American naval staff in Paris.[36]

The first dealt with the disposition of the German fleet, developing a strong case for destruction rather than distribution of the ships among the Allied and Associated Powers. Because of their short cruising radius, it was contended, Great Britain was the only country that would benefit from such a distribution. That would place a heavy burden upon the American people, for it was essential that we have a navy "as large as that of Great Britain." Only thus would the proposed league of nations have the power "to restrain, if necessary, its strongest member." And only thus would the "national safety" of the United States be assured against a possible combination of the sea power of Great Britain and Japan.

The second memorandum opened with a lengthy disquisition on power politics. "The smooth and leisurely phrases of diplomacy," it was observed, derive "their pungency from a vision of the force in readiness that lies behind them." For the United States, because of its geographical position, naval power was the decisive factor. "Military pressure" on the territories or com-

[34] 65 Cong. 3 Sess., *H. Rept.* No. 1024, p. 3; and *Hearings, 1919*, pp. 827-8. For further interpretations of the Administration's strategy, see the *Scientific American*, Vol. 120, Feb. 22, 1919, p. 164; and *Cong. Rec.*, Vol. 57, pp. 2682*ff.*

[35] See Miller, *Diary*, Vol. 8, p. 147; and Seymour, *House Papers*, Vol. 4, pp. 417*ff.*

[36] Baker, *World Settlement*, Vol. 3, pp. 197*ff.*, 206*ff.*

merce of the United States "must be a pressure based upon possible operations by way of the sea. . . . Conversely, if we desire to retaliate or to exert opposing military pressure, we must base our efforts upon sea power."

"In the past," this paper continued, "our naval position has derived great strength from the potential hostility of the British and German fleets. Neither . . . could venture abroad without grave risk that the other would seize the opportunity . . . to crush a rival." Now, however, as a result of the war, we found arrayed against us a British fleet more powerful than ever before, and no longer restrained by the potential enmity of another strong European fleet. And this situation had arisen at the very moment when we were "setting out to be the greatest commercial rival of Great Britain on the seas."

This seemed to the American naval advisers a portentous coincidence. "Every great commercial rival of the British Empire," they recalled, "has eventually found itself at war with Great Britain—and has been defeated." They found special cause for anxiety in England's "governing policy" which was "to acquire control of the foci of the sea commerce of the world" and a "monopoly, so far as possible, of international communications"—including submarine cables,[37] radio networks, commercial air lines, merchant shipping, fuelling stations, and fuel deposits.[38]

The political relations and policies of the British Empire were likewise not without significance to the United States. "At a time when all the world is seeking to form a league of nations that will secure justice to great and small nations alike, the British Prime Minister announces that the British alliance with France will continue forever." And the Anglo-Japanese Alliance still continued in the Far East. Such combinations seemed to the authors "to contain elements of grave danger and to demand

[37] This reference was apparently to the Anglo-American struggle for control of electrical communications with South America and the Far East, which was at this very moment entering an acute stage; see L. B. Tribolet, *International Aspects of Electrical Communications in the Pacific Area* (1929).

[38] This reference was apparently to the rapid progress of the British Government and of British corporations in securing control of the world's petroleum resources. For British activities in the Near East, see E. M. Earle, "The Turkish Petroleum Company—A Study in Oleaginous Diplomacy," *Political Science Quarterly*, June 1924, Vol. 39, pp. 265*ff*.

. . . extraordinary measures." Nothing less than full equality upon the sea would enable us to hold our own, whether in conference or in armed conflict, in the clearly impending Anglo-American struggle for position, power, profit, and prestige.

Such equality, they continued, was also necessary to secure the ends of world peace and international justice. If the projected league of nations was to fulfill its mission, it must have available sufficient force to overpower "any recalcitrant member. . . ." Such force was not to be found in a "heterogeneous" collection of naval craft assembled by the league, unless "that assemblage" included "one group of a single nationality . . . equal in strength" to the naval power of the nation under coercion. Thus "as long as Great Britain insists on retaining her overwhelming naval force, the only answer for the purposes of the League is the building of an equal force by some [other] nation. . . ." And as "the United States is the only Power that is today financially and physically capable of building such a fleet," it was strongly urged in conclusion, that we should, for international as well as purely national reasons, attain to such rank without delay.

While the professionals on both sides were thus reiterating positions which left little room for compromise, the statesmen were earnestly searching for some formula which would appear to serve their respective national ends without at the same time precipitating a dangerous diplomatic crisis. These conversations were carried on with the utmost secrecy, lest publicity arouse "national spirit on both sides" and render impossible any accommodation at all.[39] And so closely was the secret guarded that several weeks elapsed before even the naval staff of the American Peace Commission learned that their political superiors, contrary to the foregoing professional advice, had entered into an agreement to withdraw Administration support from the supplementary three-year building program.[40]

Not until late in May 1919, after Secretary Daniels's return to the United States, did it become generally known that the Administration had reversed itself on this issue. This reversal was officially explained and justified on two grounds. One was that the other Powers had suspended virtually all new construc-

[39] Seymour, *House Papers*, Vol. 4, pp. 422-3.
[40] *New York Times*, June 1, 1919, p. 1.

tion; the other, that the now pending treaty of peace made definite provision for a league of nations.[41] But this explanation was not too convincing, for, as was promptly pointed out, the slackening of naval construction abroad had set in months ago, immediately following the armistice; and the prospects for a really effective league of nations were almost as uncertain as when the Administration was vigorously pressing for enactment of the program now abandoned.[42]

Presently, however, the real explanation leaked out. The Administration's about face, together with the implausibility of official statements in connection therewith, had stimulated inquiries in Paris. These inquiries brought forth guarded admissions from the American principals involved in the recent naval conversations. And from these admissions, the newspaper men were able to piece together vague and fragmentary, but substantially accurate, accounts of a provisional naval agreement between Great Britain and the United States.[43]

We now know that this agreement had been reached on April 10, the day after the American naval staff submitted its second paper to the President. It was embodied in highly confidential memoranda that passed between Colonel House and Lord Robert Cecil, acting on behalf of Wilson and Lloyd George. According to this agreement, it was mutually understood that the latter would support Wilson's plans for a league of nations, and would raise no objection to inserting in the League Covenant a clause affirming the validity of the Monroe Doctrine—a clause that meant nothing to Lloyd George, but much to Wilson as he strove to bolster his crumbling lines on the home front. In return, while the President would make no commitment as to ships already building, it was understood that he would consider postponing work on ships authorized but not yet laid down, as well as suspending the second three-year program, then before Congress, but not yet enacted.[44]

[41] 66 Cong. 2 Sess. House Naval Committee, *Hearings on Naval Estimates for 1920*, pp. 2217-19; *New York Herald*, May 28, 1919, sec. 2, p. 7; *New York Times*, May 28, p. 17.

[42] *New York Herald*, May 29, 1919, p. 10; *Literary Digest*, Vol. 61, June 14, p. 15.

[43] See, for example, *New York Sun*, May 29, 1919, p. 3; and *New York Times*, June 1, p. 1.

[44] Seymour, *House Papers*, Vol. 4, pp. 417-23; Miller, *Diary*, Vol. 8, pp. 137-47; and D. H. Miller, *Drafting of the Covenant*, Vol. 1, Chap. 30.

It seems to have been tacitly understood that this maritime truce, and it certainly was no more than a truce, was to continue in force until the two Governments should have time, after the Peace Conference, to work out a permanent agreement as to the future relative strength of their respective navies. And such an agreement, establishing a naval standard or balance of power in the Atlantic, and possibly also in the Pacific, might conceivably have been reached in the winter of 1919-1920, but for the tragic physical collapse of President Wilson, and for the bitter political struggle culminating in rejection of the League of Nations by the Senate of the United States.[45]

[45] Lord Grey of Fallodon came to the United States in the autumn of 1919 for the express purpose, among others, of negotiating a naval limitation agreement with the United States, but was prevented for the reasons mentioned in the text from accomplishing anything. Seymour, *House Papers*, Vol. 4, pp. 496, 500.

CHAPTER FIVE

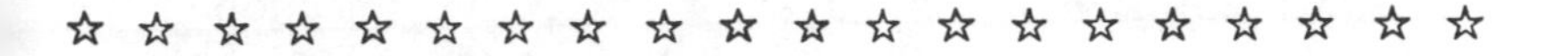

The League of Nations or the Greatest Navy

THE Wilson Administration, having employed against Great Britain the threat of unlimited naval expansion to advance the President's league-of-nations project at the Peace Conference, now turned the same weapon against the anti-league forces in America. From May 1919 until March 1921, Administration leaders, especially the President and his Secretary of the Navy, Josephus Daniels, repeatedly warned the American people that they faced a fundamental choice. Either they must accept the league or embrace militarism; they must pool their weapons with other peace-loving nations or else carry the enormous burden of incomparable armaments.

As a means of coercing the anti-league coalition in this country, these threats proved utterly unavailing. But as a means of further alienating and alarming Great Britain, the President's strategy was a decided, if undesired, success. And as the Administration's days ran out in domestic bitterness and recrimination, the two great English-speaking people were drifting toward an impasse which threatened to postpone indefinitely their collaboration in the gigantic task of world reconstruction.

The nature of the Administration's political strategy was clearly indicated in the statement, late in May 1919, announcing withdrawal of the second three-year building program which was still before Congress. This step, Secretary Daniels stated, assumed early ratification of the Versailles Treaty which embodied the Covenant of the League of Nations. "With the League in operation, composed at first of all the nations allied or associated in the World War and with provision for the admittance of all other nations opposed to conquest and militarism, it would not be necessary to impose on the taxpayers of America . . . for building more capital ships. . . ." But rejection of the Covenant, he warned, might compel the Administration to revive the abandoned program. "We have only two courses," he declared. Either we must have "a league of nations by which every nation will help preserve the peace of the world without competitive navy building, or we must have incomparably the biggest navy in the world. There is no middle ground."[1]

In terms somewhat less specific, but no less threatening, President Wilson in August warned the Senate Foreign Relations Committee what to expect if the Versailles Treaty were rejected. The Administration's future "military plans of course" awaited action on the Treaty. We could not "intelligently or wisely" decide how large an army and navy we should need, and whether or not to impose compulsory military training, until we knew "how peace was to be sustained; whether by the arms of single nations or by the concert of all the great peoples."[2]

On his last and ill-fated speaking tour through the Western States, undertaken in September 1919 in a desperate effort to stem the rising opposition, Wilson repeatedly offered the League of Nations as the only alternative to resumption of armament construction on a gigantic scale. Playing upon the historic and deeply rooted American fear of militarism, he asserted that rejection of the Covenant would leave us no alternative but to become a "nation in arms" ever ready for war. That would entail not merely "burdensome taxation" and "compulsory military service," but also the "building up of a military class" which, as in the European autocracies, would directly or indirectly dominate the civil government. There was no other choice. It was either the League with limited armaments, or isolation with militarism. And the latter course, he grimly prophesied as he tottered on the brink of physical collapse, would mean "great standing armies . . . an irresistible navy,"

[1] 66 Cong. 2 Sess. House Naval Committee, *Hearings on Naval Estimates for 1920*, pp. 2217-19.

[2] 66 Cong. 1 Sess., *Sen. Docs.* No. 106, p. 500.

and progressive decay of democracy, for civil liberty and military efficiency were fundamentally irreconcilable.[3]

With a senatorial minority blocking the entrance of the United States into the League of Nations, the Navy Department in December 1919 brought forward a new building program which clearly violated the spirit, if not the letter, of the Administration's truce with Great Britain reached at the Peace Conference. This program, which the Administration did not disclaim, but for which it took no responsibility, was not another long-term project, but rather an interim measure designed primarily to accelerate the Navy's advance to first rank upon the sea.[4]

The proposed building program called for two additional battleships, one battle cruiser, and twenty-five smaller ships of different types. The General Board, chief architect of this project, recommended laying down all these ships within the next fiscal year, and supported its recommendation with arguments which unmistakably, if tacitly, cast both Great Britain and Japan in the rôle of diplomatic and commercial rivals, if not of potential enemies.

The Board's stated objective was a navy "large enough to protect our national interests in both oceans." This objective included, of course, the defense of "our long continental coastline and our island possessions." It also implied a navy adequate "to guarantee the free use of the seas at all times to our merchant marine," and conversely, to imperil the commercial life lines of potential enemies. "The strength necessary" to realize these objectives depended "upon the strength of the navies of the Powers in position to challenge our legitimate commercial expansion upon the high seas. . . ." And so long as there existed "no agreement limiting naval armaments," it would be "necessary for the United States to steadily add to the number and power of its naval ships . . . and also to provide replacements for ships which by reason of the rapid development in naval construction will have to be relegated to the second line or scrapped."[5]

[3] Speeches at St. Louis, Kansas City, Billings, Seattle, Portland, Denver, and Pueblo. R. S. Baker & W. E. Dodd, *The Public Papers of Woodrow Wilson* (1927), Vol. 5, p. 638; Vol. 6, pp. 4, 112, 189, 196, 392, 412.

[4] Navy Department, *Annual Reports, 1919*, pp. 107, 149*ff*. [5] *ibid.*, pp. 149, 151.

Such a view necessarily envisaged a fleet sufficient not merely to command the marine approaches to the continental United States and to the Panama Canal, but also to dominate the western Pacific and even the principal sea lanes of the Old World.[6] This challenge to the sea power of Japan and of England was implicit in the testimony of Admiral Robert E. Coontz, Chief of Operations, before the House Naval Committee in January 1920.[7] And the challenge was made explicit six weeks later when Admiral Charles J. Badger, spokesman for the General Board, pressed Congress for ship authorizations that would result in giving the United States the largest navy in the world.[8]

In the meantime, Administration leaders were again threatening unlimited naval expansion in a continuing effort to beat down the Senate minority which was still blocking American entry into the League. On January 31 Assistant Secretary of the Navy Franklin D. Roosevelt publicly warned that the Navy would henceforth cost the American people a billion dollars a year in case international relations went "back to what they were before" the war.[9] And on March 6 Secretary Daniels told the House Naval Committee that the Administration's future naval plans were contingent upon the Senate's vote on the still pending Versailles Treaty. If that body passed the treaty, thereby assuring United States membership in the League of Nations, he would recommend no more than completion of the 1916 program. But if the Senate failed to take action during that session, he would have to advise some additional construction. And if that body rejected the treaty, he intended to revive the original post-war program, duplicating that of 1916, with a view to making the United States Navy "incomparably" the strongest in the world.[10]

[6] This prospectus of world domination drew a sharp protest from even the traditionally big-navy *New York Times*, which declared that the "Atlantic Coast is as secure as if there were no fleets in Europe." Dec. 11, 1919, p. 12.

[7] *Hearings, 1920*, p. 299; and see *New York Times*, Jan. 16, 1920, p. 3.

[8] *New York Times*, March 2, 1920, p. 12; *Hearings, 1920*, pp. 2045*ff*.

[9] *New York Times*, Feb. 1, 1920, p. 21.

[10] *Hearings, 1920*, pp. 2219*ff*.; *New York Times*, March 7, 1920, p. 1. On cross examination Daniels became involved in numerous contradictions and inconsistencies. He refused to say that the United States was building against Japan, although he expressly asserted that we would always have a moral responsibility to defend the Philippines, even if those islands were given a nominal independence. He was equally vague as to Great Britain, although he was forced to admit that the

GREAT BRITAIN—FRIEND OR RIVAL

Although Congress disregarded the Administration's threats, and rejected the Navy Department's ship recommendations, both in 1919 and in 1920, public discussion of the proposed building programs, together with English criticism of Wilson's peace terms and naval policy, reawakened the suspicion, distrust, and ill-will which in times past had recurrently dominated American opinion of, and relations with, Great Britain.[11]

As early as January 1919, "British-American discord" and "British-American naval rivalry" were becoming popular newspaper topics.[12] This trend was reflected in, and probably accentuated by, the provocative utterances of certain politicians. The American people, whose armed forces "had as much to do . . . in forcing the Hun fleet to surrender as England had," would never, it was asserted, "submit to a policy which would force them to sit supinely with fetters on their hands, and . . . permit Great Britain to be the bully of the world. . ." The public was reminded that "Great Britain has threatened our interests oftener and more seriously than all the other nations of the earth combined." To the suggestion that "we can rely upon the British Navy for protection" it was retorted that "those who are impractical enough to advocate such a policy either must have forgotten or do not know that we have had more wars and complications with England than with all the other nations of the world combined." Wars were generally "the result of a desire for commercial supremacy," and the United States was today the "one great commercial rival of England. . . ."[13]

The Administration's naval truce with Great Britain, announced late in May 1919, drew a blast of indignation from the ultra-nationalistic newspapers in America.[14] Anti-British utterances figured conspicuously in the anti-League-of-Nations drive that was rapidly gaining momentum in the summer and autumn of 1919. Anti-Leaguers intemperately assailed Great

possibility of future controversies with that Power was a factor, and that Great Britain was the "only other nation that has now a great navy."

[11] For some early post-war indications of this trend in American newspapers, see the *Literary Digest*, Vol. 59, Dec. 21, 1918, p. 5.

[12] See, for example, *Literary Digest*, Vol. 60, Jan. 4, 1919, p. 9; and Jan. 11, p. 12.

[13] 65 Cong. 3 Sess., *Cong. Rec.* (Vol. 57), pp. 2718, 3098, 3167.

[14] See, for example, *New York American*, May 28, 1919, p. 5; May 29, pp. 3, 20.

Britain's alleged oppression of Ireland, and vented their fury on that provision of the League Covenant which gave an Assembly-vote to each of the British self-governing Dominions, or six to the British Empire as a whole, in contrast to only one for the United States.

The same trend was perceptible in the naval debate of 1919-1920. Members of Congress continued to picture Great Britain as a dangerous rival and possible enemy. Much was made, for example, of the strategic advantage which we had formerly derived from the Anglo-German naval deadlock. England, it was pointed out, was now freed from the restraining influence of German sea power; and this strategic emancipation had come at the very moment when the United States was embarking upon a voyage of commercial expansion, with England as our only serious rival. Under these circumstances, it was contended, the only safe course was to continue enlarging our navy until we had the "dominant navy of the world"; and then, "having taken control of the sea," we could "keep it for generation after generation."[15]

It was also recalled that Great Britain had consistently flouted American neutral rights in the past. Prior to our entry into the late war, "our peaceful commerce with neutral countries" had been stopped "on the high seas by a superior naval power and carted all over the world to prize courts and used as a commercial football, notwithstanding our strenuous objections. . . ." Thus the exigencies of neutrality as well as of possible belligerency called for the greatest navy in the world.[16]

It was even publicly asserted by a member of the lower House, that until Great Britain could "pay interest on her bonded indebtedness . . . to her foreign creditors, she would not be justified in going ahead with a costly competitive battleship program, and particularly so not with us, when she realizes fully that we have no designs upon anything she may have. While the pride of England may be hurt by her slide into second place among the naval Powers, she certainly cannot hope to successfully compete against us if we are really determined to take the place we are entitled to on the seas as the world's foremost nation. . . ."[17]

[15] 66 Cong. 2 Sess., *Cong. Rec.* (Vol. 59), p. 4660. [16] *Hearings, 1920*, p. 2221.
[17] Quoted in *Army and Navy Journal*, Vol. 57, April 17, 1920, p. 996.

A section of the press took up the attack, dwelling on the assumed menace of British sea power. And after comparative quiescence during the later months of 1919, the growth of Anglo-American discord again became a popular topic of editorial comment and discussion.[18]

Public disclosure at this juncture that the British Government and British corporations with government support, had succeeded in cornering most of the then known petroleum reserves of Europe and Asia, and some of those in Latin America as well, gave fresh impetus to the anti-British current in the United States. A highly indiscreet public boast uttered, in March 1920, by the First Lord of the Admiralty, that control of the world's oil resources would place the British Government in a position to "do what we like," associated the oil problem with the naval issue.[19] And revelations of anxiety in American official circles, lest our warships soon become dependent upon British-controlled supplies of fuel oil, stirred the smoldering fire of American distrust, resentment, and growing indignation.[20]

So did the annual drive for larger naval appropriations which once more got under way in the autumn of 1920. This time the naval authorities returned to the idea of a three-year building program. And the project which the General Board offered this year as a "rounding out" program, embraced eighty-eight vessels, including three battleships, one battle cruiser, thirty light cruisers, six long-range cruising submarines, and four aircraft carriers.[21]

In support of this project, the Board reviewed its previous utterances, and went on to emphasize its view as to the "importance of unimpeded ocean transportation for commerce," in peace as well as in war. In language strongly flavored with Mahan, it was contended that "a great and developing country needs a proportionately great merchant fleet of its own to insure its markets and preserve its commerce from subservience to rival nations and their business. Our Navy and our merchant service are inextricably associated in the economic progress

[18] See, for example, *Literary Digest*, Vol. 64, March 27, 1920, pp. 20*ff*.

[19] *New York Times*, March 26, 1920, p. 12; *Hearings, 1920*, pp. 3309*ff*.

[20] *New York Times*, Feb. 25, 1920, p. 23; May 18, p. 23; May 19, p. 15; *Commercial and Financial Chronicle*, Vol. 110, May 22, 1920, pp. 2146*ff*.; *Literary Digest*, Vol. 65, June 12, 1920, p. 23; and Vol. 67, Dec. 11, p. 18.

[21] Navy Department, *Annual Reports, 1920*, pp. 211, 216.

and prosperity of the people. A combatant Navy supporting and protecting a great merchant fleet, such as the country requires both in peace and war, appears to the General Board as an essential condition of national progress and economic prosperity."

"The large increase in our merchant marine and our rapidly extending commercial interests," together with our long coastlines and widely separated possessions in two oceans, left the Board in no doubt as to need of a navy "equal to the most powerful maintained by any other nation of the world." But there was "no thought of instituting international competitive building." No other country could reasonably "take exception to such a position." The United States threatened no one "by the mere act of placing itself on an equality with the strongest." None could "justly" construe it "as a challenge." On the contrary, it was contended, "a policy of equal naval armaments may well tend to diminish their growth and would certainly work to lessen the danger of sudden war."[22]

As in the preceding year, the Wilson Administration took an equivocal stand, professing neutrality toward the General Board's recommendations, but threatening to give them full support unless the United States joined the League of Nations and collaborated in a world-wide effort to reduce armaments.

This theme recurred with monotonous regularity. It was iterated in the annual report of Secretary Daniels.[23] On December 13, he released a statement to the press, in which he asserted that "unless the United States is ready to go into an association of all nations, or of practically all nations, we cannot quit our building program. The world today is in chaos. Nobody knows what will happen within the next year, and the United States should complete its building program, already started, without interruption."[24]

Daniels criticized a Senate Resolution, introduced by Senator Borah, which urged the President to conclude an agreement with the two other leading naval Powers—Great Britain and Japan—to reduce naval expenditures by 50 per cent during the next five years. Such an agreement, he held, "would be a blunder equal to a crime. . . ." Such a three-Power agreement

[22] *ibid.*, p. 211.
[23] *ibid.*, pp. 2*ff*.
[24] *New York Times*, Dec. 14, 1920, p. 19.

would excite suspicion in countries not included. Unless we could have an agreement that included practically all the world, "then we must in America, having the longest shore line of any nation on earth, have the largest navy."[25]

Two days later, Daniels offered the further explanation that the Administration had recommended no building program the preceding year in the "sublime belief that we should be in the League of Nations." But that belief had proved to be unfounded. Now he did not know what conditions would "be as to our world relations." But he was convinced "it would be fatal for the United States" to agree at this juncture to a naval building holiday, since that would prevent the United States from achieving parity with Great Britain. He was likewise certain that if we were determined to go our way "alone, joining no League or association of nations, we must keep on building up our Navy."[26]

On December 27, in reply to a growing volume of hostile criticism, Secretary Daniels issued another extended defense of the Administration's course. Contrary to popular impression, they were not unconditionally supporting the building program advocated by the General Board. "The suggestion for another large naval building program was contingent wholly upon the theory that there might be no . . . League of Nations, and no agreement for a limitation of armaments." The main purpose of the League, he held, was to stop armament competition. Every member was pledged to that effect. All that was needed to make this pledge effective was to get the United States into the League. And as long as there was any chance of doing that, the Administration's naval plans went no further than completing the ships already authorized.[27]

In a supplementary statement Daniels emphasized the Administration's unqualified opposition to any three-Power agreement to halt naval construction. Great Britain would be the chief beneficiary of a naval holiday. England "could well afford to favor an agreement to curtail naval building today, for such an agreement would leave her with a navy almost twice as powerful as any other in the world, in addition to the fact that she has an alliance with Japan." That Alliance was probably not directed

[25] 66 Cong. 3 Sess. House Naval Committee, *Hearings on Sundry Legislation, 1920-1921*, p. 86.

[26] *New York Times*, Dec. 17, p. 11.

[27] *ibid.*, Dec. 28, p. 3.

at the United States, but we could not overlook its existence. And we should not ignore the fact that the "combined Japanese and British navies would overshadow the American sea forces."[28]

On January 11, this naval spokesman of the defeated outgoing Administration returned once more to the attack. In a long and rambling statement before the House Naval Committee, he reiterated that the United States must choose either navalism or the League of Nations, and reviewed his objections to any tripartite or other agreement that would leave Great Britain with the largest navy. While he would not quite admit that the Administration regarded England as a dangerous potential enemy, he nevertheless argued, in palpable disregard of elementary strategic and political facts, that the American people could no longer safely view the two oceans as great protective barriers against foreign aggression.[29] A few days later in a valedictory statement, Daniels solemnly warned that if we were "going it alone," it would be necessary not only to complete the ships under construction, but also to authorize and build many more, with a view to seizing virtually a world-wide command of the sea.[30]

Throughout these and other pronouncements ran the two threads of Administration strategy, first perceptible in the winter of 1918-1919. One was a fixed purpose to coerce Great Britain into a clear and unequivocal acceptance of naval parity with the United States. The other was a continuing effort to frighten the American people into joining the League of Nations. In retrospect, it seems fairly clear that the Administration was waving a stuffed club. As we shall see in a later chapter, there was no hope of further expanding the Navy during the last months of the Wilson Administration.[31] And if acts speak louder than words, there is very little evidence that the political authorities, as distinguished from the professional naval authorities, really desired any further increase. In May 1919, it will be recalled, the Administration had publicly withdrawn support from the supplementary three-year building program framed after

[28] *ibid.*, Jan. 4, 1921, p. 4.

[29] *Hearings on Sundry Legislation, 1920-1921*, pp. 542-3.

[30] 66 Cong. 3 Sess. House Appropriations Committee, *Hearings on Naval Appropriation Bill for 1922*, p. 936.

[31] Chap. 7, *infra*.

the armistice. In the winter of 1919-1920, the Administration had threatened and blustered, but asked for little beyond continuance of work on ships already building or authorized. And this, as we have just seen, was about what happened in the congressional session of 1920-1921.

Whether intended or not, the residual effect of the Administration's insinuations, threats, warnings, and alarms was to cast Great Britain and Japan in the rôle of dangerous rivals and possible enemies. From all the evidence available, one gathers that the idea of armed conflict with England was abhorrent to the vast majority of the American people. But there was no denying that the historic anti-British trend in the United States received additional impetus from the continuing agitation for a navy second to none.

Advocates of further naval expansion were repeatedly asked why the United States should try to outstrip Great Britain. No one put this question more trenchantly than did Admiral William Sowden Sims, commander of American forces in European waters during the World War, and a lifelong exponent of Anglo-American friendship and solidarity. "A navy is built for only one purpose," he declared, "and that is to fight an enemy. . . . I do not see why it is a thing about which there should be any pussyfooting." If the President, State Department, and Congress were convinced that we were "in more or less imminent danger of getting into armed conflict with Great Britain, or with Great Britain and Japan combined," then we were certainly justified in building the world's greatest navy. Otherwise he failed to see why a navy second to England's was not just as adequate now as it had been prior to the war when nobody seriously contemplated challenging the naval primacy of Great Britain.[32]

Others professed to agree with Sims in principle, but disagreed sharply with the conclusion implicit in his language. The *Army and Navy Journal*, claiming to voice dominant Service opinion, declared: ". . . no Senate, no Administration, not ourselves as a nation, can wholly read the future. Granting the good-will of the world at the present moment toward a policy of reduction in armament; none can determine when economic conditions or self-interest may tempt some nation to seek to

[32] *Hearings on Sundry Legislation, 1920-1921*, p. 643.

evade . . . any agreement on the subject of disarmament. In the future, as the past has shown, there is only one adequate policy for this country, and that is to be prepared . . . to meet any eventuality that may arise." In short, we must have a navy "powerful enough to win in any field of battle a naval war into which this nation may be drawn," even in the far western Pacific 7,000 miles from our nearest continental base.[33]

Admiral H. McL. P. Huse, who had served on the American naval staff at the Peace Conference, went so far as to recommend frank discussion regarding ways and means of waging war against Great Britain allied with Japan. And as a necessary step in preparation for that eventuality, he urged immediate construction of a navy equal to the combined strength of "any other two navies in the world."[34]

Others were equally positive that the United States should hasten to seize the trident from Great Britain. One of these, Representative H. C. Pell (Democrat, from New York), emphatically asserted that our succession to Germany's rôle as "chief commercial competitor of Great Britain" also placed us in "Germany's position as the chief [potential] enemy of England. . . ." But if the peril was great, so was the opportunity. An Anglo-American war was not an "ineluctable necessity." With Britain exhausted from the last war, we could now seize "the maritime control of the world without a struggle." And with that achieved, he declared, "our commerce may develop in peace and the United States can be for centuries to come what England has been for centuries past—the dominant country of the world, in whose strength will lie the ultimate arbitrament of mundane destiny."[35]

There were numerous indications that such ideas were also acceptable to the incoming Republican Administration. President-elect Harding's newspaper, the *Marion* [Ohio] *Daily Star* enthusiastically hailed the prospect of the United States soon having "by far the most powerful navy in the world."[36] The incoming Secretary of the Navy, Edwin Denby, publicly declared for a navy strong enough to defend all our insular posses-

[33] Vol. 58, Jan. 27, 1921, pp. 620, 621.

[34] *New York Times*, Feb. 23, 1921, p. 1; March 9, p. 13.

[35] 66 Cong. 3 Sess., *Cong. Rec.* (Vol. 60), p. 2959; and see also, pp. 3161, 4166.

[36] Quoted in *New York Times*, Jan. 1, 1921, p. 1.

sions, including the Philippines which "must be held at whatever cost. . . ."[37] And it was authoritatively stated soon after his inauguration, that President Harding himself favored building the "most powerful navy in the world as a guarantee, not only to the world, but to American citizens of the sincerity of the Administration when it proposes changed international relations and reduction of armaments."[38]

IMPENDING CRISIS IN THE ATLANTIC

Although a combination of domestic political forces not only prevented further ship authorizations in the winter of 1920-1921, but also raised doubts as to the possibility of even completing those ships already in hand,[39] it was impossible to ignore the disturbing trend of Anglo-American relations. Naval officers and civilian statesmen might reiterate that the United States was "not building against any nation." But as Admiral Sims and others pointed out, governments do not usually prepare for war in the abstract. On the contrary, they prepare for specific possible future conflicts. The Navy Department's formula of equality with the strongest, could only mean equality with Great Britain. Redefinition of American naval policy in those terms, especially in view of the British Navy's post-war emancipation from the menace of German sea power, tended naturally to cast Great Britain in the rôle, not of friend or ally, but of potential enemy.[40] Frequent charges that the Government was actively preparing for war with England,[41] together with big-navy propaganda which openly dwelt on the possibility of such a conflict, in turn gave color to irresponsible assertions that the Anglo-Japanese Alliance, originally directed against Russia, and

[37] *New York Times*, March 1, 1921, p. 6. [38] *ibid.*, March 14, p. 3.

[39] A filibuster, led by Senator Borah, prevented the passage of even routine appropriations for the Navy, in the closing days of the short session—Feb. 28, to March 4, 1921. *Cong. Rec.*, Vol. 60, pp. 4043-8, 4055-8, 4114-17, 4130-51, 4162-72, 4243-85, 4360-5, 4367-9, 4381-92, 4525.

[40] See, for example, press comment quoted in the *Literary Digest*, Vol. 64, March 27, 1920, p. 20; and Vol. 65, June 19, 1920, p. 24.

[41] See, for example, editorials in *The Nation*, "More Naval Folly," Vol. 107, Nov. 30, 1918, p. 637; and "Our Naval Policy," Vol. 110, April 10, 1920, p. 453; and also statements in Congress, *Cong. Rec.*, Vol. 57, pp. 2717, 2908, 3087, 3098, 3100, 3150, 3151.

later against Germany, was now becoming a symbol of the potential hostility of Great Britain toward the United States.[42]

British opinion was simultaneously passing through a comparable transition. Prior to the war, the United States Navy had entered scarcely at all into the calculations of British statesmen and professional strategists. This happy neglect, as previously noted, had come to an end with the destruction of German sea power and the prospective advance of the United States to first place upon the sea. As early as July 1919, Colonel House, in London, remarked that "the relations of the two countries are beginning to assume the same character as that of England and Germany before the war."[43] There were unmistakable indications of a growing apprehension of the United States, frequently disguised by protestations of confidence and good-will, but none the less implicit in British discussion of American post-war naval policy and development.[44] The same could also be said of the British Government's announcement in March 1921 of plans for resuming naval construction with a view to maintaining at least a one power standard upon the sea.[45]

Although British as well as American statesmen solemnly iterated that their naval plans were neither competitive nor framed with the other country specifically in view,[46] such assertions could only partially conceal a corroding anxiety that was rapidly destroying that mutual trust and confidence which had largely characterized Anglo-American relations during the final months of the late war. While other considerations entered into the post-war naval plans of both Governments—in particular

[42] See, for example, the views of Admiral Huse, previously cited, from *New York Times*, Feb. 23, 1921, p. 1; and March 9, p. 13; also A. G. Gardiner, "Anglo-American Issues," *Contemporary Review*, Vol. 118, Oct. 1920, p. 609; also "What the Anglo-Japanese Alliance Means to Us," *Literary Digest*, Vol. 70, July 2, 1921, p. 11; and "The United States and the Old World," *Round Table*, Vol. 11, June 1921, pp. 558, 574.

[43] Charles Seymour, *Intimate Papers of Colonel House* (1928), Vol. 4, p. 495.

[44] See, for example, articles by Archibald Hurd in *Fortnightly Review*, "The United States and Sea Power: A Challenge," Vol. 111, Feb. 1919, p. 175; "Shall We Suffer Eclipse by Sea? American Progress," Vol. 113, June 1920, p. 849; "Naval Supremacy: Great Britain or the United States," Vol. 114, Dec. 1920, p. 916; and see British comment quoted from time to time in the *New York Times*, and cited in *New York Times Index*, title: "England, Navy"; "Sea Power"; etc.

[45] See *Brassey's Naval Annual, 1921-1922*, pp. 405*ff*., 412*ff*.; and R. A. Chaput, *Disarmament in British Foreign Policy* (1935), pp. 79*ff*., 93*ff*.

[46] *Brassey, 1921-1922*, pp. 406, 413.

the developing Japanese-American crisis in the Pacific—the residual effect, in both Great Britain and the United States, of the events reviewed in these pages was certainly not conducive to Anglo-American solidarity. And while armed conflict between the English-speaking peoples was still generally regarded as an extremely remote contingency, the utterances of many of their official and unofficial spokesmen both reflected and aggravated a growing estrangement which, unless speedily checked, might have repercussions vitally affecting peace and political stability throughout the world.

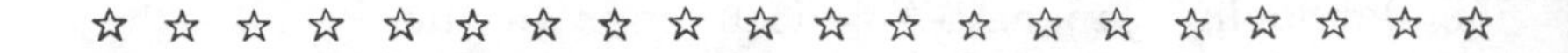

CHAPTER SIX

Power Politics in the Pacific

THE defeat of Germany, which had such unexpected and alarming repercussions in the Atlantic, set the stage for even graver events in the Pacific. When the Armistice suspended hostilities, American policy and opinion were undeniably hardening into uncompromising opposition to Japan's advance in the Far East. The Wilson Administration was attempting to mobilize American finance to combat Japanese economic monopolies in Asia. American troops in Siberia were blocking Japan's thinly disguised designs on Russian territory. American naval authorities were unreconciled to Japan's permanent occupation of the former German islands north of the equator. And the President and his intimate advisers were framing a program of world reconstruction which, if carried out at the forthcoming peace conference, would go far toward depriving Japanese imperialists of their spoils of war and victory.[1]

WAR SPOILS AND SEA POWER IN THE PACIFIC

In the eyes of Japanese statesmen and naval experts, their country's long sought primacy in the Far East depended in no small degree on permanent occupation of the Marianas, Caroline, and Marshall archipelagoes seized from Germany in the early weeks of the World War.

It is impossible to say, from evidence yet available, just when Japanese policy hardened on this question. The United States was repeatedly assured, in 1914, that Japan's occupation of

[1] See, in general, A. W. Griswold's *Far Eastern Policy of the United States* (1938), Chap. 6.

these islands was only for duration of the war.[2] Early in 1916 there were intimations from Tokio that the future of the islands was still unsettled. The following December the press commented on a growing insistence that Japan retain control after the war. And in August 1917, it was publicly reported that Viscount Ishii, en route to the United States, would seek an understanding on this question.[3]

No such understanding was reached. But it was secretly disclosed to Secretary of State Lansing that Japan had entered into an agreement with Great Britain (contrary to previous assurances from London to the United States) whereby the British Government would support Japan's claim to all former German colonies in the Pacific north of the equator, in return for Japanese support of British colonial claims south of that line.[4] This agreement, it subsequently transpired, dated from February 1917. It had been wrung from England as the price of Japanese aid against German submarines in the Mediterranean. The Japanese Government had taken the further precaution of securing the assent of France. And fortified with this support, the Japanese delegation went to the Peace Conference with the demand, among others, for outright and unqualified transfer of the Marianas, Caroline, and Marshall Islands.[5]

Not until it was too late did the United States make a stand against this eastward expansion of the Island Empire. But this is not to say that all American observers were oblivious to the strategic implications of what was happening.

As previously noted, the Wilson Administration fervently desired to exclude the war from the Pacific and Far East, though it was unwilling, and perhaps unable, to assume any large responsibility for doing so.[6] Representative Fred Britten (Republican, from Illinois) introduced on August 18, 1914, a little noticed resolution which declared that the House viewed with

[2] *For. Rels. 1914, Supplement*, pp. 184, 185; *New York Times*, Oct. 8, 1914, p. 1; Oct. 9, p. 3; Nov. 19, p. 1; Nov. 20, p. 2.

[3] *New York Times*, Feb. 26, 1916, p. 2; Dec. 30, 1916, p. 1; Aug. 2, 1917, p. 2.

[4] *War Memoirs of Robert Lansing* (1935), p. 291.

[5] W. W. Willoughby, *Foreign Rights and Interests in China* (1920), pp. 397*ff*.; R. S. Baker, *Woodrow Wilson and World Settlement* (1922), Vol. 1, p. 60; Vol. 2, pp. 229, 247.

[6] *For. Rels. 1914, Suppl.*, pp. 161*ff*.

concern Japan's attack on Kiaochow, the German naval base in Shantung.[7] This attack, Britten feared, foreshadowed early Japanese seizure of Germany's Pacific islands, which he would regard as a "distinct menace" to the Philippines, Guam, and even Hawaii, and "not to be countenanced without severe opposition."[8]

The press, on the whole, either ignored or belittled the danger. Britten's resolution attracted little attention. And the general attitude seemed to be that summed up in the *New York Evening Sun* which observed that "the prospect of the acquisition by Japan of all the long stretch of German island colonies from the Yellow Sea south to Samoa must give the statesmen of our own country cause for present and future concern. But there is no warrant for American protest, much less intervention."[9]

A few editors, however, took a more serious view of the storm gathering over the western Pacific. The *New York Times*, for one, emphasized that occupation of Germany's islands would give Japan "naval stations on the direct line between the Panama Canal and the Philippines." It was feared that Japan aimed at exclusive control of Asiatic waters. It was "not to be supposed that we could view" that prospect "without anxiety." But even the *Times* had no specific counter-measures to suggest.[10]

When, however, it was learned a few weeks later that Japanese forces had occupied Jaluit Island, a partially developed German naval station in the Marshall archipelago, approximately 2,000 miles southwest of Hawaii, the *Times* again raised a warning voice. This group of islands lay "directly between" Hawaii and the Philippines "in the middle of the Pacific, remote from the coast of Asia and the China Sea."[11] Still later, when it was becoming clear that something stronger than words would be required to loosen Japan's grip on these strategic islands in the western Pacific, the American public was once more reminded that the Japanese occupation seriously weakened our Government's ability to protect American territories and other interests in the Far East.[12]

[7] 63 Cong. 2 Sess., *Cong. Rec.* (Vol. 51), p. 13896.
[8] *New York Times*, Aug. 8, 1914, p. 2.
[9] *ibid.*, Aug. 17, 1914, p. 8.
[10] *ibid.*, Aug. 18, p. 8.
[11] *ibid.*, Oct. 7, p. 8.
[12] *ibid.*, July 9, 1916, sec. 7, p. 2.

This was likewise the position of American naval authorities who were giving attention to developments in the Pacific. A committee of naval officers who drew up a memorandum on peace terms in the autumn of 1918, fully appreciated the strategic implications of Japan's eastward expansion. These experts strongly opposed leaving the Marshall and Caroline Islands in the hands of that Power. Yet they suffered no delusions as to the difficulty of now transferring them to any other country. The only solution they could see was to ask Japan to accept international control in return for a "free hand in eastern Siberia."[13]

The strategical consequences of leaving Japan in possession of the German islands were developed still more forcefully in a memorandum prepared by Assistant Secretary of State Breckinridge Long for the American delegates to the peace conference. The United States, he wrote, had a "material interest" in those islands. They surrounded Guam, "the principal cable station in the Pacific Ocean" connecting San Francisco with Manila, Shanghai, and Yokohama. In case of war, ships operating from those surrounding islands could cut the cable and sever all direct communications with the Philippines. In addition, the German islands formed a "screen separating the Philippines from the Hawaiian Group and from the United States." In consequence, "it would be impossible to send any military force to the Philippines with any safety, if the convoy were directed through the usual channels. Also, they would be a constant menace to naval ships moving through the Pacific and between the Philippines and the United States."

In Japanese hands those islands were a serious menace to American interests in the Pacific Ocean. But Japan had possession, and there was no hope of persuading Japan to yield possession to the United States. It was therefore proposed to return the islands to Germany. In this way the United States might have a chance to acquire them later, perhaps as part payment of America's share in the war indemnity that would be imposed on Germany. Even if Germany kept the islands, no harm would result, since Germany in the future would command no naval force sufficient "to disturb the peace of the Pacific."[14]

[13] D. H. Miller, *My Diary at the Conference of Paris, with Documents* (1924), Vol. 2, pp. 101, 106-7.

[14] *For. Rels. 1919: Paris Peace Conf.*, Vol. 2, pp. 512-15; and see E. T. Williams,

President Wilson himself seems to have felt comparatively slight concern for the purely strategic aspects of this problem. He appreciated that the north Pacific islands lay "athwart the path from Hawaii to the Philippines"; that some of them "were nearer to Hawaii than the [United States] Pacific coast was"; that Japan could fortify and build naval bases in them; "that indeed they were of little use for anything else; and that we had no naval base except at Guam."[15] But Wilson favored early withdrawal from the Philippines. And he was vastly more concerned with Japanese aggressions in Shantung and elsewhere in eastern Asia, than he was in safeguarding the long and exposed line of military communications upon which, in no small degree, American influence in the Far East ultimately depended.[16]

In theory, the settlement finally reached at Paris did safeguard our military road across the Pacific. Japan retained possession of the former German islands north of the equator, not as full and unlimited sovereign, but as the administrator of a mandate, or commission, from the Allied and Associated Powers. The terms of this mandate specifically prohibited the construction of fortifications or the establishment of military bases anywhere in the mandated islands. And the Japanese Government, as mandatory, was expressly charged with presenting annual reports "containing full information" as to conditions in the islands.

This paper solution might or might not fulfill the hopes of its authors and advocates. With no modern fortified naval base west of Hawaii, it would be extremely difficult for the United States to carry war against Japan into the western Pacific. As long as this situation continued, it was quite conceivable that Japan would faithfully honor the non-fortification clause of its mandate. With Japanese authorities in complete and exclusive possession, however, there could be no positive assurance that such was in fact the case. It was certainly unlikely, to say the least, that

"Japan's Mandate in the Pacific," *Amer. Journal of International Law*, Vol. 27, July 1933, pp. 428, 429. It is perhaps significant that earlier reports of preparatory studies for the American peace conference delegation made frequent reference to the Pacific Islands, though more frequently in connection with the treatment of "weak peoples" than with the problem of American strategy in that Ocean. See *For. Rels. 1919: Peace Conference*, Vol. 1, pp. 19, 20, 39, 82.

[15] Miller, *Diary*, Vol. 1, p. 100.

[16] 66 Cong. 1 Sess., *Sen. Docs.* No. 106, pp. 505-6; Williams, "Japan's Mandate in the Pacific," p. 429; P. H. Clyde, *Japan's Pacific Mandate* (1935), pp. 32*ff*.

Japan would leave these insular outposts undefended should the United States undertake extensive military developments in either Guam or the Philippines. And there was no denying the possibility that Japanese forces operating from the mandated islands might completely disrupt American military communications from the International Date Line to the coast of China.

All this was well known to intelligent and informed students of naval strategy. Early in 1920 it was reported that American experts analyzing the situation had reached the conclusion that the Pacific islands "have furnished Japan with an insular barrier of defense against naval attack . . . over the whole Pacific Ocean front of Asia."[17]

In a remarkable book published in 1921, and well received in American naval circles, Hector Bywater, a thoroughly competent British naval critic, described in detail the strategic consequences of American acquiescence in Japanese occupation of the former German islands. The effect, he pointed out, was "to surround Guam with a cordon of potential Japanese strongholds and naval bases." That Japan "would forego the use of such invaluable bases in case of emergency was not to be believed." Japanese submarines "working from a base at Saipan Island" just north of Guam "would be within a few hours' sail" of the American island. The Island of Yap, "a few hundred miles to the southwest" was "admirably adapted for use as a base for submarines or other vessels operating against the Guam-Manila line of communications, and so long as it remained in enemy occupation this route would never be safe."

"Even if . . . driven out of Yap," Bywater continued, "Japan would still have the Pelew Islands" still farther to the southwest, where there was at least one good harbor for naval craft. Also to the south and east of Guam there was a large number of suitable havens. As long as these positions remained in the hands of a hostile Japan, an American fleet based on Guam would operate under difficulties comparable to those that would have confronted England's Grand Fleet in the late war if Germany had possessed a submarine base in the Shetland Islands at the threshold of Scapa Flow.[18]

[17] *New York Times,* Jan. 21, 1920, p. 3.
[18] *Sea Power in the Pacific* (1921), pp. 266-8.

Recent developments in naval warfare added to the handicap which the United States suffered as a result of Japan's possession of the mandated islands in the western Pacific. The remarkable wartime development of marine mines, automotive torpedoes, and submarines multiplied the difficulties involved in maintaining intact any long and exposed line of oversea communications. Air power, especially shore based air power, though still in its infancy, had already revealed immense potentialities for interrupting sea communications. And the mandated islands, provided not only refuges for submarines but literally scores of havens for naval aircraft which in the event of war in the western Pacific, might conceivably be loosed with devastating effect.[19]

Storm Signals in the Pacific

While acquiescing in permanent Japanese occupation of the former German islands, and thereby further undermining our already unsound military position in the western Pacific, the Wilson Administration was simultaneously driving ahead on a course which progressively embittered American political relations with Japan.[20]

We have previously noted the Administration's efforts to mobilize investment capital to break Japan's growing financial grasp on China. And we have also mentioned the military impasse in Siberia where American troops remained from 1918 until early 1920, a constant reminder of the President's disapproval of Japan's suspected designs on Russian territory in eastern Asia.

The Shantung controversy offered still clearer evidence of the anti-Japanese current in America. Early in the war, it will be recalled, Japanese forces had besieged and taken the German naval base on Kiaochow Bay in the Shantung peninsula. By the end of 1918 they had fastened an iron grip on the German leasehold in the port of Tsingtau, and had extended their control far back into the interior. And by the secret agreements of

[19] According to a Washington dispatch to the *New York Times*, American naval authorities held that "these newly acquired islands, in conjunction with those which were previously owned by Japan, are regarded as giving that nation immunity from naval coercion by sea and the opportunity to throw a submarine barrier between the United States and the Philippines." Jan. 21, 1920, p. 3.

[20] For a concise, documented account of the episodes mentioned in this section, see Griswold, *Far Eastern Policy*, Chap. 6.

February 1917, France and Great Britain were pledged to support Japan's claim to all German rights in Shantung as well as in the Pacific islands.

All this, it is obvious, was utterly repugnant to President Wilson's peace program. But the Japanese would not withdraw. They enjoyed at least the passive support of the French and British delegations who were committed by the secret agreements just mentioned. And the most Wilson could do without driving the Japanese delegation from the Peace Conference was to acquiesce in Japan's succession to all German rights in Shantung, in return for a verbal pledge to hand back political control of the province to China at some unspecified future time.

This compromise could be interpreted as a surrender to Japan. It was so interpreted by thousands of Americans who either felt a strong sympathy for China or desired to discredit and humiliate the Administration. And the senatorial and popular outcry which went up in the United States had an ominous and sinister ring in Japanese ears.[21]

A teapot-tempest over the Island of Yap further embittered Japanese-American relations. Two submarine cables joined North America with eastern Asia. One, under British control, crossed the Pacific from Vancouver, by way of New Zealand, Australia, and the East Indies. The other, an American cable, stretched from San Francisco to Hawaii, Guam, the Philippines, and Shanghai. A branch ran north from Guam to the Bonin Islands where it connected with the Japanese cable to Tokio. Another cable, formerly under German control, connected Guam with Yap Island, 500 miles to the southwest. And from Yap, two other lines ran to Menado, in the Dutch East Indies, and to Shanghai. The Yap cables thus offered alternative routes from Guam to China, the East Indies, and indirectly to the Philippines.

Past experience indicated that it was virtually impossible to insure the inviolability of diplomatic, military, or commercial communications over lines that passed through the territory of

[21] See D. F. Fleming, *The United States and the League of Nations, 1918-1920* (1932), index, title: "Shantung"; and E. Tupper and G. E. McReynolds, *Japan in American Public Opinion* (1937), pp. 145*ff*.; and, for example, *Literary Digest*, Vol. 62, July 5, 1919, p. 31; and Vol. 63, Dec. 13, 1919, p. 22.

other countries. At relay stations and junction points, messages could be intercepted, censored, delayed, or even suppressed, as might suit the interests of the local sovereign. With the United States deeply involved with Japan in Asia, and with Americans growing apprehensive as to the future security of the Philippines, it was only natural that President Wilson, at the prompting of his naval advisers, should oppose Japan's exclusive occupation of Yap, even in the rôle of mandatory under the League of Nations.[22]

The alternative which Wilson proposed, some kind of international administration and control, was just as obviously unacceptable to Japan. The European Allies sided with that Power. And despite repeated verbal objections on behalf of the United States, Yap was not reserved from the mandate which the Allied and Associated Powers conferred on Japan in May 1919.[23]

The United States Government refused to recognize Japan's right to mandatory authority over Yap. The question dragged along through 1919 and on into 1920. It flared into open controversy at the international communications conference which met in Washington late in that year to consider what should be done with the cables seized from Germany during the war. Yap became front-page news. And while this question was intrinsically less important than certain other phases of the Pacific crisis (and destined to become still less important with the further development of radio), it dramatically symbolized the growing American antipathy to Japan.

Still other events contributed to the gathering storm. Heaping insult on injury, as it appeared in Japan, President Wilson refused at the Peace Conference to support a clause affirming racial equality in the League of Nations. His Administration failed to check a rising anti-Japanese agitation in America, especially on our Pacific slope, which demanded, among other things, the complete exclusion of Japanese immigrants from the United States. And finally, to deprive Japanese imperialism of any semblance of moral support from Great Britain, as well as to remove the remote menace of a naval war in two oceans, the

[22] 66 Cong. 1 Sess., *Sen. Docs.* No. 106, p. 506; L. B. Tribolet, *The International Aspects of Electrical Communications in the Pacific Area* (1929), pp. 230*ff*., and *passim*.

[23] Baker, *World Settlement*, Vol. 2, pp. 247, 470, 480-1; *For. Rels. 1921*, Vol. 2, pp. 263*ff*.

Government at Washington strove with growing intensity of purpose to drive a wedge into the Anglo-Japanese Alliance which was due for renewal in the year 1921.

Naval Repercussions in Japan

American opposition to Japan's Asiatic and Pacific program, the increasingly hostile tone of American public opinion, as well as our Navy Department's widely publicized plans for building up as soon as possible to a total of more than fifty capital ships, all tended to accelerate the pace of Japanese naval expansion.[24]

The naval standard, toward which the Japanese Admiralty had aimed after the Russo-Japanese War (1905), was a fighting fleet built around eight battleships and eight armored cruisers, all less than eight years old. Advent of the all-big-gun, dreadnought-type battleship in 1906 rendered obsolete every armorclad in the Japanese Navy, as in other navies also. Limited financial and industrial resources, however, retarded the construction of a dreadnought fleet. Thus the outbreak of war in 1914 caught Japan with but two dreadnought battleships and two battle cruisers in commission, and with only two battleships and two battle cruisers under construction.[25]

As late as 1917, Japan's immediate building program included only eight battleships and four battle cruisers. The following year the number of battle cruisers was increased to six. A further increase was projected in 1919. In 1920, the Japanese Parliament accepted a building program designed to give Japan, by 1927, a fleet of eight super-dreadnought battleships and eight giant battle cruisers, all less than eight years old, in addition to five older dreadnoughts and four battle cruisers—a total of twenty-five capital ships completed since 1913.[26]

In addition to capital ships, the Japanese Navy in 1921 included a long list of auxiliary combatant craft, built, building, and authorized. Counting no ships authorized earlier than 1910, the totals were twenty-five light cruisers, 102 destroyers, and 113

[24] Bywater, *Sea Power in the Pacific*, pp. 150*ff*.; and *Literary Digest*, Vol. 63, Dec. 27, 1919, p. 23.

[25] *Jane's Fighting Ships, 1916*.

[26] Bywater, *op. cit.*, pp. 328-9; Bywater, "Japanese and American Naval Power," *Atlantic Monthly*, Vol. 128, Nov. 1921, pp. 704*ff*.; *Japan Year Book, 1921-1922*, pp. 300-1; and *Proc. U.S. Nav. Inst.*, Vol. 47, Dec. 1921, pp. 1959*ff*.

submarines. And there were clear intimations that all these totals might undergo further upward revision depending on the course of American naval construction.[27]

There were also recurrent rumors, officially denied,[28] that Japan was fortifying strategic positions in the former German islands, in violation of the mandate received from the Allied and Associated Powers. And authorities in Washington possessed information which led them to believe that the Japanese Admiralty was studying "the possible use of submarines based on this long chain of islands"; and that it was "training submarine officers, and making a special study of the operations of German submarines in the World War," all with a view to "setting up an elaborate system of submarine torpedo boat defense" which would insure "control over the whole Pacific Ocean front of Asia."[29]

Naval Repercussions in America

The quickening pace of Japanese naval construction, coinciding with the political impasse in the Far East, completed the vicious circle of armament competition. By the end of 1919, there was a perceptible tendency to shape American naval plans toward the possibility of an early war in the western Pacific. This was reflected in the Navy Department's building program. It was more or less implicit in the actual disposition of ships in commission. It also clearly underlay the growing emphasis, noticeable after 1919, on the need for large-scale shore developments on our western seaboard and at various points in our oversea possessions in the Pacific.

There were a number of indications that the Navy Department was pointing its building program toward a possible war in the western Pacific. The estimates for 1920 called for larger cruisers with a fuel endurance of more than 10,000 miles.[30] A strong plea was made for submarines of 2,000 tons displacement that could function as "scouts, or blockaders at long distance from our home bases. . . ."[31] And the large proportion of battle

[27] Bywater, *Sea Power in the Pacific*, pp. 151, 155, 330*ff*.

[28] See, for example, *New York Times*, April 6, 1920, p. 1; Nov. 15, p. 15.

[29] *New York Times*, Jan. 21, 1920, p. 3.

[30] Navy Department, *Annual Reports*, *1919*, pp. 150, 151; 66 Cong. 2 Sess. House Naval Committee, *Hearings on Estimates for 1920*, pp. 2048-9.

[31] *Hearings*, *1920*, p. 2049; *Ann. Repts. 1919*, pp. 150, 151.

cruisers to battleships in the Japanese Navy was cited as one reason for authorizing additional battle cruisers for our own.[32]

Likewise symptomatic was the Wilson Administration's decision to establish a separate battle fleet in the Pacific. This step, foreshadowed in January 1919, was a radical departure from concentration of all battleships in the Atlantic Fleet. When formally announced the following June, it was officially explained that one of the reasons, "possibly the paramount one," for stationing a strong fleet in each ocean was to stimulate a spirit of rivalry within the Service, and thus to promote the efficiency of the Navy as a whole.[33]

This explanation provoked a good deal of comment. It was widely contended that division of the fleet weakened rather than strengthened the total naval power of the United States.[34] It was cynically suggested that this move was a political stratagem contrived "to make votes for the Democratic party in the coming presidential election."[35] It was also hinted that the ulterior purpose was to put pressure on Japan.[36]

It is impossible to discover precisely to what extent this last motive may have influenced the Administration. It is difficult to believe that it was wholly absent from the decision to assign all the newest and most powerful battleships to the Pacific Fleet.[37] It was also significant that all six of the great battle cruisers under construction were earmarked for the Pacific, their "speed and long cruising radius" rendering them "peculiarly suitable to conditions" in that ocean.[38] And it was a notable fact that, by the end of 1919, the United States had assembled in the Pacific a fighting fleet numbering nearly 200 units, with a total displacement of almost 800,000 tons—a force nearly, if not quite, as formidable as the entire navy which Japan then had in commission.[39]

[32] Navy Dept., *Ann. Repts. 1920*, p. 213.

[33] *New York Times*, Jan. 2, 1919, p. 2; June 17, p. 19; *Ann. Repts. 1919*, p. 11.

[34] For representative arguments on both sides, see "The Folly of a Divided Fleet," *Scientific American*, Vol. 123, July 17, 1920, p. 56; and Lieutenant P. H. Hutchinson, "The Fleet in the Pacific," *Sea Power*, Vol. 8, April 1921, p. 171.

[35] "The Navy Repudiates Mahan," *World's Work*, Vol. 38, Oct. 1919, pp. 569-71; and "Dividing the Fighting Fleet," *ibid.*, Sept. pp. 461-2.

[36] See, for example, "Our Peaceable Pacific Fleet," *Literary Digest*, Vol. 62, Aug. 9, 1919, pp. 13-14.

[37] *New York Times*, June 23, 1919, p. 7.

[38] *ibid.*, June 18, 1919, p. 19.

[39] Navy Dept., *Ann. Repts. 1919*, pp. 234-5.

The United States, moreover, continued its concentration of force in the Pacific. Early in 1921 the Atlantic Fleet joined the Pacific Fleet for combined maneuvers.[40] And in June of that year it was announced that the recently inaugurated Republican Administration had decided, on the advice of the naval authorities, to station most of our fighting ships permanently in the Pacific.[41]

The official explanation was as significant as the decision itself. The United States, it was pointed out, had "nothing to fear from the Atlantic side," but had "certain definite interests in the Pacific." In particular, there were "Hawaii and the Philippines, to say nothing of Yap," in addition to the "natural tendency of American commercial development [which was] toward the South and West"; and it was "believed that the maintenance of an imposing fleet in the Pacific would immeasurably enhance the prestige of America there."[42]

An almost identical argument had been used in the preceding session of Congress, in support of liberal appropriations for naval-construction. Senator Lodge was reported to have said in executive session that the Government "intended to maintain a strong policy in the Pacific and that if this policy was to prevail the naval arm must not be weakened." And the press was given to understand that the Sena or's full statement which was not released for publication not only reflected executive policy, but actually contained information furnished by a representative of the State Department.[43]

The trend of power politics in the Pacific was further reflected in growing concern over the inadequacy of the Navy's shore facilities in that ocean. On the basis of previous surveys, the Navy Department prepared plans for greatly enlarging existing yards and for developing additional stations on our West Coast.[44] The Secretary of the Navy laid these before Congress in December 1919, together with an urgent plea for action.[45] And this plea was renewed in 1920, with the assertion that there

[40] Navy Dept., *Ann. Repts. 1921*, p. 19.
[41] *New York Times*, June 5, 1921, p. 6; June 19, p. 2; June 21, p. 19.
[42] *ibid.*, June 5, 1921, p. 6.
[43] *ibid.*, March 2, 1921, p. 1. [44] Navy Dept., *Ann. Repts. 1919*, pp. 69*f.*, 175*ff.*
[45] *ibid.*, pp. 9, 69*f.*

was "no more pressing problem in connection with the national defense than the provision on the Pacific of ample bases . . . for the maintenance and operation of the fleet. . . . The day will never come," the Secretary predicted, "when a powerful [American] fleet will not be based in the Pacific, and it is essential that ample provision be made not only for the Pacific Fleet, but for the whole American fleet in its stated period of tactical exercises on the west coast."[46]

Recommendations for expanding the naval base at Pearl Harbor, in the Hawaiian Islands, revealed even more plainly the trend of American preparations. Pearl Harbor, it was pointed out, was not only the "key situation" in the eastern Pacific; it was also an indispensable way station on our military road to the Far East. The existing facilities in Hawaii were "entirely inadequate to care for the Pacific Fleet in time of peace and, of course, totally inadequate to take care of the *whole* fleet in any movement, offensive or defensive, across the Pacific."[47]

It was also disclosed that the Navy Department was planning large-scale developments in the western Pacific. These plans envisaged a "strongly fortified naval base" at Guam, and an improved secondary base in the Philippines.[48] Official discussion of these projects, loaded with international dynamite, was naturally guarded, at least in public. But enough was said in published reports and in congressional hearings to indicate the trend of official opinion. This opinion rested mainly on two assumptions. One was that the United States could never escape "moral responsibility" for the defense of the Philippines, even though Congress should make the Islands nominally independent. The other assumption that trembled beneath the surface of deliberately vague official statements was that the American people were headed toward armed conflict with Japan. And on the basis of these two assumptions, American naval authorities could see no justification for congressional delay in voting the appro-

[46] *Ann. Repts. 1920*, p. 10. A joint Senate-House Committee, appointed to study the problem, brought in a favorable report in January 1921, which did not, however, produce any large immediate results, 66 Cong. 3 Sess., *Sen. Docs.* No. 366; and *Navy Yearbook, 1920-1921*, pp. 668-9.

[47] *Ann. Repts. 1919*, p. 184; and see *ibid., 1920*, p. 12.

[48] *ibid., 1919*, pp. 141, 176; *ibid., 1920*, p. 13.

priations necessary to retrieve past blunders and to push our military road into the far western Pacific.[49]

Crisis in the Pacific

The accelerating tempo of naval development on both sides of the Pacific not only reflected but also aggravated popular indignation and a growing sense of insecurity both in Japan and in the United States. Japanese and American statesmen and naval authorities might and did reiterate that their respective armament programs were purely defensive. And they solemnly denied that their warlike preparations were directed against any nation in particular.[50] But such formal protestations of non-aggressive intent did little to relieve the tension. They could not explain away the fundamental conflict of national interests and policies. Japan's program of expansion, defended on strategic as well as on economic grounds, seemed absolutely incompatible, in Western eyes, with the open door for commerce and investment and with the political, territorial, and administrative integrity of China, to all of which American statesmanship was still avowedly committed.

A navy strong enough to compel respect for American interests and policies in the Far East would inevitably appear in Japanese eyes, not only as a challenge to Japanese Asiatic expansion, but also as a menace to the political existence of the Island Empire. Conversely, a navy powerful enough to defend the territory and support the policies of Japan would just as inevitably appear, to Americans, as a menace to their insular possessions and other national interests in the Far East.

As long as this conflict of interests and proximity of national territories existed in an atmosphere charged with mutual distrust and misunderstanding, naval expansion by one Power would certainly provoke a comparable or greater increase by the other.[51] While the relative naval strength of the two might re-

[49] See, for example, *Hearings, 1920*, p. 2275; 66 Cong. 3 Sess. House Appropriations Committee, *Hearings on Naval Appropriation Bill for 1922*, pp. 366-71, 939.

[50] For Japanese declarations to this effect, see, for example, *New York Times*, Jan. 8, 1921, p. 4; March 26, p. 2; *Japan Year Book, 1921-1922*, p. 301; and Bywater, *Sea Power in the Pacific*, p. 155.

[51] In December 1920, for example, Viscount Ishii flatly told the League of Nations that it was useless to try to get Japan to reduce its armaments in the face of

main fairly constant, each stage in the process of competitive building would add to the fiscal burden and also accentuate the sense of insecurity which naval preparedness was supposed to relieve.[52] Though no one could foresee the ultimate outcome, there was a widespread and growing conviction, in the winter of 1920-1921, that only restoration of a Far Eastern balance of power, redefinition of national interests and policies in that region, and limitation of naval armaments, could avert a costly, if not utterly ruinous, war in the western Pacific.

continued naval expansion on the part of the United States. *New York Times*, Dec. 12, 1920, p. 1.

[52] The Tokio correspondent of the *Morning Post* (London) reported in the winter of 1920-1921, that "there is profound resentment in Japan against what is supposed to be the American design of compelling Japan to waste her national substance in a ruinous outlay on defenses." Quoted in *New York Times*, Jan. 1, 1921, p. 4.

CHAPTER SEVEN

The Popular Revolt Against Navalism in America

THE deepening shadow on Anglo-American relations and the gathering storm over the Pacific, forced the question of naval disarmament[1] into the sphere of practical politics.

Disarmament was not a new prescription for peace. Before the war people in many lands had watched with rising anxiety the competitive struggle for armed security which, instead of producing a feeling of security, had practically everywhere heightened the sense of insecurity. The war momentarily discredited the ancient dogma that armaments insure peace. And the post-war reaction gave wide vogue to the antithetical doctrine, embodied in President Wilson's peace platform, that an enduring peace required reduction of national armaments to the "lowest point consistent with domestic safety."

With many practical men of affairs, however, peace was not the only consideration, or even the most compelling one. A widespread fear that national bankruptcy might be the price of armed security gave added impetus to the post-war movement for naval limitation. And nowhere did the public demand fiscal relief with greater insistence than in the United States as this country slid from the heights of war prosperity to the depths of post-war depression, and people contemplated an uncertain future burdened by unprecedented debts and taxes.

[1] Strictly speaking, the term disarmament was a misnomer, since it rarely connoted abolition or even radical reduction of armed forces, but rather their moderate reduction and agreed future limitation. It is in the latter sense that the term is used in this and in succeeding chapters.

Appealing as was the ideal of peace, and compelling as was the demand for fiscal relief, statesmen of the great naval Powers approached the question of disarmament cautiously and with qualifications. Navies were not merely agencies of defense, but also instruments of policy, as well as vested interests of certain important groups in society.

They were, first of all, instruments of internal policy. Naval construction had come to play an extremely important rôle in the "normal" political economy of Great Britain, Japan, and the United States. Government expenditures on armaments cushioned the post-war slump which threatened to disrupt shipyards, steel mills, and many other industries. Drastic naval limitation, despite the pressure for fiscal retrenchment, presented internal economic and political hazards that statesmen might well hesitate to risk.

Navies were also instruments of external policy. Far from a simple problem of scrapping tons and guns, and cutting expenditures by some easily determined formula, naval limitation involved for each Power a reconsideration of time-honored interests and policies. Progress toward that goal depended upon the ability of statesmen to reconcile or to compromise conflicting national aims. And to understand the complicated chain of events which ultimately brought the naval powers together at the Washington Conference on the Limitation of Armament (November 1921—February 1922), it is necessary first, to analyze not only the trend of public opinion, but also the rôle of naval limitation in the internal and foreign politics of Great Britain, Japan, and especially the United States during the critical years immediately following the war.

Post-War Reaction Against Navalism

In 1914 the United States ranked a poor third among the naval Powers. Four years later the American Navy stood second only to England's, with sufficient work in hand or authorized to assure first place within six or seven years at the latest. Whether viewed from the standpoint of ships, personnel, or expenditures, the growth of American naval power attributable directly or indirectly to the war had been impressive.

Likewise impressive were the Navy Department's plans for future development. These plans, it will be recalled,[2] envisaged a peace time establishment without precedent in naval annals. Appropriations voted in the summer of 1918, at the peak of the Government's war effort, totalled $1,693,804,405. The Navy Department's estimates for 1919-1920, *revised after the armistice*, called for $1,414,064,090. The original estimates had allocated over $400,000,000 for new construction. In the revised estimates, as reported in the press, this item was increased to $600,000,000, or nearly twice the sum voted for all naval purposes in the Act of 1916. And it was obvious that the total cost of building, not to mention maintaining, the post-war fighting fleet envisaged in American naval plans would eventually run into billions.[3]

These plans which, with ships previously authorized but not yet built, contemplated adding twenty new super-dreadnoughts, twelve giant battle cruisers, and nearly 300 other vessels, to several hundred craft already in service, would necessarily involve a large permanent increase of personnel. By the end of 1918, the Navy Department was tentatively estimating 250,000 as the minimum personnel that would satisfy post-war requirements, nearly 200,000 more than the number actually in service in 1914.[4]

The Navy Department's plans began to encounter resistance immediately after the armistice.[5] This opposition which developed rapidly during the winter of 1918-1919 deplored any attempt to outbuild Great Britain. Ex-President Theodore Roosevelt publicly described the British Navy "as probably the most potent instrumentality for peace in the world," and declared that we should "not . . . try to build a navy in rivalry to it," but should be satisfied to "have the second navy in the world."[6] The influential *New York Times* opposed doing anything

[2] See pp. 48*ff*.

[3] See Navy Department, *Annual Reports, 1918*, p. 385; 65 Cong. 3 Sess., *H. Reports* No. 1024; *New York Times*, Nov. 26, 1918, p. 5; *New York Herald*, same date, sec. 2, p. 2; *Navy Yearbook, 1920-1921*, p. 805.

[4] See *New York Times*, Jan. 1, 1919, p. 16; and *Navy Yearbook, 1920-1921*, p. 945; 65 Cong. 3 Sess., *H. Repts*. No. 1024.

[5] This opposition came not only from little-navy sources, but also from traditional advocates of a big navy. Compare, for example, the remarkably similar reactions of *The Nation*, Vol. 107, Nov. 30, 1918, p. 637, and *The Scientific American*, Vol. 119, Nov. 30, 1918, p. 432.

[6] Quoted in *New York Times*, Dec. 11, 1918, p. 14.

that might jeopardize our close relations with Great Britain.[7] The *Scientific American*, traditional advocate of naval expansion, likewise joined the opposition.[8] Even the Navy League reported, after a canvass of its members, that there was very little support for a policy of competitive building against Great Britain whose insular position and scattered empire were believed to justify a navy larger than that of the United States.[9]

By the end of January 1919, Administration leaders were convinced that it would require strong presidential pressure to force the new building program through Congress.[10] A cable from Wilson, then in Paris, secured from the House Naval Committee a unanimous and ostensibly favorable report. But it was subsequently disclosed that the price of this unanimity was virtual assurance from the Administration that the proposed building program would be modified or abandoned as soon as there was reasonable certainty of a league of nations and a general reduction of armaments.[11] And the legislation which the Committee recommended fell very far short of the Navy Department's original estimates.

Although the Administration had already cut down those estimates from $1,414,064,000 to $975,903,000, the Committee recommended a further decrease to $746,457,000. Instead of the $600,000,000 or $400,000,000, urged at different times by the Department for new construction, the Committee recommended only $179,000,000, to be spent chiefly on ships already under construction or previously authorized.[12]

But even this qualified program met stubborn resistance in the House. There was a long and heated debate. And only after a still further reduction of nearly $26,000,000 did the Administration leaders succeed in passing the bill on February 11, 1919.[13]

[7] See issues of Dec. 8, 1918, sec. 3, p. 1; Dec. 10, p. 12; Dec. 11, p. 14; Jan. 30, 1919, p. 10.

[8] See issues of Nov. 30, 1918, Vol. 119, p. 432, and Jan. 4, 1919, Vol. 120, p. 4.

[9] *Sea Power*, Vol. 6, March 1919, pp. 149, 151. For a fairly comprehensive survey of press opinion at the turn of the year, see *Literary Digest*, Vol. 60, Jan. 4, 1919, pp. 11*ff*.

[10] See *New York Times*, Jan. 31, 1919, pp. 1, 3.

[11] *New York Tribune*, May 28, 1919, pp. 1, 8.

[12] 65 Cong. 3 Sess., *H. Repts*. No. 1024, pp. 1, 3, 11.

[13] *New York Times*, Feb. 12, 1919, p. 1; 66 Cong. 1 Sess., *H. Repts*. No. 35, p. 1.

Some of the rising opposition in Congress undoubtedly sprang from a partisan desire to discredit and humiliate the President and his Administration who, for reasons previously analyzed, were supporting the proposed building program. The debate was permeated with party politics. And in the critical divisions, the Republicans averaged three to one against the Administration.[14]

There was also a clear desire to shake off the heavy hand of executive, and especially of military, domination. The country was "no longer on a war basis, although naval and military experts sought to keep us there." There was no excuse any longer for the President to keep Congress under "whip and spur." Senators and Representatives had acquired the dangerous habit during the war, of voting "every appropriation that those in executive authority demanded or requested." It was time for this to cease. With the war over, Congress had no right "to sublet" its constitutional prerogatives "to anyone, not even to the President of the United States."[15]

Important as were these motivations, they were subsidiary, in many instances at least, to other considerations. Those who advocated piling up armaments for the future were repeatedly challenged to show what existing menace required building any such fleet as was now proposed. Naval construction on this scale, it was contended, would produce but one inevitable result—a race to the finish with Great Britain. There was declared to be no valid reason for building a navy second to none. Rather there were pressing reasons for cutting armament expenditures to the lowest possible level at a time when the country was crying for relief from the fiscal burdens of war and of preparation for war.

No mere summary can give any impression of the moral intensity of that debate. Only by translating these arguments into parliamentary rhetoric is it possible to recapture something of the atmosphere of revolt that was sweeping Congress in the winter of 1918-1919. Representative Huddleston, Democrat, from Alabama, wanted to hear one sound argument for building against Great Britain. Sea power was vital to the life of that country, but not to the United States. We were "self-sustaining."

[14] 65 Cong. 3 Sess., *Cong. Rec.* (Vol. 57), pp. 3152, 3171.
[15] *ibid.*, pp. 2783, 2910, 3086, 3102, 3163.

We could subsist even though cut off from the outside world. We had no scattered empire, no policy of imperialism. But a great navy and a greater naval program might well lead us along the road to imperialism—a course trending inexorably toward head-on collision with Great Britain.[16]

Had we won the last war only to lose it? asked Congressman Little, Republican, from Kansas. Had we overthrown Germany's "military caste" only to "build another" of our own? Had we destroyed militarism abroad only to succumb to that dread disease at home? "Why this call upon the House by the naval department? . . . Have they in mind to challenge the naval supremacy of the British Empire? . . . What have we to fear from them? . . . On this floor a gentleman said yesterday that New York would be an immediate object of attack in case of such a war by that great fleet which never dared venture within sight of the . . . German coast" in the last war. This prospectus of naval aggrandizement "would appear to be nothing but the vain dreams of professional seamen obsessed with their own theories of the importance of their profession, who have no practical experience in collecting or conserving revenues, but simply think that they hold Aladdin's lamp . . . and have but to rub it."[17]

"Is it the logic of the situation," asked Representative Saunders, Democrat, from Virginia, "that as dangers recede, our preparations for war shall multiply?" Advocates of the pending bill, "the most prodigious naval bill in the history of our country," rested on the argument that we needed an "adequate navy—a magnificent platitude but hardly an illuminating statement." Why, "at this time when our enemies are prostrate," should we "increase the public burdens in the name of national defense? What are the dangers that render necessary these prodigious preparations?"

What do we find, he asked, if we look abroad? "England has deferred her naval program. Neither in France, Italy, or Spain do we find any lurking dangers, or any quickening activities. . . . Germany is in sackcloth and ashes. Look to Japan, China, South America, take in the whole circle of the world, and tell me where you find the evidence of any present, or prospective prep-

[16] *ibid.*, p. 2717.

[17] *ibid.*, p. 2771.

aration so extensive, and so alarming, as to make it necessary for this Congress to proceed with feverish haste to establish new armaments in the name of proper and adequate defense."[18]

Representative Frear, Republican, from Wisconsin, was another who rebelled against the proposed pyramiding of armaments upon the backs of the American people. He had consistently voted for naval increases in the past. But he now drew the line. We had just emerged from war in a bankrupt world, with a navy "as large and powerful as the navies of France, Japan, and Italy combined." He for one would not vote to add "this enormous tax burden . . . to the heavy burdens we have already laid upon the people of this country." And he would take this stand despite "criticisms . . . from navy leagues, 'security leagues,' . . . naval construction interests, steel interests, publicity bureaus, and others who thrive on such appropriations."[19]

Representative Currie, Republican, from Michigan, was astounded at the "spectacle of our President preaching disarmament to the world and sending a mysterious message back to his own country asking us to authorize him to launch the greatest naval program in the world's history." For what purpose was this navy to be built? Germany was "humbled in defeat." Our navy was already "equal in strength to the combined navies of Japan, France, and Italy." Were we to prepare for a possible "test of strength with the British Navy"? Such an idea was almost inconceivable. Or was this simply "one of the meanest, crudest bluffs ever recorded?" To take the course here proposed, whatever the purpose of its framers, was to "follow in the footsteps of Germany and proclaim our belief that 'might makes right,' and that brutal force is yet destined to rule the world."[20]

Representative Campbell, Republican, from Kansas, held that passage of the Administration's program would be a "challenge to England, a challenge to France, a challenge to Japan, a challenge to Italy, a challenge to every nation in the world to increase their armament, to increase the number of their battleships, and to prepare for war, because the greatest, the richest, the most powerful nation in the world, the nation which has the most unlimited resources, is today, while urging all . . . other nations . . . to disarm and to enter into covenants of

[18] *ibid.*, pp. 2822, 2823.
[19] *ibid.*, p. 2909.
[20] *ibid.*, pp. 3085, 3086.

peace, preparing to control the seas and for arbitrament by arms with the greatest navy the world has ever seen."[21]

Running through the debate from beginning to end was the recurring theme of debts and taxes. Many a Congressman who had regularly supported naval increases in the past simply could not justify spending additional millions and billions to wrest the trident from Great Britain. As Representative Dennison, Republican, from Illinois, emphatically put it, our people had already felt the heavy burden of taxation resulting from the war. To enter upon a "policy of naval competition with Great Britain" would postpone "any hope of a lessening of the burden for generations to come."[22]

Thus the congressional revolt against navalism flared and spread. From first to last nearly three dozen members of the lower House raised their voices in protest.[23] And as previously stated, it taxed all the resources of the Administration organization to pass a bill that fell far short of the hopes and expectations of the President and the Navy Department.

An attempt was made in the Senate to repair some of the damage which the House had inflicted upon the Administration's program.[24] The Senate Naval Committee in which big-navy sentiment still predominated, added more than $100,000,000 to the sum voted by the House.[25] But the flight of time and a senatorial filibuster prevented further action. And on March 4, 1919, the Sixty-fifth Congress expired with the controversy over naval policy still raging unabated.[26]

The outlook for naval expansion was no brighter when the new Congress convened in special session a few weeks later. With the Republicans now in control of both branches, with the President and Republican leaders at loggerheads over foreign policy, and with the post-war reaction against navalism and militarism still gaining momentum, it was easily predictable that Congress would continue its assault on the naval program.

The growing possibility of defeat at the hands of a hostile and intransigent Congress may well have influenced President

[21] *ibid.*, p. 3143. [22] *ibid.*, p. 3164.

[23] For the full debate, see *ibid.*, pp. 2674-710, 2770-85, 2821-66, 2898-933, 3076-102, 3141-72.

[24] *New York Times*, Feb. 21, 1919, p. 10; Feb. 27, p. 3.

[25] 65 Cong. 3 Sess., *Sen. Repts.* No. 777.

[26] *New York Times*, March 9, 1919, sec. 4, p. 1.

Wilson, contrary to the advice of his naval staff, to abandon that program in return for relatively minor concessions which British statesmen at Paris would probably have had to make in any event. And it is a notable fact that the revelation, late in May 1919, of the naval truce concluded at the Peace Conference, evoked considerable criticism of the Administration's alleged surrender to Great Britain, but almost no public complaint against the downward revision of the Government's naval program.[27]

With the Administration no longer sponsoring the supplementary three-year building program, the House Naval Committee, in June 1919, reported out a revised appropriation bill for the ensuing fiscal year. This bill carried items aggregating less than $600,000,000. This was a gigantic sum compared with the annual outlays before the war. But it was a mere fraction of the Navy Department's original estimates; and it was actually less than the sum demanded by the Department for new construction alone.

The revised bill made no provision for additional ships. It provided for a progressive reduction through the year, from 241,000 to 170,000 in the regular enlisted personnel of the Navy. And despite protests from the naval authorities, this bill after a few slight changes was promptly enacted into law.[28]

The reaction against navalism continued unabated during the congressional session of 1919-1920. A revised building program which the Navy Department made public in December, was sharply criticized in the press. Typical of this criticism was a strongly worded editorial in the traditionally big-navy, but likewise decidedly pro-English, *New York Times* which deplored the incipient naval contest with Great Britain. If that Power was no menace to us in 1914, it certainly was not so now. Our Atlantic coast was declared to be "as secure as if there were no fleets in Europe" at all. It was "grotesque" even to "talk about British aggression today. . . ."[29]

[27] See, for example, *New York Herald*, May 28, 1919, sec. 2, p. 7; May 29, sec. 1, p. 10; *New York Sun*, May 28, p. 1; May 29, p. 3; *New York Times*, June 1, p. 1; *New York American*, May 28, p. 5; May 29, pp. 3, 20; and *Literary Digest*, Vol. 61, June 14, 1919, p. 15.

[28] 66 Cong. 1 Sess., *H. Repts*. No. 35; *New York Times*, June 13, 1919, p. 17; June 16, p. 4; June 19, p. 8; June 20, p. 12; *Navy Yearbook, 1920-1921*, pp. 591, 599, 944.

[29] Dec. 11, 1919, p. 12.

This sentiment was reflected in the House Naval Committee which drastically reduced the Navy Department's estimates from $647,631,000 to $425,289,000. In view of the actual shrinkage of enlisted personnel, the Committee made financial provision for only 120,000 men, 50,000 less than the strength authorized by Congress in 1918. While endorsing in principle the Department's program of expansion, the Committee postponed action on a project for enlarging the Navy's shore establishments in the Pacific, and rejected the revised building program.[30]

As in the preceding session, the Committee's bill, embodying these relatively conservative provisions, passed the House and Senate after brief debate. With but slight modification, it was enacted into law in June 1920.[31] And again Congress was reproached for its parsimony and its failure to provide for the Navy even at its existing strength, to say nothing of provision for the future.[32]

With the enactment of this legislation, the first or essentially negative phase of the post-war reaction against navalism came virtually to an end. The appropriation for 1920-1921, approximately $432,000,000, still exceeded the pre-war peak of $312,000,000, voted in August 1916 under the stimulus of war propaganda. But the larger establishment resulting from the war, and the higher costs attributable to war inflation and to the ever increasing complexity of war technology, more than offset the difference.

The atmosphere in professional circles was blue with discouragement and pessimism. This feeling was eloquently reflected in the *Army and Navy Journal* which lamented that practically all the Navy's civilian friends had deserted the ship. "No better proof of this lack of public interest in proper military preparedness can be offered," this Service organ declared editorially in November 1920, "than to call attention to the almost complete disappearance of preparedness propaganda from the columns of the daily press. The civilian societies formerly active in the field appear to have abandoned their work completely. The editorial columns of newspapers that have always been strong friends of military preparedness now and

[30] 66 Cong. 2 Sess., *H. Repts.* No. 744; *Navy Yearbook, 1920-1921*, p. 944.
[31] *Navy Yearbook, 1920-1921*, pp. 625*ff*.
[32] *New York Times*, June 7, 1920, p. 8.

again print some remarks on this subject, but these are about as inspiring as the reverberations of a slack drum."[33]

The Naval Limitation Movement in America

The post-war reaction against naval expansion entered a new phase in the winter of 1920-1921. Down to that time this reaction had been essentially negative in character. It now evolved rapidly into a positive, well directed popular movement for international action to check the competitive struggle for naval primacy which, according to a widespread and growing fear, was driving the great naval Powers toward bankruptcy or war, or both together.

This movement undoubtedly owed much of its drive and popular appeal to preparatory work which reached back into the pre-war years.[34] Early discussions of the armament problem had ranged over a wide field. In May 1914, on the eve of the European war, Mr. Denys P. Myers of the World Peace Foundation had gone so far as to suggest that the great naval Powers, in return for reduction of their armaments, should engage "jointly and severally . . . to go to the aid of any one of the contracting Powers . . . attacked on account of a reduction of armament."[35]

There had also been tentative official gestures toward limitation of armaments. In 1910, Congress had passed an innocuous joint resolution authorizing the President to appoint a commission "to consider the expediency of utilizing existing international agencies for the purpose of limiting the armaments of the nations of the world by international agreement, and of constituting the combined navies of the world an international police force for the preservation of universal peace. . . ."[36] In 1912, President Taft had advocated creating an international court as a preliminary step toward a universal reduction of armaments.[37]

[33] Vol. 58, p. 360.

[34] See, for example, the annual reports of the Lake Mohonk Conferences on International Arbitration (1895-1916), in 22 volumes; American Society for International Conciliation, pamphlet series, No. 17 (April 1909); No. 41 (April 1911); No. 60 (Nov. 1912); World Peace Foundation, pamphlet series, Vol. 2, No. 5, sec. 1 (April 1912); Vol. 3, No. 6 (June 1913); Vol. 4, No. 5 (August 1914).

[35] *Report of the Twentieth Annual Lake Mohonk Conference*, p. 117.

[36] *Stat. at Large*, Vol. 36, pt. 1, p. 885.

[37] Navy Dept., *Ann. Repts. 1912*, p. 19.

This idea had captured the imagination of Josephus Daniels who presided over the Navy Department from 1913 to 1921. In his first annual report, Daniels had recommended calling an international conference to formulate a plan "for lessening the cost of preparation for war." Year after year he had reiterated this proposal which, by 1917, had evolved into a project for an "international navy to keep the peace of the world."[38]

In the meantime, Congress, at the insistence of Representative W. L. Hensley (Democrat, from Missouri), a leader in the pre-war peace movement, had inserted a clause in the Naval Act of 1916, deploring the "general increase of armament throughout the world," and authorizing and requesting the President "at an appropriate time, not later than the close of the war in Europe" to invite "all the great Governments of the world to send representatives to a conference" to formulate "a plan for a court of arbitration or other tribunal" for peacefully settling international disputes and "to consider the question of disarmament. . . ."[39] And as previously noted, one of the planks in President Wilson's platform of a just and enduring peace called for reduction of armaments to the "lowest point consistent with domestic safety."

The transference of disarmament from the realm of theory and discussion to the practical world of affairs came about largely, it would appear, through a remarkable and also alarming concurrence of events. In December 1920, as we have seen, the Navy Department brought forward another building program which called for laying down within three years a total of eighty-eight additional naval vessels, including four capital ships and thirty light cruisers. This project, coming on top of agitation for naval increases extending back to the armistice, stimulated a demand in Great Britain to resume capital-ship construction. And this demand resulted in the British Admiralty's announcement in March 1921 of a building program designed to keep pace with American naval expansion and to maintain at least a one-Power standard.

The threat of accelerated naval development in America also aggravated the situation in the Pacific which was rapidly ap-

[38] Navy Dept., *Ann. Repts. 1918*, pp. 386-90.
[39] *Navy Yearbook, 1920-1921*, p. 493.

proaching a crisis, with numerous observers predicting a Japanese-American war in the near future.[40] And finally, perhaps most importantly, the Navy Department's building plans collided head on with a popular demand for governmental retrenchment, which rose in volume and intensity as the American people slid headlong into the unplumbed depths of the post-war depression.

This concurrence of events, alarming in both its political and its economic ramifications, gave a strong impetus to fresh consideration of the armament problem. And this, under the guidance of vigorous leaders, evolved rapidly into an organized movement which enlisted the support of many individuals and groups, including peace societies and foundations,[41] churches of all denominations,[42] the recently founded National League of Women Voters,[43] the American Federation of Labor,[44] a large and influential group of daily newspapers,[45] and eventually also the conservative editorial spokesmen of American industry and finance.[46]

In mid-December 1920, Senator Borah assumed the parliamentary leadership of the arms limitation movement, by sponsoring a congressional joint resolution requesting the President

[40] See pp. 94*ff.*, *supra*.

[41] The World Peace Federation and the American Association for International Conciliation published timely and important pamphlets. The Carnegie Endowment for International Peace played a conservative, though extremely helpful rôle in the later stages. More active in the early stages were a number of newly founded organizations, including the Women's Peace Society, The Women's World Disarmament Committee, the Women's International League, the Church Peace Union, and others whose activities can be followed through the columns of the *New York Times* and other metropolitan newspapers.

[42] The Federal Council of Churches of Christ in America was especially active, and in the opinion of one competent authority, this organization was more responsible than any other for mobilizing public opinion behind the drive to limit armaments. See M. E. Curti, *Peace or War* (1936), pp. 291-3. For surveys of the religious press, see *Literary Digest*, Vol. 68, Feb. 12, 1921, p. 30; Vol. 69, June 4, p. 34.

[43] See *New York Times*, April 14, 1921, p. 16; and April 15, p. 16.

[44] *Proc. of 41st Convention, Amer. Fed. of Labor*, p. 372.

[45] The outstanding leader was the *New York Times* which gave the widest possible publicity to the arms limitation movement, and published a barrage of editorials urging action. For surveys of press opinion, see the *Literary Digest*, Vol. 67, Dec. 25, 1920, p. 10; Vol. 68, Jan. 15, 1921, p. 7; March 12, p. 10; Vol. 69, June 11, p. 7; Vol. 70, July 23, p. 5.

[46] See, for example, *Commercial and Financial Chronicle*, Vol. 112-2, April 2, 1921, p. 1338; Vol. 113-1, Aug. 27, p. 891; and *Wall Street Journal*, July 12, 1921, p. 1.

to open negotiations on the subject with Great Britain and Japan. This resolution noted in its preamble that these were the only Powers which entered into the naval calculations of the United States; that American naval expansion was reputedly the cause of Japan's reluctance to modify its own naval program; that the Japanese Government was said to desire a naval building holiday; and that the United States Government had long emphasized its desire for limitation of armaments.

For these reasons, therefore, it was resolved that the President of the United States "is requested, if not incompatible with the public interest, to advise the Governments of Great Britain and Japan respectively, that this Government will at once take up directly with" them "and without waiting upon the action of any other nation the question of disarmament, with a view of quickly coming to an understanding by which the building naval programs of each . . . shall be reduced annually during the next five years by 50 per cent of the present estimates or figures."

Adoption of this resolution, it was further resolved, would pledge Congress to "conform its appropriation and building plans to such agreement." And it was expressly stated that "this proposition is suggested . . . to accomplish immediately a substantial reduction of the naval armaments of the world."[47]

The *New York Times* promptly entered the campaign with a vigorous editorial strongly supporting the Borah Resolution, the first of a long series which placed this great daily in the forefront of the arms limitation movement. The *Times* was followed by the *New York World* whose denunciation of the "crime of competitive armament" put the incompatibility of capitalism and militarism still more dramatically before a receptive public.[48] And on December 29, General Pershing threw his immense influence into the campaign, with an eloquent plea for armament limitation to prevent us from plunging "headlong down through destructive war to darkness and barbarism."[49]

The movement was now rapidly gathering momentum. A rising flood of publicity swept over the country, while a determined group of Senators and Representatives waged an unrelenting

[47] 66 Cong. 3 Sess., *Cong. Rec.* (Vol. 60), p. 310.
[48] See, for example, Dec. 19, 1920, sec. E, p. 2.
[49] *New York Times*, Dec. 30, 1920, p. 8.

struggle not only to curtail armament appropriations but also to force the Administration to take the initiative in calling a conference of the principal naval Powers.

Commencing on January 11, the Naval Affairs Committee of the House of Representatives held extended hearings which provided a splendid sounding board for the utterances of numerous distinguished persons, and many excellent texts for the journalistic crusaders against militarism.[50] One of these witnesses was General Tasker H. Bliss, a lifelong professional soldier, who had served as one of the American delegates at the Paris Peace Conference. His proposal, which accurately foreshadowed and may well have influenced American preparations for the Washington Conference a few months later, was that the United States should hold an international arms conference at Washington "where the representatives of other nations would better realize what confronts them if they force the United States into a real competition with them in the matter of armaments."

The United States, Bliss held, should open the conference with a "reasonable proposition tending to remove mutual fear." The proceedings should be carried on with the maximum publicity possible. And Bliss, as well as General Pershing who appeared before the committee a few days later, firmly believed it would greatly enhance the prospect for success if the delegates to such a conference were civilians exclusively, rather than "military men" who were the "concrete expression . . . of the mutual fear dominating their respective countries."[51]

Somewhat earlier the House had quietly pigeonholed a resolution recommending that "all warship construction authorized to date be completed in the shortest practicable time commensurate with the nation's desire for economy. . . ."[52] On January 15 a measure similar to the Borah Resolution in the Senate, was reported favorably from the Foreign Affairs Committee of the lower chamber.[53] And a few days later the Senate Foreign

[50] 66 Cong. 3 Sess., *Hearings on Disarmament: Its Relation to the Naval Policy and the Naval Building Program of the United States*; reprinted in *Hearings on Sundry Naval Legislation, 1920-1921.*

[51] *ibid.*, pp. 554, 557, 560, 600.

[52] *New York Times*, Jan. 7, 1921, p. 2; *Cong. Rec.*, Vol. 60, p. 1083.

[53] *New York Times*, Jan. 16, 1921, p. 7; *Cong. Rec.*, Vol. 60, pp. 616, 2478; the formal report, dated Feb. 2, is in 66 Cong. 3 Sess., *H. Repts.* No. 1283.

Relations Committee recommended passage of the Borah proposal in slightly amended form.[54]

This was no sooner accomplished than Borah launched another attack on the parliamentary citadel of navalism. In a resolution, introduced and adopted on January 25, the Senate Naval Committee was requested to consider and report on the expediency of suspending all naval construction for six months, pending a thorough reexamination of naval policy and the outcome of the current movement for limitation of armament. He followed this up two days later with a provocative speech in which he urged arms limitation and read one quotation after another questioning the continued utility of capital ships.[55]

On February 9 the big-navy majority which controlled the Senate Naval Committee, brought in a report which played right into the hands of the advocates of naval limitation and retrenchment. This report, which embodied a carefully phrased statement by the General Board, unqualifiedly endorsed the view that capital ships were still the backbone of naval power, and that the United States should lose no time in building up its fighting fleet to equality with the strongest.[56]

Under different conditions, this report might have provided the stimulus necessary to mobilize support for the lagging naval program. But with the temper then prevailing in Congress and in the country, it produced just the opposite effect. It was denounced in the press as a "General Board document." It offered a target for another parliamentary attack led by Senator Borah. And it drew a minority report, prepared by Senator King of Utah, which fairly represented the wave of anti-navalism that was sweeping the United States in the spring of 1921.[57]

This dissenting opinion opened with an attack both on the majority report and on the evidence upon which it rested. The expert witnesses called by the majority had showed hostility and prejudice against the very idea of arms limitation. Their testimony represented a reactionary view contrary to the drift of competent opinion. And the majority, accepting this view, had

[54] *New York Times*, Jan. 21, 1921, p. 17; 66 Cong. 3 Sess., *Sen. Repts.* No. 709.

[55] *Cong. Rec.*, Vol. 60, pp. 1796, 2112*ff.*; *New York Times*, Jan. 28, 1921, p. 6.

[56] *Cong. Rec.*, Vol. 60, pp. 2825*ff.*; the enclosure from the General Board is also printed in 66 Cong. 3 Sess. House Naval Committee, *Hearings on Sundry Naval Legislation, 1920-1921*, pp. 925*ff.*

[57] *New York Times*, Feb. 11, 1921, p. 10; *Cong. Rec.*, Vol. 60, pp. 2983*ff.*, 4273*ff.*

taken the position that we must go on building battleships "in increasing numbers, notwithstanding the enormous cost" and the manifest desire of England and Japan, our only naval rivals, to reach an agreement limiting armaments.

"The day has come," King declared, "when the United States must cease its prodigal and useless outlays in time of peace. . . . Our naval policy must cease to be dominated by the professional naval view, and the influence of men who have a more comprehensive conception of the advantage and welfare of our country must become dominant in the naval policy of the Government."

Specifically, he concluded, "we should suspend the naval program to the extent herein indicated,[58] and either enter the League of Nations or address ourselves to obtaining an agreement with the Great Powers for the limitation of armaments and the establishment of tribunals for the settlement of international controversies."[59]

Meanwhile, the House Committee on Appropriations had reported a naval supply bill which cut the Navy Department's estimates nearly in half. This bill made provision for only 100,000 enlisted men, 35,000 less than the number actually enrolled, and 43,000 less than the minimum asked for. The Department's request for authorization of a new building program was completely ignored. Only $90,000,000 was allotted for continuing work on ships already under construction, in place of the $184,000,000 demanded. And the Committee had reduced the total estimates from $679,000,000 to $395,000,000.[60]

The item of $90,000,000 for new construction, though less than one-half the amount asked for, and not more than one-fourth the amount needed to complete the 1916 building program, was still too much for the advocates of retrenchment and disarmament. An amendment to withhold the entire amount until after the President should have called an arms conference developed remarkable strength in debate. And this amendment, as well as others less drastic, would almost certainly have commanded a majority, but for the disinclination of the Republicans to weaken or to force the hand of their incoming President who

[58] Six battleships and five battle cruisers, with an aggregate displacement of nearly 500,000 tons.

[59] *Cong. Rec.*, Vol. 60, pp. 4273*ff*.

[60] 66 Cong. 3 Sess., *H. Repts.* No. 1281; *Cong. Rec.*, Vol. 60, pp. 2939*ff*.

was reported to be planning definite steps toward an international limitation of armaments.[61]

The bill passed the House on Feburary 14. And though denounced in the press as a "big-navy" measure, its passage really marked another substantial and important victory for the naval limitation movement in America.[62]

A further victory was won in the Senate against an attempt to increase the naval appropriation by $100,000,000. A determined filibuster, again led by Senator Borah, not only frustrated this attempt, but also brought forth a whole crop of resolutions and amendments designed to force the hand of the incoming Administration.[63] An appeal by Senator Lodge, in executive session, for a strong navy to enforce a firm foreign policy, especially in the Far East, was ignored. On March 3, the sponsors of the bill gave up in despair. And the following day the Sixty-sixth Congress, like its predecessor two years before, expired without making any provision whatever for the support of the naval establishment.[64]

In this outcome, the *Army and Navy Journal* saw "repeated" the "old, depressing and costly story of the refusal of our Legislators to heed the best professional opinion of our most highly trained and experienced officers. . . ." Against the advice of the General Board, the Senate had insisted on demanding a conference for reduction of armaments. In this action, as well as in its failure to make adequate provision for the Services, the Sixty-sixth Congress had passed into history "leaving behind it in the Army and Navy a feeling of injustice and foreboding. . . ."[65]

Senator Borah, on the contrary, viewed the outlook with optimistic satisfaction. There would be ample time, he insisted, to enact a supply bill before the new fiscal year opened on July 1. And the Senate's failure to pass the big-navy bill reported from its Naval Committee served notice on the incoming Administration that the demand for arms limitation would be renewed and "urged at the opening of the next session."[66]

[61] *Cong. Rec.*, Vol. 60, pp. 3145*ff*.

[62] *ibid.*, p. 3165; and see *New York Times*, Feb. 16, 1921, p. 8.

[63] Feb. 15, Borah amendment, embodying substance of his resolution of Dec. 14; Feb. 28, Pomerene amendment; March 1, Edge and Walsh amendments. *Cong. Rec.*, Vol. 60, pp. 3171, 3740, 4043, 4114, 4141, 4162.

[64] *New York Times*, March 2, 1921, p. 1; March 4, p. 1; *Cong. Rec.*, Vol. 60, pp. 4360*ff*.

[65] Vol. 58, March 12, 1921, pp. 780-1.

[66] *New York Times*, March 4, 1921, p. 2.

CHAPTER EIGHT

☆ ☆ ☆ ☆ ☆ ☆ ☆ ☆ ☆ ☆ ☆ ☆ ☆ ☆ ☆ ☆ ☆ ☆ ☆ ☆

The Road to Washington

PRESIDENT HARDING entered the White House on March 4, 1921, with public commitments which were widely interpreted as a pledge to take early steps toward limitation of armaments by international agreement. The Republican platform and the President's preelection utterances had foreshadowed American cooperation in some kind of "association of nations" to preserve peace. Prior to his inauguration, Harding had repeatedly intimated that he favored an arms conference as the most effective step in that direction. Though he had studiedly avoided making clear and unequivocal statements, there was an all but universal popular expectation that the incoming Republican Administration would promptly announce plans for an international conference for the limitation of armaments.

Weeks passed, however, without much perceptible progress in this direction. There were vague intimations that the Administration was exploring the problem.[1] The President's message to the new Congress which met in special session early in April, noted the popular "call for reduced expenditure for . . . national defense." The Administration too wished "to eliminate the burdens of heavy armament." And while the "merest prudence" forbade that we "disarm alone," the President was "ready to cooperate with other nations to approximate disarmament."[2] But certain other things, it soon appeared, must come first.

On April 18, the President announced that any move toward arms limitation would have to await conclusion of peace

[1] See, for example, *New York Times,* March 5, 1921, p. 4; March 8, p. 2; March 14, p. 3; April 7, p. 19.

[2] 67 Cong. 1 Sess., *Cong. Rec.* (Vol. 61), p. 172.

negotiations between the United States and Germany, still technically at war because of the Senate's refusal to accept the Versailles Treaty. Two days later, it was disclosed that the Administration was opposing any curtailment of the shipbuilding program authorized back in 1916. And the following day, it was intimated that the President and his intimate advisers desired to postpone limitation of armaments until after completion of that program, probably about 1924.[3]

This procrastination meanwhile gave fresh impetus to the disarmament movement. The barrage of publicity which had slackened somewhat in anticipation of action, was resumed. Senator Borah reintroduced his resolution which called for early naval negotiations with Great Britain and Japan. And similar proposals were again offered in the House of Representatives.[4]

These and other developments resulted in a parliamentary struggle in which the Administration, despite its avowed policy of arms limitation, appeared publicly as the ally and leader of those groups favoring naval expansion and opposing limitation of armaments. The Administration's position was duly explained and defended in Congress after the House Committee on Appropriations reported out the naval bill which the House, but not the Senate, had passed in the preceding session. This bill, contrary to the wishes of many Representatives, still carried the item of $90,000,000 for continuing work on the 1916 program. And this item, retained at the instance of the Administration, was justified and defended on the ground, among others, that early completion of the capital ships begun under that program would hasten rather than retard progress toward universal reduction of armaments.[5]

Completion of these ships, it was contended, would give the United States naval parity with Great Britain. Then and then only could we safely agree to proportionate reduction of armament. Then and only then would England assent to reduction on the basis of formal parity with the United States. Then and not

[3] *New York Times*, April 19, p. 18; April 21, p. 22; April 22, p. 17.

[4] *Cong. Rec.*, Vol. 61, pp. 99, 188, 357; *New York Times*, March 24, p. 10; March 28, p. 10; March 29, p. 9; April 7, p. 19; April 14, p. 3; April 16, p. 10; April 22, p. 17; April 23, p. 10.

[5] See *New York Times*, April 21, p. 22; April 22. p. 12.

till then would the United States occupy a favorable bargaining position. For the Administration had no intention of scrapping these new ships. "Nobody would be foolish enough to reduce armament by scrapping his latest weapon." We had "old ships by the hundred." With the new ships completed, we could dispose of these older vessels, which had little fighting value and were a constant expense, without materially weakening our naval power. Thus, argued one congressional spokesman of the Administration, "whether we have reduction of armament or not, I can not see any escape from completing this program, if we are wise and if we are to play the part in shaping the future of the world that events and Providence have put upon us."[6]

This argument made no impression on the militant advocates of naval limitation. So rapidly were their demands growing, that the naval bill carried over from the preceding session, was now as unacceptable to them as it had been formerly to the exponents of continued naval expansion. One after another, they challenged the good faith of the Administration; scouted the argument that further naval expansion was a necessary preliminary to naval limitation; and denounced the Administration's bill as an incitement to navalism, as a menace to our peaceful relations with Great Britain and Japan, and as an intolerable burden upon the groaning taxpayers of America.[7]

Arguments proved insufficient, however, to halt the majority steam roller. And on April 28, the lower house, under firm Administration leadership and control, pushed through its bill, defeating repeated assaults designed either to reduce appropriations or to whip the executive into calling an arms conference.[8]

The President followed up this victory with a direct attack on the Borah Resolution, and a public warning to Congress to cease its attempts to "force the hand of the Executive" in relation to disarmament.[9] Administration leaders in Congress hastened to carry out this command. The House Committee on Foreign Affairs dropped all proceedings on the disarmament resolutions previously referred to it. The Senate Naval Committee ignored the pending Borah Resolution. And the Republican majority of that Committee, in accord with the Administration's policy,

[6] *Cong. Rec.*, Vol. 61, p. 613.

[7] *ibid.*, pp. 606*ff.*, 665*ff.*, 756*ff.*

[8] *ibid.*, pp. 680*ff.*, 683*ff.*, 756-66.

[9] *New York Times*, May 4, 1921, pp. 1, 2.

added $100,000,000 to the appropriation bill received from the lower chamber.[10]

The opponents of navalism met these setbacks with redoubled efforts. The clergy of practically all denominations urged disarmament from the pulpit.[11] The cause was agitated in secular forums throughout the country.[12] And its leaders mobilized their resources for a fight to the finish in Congress.[13]

Whether or not as a result of this fresh onslaught, the Administration presently staged a strategic retreat. On May 18, the President was reported to have withdrawn his opposition to the Borah Resolution, now offered as an amendment to the naval appropriation bill, on the understanding apparently that the intransigent Idaho Senator would acquiesce in the increased appropriations recommended by the Naval Committee.[14] Then on May 25, the Senate voted this resolution into the bill without a dissenting vote.[15]

But the fight for arms limitation was not yet won. The Administration blocked a proposal authorizing suspension of the naval construction program for six months pending the outcome of the conference envisaged by the Borah Amendment.[16] And on July 1, the Administration leaders in the Senate forced through the supply bill with appropriations totalling $494,000,000, after defeating repeated attempts to cut down or restrict the expenditure of funds allocated for continuing work on the ships under construction.[17]

[10] *ibid.*, May 4, 1921, p. 2; May 5, p. 1; 67 Cong. 1 Sess., *Sen. Repts.* No. 35.

[11] See, for example, *New York Times*, May 9, 1921, p. 8; May 14, p. 3; May 19, p. 14; May 26, p. 6; June 6, p. 13; and *Literary Digest*, Vol. 69, June 4, 1921, p. 34.

[12] See, for example, *New York Times*, May 15, 1921, p. 10; May 18, p. 2; May 19, p. 14; May 20, p. 17; May 23, p. 2; May 27, p. 3; May 31, p. 3.

[13] *ibid.*, May 10, p. 1.

[14] *ibid.*, May 18, p. 1.

[15] *Cong. Rec.*, Vol. 61, pp. 1757-8; *New York Times*, May 26, p. 1. As thus adopted, the Borah Amendment provided: "That the President is authorized and requested to invite the Governments of Great Britain and Japan to send representatives to a conference, which shall be charged with the duty of promptly entering into an understanding or agreement by which the naval expenditures and building programs of each of the said Governments, . . . shall be substantially reduced annually during the next five years to such an extent and upon such terms as may be agreed upon, which understanding or agreement is to be reported to the respective Governments for approval."

[16] This was known as the Pomerene Amendment. *New York Times*, May 28, 1921, p. 2; *Cong. Rec.*, Vol. 61, pp. 1007, 1840-7.

[17] *Cong. Rec.*, Vol. 61, pp. 1901-12, 1940-72.

The Administration now returned to the attack on the Borah Amendment. When the amended bill was presented to the House for ratification, two further amendments were proposed—one apparently, and the other certainly, with the support of the Administration. The first, proposed as a substitute for the Borah Amendment, broadened the scope of the requested conference to include numerous other Powers besides Great Britain and Japan. This would probably have the effect of so complicating the limitation problem as to prevent any constructive achievement at all.[18] The other, also offered as a substitute for the Borah Amendment, further watered down the mild terms of that proposal to an extent that would relieve the executive from all obligation to take any action whatsoever.[19]

Against these assaults, the disarmament forces, supported by a rising public sentiment, held their lines. The Administration once more yielded, enabling the House to ratify the Borah Amendment with only four dissenting votes.[20] And on July 8, a conference committee of Senators and Representatives reached an agreement, with the advocates of smaller appropriations and international limitation of armaments winning all along the line.[21]

External Pressures and Complications

While the popular revolt against navalism within the United States was unquestionably an important factor shaping the naval policy of the Harding Administration, it would be a serious mistake to interpret the President's call to an arms conference as a product solely of American internal politics. This action was also a response to external pressures and to developments abroad which removed certain obstacles to effective cooperation with the other naval Powers.

The chief source of external pressure was Great Britain where the proposed naval program of the United States was viewed with anxiety often verging on consternation and alarm. Posses-

[18] *New York Times*, June 4, 1921, p. 1. [19] *ibid.*, June 5, p. 1.

[20] *ibid.*, June 30, 1921, p. 1; *Cong. Rec.*, Vol. 61, pp. 3225-6.

[21] *New York Times*, July 9, p. 6. For the conference report formally presented on July 11, see 67 Cong. 1 Sess. *H. Repts.* No. 258. As finally passed, the bill represented a reduction of about $86,000,000 from the total voted by the Senate. See *New York Times*, July 13, p. 19.

sion of the world's greatest navy had long symbolized the unity, power, and prestige of the British Empire. Loss of first place upon the sea would not only wound the pride of the British peoples but also have disturbing repercussions on the external relations of Great Britain and the Empire. Yet to maintain even a nominal naval equality with the United States, in open and unrestricted competition, would require a financial outlay which Great Britain's war-weakened and seriously depressed economy was then in no condition to bear. Also it could scarcely be doubted that any large British effort in this direction would further stimulate navalism within the United States, accelerating the pace of American naval development, and requiring still larger expenditures by Great Britain. Accelerated naval development in the United States, moreover, would inevitably aggravate the Japanese-American crisis which was already threatening to result in a war that would certainly produce grave consequences throughout the British Empire even if it did not irreparably injure British interests in the Pacific. And even if these disasters were avoided, a naval building contest with the United States would destroy any possibility of that Anglo-American entente which after the war appealed to many Englishmen as the only firm foundation upon which to rebuild a shattered world order.

For these and other reasons, a naval limitation agreement with the United States became an important objective of British diplomacy after the war. We have previously noted the first effort in this direction made at the Peace Conference, where a naval truce was reached with the United States.[22] But that understanding was no more than a *modus vivendi* pending the negotiation of a permanent agreement. And months stretched into years without visible sign of further progress toward that end. On the contrary, there were alarming indications,[23] especially after the British Government's decision, in the winter of 1920-1921, to resume capital ship construction,[24] that the two countries were in danger of drifting into a financially if not politically ruinous struggle for a nominal primacy upon the sea.[25]

[22] See pp. 62*ff.*, *supra*. [23] See pp. 86*ff.*, *supra*.

[24] The British Government's capital ship "replacement" program, while not formally announced until March 1921, had been under discussion for several months.

[25] In a forthright editorial, *The New Statesman*, radical London weekly, tersely declared: ". . . the problem of naval construction today is simply and exclusively

The prospect of such a struggle stimulated a widespread British demand that their Government come to a settlement with the United States.[26] And this agitation, coinciding with the rapid development of the disarmament movement in America, encouraged British statesmen to renew their efforts to reach a permanent naval limitation agreement with the United States. But the problem of securing such an agreement presented serious difficulties.

To approach the United States as a suppliant would only damage British prestige and bargaining power. To make threats would only accelerate the pace of American naval development. For the British Government itself to institute formal negotiations, might easily so strengthen the anti-British drift in America as to render impossible any agreement at all. And British statesmen had always to consider the possible repercussions on the imperial and external relations of Great Britain. It was therefore desirable, if not absolutely necessary, that the United States should assume the responsibility for instituting formal negotiations or for calling an arms conference.[27]

During January and February 1921, the British Government seems to have confined its efforts to preparing the way for positive steps to be taken after the inauguration of the Harding Administration March 4, 1921. In January, Sir Auckland Geddes, the British Ambassador in Washington, was called home to consult on the armament problem, and his return a few weeks later was heralded as a prelude to Anglo-American naval negotiations.[28] Late in February, Lord Lee of Fareham, a conspicuous advocate of close relations with America, was put at the head of the British Admiralty.[29]

a problem of preparation for a hypothetical war against America." Dec. 18, 1920, Vol. 16, pp. 328, 329.

[26] This movement embraced groups as far apart, ideologically, as the British Navy League (see *New York Times*, Jan. 2, 1921, p. 10) and *The New Statesman* (see preceding note). For other typical samples of this agitation, see *The Times* (London, moderate conservative), Feb. 10, 1921, pp. 10, 11; Feb. 22, p. 11; March 17, p. 14; March 18, pp. 11, 14; May 11, p. 11; June 15, p. 11; June 17, pp. 10, 11; June 18, p. 11; *The Manchester Guardian Weekly* (liberal), Jan. 7, 1921, Vol. 4, p. 2; March 18, p. 207; and *The Spectator* (conservative), Dec. 11, 1920, Vol. 125, p. 765.

[27] See R. A. Chaput, *Disarmament in British Foreign Policy* (1935), p. 97; E. J. Young, *Powerful America* (1936), Chap. 3.

[28] See *New York Times*, Jan. 18, 1921, p. 1; Feb. 9, p. 1; Feb. 10, p. 6.

[29] See Young, *Powerful America*, pp. 46*f*.

Twelve days after the inauguration of President Harding, Lord Lee made the first public bid for American initiative. Speaking before the British Institute of Naval Architects, he strongly urged naval limitation on the basis of equality with the United States. Welcoming the "hint . . . thrown out" in President Harding's inaugural address,[30] he declared "that if an invitation comes from Washington, I am prepared personally to put aside all other business . . . in order to take part in a business than which there can be nothing more pressing in the affairs of this world."[31]

When this gesture produced no decisive result,[32] Lord Lee tried a different approach. Adolph Ochs, publisher of the *New York Times*, was one of the leading American advocates of a naval limitation agreement with Great Britain. Early in April, *The Times* (London) printed an interview with Mr. Ochs, who was then visiting in England, in which the latter reiterated his belief that the "peace of the world" depended upon Anglo-American friendship and solidarity.[33] On April 22, Lord Lee secured a conference with Mr. Ochs, which resulted in the latter's relaying to the Navy Department the British Government's desire to co-operate in any arms limitation project which the United States might initiate.[34]

Though the Ochs memorandum never reached the Secretary of State who was handling the problem, plans for an arms conference were definitely taking shape during May and June.[35] But the Administration moved with great caution. Account had to be taken of the hostility with which certain influential American groups viewed all proposals for naval limitation.[36] And even more important, the Administration had to steer carefully through a maze of international pitfalls and complications.

[30] This was obviously a reference to Harding's statement that "we are ready to associate ourselves with the nations of the world, great and small, for conference, for counsel; to seek the expressed views of world opinion; to recommend a way to approximate disarmament and relieve the crushing burdens of military and naval establishments."

[31] See *New York Times*, March 17, 1921, pp. 1, 2.

[32] Its only apparent result was an unofficial and unconfirmed newspaper report that the United States Government, late in March, was carrying on secret conversations with Great Britain. See *New York Times*, March 29, 1921, p. 2.

[33] April 2, 1921, p. 7.

[34] See Young, *Powerful America*, pp. 48*ff*.

[35] Chief Justice Hughes to the authors, Aug. 5, 1940.

[36] See, for example, *New York Times*, May 1, 1921, sec. 2, p. 2; May 18, p. 2.

One complicating factor was the so-called "Anglo-Irish War." While the status of Ireland within the British Empire had nothing to do with disarmament, and while that question was technically no business of the American people, various Irish-American groups and a section of the press within the United States carried on an anti-British agitation which unquestionably embarrassed the Administration in dealing with Great Britain.[37] And in June 1921, the Secretary of State himself utilized the threat of congressional demonstration on behalf of Ireland in his efforts to force Great Britain to liquidate the Anglo-Japanese Alliance.[38]

That Alliance was the key to an even greater obstacle to naval limitation. For obvious and compelling reasons, Japanese statesmen and naval experts regarded control of the western Pacific as absolutely essential, not only to the security of their island home, but also to the execution of their program of expansion in Asia. In 1921 it was widely conceded that, north of the equator from about the International Date Line to the coast of Asia, the Japanese Navy commanded an area which surrounded the American insular possessions of Guam and the Philippines.

The naval program of the United States framed with increasing reference to defense of these outlying possessions, as well as to support of American claims and policies in the Far East, challenged Japan's entire system of policy and strategy. A navy which American experts would regard as adequate for these purposes would have to be strong enough to blockade Japan and to disrupt Japanese communications with the mainland of Asia, and hence strong enough to search out and defeat the Japanese fleet in its home waters. While the United States did not possess such a force in 1921, there was no mistaking the purpose of the Navy Department, of numerous civilian statesmen, and of a vocal section of the American press, to work toward that end as rapidly as possible.

Japan's answer to America's naval challenge, as previously noted,[39] was accelerated naval development with a view to maintaining the strategic status quo in the western Pacific. But

[37] H. W. Steed, *Through Thirty Years* (1924), Vol. 2, p. 362.
[38] *For. Rels. 1921*, Vol. 2, pp. 314-16.
[39] See pp. 97*ff*., *supra*.

the insatiable demands of the Emperor's armed Services which, by 1921, were consuming nearly half of his Government's revenue,[40] as well as the encroaching business depression, and the threatening international outlook, stimulated a movement within Japan for international limitation of armaments.[41] Chambers of commerce and other organized groups carried on active propaganda for arms limitation.[42] The question was agitated in the Japanese Parliament during the winter of 1920-1921.[43] The movement received increasingly favorable publicity in the Japanese press.[44] And Japanese statesmen repeatedly iterated their readiness to cooperate in any feasible project to that end. While they flatly refused to curtail Japan's defense program in the face of continued American naval expansion,[45] and while they showed aversion to taking any initiative,[46] all but a small minority, consisting chiefly, it would appear, of incorrigible militarists, were receptive to the idea of limiting armaments. They were even prepared to cut down their own settled naval program provided this could be done without impairing Japan's prestige or seriously disturbing the naval status quo upon which depended not only the strategic security of the Island Empire but also its future destiny in Asia.[47]

These provisos, however, raised serious if not insuperable obstacles in the way of Japanese-American cooperation. They meant, in effect, that naval limitation was contingent on American acceptance of political and strategic terms calculated to clinch Japan's hold on the western Pacific. Such terms would

[40] *New York Times*, Dec. 1, 1920, p. 1; Feb. 4, 1921, p. 15.

[41] See, for example, Captain M. D. Kennedy, *Some Aspects of Japan and Her Defense Forces* (1928), p. 107.

[42] See, for example, *New York Times*, March 7, 1921, p. 2; June 11, p. 6; June 25, p. 3; June 27, p. 1; June 28, p. 4; and June 30, p. 1.

[43] Tatsuji Takeuchi, *War and Diplomacy in the Japanese Empire* (1935), pp. 227*ff*.

[44] At least such is the inference clearly deducible from quotations from Japanese newspapers, published in the *New York Times* and other American newspapers. For a survey of Japanese press opinion, see *Literary Digest*, Vol. 69, May 7, 1921, p. 18.

[45] See, for example, Viscount Ishii's statement before the League of Nations Armament Commission. *New York Times*, Dec. 12, 1920, p. 1.

[46] See, for example, *New York Times*, Jan. 26, 1921, p. 4; March 7, p. 2; and June 23, p. 10.

[47] This conclusion is derived from a large number of contemporary utterances to which one may have ready access through the *New York Times Index*, titles: Japan, Navy; Disarmament; and Naval Disarmament.

necessitate radical contraction of the American political and naval program in the Pacific. Any treaty that could be construed as a surrender to Japan would encounter senatorial and popular opposition which might easily prevent ratification. And the state of American opinion in 1921 practically forbade any formal negotiations at all as long as the Anglo-Japanese Alliance continued in existence.

The original objects of Great Britain's military partnership with Japan had disappeared with the collapse of the Russian Empire and the forcible elimination of Germany from the Far East. Continuance of the Alliance after the World War had naturally aroused distrust and suspicion within the United States. American statesmen had repeatedly indicated their opposition to its renewal.[48] By 1921 popular feeling had grown to such proportions that renewal of the Alliance, which was now due for reconsideration, would certainly have given fresh impetus to navalism in America, and would almost certainly have put naval limitation beyond the sphere of practical politics for an indefinite time to come.

Although British spokesmen repeatedly denied that the Alliance involved any menace to the United States, they nevertheless showed little inclination to relinquish it as long as the United States continued to follow an intransigent naval policy. While it was almost unthinkable that Great Britain would ever join Japan in a war against the United States, the Alliance unquestionably strengthened Japan's political position, and its renewal at this juncture would have been widely construed in America as a gesture of British toleration, if not support, of Japanese aggressions in Asia against which the American political and naval program in the Pacific was in some measure directed. On the other hand, summary abrogation of the Alliance would tend to isolate Japan, and might even prevent the absolutely essential cooperation of that Power in any naval limitation project. In short, the United States would not agree to limit its navy as long as the Anglo-Japanese Alliance existed; Japan might well reject naval terms acceptable to the United States without the support which the Alliance afforded; and Great Britain was reluctant to sacrifice its long-standing association

[48] See A. W. Griswold, *The Far Eastern Policy of the United States* (1938), pp. 275*ff*.

with Japan for an uncertain naval agreement with the United States.[49]

This was substantially the situation when, late in June 1921, the Governments of Great Britain and the oversea Dominions met in London to consider problems of empire and foreign policy. Despite efforts to enforce secrecy, it soon leaked out that the British Government's proposal to renew the Anglo-Japanese Alliance was arousing strong protest, especially on the part of the Right Honorable Arthur Meighen, Prime Minister of Canada.[50] So determined was this protest and so ominous were the signs of growing opposition to the Alliance in the United States,[51] that the British Government, under the facile leadership of Mr. Lloyd George, presently executed an about-face behind a smoke screen of juridical verbiage, specious publicity, and diplomatic maneuvering. The Alliance, previously construed as lapsing unless renewed by July 13, was now reinterpreted as automatically continuing for another year unless denounced sooner.[52] This move was followed by a barrage of rumors and speculations which served to confuse the issue and gain time while British statesmen explored the possibilities of transmuting the Anglo-Japanese Alliance into some broader and less specific commitment which would avoid offense to Japan, and at the same time serve the purposes of imperial unity, as well as satisfy and perhaps include the United States.[53]

These efforts were directed chiefly toward maneuvering the United States into sponsoring this distinctly political enterprise with which the question of naval limitation might or might not be joined.[54] It was secretly proposed that the United States sponsor a political conference of the Powers "directly con-

[49] See R. A. Chaput, *Disarmament in British Foreign Policy* (1935), pp. 99*ff.*; and R. L. Buell, *The Washington Conference* (1922), pp. 124, 146.

[50] See J. B. Brebner, "Canada, the Anglo-Japanese Alliance and the Washington Conference," *Political Science Quarterly* (1935), Vol. 50, pp. 45*ff.*

[51] See, for example, the following editorials in the notoriously pro-British *New York Times*, June 24, 1921, p. 14; July 2, p. 8; July 5, p. 14.

[52] See Brebner, "Canada and the Anglo-Japanese Alliance," p. 54; and *New York Times*, July 2, 1921, p. 3.

[53] See *New York Times*, July 4, 1921, p. 1; July 5, p. 17; July 6, p. 17; July 8, p. 1; July 9, p. 3.

[54] See Brebner, "Canada and the Anglo-Japanese Alliance," p. 56; and *New York Times*, July 5, 1921, p. 17; July 8, p. 1.

cerned" (i.e. Great Britain, Japan, the United States, and possibly China), "to consider all essential matters bearing upon [the] Far East and Pacific Ocean. . . ."[55] And on Thursday, July 7, Lloyd George, in response to questions in the House of Commons, made a public statement which virtually committed the British Government itself to assume the initiative if the United States failed to act within the next four days.[56]

These developments, together with the announcement, on July 8, of a truce in Ireland, cleared the way for action in Washington. With the irrelevant but none the less disturbing Irish question on the road to settlement, and with the Anglo-Japanese Alliance apparently in process of liquidation, the Harding Administration could now take the initiative so insistently urged both at home[57] and abroad.[58] And it was increasingly apparent that the Administration must act quickly or lose the initiative to the British Government whose interest in naval limitation had become at least temporarily subordinate to its desire to preserve unity within the Empire without too seriously disturbing its relations with Japan.

On July 8, the same day that the House and Senate conferees inflicted the final defeat on the naval program hitherto supported by the Administration,[59] the State Department dispatched a tentative proposal for an arms conference to the Governments of Great Britain, France, Italy, and Japan.[60] On July 9, in view of developments in London, and in order to keep the initiative in American hands, the scope of the proposed conference was widened "to include discussion of all Far Eastern problems by [the] Powers interested [therein]. . . ."[61]

[55] *For. Rels. 1921*, Vol. 1, p. 19.

[56] *ibid.*, pp. 19*ff*.; and *New York Times*, July 8, 1921, p. 1.

[57] The developments related in this section, it should be remembered, were occurring simultaneously with the disarmament campaign and congressional struggle described in the preceding section.

[58] For examples of continuing British agitation for the United States to take the initiative in calling a naval conference, see *New York Times*, May 27, 1921, p. 3; May 31, p. 7; June 18, p. 1; June 21, pp. 1, 3; July 5, p. 2. For Japanese official gestures toward the United States, see June 4, 1921, p. 2; July 4, p. 1.

[59] See *New York Times*, July 9, 1921, p. 6.

[60] See *For. Rels. 1921*, Vol. 1, p. 18. According to press reports, informal discussion of naval limitation had been proceeding in diplomatic circles for several weeks. See *New York Times*, June 1, 1921, p. 1.

[61] *For. Rels. 1921*, Vol. 1, p. 23; and Chief Justice Hughes to the authors, Aug. 5, 1940.

On July 10, President Harding approved a formal statement announcing these developments.[62] And on Monday morning, July 11, this statement informed newspaper readers the world over, that the United States Government had at last extended the long awaited invitation to the principal naval Powers and to China, to participate in a conference at Washington, for the "limitation of armament" and for "reaching a common understanding with respect to principles and policies in the Far East."[63]

Conference Preparations

The next task was to prepare for constructive achievement at the arms conference to which the Harding Administration was now committed. This task was admirably executed under the direction of the American Secretary of State, Mr. Charles Evans Hughes, in the face of formidable and discouraging obstacles.

It was indisputable that the President's announcement of July 11 voiced the desire of articulate opinion in the United States. It was also true that the Administration had received informal assurances of cooperation from the other naval Powers. But there was no certainty that those Powers and the United States could reach agreement either as to armaments or as to the Far East. Indeed, there was grave danger, as events promptly demonstrated, that the conflicts of national interest and policy, and the prevailing atmosphere of suspicion and distrust, all of which had contributed to the politico-naval crisis, would now present insuperable obstacles to effective cooperation for liquidating that crisis.

The first difficulty arose with Great Britain. As soon as President Harding had definitely taken the initiative in calling a conference, British statesmen proposed a preliminary meeting in London with a view to reaching a "settlement of Pacific and Far Eastern problems. . . ." In support of this, they contended that such a settlement must precede any attempt to limit naval armaments and that an early meeting in London would accom-

[62] *ibid.*, p. 24; and J. E. Watson, *As I Knew Them*: *Memoirs of James E. Watson* (1936), p. 230.

[63] *For. Rels. 1921*, Vol. 1, p. 24.

modate the Dominion prime ministers who were attending the Imperial Conference there.[64]

Though it was perfectly clear that a Pacific and Far Eastern settlement involving liquidation of the Anglo-Japanese Alliance, would have to precede or at least accompany a naval limitation agreement, there were compelling reasons for rejecting the British proposal. For the United States to participate in the proposed meeting would almost certainly evoke public protest and criticism within this country, and give rise to charges that the Administration was deliberately sidetracking the armament problem. The very possible failure of such a meeting would certainly jeopardize the prospects of the subsequent arms conference. There was also the danger, of which the Administration was apparently not unaware, that the British and Japanese Governments might present joint demands which would decidedly embarrass the United States, render agreement impossible, and further obstruct American opposition to Japanese aggressions in eastern Asia. And it was practically inevitable that the United States Government would lose exclusive control over, and be forced into a subordinate position as to, preparations for the later arms conference. For these and perhaps other compelling reasons, Secretary Hughes refused to transfer the negotiations to London, or indeed to participate in any preliminary meeting at all.[65]

This stand safeguarded the Administration's freedom of action and kept guidance of the main enterprise firmly in American hands. But the protracted conversations and correspondence which took place before the British Government acquiesced in this decision, produced annoyance and irritation on both sides, and left British statesmen decidedly embarrassed, somewhat resentful, and at least temporarily uncooperative.[66]

Another controversy, this time with Japan, arose over the last-minute broadening of the naval limitation project at the instance of Great Britain. In the light of all available evidence, it seems a fair inference that the British proposal of a conference to deal with "all essential matters bearing upon [the] Far East and

[64] *ibid.*, pp. 25, 26.
[65] *ibid.*, pp. 28*ff.*; and see Griswold, *Far Eastern Policy*, pp. 294*ff.*
[66] *For. Rels. 1921*, Vol. 1, pp. 32, 36, 37, 45, 46, 47, 50, 51, 53.

Pacific Ocean"[67] implied little more than a meeting to find ways and means for transmuting the Anglo-Japanese Alliance into some new association tolerable to Japan, and at the same time acceptable to all the British Dominions and to the United States. As incorporated into the American naval limitation project, however, this addition rather clearly involved something more. In supplementary notes to the Powers, it was proposed to include "*all* Far Eastern questions." And in the President's public announcement of July 11, it was explained that the "manifest . . . close relation" between "limitation of armament" and "Pacific and Far Eastern problems" made it necessary, "in connection with this conference," to consider "*all* matters bearing upon their solution with a view to reaching a common understanding with respect to principles and policies in the Far East."[68]

In view of American popular hostility and the United States Government's active opposition to Japan's advance in China, Manchuria, and Siberia, not to mention the pending dispute over cable rights in the former German Island of Yap, it was an easy and perfectly logical inference that American statesmen were planning a concerted attack not only on the naval but also on the political expansion of Japan. At any rate, the President's proposal immediately aroused the apprehension of Japanese leaders who desired to secure a proportional reduction of armaments, but had no desire to have any international assemblage sit in judgment on Japan's political program in Asia. Accordingly they delayed acceptance, and attempted to maneuver the United States into excluding from the agenda all "accomplished facts" (as, for example, Japan's occupation of various Chinese and Russian territories), as well as all questions still pending between particular governments (as, for example, Japan and China).[69]

These maneuvers, designed to tie American hands, made little headway in Washington. Mr. Hughes declined courteously but firmly to settle the agenda until the Japanese Government should have formally pledged its participation in the conference. That Government, therefore, faced the embarrassing alternative of capitulating to the United States or of assuming responsibility for wrecking the whole project. Although the Tokio Cabinet contrived a formula calculated to save its face, and though

[67] *ibid.*, p. 19.
[68] *ibid.*, p. 24. (Our italics.)
[69] *ibid.*, pp. 45, 63.

Hughes made Japan's retreat as easy as possible, this episode, like the simultaneous negotiations with Great Britain, certainly did not augur any too well for the conference with which the domestic political fortunes of the Harding Administration were now thoroughly involved.[70]

These two diplomatic skirmishes, however, left the United States in indisputable control of the preparations for the conference. And while they were costly victories, it is clear in retrospect that any other strategy would have placed the Administration in the vulnerable position of assuming responsibility without power. Now, having successfully asserted full direction of the preliminaries, it remained for the President and his counsellors to determine the size and scope of the conference, to formulate a program in accord with American policy and opinion, to calculate the limits beyond which the other Powers would probably not compromise their respective policies, and above all to conjure into being a diplomatic atmosphere of mutual confidence and good-will absolutely essential to the achievement demanded by public opinion and by the exigencies of American internal politics.

The first task was to settle the composition of the conference within limits compatible with the practical achievement desired. To this end, the naval limitation project was restricted to the five principal naval Powers: The United States, Great Britain, Japan, France, and Italy. For the discussion of Far Eastern questions, it was decided also to include China, the Netherlands, Portugal, and Belgium, all with territorial or substantial economic interests involved. Soviet Russia was excluded despite its Government's repeated protests and manifest concern with any political settlement in eastern Asia.[71]

Another problem was that of personnel. Secretary Hughes early took the position that it would facilitate matters at the conference if only civilian statesmen were appointed to the official delegation of each state, with professional army and navy experts serving only as technical advisers to their respective delegations.[72] All of the principal Powers except Japan followed this suggestion, much to the dissatisfaction of the armed Ser-

[70] *ibid.*, pp. 31, 39, 44, 45.

[71] *ibid.*, pp. 41, 69, 86.

[72] *ibid.*, p. 61.

vices.[73] And it must be admitted that Japan's chief delegate, Admiral Baron Tomosaburo Kato, Minister of the Navy, attempted from the outset to disassociate himself from the narrow professionalism which characterized the outlook of the Japanese naval bureaucracy.[74]

The United States delegation was notable for both its inclusions and its omissions. Senator Borah, who was more responsible perhaps than any other American statesman for forcing naval limitation into the sphere of practical politics, was conspicuously omitted.[75] This was doubtless a justifiable omission, however, in view of the Administration's desire to have a small delegation so composed as to insure unity and team work.[76] The selection of Elihu Root, distinguished lawyer and citizen, as well as former Secretary of War, Secretary of State, and Senator, gave the United States delegation not only an experienced diplomatist but also at least one member with a generally sympathetic attitude toward Japan. If the inclusion of Henry Cabot Lodge, chairman of the Senate Committee on Foreign Relations, and of Oscar W. Underwood, ranking minority member of that Committee, gave the delegation a decidedly conservative cast, it had the compensating effect of practically insuring senatorial assent to whatever treaties issued from the conference.[77] From beginning to end, the guiding hand was that of Secretary Hughes, who proved fully as skilful and astute a negotiator as Baron Kato of Japan, or as Arthur Balfour, chief of the British delegation, former First Lord of the Admiralty, and a statesman and diplomatist of great ability and long experience.

A third problem was that of scope and emphasis. With unerring political instinct, Hughes focused the conference preparations on naval limitation. This strategy, which subordinated

[73] See, for example, Steed, *Through Thirty Years*, Vol. 2, p. 374; Lord Riddell's *Intimate Diary of the Peace Conference and After* (1933), p. 344.

[74] See, for example, *For. Rels. 1921*, Vol. 1, pp. 179-80.

[75] Professor C. O. Johnson quotes Borah as replying, in answer to an inquiry if the President had asked him to serve on the American delegation: "Not loud enough for me to hear it, although I wasn't expecting to hear anything of that kind and I might have overlooked it. I rather suspect he will not repeat it, however, if he has." *Borah of Idaho* (1936), p. 270.

[76] Chief Justice Hughes to the authors, Aug. 5, 1940.

[77] P. H. Jessup, *Elihu Root* (1938), Vol. 2, pp. 447, 450.

without ignoring the political crisis in the Far East, placed the Administration at the head of the popular disarmament movement which was still gaining strength both at home and abroad. It gave the United States, with its great fleet of super-dreadnoughts nearing completion, a stronger bargaining position than could have been achieved under any other strategy that Hughes could have devised. And it unquestionably helped to relieve Japanese anxiety, and hence to overcome Japanese intransigence which threatened for a time to wreck the whole enterprise.

In accord with this statesmanlike strategy, the formal invitations, issued August 11, dwelt on the political and economic consequences of continued armament competition—"an economic burden too heavy to be borne"; an "encumbrance upon enterprise and national prosperity"; "a constant menace to the peace of the world rather than an assurance of its preservation." It was recognized that there was little ground "to expect the halting of these increasing outlays" on armaments "unless the Powers most largely concerned find a satisfactory basis for an agreement to effect their limitation." The time was now believed "opportune" for these Powers "to approach this subject directly and in conference. . . ." The success of such an effort would depend not only on a "desire for peace" but also on "this desire" finding "expression in a practical effort to remove causes of misunderstanding and to seek ground for agreement as to principles and their application." Thus, with the object (inferred if not expressly stated) of facilitating the reduction and future limitation of armaments, the United States had proposed and still desired to "find a solution of Pacific and Far Eastern problems. . . ." But it was "not the purpose of this Government to attempt" arbitrarily "to define the scope of the discussion in relation to the Pacific and Far East. . . ." On the contrary, it was proposed "to leave this to be the subject of suggestions to be exchanged before . . . the Conference, in the expectation that the spirit of friendship and a cordial appreciation of the importance of the elimination of sources of controversy, will govern the final decision."[78]

These preliminaries showed the determination of the Administration to keep the Conference centered on the armament

[78] *For. Rels. 1921*, Vol. 1, pp. 56-7.

problem, but afforded no indication whatever as to the specific procedure which the American delegation might follow in dealing with that problem.

The conventional procedure would be to open the Conference with the usual diplomatic amenities, and then refer the agenda to committees for study. This was the procedure for which the other participating Powers would come prepared. It was also the course most strongly favored in certain official circles in Washington.

Such a course had serious disadvantages, however. Past experience indicated that each delegation would tend to put forward its maximum demands, with a view to driving as hard a bargain as possible. All this would emphasize the clashing interests and policies of the Powers, rather than the universal popular desire for relief from the armament burden. It would stimulate endless bargaining which would almost certainly prevent any large reduction of armaments. And there would be constant danger of the Conference becoming mired in a morass of conflicting claims and technicalities that might break it up without any agreement at all.

As an alternative, the American delegation might lay their cards on the table at the outset, stating publicly the maximum concessions which the United States was prepared to make, and inviting equally frank response from the other Powers in their turn. But this had its dangers. There was no assurance whatever that the others would reciprocate in kind. It was just as likely that they would counter with maximum demands, and then attempt to wring still greater concessions from the United States.

The third possibility was to confront the Conference at its opening session with a concrete proposal for reducing and limiting the armaments not only of the United States but of the other participating countries as well. Such a course had manifest tactical advantages. It would keep the initiative from slipping out of American hands. It would exploit to the fullest the popular demand for arms limitation, a demand which was still gaining weight and momentum. It would enable the Administration to escape blame for possible failure. Refusal of the foreign delegations to go along with the United States would tend to place Congress and country squarely behind whatever naval plans the Administration might thereafter recommend.[79]

This third course was the more attractive because of the extraordinary bargaining power of the United States at this particular juncture. This advantage arose mainly from the possession of sixteen "post-Jutland" capital ships, built and building. These ships, authorized in the summer of 1916, embodied the so-called lessons of the Battle of Jutland, the only major fleet action during the late war.[80] The first four were battleships of 32,600 tons, eight 16-inch guns, and a speed of twenty-one knots. The next six were battleships of 43,200 tons, twelve 16-inch guns, and twenty-three knots. And the last six were 43,500-ton battle cruisers, with eight 16-inch guns and a designed speed exceeding thirty-three knots. Though only one in the first group, the *Maryland*, and none in the second and third groups, was ready for service in the summer of 1921, the remaining fifteen were all scheduled for completion by 1924.

Completion of these ships on schedule would give the United States by far the strongest battle line in the world for a considerable number of years at least. Great Britain had only one post-Jutland ship in commission, none under construction, and only four authorized.[81] Japan had one post-Jutland ship in service, another nearly ready, and four under construction. And while the Japanese Admiralty had authority to build ten additional capital ships over a period of seven years, there were grounds for doubt as to Japan's ability to execute so huge a program on schedule.[82]

[79] On October 20, Colonel Theodore Roosevelt, Assistant Secretary of the Navy, who played a leading part in the conference preparations, recorded in his diary: ". . . the original American propositions must be sufficiently drastic in their nature to prove the honesty of our intentions to the country and to place us therefore in a position where, if any refusal came on the part of any European Powers, Congress and the Senate would be behind the Administration's plans."

[80] The Battle of Jutland occurred May 31, 1916, while the naval expansion bill was before Congress. For the repercussions on that legislation, see our *Rise of American Naval Power* (1939), pp. 333*ff*.

[81] Technically the battle cruiser *Hood*, completed in 1920, was only partially a post-Jutland ship in its basic design, and it mounted 15-inch instead of 16-inch guns as in the new American ships. The four authorized ships, still in the blueprint stage, were to be battle cruisers somewhat larger and more powerful than the *Hood*.

[82] The post-Jutland ship in service was the *Nagato*; the ship nearly finished, the *Mutsu*. Both were battleships similar in displacement and battery to the *Maryland*

With the United States thus setting the pace of naval construction, and with the Navy Department annually pressing Congress for authority to replace older but still serviceable ships, any proposal put forward by the American delegation at the forthcoming conference was bound to receive serious consideration.

It was important, however, for the Administration to avoid overplaying its hand. American naval development was rapidly losing its abnormal war-induced momentum. Congress had rejected three successive building programs recommended by the Navy Department. No new combatant ships had been authorized since the armistice of November 1918. To an extent nowhere fully appreciated abroad, the ships under construction, especially the capital ships just described, were gradually becoming frozen assets. In January 1921, only one of the ten battleships authorized back in 1916 was approaching completion; only three were as much as 50 per cent along; six were less than 20 per cent. The battle cruisers were still less advanced, ranging from 1 to 11 per cent of completion.[83]

Each session of Congress, moreover, revealed a growing movement to further curtail this lagging program of construction.[84] It was becoming more and more difficult to secure the funds necessary to proceed even with those ships that were well along toward completion. Appropriations for new construction had dwindled from $133,000,000 in 1919, to $104,000,000 in 1920. In the summer of 1921 it taxed the leadership and political resources of Administration leaders to pass an appropriation of $90,000,000 for this purpose.

A canvass of Senators and Representatives indicated a still more discouraging outlook for the session that would open in December 1921. There was even talk of scrapping many of the

class; but they differed from the American ships in having greater speed and considerably less armor protection. Two of the four ships under construction were battleships of 40,000 tons, ten 16-inch guns, and twenty-five knots speed. The remaining two were battle cruisers of 44,000 tons, ten 16-inch guns, and thirty-five knots speed.

[83] 66 Cong. 3 Sess. House Appropriations Committee, *Hearings on Naval Appropriation Bill for 1922*, p. 543.

[84] See, for example, 66 Cong. 2 Sess. House Naval Committee, *Hearings on Estimates for 1920*, p. 857; 66 Cong. 3 Sess. House Appropriations Committee, *Hearings on Naval Appropriation Bill for 1922*, pp. 546, 550; 66 Cong. 3 Sess. S. Res. 433 and H. Res. 653; 66 Cong. 2 Sess. *Cong. Rec.*, Vol. 59, pp. 4651-2, 4699, 4759*ff*.; 66 Cong. 3 Sess. *Cong. Rec.*, Vol. 60, pp. 2952, 3003, 3148*ff*.

unfinished ships without waiting for an arms conference. Congressional leaders—including Henry Cabot Lodge, big-navy leader in the Senate—frankly recognized this situation. And the American delegation at one of their preliminary meetings secretly admitted the practical impossibility of completing the building program on schedule, if indeed it could be completed at all under conditions then prevailing in Congress and in the country at large.[85]

Another arresting consideration was the weakness of the American position for bargaining with respect to land armaments. That subject was expressly included in the agenda which the United States Government circulated in September 1921. But the American delegation had nothing to offer in the way of military concessions. It could be foreseen that any proposal for limiting land armaments would lead the conference straight into the morass of European international politics. France was the dominant Continental Power, and with France it was either military hegemony, or military guarantees from England and America.

The French Government would almost certainly counter any American proposal for the reduction of its land forces, by demanding a security pledge utterly abhorrent to the United States Senate. Such a demand would reopen the League of Nations controversy, embarrass the Republican Administration, give fresh impetus to American isolationism, and seriously jeopardize the outlook for naval limitation which was the primary concern of the American people at this particular juncture.

The problem of naval limitation alone presented sufficient difficulty, as was immediately discovered when the Navy Department commenced preliminary studies in preparation for the Conference. The Department's point of departure was the concept of national needs. And this led to a recommendation that "if the Anglo-Japanese Alliance is to be continued, the minimum strength that the United States can safely accept for its Navy is equality with that of the two nations combined. This means a two-Power standard and a Navy the greatest in the world."[86]

[85] Information furnished by Colonel Theodore Roosevelt; to the same effect, Jessup, *Elihu Root*, Vol. 2, p. 449; and Diary of Chandler P. Anderson, Nov. 26, 1921.

[86] 67 Cong. 2 Sess., *Cong. Rec.*, Vol. 62, p. 4682.

While there were grounds for hoping that the Anglo-Japanese Alliance could be liquidated at the forthcoming conference, the American proposal could scarcely assume this liquidation as a fact. At the same time, any proposal designed to give the United States a navy equal to those of England and Japan combined, would certainly foredoom the Conference to complete and ignominous failure. After extensive study and much discussion, it was decided that only one procedure offered any prospect of success. That was to reduce and limit armaments on the basis of existing strength.[87]

Existing strength, however, was susceptible of various interpretations. Should a navy's existing strength be measured in capital ships alone? Or capital ships in combination with some or all of the auxiliary combatant craft—cruisers, destroyers, submarines, and aircraft carriers? Did existing strength comprise only ships ready for service? Did it embrace some or all of those under construction? And should account be taken of ships authorized or projected but not yet laid down?

In dealing with these technical questions, Secretary Hughes and his fellow delegates relied consistently on their professional naval advisers. These latter started with the assumption that capital ships were the true index of a navy's power. They then took the eminently reasonable position (which the Japanese delegation later contested), that some weight should be given to ships under construction. Starting with these two general principles and using various technical criteria—such as number, advancement, and cost of ships building; number and age of ships in service; gun power, armor protection, speed, etc.—American naval authorities reached the conclusion that the existing relative strength of the British, American, and Japanese navies was in approximately the ratio of 5:5:3. It then remained to decide at what tonnage levels to stabilize for the future these three leading navies.[88]

[87] In the debate on ratification, Senator Lodge stated that "it was very clear to the American delegation, and they stood firmly on that point, that the only basis for starting the limitation of navies must be the naval armament which actually existed. . . . The moment we left that ground and got into the very cloudy region of each country's deciding what its peace and safety demanded, there would be no standard, and we could get nowhere." *Cong. Rec.*, Vol. 62, p. 4678; and to the same effect, Jessup, *Elihu Root*, Vol. 2, p. 450.

[88] The Navy Department had been working on the general problem since midsummer. On July 27, the Assistant Secretary of the Navy, Colonel Theodore

The first concrete proposal came from the General Board. This contemplated fixing capital-ship quotas at approximately 1,000,000 tons for Great Britain; 1,000,000 tons for the United States, and 600,000 tons for Japan. The figure for the United States, 983,000 tons to be exact, would be reached by completing all of the fifteen super-dreadnoughts and battle cruisers still under construction, and scrapping only the older capital ships with smaller than 14-inch guns in their main batteries.[89]

For political as well as fiscal reasons, this plan did not meet the requirements of the Administration. To answer these objections, the General Board suggested scrapping four or five new ships, thereby reducing the total to 820,000 tons.[90] This too was rejected, and a smaller group, consisting of Colonel Theodore Roosevelt (Assistant Secretary of the Navy), Admiral Robert E. Coontz, and Captain (soon to become Rear Admiral) William V. Pratt, prepared a third plan which contemplated scrapping eight and completing seven of the new ships.[91] Conference plans went forward on this basis until October 24, when Mr. Hughes, with the support of his fellow delegates, decided to explore the possibilities of making still larger reductions.[92]

In order to "create a proper impression," it was felt, the Administration "must come forward with a plan which indicates to the country at large the sincerity of our intentions. . . ." Objections from the "other Powers should be along the line that they could not stand the coincident reduction rather than that we are unwilling to go further. . . . Only in this way . . . could we keep our people in sympathy with our undertaking."[93]

A scheme for scrapping all capital ships less than 60 per cent completed, and retaining the older 12-inch gun dreadnoughts, worked out to approximately 600,000 tons, but was deemed still too high.[94] And on October 31 it was definitely decided at an-

Roosevelt, had directed the General Board to make a "preliminary investigation" of the question of naval limitation and to report thereon not later than September 20. This had been followed on September 1 by a letter from the Secretary of State requesting information bearing on the naval armaments of the other Powers. Pursuant to these instructions, the General Board had prepared a number of reports, and was preparing still others. 71 Cong. 2 Sess. Senate Naval Committee, *Hearings on the London Naval Treaty of 1930*, pp. 432, 465; and information from Admiral W. V. Pratt.

[89] *Hearings, 1930*, pp. 437, 465.
[90] *loc. cit.*
[91] *loc. cit.*; and Colonel Roosevelt's diary, Oct. 24, 1921.
[92] Diary, Oct. 21, 24.
[93] *ibid.*, Oct. 24.
[94] *Hearings, 1930*, pp. 471-2.

other meeting of the American delegation to frame the conference proposal on the principle of "stop-building-now," with all the naval Powers scrapping all ships under construction.[95]

The work was now pushed along rapidly. The newspapers reported almost daily meetings of the American delegation.[96] What took place at these meetings was a closely guarded secret. Senator Lodge afterwards claimed that the American conference proposal was framed therein.[97] But we now know that the pre-conference meetings of the American delegation were confined in the main to generalities.[98] Mr. Hughes consulted with his fellow delegates as well as with President Harding on every vital point. These men were fully informed and in complete accord as to the underlying principles to be observed. But they had very little to do with the actual framing of the American conference proposal. That was largely the work of just four men—Secretary of State Hughes, Assistant Secretary of the Navy Theodore Roosevelt, Admiral Coontz, and Captain Pratt.[99]

On November 4 the proposal was taking shape. The technical details were finished five days later. The following day, Hughes and Roosevelt went over the former's opening speech and the final draft of the American proposal. Later the same day, that draft with Hughes's last-minute changes was taken to the Navy Department and mimeographed in the offices of the General Board under the immediate supervision of Captain Pratt. The mimeographed copies were delivered to Colonel Roosevelt who personally took them, together with the stencils from which they were made, to Mr. Hughes's office in the State Department where they were securely locked up until the opening session two days later.[100]

With no real news available, the press fed on rumors. The impression spread that something out of the ordinary was impending. Washington buzzed with speculation and gossip. But the visiting delegations which began to arrive early in November

[95] Colonel Roosevelt's diary.

[96] Senator Lodge afterward stated that the American delegation met twelve times prior to the opening day. *Cong. Rec.*, Vol. 62, p. 4677.

[97] *loc. cit.*

[98] For one account of these meetings, based on the recollections and papers of Elihu Root, see Jessup, *op. cit.*, Vol. 2, pp. 448*ff*.

[99] Colonel Roosevelt's diary.

[100] *ibid.*; and information from Admiral Pratt.

could learn practically nothing. On November 11, Mr. Hughes conferred for two hours with Mr. Balfour. He said he intended to make an important "statement of policy" at the opening session, but divulged no details, and gave no "indication of the real importance of his statement."[101] When the curtain rose on the opening session at 10:30 o'clock on the morning of November 12, only four men knew the full details of the American proposal, and not more than half a dozen others had any forewarning whatsoever of the staggering surprises that were unfolded with bewildering speed in the great hall of the Daughters of the American Revolution.[102]

[101] For one account of this conversation, see Lord Riddell's *Intimate Diary*, p. 337.

[102] Colonel Roosevelt's diary; and *New York Times*, Nov. 15, 1921, p. 3. On November 13, Colonel Roosevelt recorded in his diary: "An amusing incident happened yesterday. Just before the opening of the conference, Lord Lee (First Lord of the British Admiralty) said he understood I had been working on the naval plan, and asked if he and I couldn't get together at four in the afternoon in order to discuss the basis of the plan and see if we couldn't arrive at some understanding between our countries. Knowing that the plan would be public property within half an hour, I agreed. When the conference [session] was over, he turned to me and said that he would have to think now and not talk for a number of days."

CHAPTER NINE

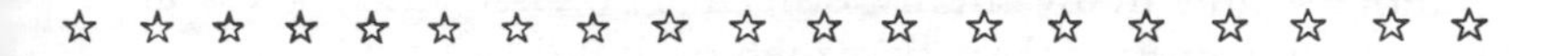

The Washington Conference: The Great Beginning

THE day was Saturday, November 12, 1921. The hour was approaching 10:30 o'clock in the morning. The place was the City of Washington. The occasion was the formal opening of the Conference on Limitation of Armament, called to halt the incipient struggle for naval primacy in the Atlantic, to check the ominous drift toward armed conflict in the Pacific, and to fashion, if possible, a stable balance of power upon the sea.

For two hours on this "chilly November morning" eager throngs had crowded the avenues and parkways leading to Continental Hall on Seventeenth Street about midway between the White House and the Washington Monument. Even a "sharp wintry wind" had failed to discourage the thousands who lined the curbs to catch momentary glimpses of the distinguished statesmen cast for leading rôles in the great impending drama.

Inside the white-walled auditorium nearly a thousand invited guests and newspaper correspondents were taking their places. The rear section of the balcony (which extended around three sides of the room) was filling with Senators. In one side section sat the members of the House of Representatives; across from them, the Cabinet and Diplomatic Corps. On the main floor beneath the balcony, the two sides of the room were filled with newspaper men, and in the rear were the assistants, experts, and secretaries of the various delegations.

A glance over the press sections immediately confirmed the importance of the occasion. Here were several hundred journalists, including some of the world's foremost editors and correspondents. One discovered Wickham Steed, editor of *The Times* of London; Stephanne Lauzanne, editor of *Le Matin* of Paris, Edwin James of the *New York Times*, Mark Sullivan, Frank Simonds, and many, many others. The Associated Press alone had fully twenty of their best men on hand.[1]

On all sides one beheld men and women of official and social importance. In a box at the front sat Mrs. Harding, wife of the President, with Vice-President Coolidge at her side. Nearby was Mrs. Longworth, daughter of Theodore Roosevelt who had played so large a rôle in the rise of American naval power. To H. G. Wells, the noted British writer, it all seemed "extraordinarily like a very smart first night in a prominent London theater." Indeed, Wells found it "difficult to believe that this gathering could be the beginning of anything of supreme historical importance."[2]

Others, however, noted an undercurrent of excitement and anticipation. For days official and social Washington had seethed with rumors and speculations. One of the visiting journalists had found the prevailing mood "one of intense nervousness, even anxiety."[3] It was noted on this morning that Mrs. Harding sat "erect and watchful"; and that the "austere" Vice-President's "cold blue eyes" never left the "forum." In the section reserved for the Supreme Court, Mr. Justice Brandeis was observed to be taut with "tense watchfulness." To one of those present, William Jennings Bryan seemed the very embodiment of the prevailing mood. "Entering in his silk hat and old-fashioned cape," the former Secretary of State and anti-war crusader reminded him of an "Old Testament prophet, not quite sure, yet, whether to shed benevolence on the occasion or to thunder anathema if things should go wrong."[4]

Meanwhile, the leading characters were arriving and exchanging greetings in the anteroom. The first to appear in the auditorium was Senator Henry Cabot Lodge who "strolled" in about 10:25, with the "listless manner of having done this sort of thing very often, quite in the course of the day's work." Others soon followed, and busied themselves finding their places

[1] Mark Sullivan, *The Great Adventure at Washington* (1922), p. ix.
[2] *Washington and the Riddle of Peace* (1922), p. 69.
[3] J. G. Hamilton, in *New York Times*, Nov. 12, 1921, p. 7.
[4] Sullivan, *op. cit.*, pp. 3-4.

The Washington Conference in Plenary Session

around a rectangular arrangement of green cloth-covered tables in the center of the main floor.[5]

At the head of the rectangle sat Mr. Hughes, Secretary of State, and chief of the American delegation. On Hughes's right, Senator Lodge, Mr. Root, and Senator Underwood.[6] The British delegation, seven strong, occupied chairs to the left of Hughes, at the head of the rectangle and part way down one side. Its chief, in the absence of Prime Minister Lloyd George, nominal head of the British delegation, was Mr. Arthur Balfour. The French delegates, headed by Premier Aristide Briand, sat on the right side around the corner from the Americans. Beyond the French came the three Japanese delegates, under the nominal leadership of Prince Tokugawa, but under the actual direction of Admiral Baron Tomosaburo Kato, impassive, immensely competent Minister of the Navy. Across from them sat the Italians, with the representatives of the smaller states ranged along the foot of the rectangle.

Prolonged applause greeted the entry of President Harding who took a seat next to Mr. Hughes. The latter, as temporary chairman, rapped for order. Prayer was offered. The chair announced: "The President of the United States." And Harding arose to deliver his address of welcome.

The President offered no plan or prescription. Rather, continuing a theme which he had eloquently developed at Arlington Cemetery the preceding day in the solemn burial service for America's "Unknown Soldier," he pleaded for a concerted effort to build a new world order upon the ruins of the old. A cynical minority might belittle this plea, and sniff at the "religious" atmosphere.[7] But it would have been difficult to contrive a more effective prelude to the astounding thing that was soon to follow.

After a stirring demonstration in which the galleries (contrary to all diplomatic precedents) enthusiastically joined, the President departed. Mr. Hughes proposed that French and English be the official languages of the Conference. Mr. Balfour

[5] *ibid.*, pp. 5-6.

[6] For descriptive comments on the American delegates, see p. 139, *supra*.

[7] J. G. Hamilton, *New York Times*, Nov. 13, 1921, p. 4: Lord Riddell, the British journalist, thought Harding's speech "rather poor stuff." *Intimate Diary of the Peace Conference and After* (1933), p. 335.

in a graceful little speech announced the unanimous wish of all the delegations that Hughes become the permanent chairman.[8] And as the latter arose to accept the honor, "it was manifest from the casual attitude of the delegates from the important Powers . . . that they had expected merely a cordial word of welcome, with possibly a general outline of the purposes of the Conference."[9]

This impression was not immediately dispelled. After a perceptible pause in which he silently studied the audience before him, Hughes began to speak in a voice variously described as cold, hard, and even harsh. He delivered the anticipated words of welcome and reviewed briefly the background and purposes of the Conference. "The world looks to this Conference," he declared, "to relieve humanity of the crushing burden created by competition in armament, and it is the view of the American Government that we should meet that expectation without any unnecessary delay."[10] This drew applause, and many thought he had finished. But such was not the case.

Contrary to all expectation, Hughes now launched into an extended résumé of the Hague Conferences of 1899 and 1907, called ostensibly to check the ruinous pre-war struggle for armed security on land and sea. He described the failure of those efforts, and read the pious and utterly futile resolution in which the second Hague Conference had recommended further study of the armament problem. These "futile suggestions," he carefully noted, had had no practical effect. The arms race had continued "until it fittingly culminated in the greatest war in history; and we are now suffering from the unparalleled loss of life, the destruction of hopes, the economic dislocations, and the widespread impoverishment which measure the cost of victory over the brutal pretensions of military force."[11]

[8] "Balfour himself was very impressive, with his great height, his ungainly build, and the very fine head with the rather long, white hair." Unpublished diary of Colonel Theodore Roosevelt, Assistant Secretary of the Navy, entry of Nov. 12, 1921.

[9] Louis Siebold, *New York Herald*, Nov. 13, 1921, p. 5.

[10] *Conference on Limitation of Armament*, p. 52. This document, with parallel texts in English and French, contains, among other things, the record of the plenary sessions. For a guide to other sources on the Washington Conference, see Appendix A.

[11] *Conference*, p. 56.

By this time the audience was completely off guard. This was "old stuff" to the newspaper men who had settled back in their chairs or were carrying on whispered conversations with their neighbors. And the "same sense of relaxation" was observed in the galleries where people were "looking about the room, recognizing acquaintances, and nodding to them."[12]

But all this was suddenly cut short as the speaker whose voice now took on an imperious tone, abruptly declared: "If we are to be spared the uprisings of peoples made desperate in the desire to shake off burdens no longer endurable, competition in armament must stop." The applause which greeted this had scarcely died down before it burst forth again as the speaker cried: "The time has come, and this Conference has been called, not for general resolutions or mutual advice, but for action." Then in a moment: "Competition will not be remedied by resolves with respect to the method of its continuance. . . . There is only one adequate way out and that is to end it now.

"It is apparent," Hughes continued, "that this cannot be accomplished without serious sacrifices. Enormous sums have been expended upon ships under construction, and building programs which are now under way can not be given up without heavy loss. Yet, if the present construction of capital ships goes forward, other ships will inevitably be built to rival them and this will lead to still others. Thus the race will continue so long as ability to continue lasts. The effort to escape sacrifices is futile. We must face them or yield our purpose.

"It is also clear that no one of the naval Powers should be expected to make these sacrifices alone. The only hope of limitation of armament is by agreement . . . fair and reasonable in the extent of the sacrifices required of each of the Powers. In considering the basis of such an agreement and the commensurate sacrifices to be required, it is necessary to have regard to the existing naval strength of the great naval Powers, including the extent of construction already effected in the case of ships in process. . . .

"It would also seem to be a vital part of a plan for the limitation of naval armament that there should be a naval holiday." Even then, few in that increasingly bewildered audience were

[12] Sullivan, *Great Adventure*, pp. 19, 20.

prepared for the specific proposal, "that for a period of not less than ten years there should be no further construction of capital ships." And their surprise turned to amazement when he continued: "I am happy to say that I am at liberty to go beyond these general propositions, and, on behalf of the American delegation acting under the instructions of the President of the United States, to submit to you a concrete proposition for an agreement for the limitation of naval armament."[13]

This proposal, he explained, dealt only with the United States, Great Britain, and Japan. It did not seem necessary at this point to consider the special positions of the French and Italian Navies whose "existing strength" was a result of "extraordinary conditions" arising from the late war. Reserving this matter for later consideration, he laid down four general principles on which the American proposal was founded: "(1) That all capital ship building programs, either actual or projected, should be abandoned; (2) That further reduction should be made through the scrapping of certain of the older ships; (3) That, in general, regard should be had to the existing naval strength of the Powers concerned; (4) That the capital-ship tonnage should be used as the measurement of strength for navies and a proportionate allowance of auxiliary combatant craft prescribed."

Specifically, it was proposed that the United States should scrap its fifteen capital ships—nine battleships and six battle cruisers—still in course of construction, although some of these ships were now more than 80 per cent completed, and two were already launched. In addition, the United States was to scrap all fifteen of its pre-dreadnought battleships, up to but not including the *Delaware*.[14] The United States, in short, was prepared to destroy thirty capital ships, built and building, with a total displacement of 845,740 tons.[15]

Hughes paused at this point. One observer noted that "everybody thought the speech was over. Hughes had stated what

[13] *Conference*, pp. 56, 58, 60; and see Sullivan, *op. cit.*, pp. 20-2.

[14] The *Delaware* was the first American battleship to carry as many as ten big guns. For a description and illustration of this ship, completed in 1910, see our *Rise of American Naval Power* (1939), pp. 263-4, or (1942), pp. 263-4.

[15] *Conference*, pp. 60, 62. It should be noted, however, that most of the older ships to be scrapped had ceased to have any fighting value in the battle line, and would sooner or later have been scrapped in any event.

America proposed to do. That he should have done this at all on the opening day was a thrilling fact; the sweeping character of what he proposed added thrill to thrill. It was more than any person in the audience had expected. . . ."

The applause, at that point impressed this observer as "in the nature of an immense and burning ceremonial for the close of a day that had made unprecedented history. That the day was over was taken for granted. That there might be more yet was beyond the dreams of anybody in the room except nine men. . . ."[16]

But more there was. "The plan contemplates," Hughes resumed, "that Great Britain and Japan shall take action which is fairly commensurate with the action on the part of the United States." Specifically, he proposed that the British Government abandon its four new capital ships (the so-called super-*Hoods*), authorized but not yet laid down; and that it scrap nineteen older capital ships, a total altogether of 583,375 tons.[17]

This produced a sensation. Admiral Beatty, First Sea Lord of the British Admiralty, was seen to come forward in his chair, a "slightly staggered and deeply disturbed expression" on his countenance, reminding one of a "bulldog, sleeping on a sunny doorstep, who has been poked in the stomach by the impudent foot of an itinerant soap-canvasser seriously lacking in any sense of the most ordinary proprieties. . . ."[18] Admiral Chatfield, one of Beatty's colleagues, "turned red and then white, and sat immovable." Lord Lee of Fareham, civilian head of the Admiralty, betrayed intense excitement, "half rose and whispered to Balfour" who alone maintained a calm and placid exterior, as he "made notes on an envelope, according to his custom."[19] Others noted the "deep silence" that prevailed while Hughes sank more British battleships "than all the admirals of the world had destroyed in a cycle of centuries."[20] Still another saw the "naval experts of the various nations leaning forward and drinking in every word with avid attention."[21]

[16] Sullivan, *Great Adventure*, pp. 23-4.

[17] *Conference*, p. 62.

[18] Sullivan, *op. cit.*, pp. 26-7.

[19] Colonel Roosevelt's diary, Nov. 12; Lord Riddell's *Intimate Diary*, p. 335.

[20] Colonel A. à C. Repington, *After the War* (1922), p. 433; H. W. Nevinson, *Manchester Guardian Weekly*, Nov. 18, 1921, p. 384.

[21] J. G. Hamilton, *New York Times*, Nov. 13, 1921, p. 4.

Giving his listeners no time to recover from this shock, Hughes passed on to Japan. That Power, it was proposed, should "abandon her program of [eight capital] ships not yet laid down"; and scrap seven ships under construction, as well as ten "pre-dreadnoughts and battleships of the second line," altogether a total of 448,928 tons.[22]

Although warned by what had gone before, "there was no discounting the surprise of Prince Tokugawa, Baron Kato, and Ambassador Shidehara, the delegates from Japan."[23] One observer remarked that these Japanese statesmen "stirred in their seats and drooped close to the table."[24] Another noted that they sat with "immovable faces"[25] "looking straight ahead." As for their naval experts—it was remembered that they had been "all one broad happy smile when Hughes announced what America proposed to scrap"; but this was something else.[26]

Meanwhile, the speaker was developing additional phases of the American plan. The proposed reductions would leave the United States with eighteen capital ships (500,650 tons), Great Britain with twenty-two (604,450 tons), and Japan with ten (299,700 tons). Because of differences in age and in technical details, the larger tonnage allotted to Great Britain was deemed substantially equivalent to that of the United States. No capital ship replacements were to be laid down until after ten years. No ship built in replacement was to displace more than 35,000 tons. Subject to the ten-year restriction, capital ships might be replaced when they became twenty years old. And replacements were to remain within an "agreed maximum of capital ship tonnage" of 500,000 for the United States and Great Britain, and 300,000 tons for Japan. Further details as well as provisions relating to auxiliary surface craft, submarines, and aircraft carriers were to be found in the "formal proposition" which was "ready for submission to the delegates."[27]

"With the acceptance of this plan," Hughes concluded, "the burden of meeting the demands of competition in naval armament will be lifted. Enormous sums will be released to aid the progress of civilization. At the same time the proper demands of national defense will be adequately met and the nations will

[22] *Conference*, pp. 62, 64.
[23] Louis Siebold, *New York Herald*, Nov. 13, p. 5.
[24] Sullivan, *Great Adventure*, p. 29.
[25] Colonel Roosevelt's diary, Nov. 12.
[26] Repington, *After the War*, p. 433.
[27] *Conference*, p. 64.

have ample opportunity during the naval holiday of ten years to consider their future course. Preparation for offensive naval war will stop now."[28]

These final words evoked a "tornado of cheering" from the galleries, especially from those sections occupied by the Senate and House of Representatives.[29] From this point on, the scene reminded one veteran reporter of an "American political convention."[30] Diplomatic precedents and proprieties were thrown to the winds. Someone in the congressional galleries shouted for Briand, and Hughes, catching the spirit of the moment, "made a smiling gesture" to the distinguished Frenchman who responded with a few graceful remarks. Further calls from the galleries brought similar responses from the other delegations, each received with prolonged and enthusiastic applause. No such demonstration had ever swept a grave international assembly before. "To all Europeans present, probably also to the Asiatics," commented one foreign journalist, "all this must have seemed irregular and undisciplined, even childish. Americans and those who knew America realized its significance. . . . American democracy had stormed the hall and taken a grip upon the Conference."[31]

A few minutes later, Hughes had adjourned the Conference until the following Tuesday, giving the startled delegations three days in which to recover their equilibrium, to study and digest the American plan, and also to feel the world-wide popular repercussions from this extraordinary beginning.

The Popular Verdict

Not only in technique but also in timing was the opening session of the Conference a masterpiece of political strategy calculated to mobilize public opinion behind the American proposal to reduce and limit naval armaments. From Saturday noon until the following Tuesday, the all-absorbing topic of popular discussion was the Conference at Washington. More words were cabled to Europe that Saturday, it was estimated, than on any previous day in history. The single wire across the Pacific to Japan proved utterly inadequate to carry the unprec-

[28] *ibid.*, p. 66. [29] J. G. Hamilton, *New York Times*, Nov. 13, 1921, p. 4.
[30] Sullivan, *Great Adventure*, pp. 29-30.
[31] *ibid.*, p. 30; and J. G. Hamilton, *New York Times*, Nov. 13, p. 4.

edented load of diplomatic and press dispatches. By Sunday the popular verdict was pouring in from all parts of the United States. The following day the stream was swollen by a flood of reports from abroad. And when the Conference reconvened on Tuesday, the returns, while still far from complete, left no room for doubt that the news from Washington had aroused the hopes and captured the imagination of war-weary peoples the world over.

The response within the United States was immediate and overwhelming. A canvass of Congress revealed all but unanimous support for the Administration's program, and assurance that a treaty embodying its terms would pass the Senate with few if any dissenting votes.[32] The country's leading dailies, with very few exceptions, enthusiastically applauded the great beginning. It was hailed as a "most astounding and stupendous move"; an experiment in "practical idealism"; a "drastic but workable" plan; a "plain business statement" with "no equivocation, no shuffling, and nothing . . . concealed"; a "practical" proposition, "not visionary and footless evangelism"; a "master stroke for peace"; etc., etc.[33]

The clergy were no less outspoken. Bishop William T. Manning, from the pulpit of the Cathedral of St. John the Divine, in New York City, called the Hughes plan "one of the greatest events in history . . . the very boldness of it . . . its assurance of success." Churches of all denominations joined in the paean, the exaltation in some quarters reaching an "evangelical, almost fanatic, pitch."[34]

Spokesmen for American business and finance were likewise favorably impressed. The *Wall Street Journal* declared "Mr. Hughes's proposal merits unqualified approval."[35] The *Commercial and Financial Chronicle* enthusiastically endorsed the great beginning in a long editorial on the theme that the American program should have the support of "every sane human being . . . in the whole world."[36] Elbert H. Gary, chairman of the board of the United States Steel Corporation, voiced the

[32] *New York Times*, Nov. 13, 1921, p. 1; Nov. 14, p. 1.

[33] Selected from a country-wide survey of editorials quoted in the *New York Times*, Nov. 13, p. 9; Nov. 14, p. 5.

[34] Sullivan, *Great Adventure*, p. 41; *New York Times*, Nov. 14, p. 4; and *New York Herald*, Nov. 14, p. 3.

[35] Nov. 15, p. 1.

[36] Vol. 113, Nov. 19, 1921, pp. 2117-18.

general conviction that arms limitation would in the long run benefit business.[37] And leading bankers were even more emphatic in their endorsement of the Hughes proposal, one editor noting that the "financial community has begun to understand the vast force for international business growth which would lie in an agreement for the reduction of expenditure for navies and standing armies."[38]

The average citizen might not fully appreciate the political and military implications of what had been proposed. But it was impossible to ignore the burning desire of virtually all classes in America to take what was then almost universally regarded as a long stride forward toward greater security, prosperity, and a more enduring peace. Indeed, almost the only discordant note during this week-end of applause and thanksgiving was sounded by the Communist American Labor Alliance which ridiculed the Conference and all its works, on the ground that there could be "no true disarmament until the workers have gained possession of the armies and navies" of the world.[39]

The response abroad, if slightly less spontaneous and somewhat more critical, was nevertheless impressive. "Overwhelming surprise and a disposition to reserve immediate judgment" were described as the initial reaction in England to Secretary Hughes's breath-taking proposals.[40] The conservative *Times* of London dwelt on the "many difficulties" to be overcome, but admitted that "seldom, if ever, has such a body held its first session under auspices so happy."[41] And with certain variations, depending largely on party affiliation, this sentiment was echoed in the other metropolitan papers of Great Britain.[42]

The popular response in Japan appeared even more favorable. The Associated Press reported from Tokio that "keen satisfaction and admiration today comprised the keynote of the first Japanese newspaper comment on the Hughes proposal for a naval holiday. The same satisfaction was noted in the discussions at clubs and

[37] *New York Times*, Nov. 15, p. 5.

[38] *New York Herald*, Nov. 13, sec. 2, p. 4; and see *New York Times*, Nov. 15, p. 5.

[39] *New York Times*, Nov. 14, p. 4.

[40] Associated Press dispatch from London, Nov. 14, see *New York Herald*, Nov. 14, p. 1.

[41] Nov. 14, p. 11.

[42] See, for example, the collection of English editorials assembled by the *New York Times*, Nov. 14, pp. 1, 4.

by people of various shades of political opinion. Interspersed in these discussions were many expressions of surprise that the United States was prepared to set an example of such drastic curtailment in her naval program."[43]

The initial response in France was described as one of "almost unreserved approval." And if subsequent comment showed somewhat more restraint than in certain other countries, such caution was largely inspired, it would appear, by apprehensions as to the still undisclosed sacrifices to be asked of France.[44]

Thus, both at home and abroad, the great beginning produced a profound sensation and a popular demand for constructive achievement which challenged the political vision and capacity of the statesmen as they assembled for the second plenary session on Tuesday, November 15, to reply formally to the proposals put forward on behalf of the United States.

[43] *New York Times,* Nov. 15, p. 2. [44] *ibid.,* Nov. 14, pp. 1, 2; Nov. 15, p. 2.

CHAPTER TEN

The Limitation of Battle Fleets

ACCEPTANCE "IN PRINCIPLE"

TODAY . . . a white-haired man, his shoulders bowed as if weighted down by the responsibility he bore, stood with folded arms within the walls which held the armament conference and declared in the name of Great Britain the abandonment of her traditional policy of supremacy on the sea and her willingness to accept . . . naval equality with . . . the United States. . . . And then a short, spare man, with inky hair, stood up and in the name of Japan, pledged his Government to reduce its fleet, disavowing all ambitions to rival the navies of America and England, and pledging his country against aggressiveness on the sea. . . . It was big, almost too big to grasp. . . . What was an impossibility is now a fact."

Thus wrote Mr. Edwin L. James of the *New York Times* at the close of the second plenary session. And thus also responded many another who listened that day to the speeches of Mr. Balfour and Baron Kato.[1] But not all.[2] A few ears caught their qualifying words and phrases which turned acceptance "in principle" into disagreement in application and detail; which plunged the Conference into long and involved negotiations; and

[1] *New York Times*, Nov. 16, 1921, p. 1; and see, for example, the similar reactions of Louis Siebold and Edwin C. Hill, in the *New York Herald*, Nov. 16, pp. 1, 4.

[2] See, for example, Oswald Garrison Villard, in *The Nation*, Vol. 113, Nov. 30, 1921, p. 618. Colonel Roosevelt recorded in his diary for Nov. 15, after the second plenary session: "Naturally our foolish people and papers saw in both of these speeches a complete agreement reached among the delegates. Nothing of the sort has happened, however, and many rocks are to be met with in the future, before we can be reasonably sure of any agreement."

which, in conjunction with later Conference developments, seriously narrowed the great achievement that seemed easily within reach at the close of the opening session.

Mr. Balfour was first to take the floor. Speaking extemporaneously, slowly, even haltingly, but withal very effectively,[3] he paid high tribute to Mr. Hughes, to his "admirably" guarded secret, and to his "eloquent and admirable" speech which had "worthily opened" a "new chapter in the history of world reconstruction. . . ."

This "great historical event," said Balfour, had far-reaching implications for the British Empire. The components of that Empire were scattered over the world. Every British subject lived by sea communications, and "without sea communication he and the Empire to which he belongs would perish." In this respect, the British Empire stood in decided contrast to the United States which was a "solid, impregnable, self-sufficient" country, "all its lines of communication protected, doubly protected, completely protected, from any conceivable hostile attack," "wholly immune from the particular perils to which, from the nature of the case, the British Empire is subject."

These facts, however, did not prevent the British Government from regarding with "admiration and approval" the "great scheme" put forward by the United States. "We agree with it in spirit and in principle," Balfour declared. Of course, he added, it did not cover the "whole ground of international reconstruction." There were still details to be considered and settled. For instance, the American proposal dealt only with the three principal naval Powers, and omitted "all consideration for the time being of those European nations who have diminished their fleets, and who at present have no desire, and I hope never will have any desire, to own fleets beyond the necessities that national honor and national defense require," a clear and unmistakable reference to France and Italy.

Then there was also the question of submarines—a "class of vessel most easily abused in their use. . . ." Balfour recognized that the submarine was widely regarded as the "defensive weapon" of the weaker naval Powers. For this reason, it would

[3] Colonel C. à C. Repington, *After the War* (1922), p. 440.

probably be "impossible, or, if possible, it might be thought undesirable, to abolish it altogether." But the submarine tonnage allowed under the American scheme[4] was greater than that "possessed by any nation at the present moment. . . ." He suggested that these allowances might perhaps be reduced, and that it might be "practicable" and "desirable" to "forbid altogether" the construction of large, long-range cruising submarines "whose sole purpose is attack . . . probably . . . by methods which civilized nations would regard with horror."

Turning to the question of relative fleet strength, Balfour stated that the British Government found the American proposal acceptable. Both as to capital ships and as to auxiliary combatant fleet components, "we think the limitation of amounts is reasonable; we think it should be accepted; we firmly believe that it will be accepted." However, there might be "questions of detail," relating to the "replacement" of ships, as well as to "cruisers . . . not connected with or required for fleet action." But these matters, he added, were for the technical experts, and however decided did "not touch the main outline of the structure which the United States Government desire erected and which we earnestly wish to help them in erecting."[5]

It is difficult, if not impossible, in any brief abstract to convey the charming simplicity of Balfour's speech, and the disarming casualness with which he intimated the considerations and qualifications which might influence subsequent British action. But those qualifications, however casually stated, were very important. There was a veiled warning that the British Government would enter into no naval agreement which jeopardized its historic two power standard in European waters. It was subtly hinted that there might be some objection to the proposed ten-year holiday in capital-ship construction (apparently lest it disorganize and demoralize the war-inflated shipbuilding and munitions industries of Great Britain). And there was clear intimation that the British Government would insist on a larger allowance of cruisers and destroyers, especially if no effective action was taken to limit or abolish submarines. Thus in funda-

[4] These allowances were: for the United States and Great Britain, 90,000 tons each; for Japan, 54,000 tons.

[5] *Conference on Limitation of Armament*, pp. 96-102.

mental particulars the British reply did not accept the American proposal either "in spirit" or "in principle."[6]

The same held true of the Japanese reply. Baron Kato also paid high tribute to Mr. Hughes, and endorsed the American plan "in principle." He too declared that Japan "is ready to proceed with determination to a sweeping reduction in her naval armament." But, he added, "it will be universally admitted that a nation must be provided with such armaments as are essential to its security." With this in view, "a few modifications" would be "proposed with regard to the tonnage basis for replacement of the various classes of vessels." These were questions for the experts. And he felt confident that the American and other delegations would consider any proposed modifications "with the same desire to meet our ideas as we have to meet theirs." For Japan, he reminded the Conference, had "never claimed nor had any intention of claiming to have a naval establishment equal in strength to that of either the United States or the British Empire." And Japan's "existing plan" would "show conclusively that she had never in view preparation for offensive war."[7]

Precisely what "modifications" the Japanese Government had in mind were not stated. According to rumors then circulating in Washington, these would probably include a higher fleet ratio, say 10 to 7, instead of 10 to 6; and also demolition, or at least no further development, of fortifications and naval bases in American insular possessions in the Pacific.[8] And as events soon showed, these rumors were well founded.

Statements from Senator Schanzer, chief Italian delegate, and from Premier Briand of France also cast a shadow on events to come. The former's speech, read in connection with a simultaneous news release from the Italian delegation, not only disclosed their desire (apparently for reasons of internal economy) for as much reduction of armament as possible, but also foreshadowed Italy's demand for naval parity with France.[9]

[6] See R. A. Chaput, *Disarmament in British Foreign Policy* (1935), pp. 110*ff*.

[7] *Conference*, p. 106.

[8] See, for example, *New York Times*, July 28, 1921, p. 4; Sept. 14, p. 1; Oct. 30, p. 20; Nov. 1, p. 5; Nov. 13, p. 8; Nov. 15, p. 1; Nov. 16, p. 3.

[9] *Conference*, pp. 106, 108; *New York Times*, Nov. 16, 1921, p. 4.

Briand's statement was even more disquieting. The French Premier betrayed unmistakable hostility toward the British delegation, as well as a corroding suspicion that England and America were secretly working together against France. He sounded a clear warning that France, in isolation, could not join in any scheme for reducing land armaments. And he served notice that the French Navy, "as a consequence of the war," was already "reduced to proportions quite inadequate for the defense of our national interests and geographical position."[10]

Thus the second plenary session closed on a dissonance in marked contrast to the harmony of the first. With Italy certain to insist on naval parity with France; with the latter demanding more rather than less forces afloat; with Great Britain standing on the historic two-Power standard in European waters; and with both Britain and Japan entering claims for greater relative strength than that permissable under the American proposal, it was difficult to foresee any constructive outcome.

Whether these conflicting claims could be successfully and satisfactorily compromised, only time could tell. But it was certainly doubtful whether the prospect justified the optimism of the *New York Times* which concluded an editorial on the second session: ". . . to have begun with so dramatic an achievement and so rapid and resounding a triumph is to augur the brightest outlook for what remains to be done."[11]

Japan's Bid for a Higher Ratio

On Wednesday, November 16, the day following the second plenary session, the Japanese delegation opened its anticipated drive for a higher naval ratio. The resulting struggle lasted a month, with Mr. Hughes and Baron Kato in the leading rôles, and with Mr. Balfour acting alternately as "honest broker" and as advocate for the special claims of the British Admiralty. These assaults breached the American plan at several points, and for a time it seemed doubtful if any mutually acceptable compromise could be reached.

After December 1, however, the negotiations took a turn for the better. The way to compromise was further opened by the conclusion of the Four Power Treaty, a non-aggression pact

[10] *Conference*, pp. 108, 110.

[11] Nov. 16, 1921, p. 18.

which covered the insular possessions of France, Great Britain, Japan, and the United States in the "region of the Pacific," and superseded the Anglo-Japanese Alliance. And on December 15, it was finally announced that the "Big Three"—Hughes, Balfour, and Kato—had reached a provisional understanding as to capital-ship ratios, which was to become final on conclusion of a further agreement extending the ratio principle and settling the capital-ship tonnage allowances of France and Italy.

The Japanese case and plan of action were hastily prepared over the week-end following the first plenary session. On Saturday afternoon, Baron Kato publicly praised Mr. Hughes's proposal as "concrete and logical," reiterated that he was in favor of the "general principle" of arms limitation, and promised that Japan would cooperate for that purpose to the "extent possible."[12] On Sunday, he spoke optimistically of the outlook for agreement.[13] But on Monday it was intimated that Japan would insist on certain modifications.[14] Then on Tuesday, as we have already described, Kato arose in the second plenary session to accept the American proposal "in principle," with an indefinite reservation as to details which further prepared the way for a specific bill of exceptions.

This was presented on November 16 at the first meeting of the subcommittee of naval advisers to which the American proposal had been referred for study.[15] Speaking before this group, Admiral Hiroharu Kato (to be distinguished from Baron Tomosaburo Kato, chief delegate for Japan) stated the Japanese case as follows: Every state had an inherent right of security; it alone was competent to decide what means were necessary to

[12] *New York Times*, Nov. 13, pp. 1, 8. [13] *ibid.*, Nov. 14, p. 1.

[14] *ibid.*, Nov. 15, p. 1. For one thing, it was stated, the Japanese Navy was already at least 70 per cent as strong as that of the United States. Its relative strength, moreover, would be still greater when the present building program was completed. It was further maintained that the battleship *Mutsu* (listed in the Hughes proposal as still in course of construction, and hence to be scrapped) was actually in commission. And it was intimated that, if the *Mutsu* was retained and the higher ratio recognized, the Japanese Government would not raise the issue of fortifications and naval bases in the Pacific island possessions of the United States.

[15] The members of this technical subcommittee were Colonel Theodore Roosevelt (chairman), Admiral of the Fleet Earl Beatty (succeeded by Rear Admiral Sir Ernle Chatfield), Vice-Admiral de Bon, Vice-Admiral Baron Acton, and Vice-Admiral Kato. The only known record of the proceedings of this subcommittee is that contained in the unpublished diary of Colonel Roosevelt.

that end; the proposed ratio of 60 per cent for Japan was insufficient; Japan could not accept less than 70 per cent without prejudice to her national security and defense; with respect to aircraft carriers, Japan was entitled to parity with Great Britain and the United States "because of her geographical position and special circumstances"; and finally, the battleship *Mutsu* "should be preserved because already built."[16]

The strategy and motives underlying this argument were never formally disclosed. Prestige was unquestionably a factor, as was probably the political situation in Japan where certain classes, notably the Army and Navy, were by no means united in support of either the Japanese delegation or the principle of arms limitation. Likewise important, perhaps more important, was the determination manifest in every Japanese move at Washington, to control the sea approaches to Japan and China, on which depended not only the security of the Island Empire but also the future of Japanese expansion in eastern Asia.[17]

For this very reason, among others, the counter-proposals of Japan encountered strong opposition in the United States. It was reported that assent to the higher ratio demanded would have dire effects on American plans for defense of the Philippine Islands.[18] American naval authorities were said to "feel that Japan is not entitled to such a naval force as might permit her to dominate the situation in Oriental waters should the issue in China or elsewhere in the Far East be brought at some future time to the test of war."[19]

The Japanese Government was warned directly and indirectly that refusal to accept a ratio based upon existing strength "must inevitably be taken to mean refusal of the American proposal." A stand "of this sort on the part of Japan" would have serious repercussions, if it should become necessary for the United States Government to publicly fix responsibility for the failure of the

[16] *For. Rels. 1922*, Vol. 1, p. 69n.; and Colonel Roosevelt's diary.

[17] There were indications that a more liberal current in Japanese opinion did not fully support the official position. This was clearly revealed when Baron Kato, on November 17, summoned the Japanese newspaper correspondents, and sharply reprimanded them for attempting to put pressure on the delegation to accept the Hughes proposal without reservations. *New York Times*, Nov. 18, p. 2; Mark Sullivan, *The Great Adventure at Washington* (1922), pp. 123-4. And see the reports of the United States Ambassador Warren in Tokio. *For. Rels. 1922*, Vol. 1, pp. 67, 68.

[18] *New York Herald*, Nov. 18, p. 1.

[19] *New York Times*, Nov. 19, p. 2.

Conference.[20] It was also plainly intimated that such a failure could result only in renewed naval rivalry, with the vastly superior resources of the United States leaving no doubt as to the eventual outcome.[21]

In the meantime, important developments were taking place behind the scenes. There was no disagreement over using capital ships as the index of naval power. But as already noted, the Japanese delegation raised strong objection to their tonnage allowance under the American proposal. Colonel Roosevelt met privately with the Japanese experts, and reviewed the reasoning and calculations upon which the American proposal rested. Then followed ten days of technical discussion and controversy, during which the Japanese attempted to undermine the American calculations, and to show that they were entitled to a higher ratio on the basis of existing strength as well as on the basis of national need and special circumstances. The issue finally narrowed to a definition of existing strength, and on November 30 the experts of the two countries reached a complete and irreconcilable deadlock, with the British standing on the side lines in general accord with the premises and calculations of the United States.[22]

According to the American formula, upon which the Hughes plan was founded, the existing strength of a navy included ships under construction as well as those immediately ready for service. For example, the United States had fifteen capital ships in course of construction, "averaging approximately 53 per cent completed and some of them ranging as high as 88 per cent." These ships, it was contended, represented naval power just as surely as did the ships in commission, and should count in proportion to the state of their advancement. On this basis the existing relative strength of Japan and the United States, measured in capital ships, stood almost exactly in the ratio of 6 to 10.[23]

According to the Japanese formula, existing strength consisted of ships "in being" and did not include "uncompleted ships . . . unfit for navigation and naval battle. . . ." By selecting

[20] *For. Rels. 1922*, Vol. 1, p. 67; *New York Herald*, Nov. 27, p. 1.

[21] See, for example, *New York Herald*, Nov. 19, p. 1; *New York Times*, Nov. 25, p. 3; *For. Rels. 1922*, Vol. 1, p. 64.

[22] Colonel Roosevelt's diary, Nov. 17, 21, 22, 23, 25, 27, 30.

[23] *For. Rels. 1922*, Vol. 1, pp. 72-3.

this particular formula, the Japanese experts were able to reach the desired conclusion that their naval power was somewhere between 69 and 86 per cent as great as that of the United States, the exact figure depending on the value assigned to ships of different age, size, design, and gun power.[24]

The American delegates, with tacit British approval, supported their experts' refusal to accept either the reasoning or the conclusions of the Japanese. The financial condition of Japan was so serious, it was believed, as virtually to compel its delegation to make terms with the United States. A prominent American banker with Japanese connections was persuaded to take up the matter with Japanese financiers. And it was presently learned through this channel, that the Japanese delegation would compromise, if necessary to avoid a rupture and the complete isolation of the Island Empire.[25]

This turn of events placed the Japanese Government in a decidedly embarrassing predicament. To persist much longer in its struggle for a higher ratio was to risk breaking up the Conference. On the other hand, to capitulate unconditionally would involve incalculable loss of face and prestige, dangerously weaken Japan's diplomatic and strategic position in the far western Pacific, and possibly cause a political upset within the Island Empire. The problem was therefore to find some middle road tolerable alike to Japan and to the United States.

It became increasingly evident from about the twenty-seventh of November that the way was being prepared for such a move.[26] It was intimated that the Japanese delegation had new instructions from Tokio, authorizing an accommodation with the United States.[27] And on December 1, Baron Kato, utilizing an offer of good offices from Mr. Balfour, made a gesture of conciliation which led to a series of conversations, extending through

[24] *ibid.*, pp. 70-1. [25] Diary of Chandler P. Anderson, Nov. 30; Dec. 5, 1921.

[26] On Nov. 28, the *New York Times* printed a long account under the headline, "TOKIO IS PREPARED TO YIELD ON RATIO." The next day's headline read, "NAVAL EXPERTS UPHOLD OUR RATIO AND JAPAN IS EXPECTED TO YIELD." The following day it was "CRISIS ON NAVAL RATIO PLAN PASSED; JAPAN'S CONSENT IMMINENT."

[27] *New York Times*, Nov. 28, p. 1. It now appears that these instructions directed the Japanese delegation to insist on a standstill agreement as to island fortifications and naval bases in the Pacific, in return for assent to the naval ratio of three to five.

two weeks, and culminating on December 15 in a tentative naval agreement among the Big Three.[28]

The point of departure was a suggestion from Kato that it might prove possible for Japan to accept the 60 per cent ratio in return for certain concessions on the part of the United States.

The first was retention of the new battleship *Mutsu*, listed in the American proposal as only 98 per cent complete and hence to be scrapped. This ship, Kato insisted, had been actually finished before the Conference opened. It was now in commission, and had joined the fleet. It would be difficult, if not utterly impossible, he maintained, to justify before the bar of Japanese opinion the destruction of this fine new ship, toward the construction of which even the school children in Japan had contributed their savings.

His second point related to fortifications and naval bases in the Pacific. As long as other Powers were free to develop such works in their island possessions, Kato explained, Japan could not safely accept a naval ratio of less than 70 per cent. But if it could be arranged to maintain the status quo as to fortifications and naval bases in this region, it might be possible for Japan to accept the lower ratio proposed in the American plan.

The Four Power Treaty: A Political Substitute for Sea Power in the Western Pacific

Baron Kato's proposal to halt the development of island fortifications and naval bases in the Pacific presented a fundamental problem. The United States held territorial possessions at several points in the Pacific. The American Government was pursuing an Asiatic policy which necessarily envisaged the possibility of war with Japan. Such a conflict would be first and foremost a naval war for control of sea communications in the western Pacific. But the American Navy, in 1921, had no modern base west of Hawaii, and the drydocks and other facilities even at Pearl Harbor were by no means adequate to handle a large fleet on a war footing.

[28] *For. Rels. 1922*, Vol. 1, pp. 74-5, 127-30. There are two versions of these conversations. One consists of the notes made by Sir Maurice Hankey, secretary of the British delegation, published in *ibid.*, pp. 74-83, 90-130. The other, based on the notes and recollection of Professor Yamato Ichihashi, Baron Kato's interpreter, is published in Ichihashi's *Washington Conference and After*, pp. 48-59.

Without a greatly expanded and improved shore establishment there and at one or more points in the western Pacific, it would be impossible to take the American fleet into Asiatic waters in case of war with Japan. And although Japan's succession to the Marshall, Caroline, and Marianas Islands, together with the rise of submarine and air power, raised doubts as to our ability to use or even to hold Guam in such a conflict, the Navy Department in 1921, as we have noted in a previous connection, had well advanced plans for building a major fleet base in that island and a modernized subsidiary base in the Philippines.

These plans which were publicly discussed before congressional committees in the winter of 1920-1921, had attracted attention and aroused no little apprehension in Japan. The development of modern naval bases in the American islands, especially in Guam, suggested but one thing to Japanese statesmen and naval authorities—a threat to their sea communications in the western Pacific. Japan, it was argued, could not safely reduce its armaments in the face of such a menace. And it was publicly intimated during the summer and autumn of 1921, that the Japanese delegation would come to the arms conference with instructions to demand limitation of insular naval bases, in return for reduction and limitation of the Japanese fleet.[29]

These reports did not pass unnoticed in Washington. They were studied and discussed in the Navy Department. The General Board repeatedly advised against permitting any consideration of Pacific naval bases in the approaching conference. And American naval authorities apparently understood that their Government's proposal at the opening session was framed on the assumption that the United States was to make no commitments limiting their plans as to Guam and the Philippines.[30]

This assumption, if indeed it existed at all in the minds of the American delegates, did not foreclose Mr. Hughes from considering Baron Kato's proposal as to fortifications and naval bases in the Pacific. That suggestion was conveyed to Mr. Hughes on December 1, through the good offices of Mr. Balfour. Hughes's first reaction was that American "naval and military opinion would be very strongly against this proposal." He also

[29] See, for example, *New York Times*, July 28, 1921, p. 4; Sept. 14, p. 1.

[30] 71 Cong. 2 Sess. Senate Naval Committee, *Hearings on the London Naval Treaty of 1930*, p. 469; and *New York Herald*, Dec. 13, 1921, p. 17.

observed that "naval and military opinion had a way of becoming reflected in Congress . . . as well as in the press." And he feared that the American people would be worked up to a point where they would "refuse to fetter themselves in regard to their right to fortify their own possessions." But he was willing nevertheless to "sound the President and his colleagues in regard to the proposal. . . ."[31]

The following day, the Big Three—Hughes, Balfour, and Kato—met to explore the possibilities of agreement on this basis. Kato restated his suggestion which was that Japan might be able to accept the 5 to 3 ratio, provided the United States "could agree not to increase the fortifications or naval bases at Guam, the Philippine Islands, and Hawaii." Hughes doubted his ability to make any commitment as to Hawaii which "was situated so far from Japan that it could not be regarded in any sense as an offensive base." Moreover, he could make no commitment "except as part of the acceptance by Baron Kato of a general agreement which would also embrace the proposed quadruple entente in the Pacific, as well as the proposals of the American delegation on limitation of armaments."[32]

Hughes's reference to the "proposed quadruple entente" was to negotiations then under way for something to supersede the Anglo-Japanese Alliance. As previously noted, one current of American opinion strongly opposed the United States entering into any naval limitation scheme as long as Great Britain and Japan remained even nominally joined in their twenty-year-old alliance. British desire to avoid a naval building contest with the United States, as well as the trend of opinion in Canada, had compelled British statesmen to consider ways and means of gracefully terminating their partnership with Japan. The possibility of its summary abrogation was an obstacle to Japanese cooperation before and during the early weeks of the arms conference. The Alliance, though it had been declared inoperative against the United States, did afford Japan some moral support against American pressure in the Far East. And it was feared that simple abrogation would politically isolate the Island

[31] *For. Rels. 1922*, Vol. 1, pp. 74-5; and see Ichihashi, *Washington Conference*, pp. 48-9.

[32] *For. Rels. 1922*, pp. 75*ff*.; and Ichihashi, *op. cit.*, pp. 49*ff*.

Empire, lower its prestige, weaken its diplomatic bargaining power, and jeopardize its security and future expansion in Asia.

Although unwilling to cancel the Alliance arbitrarily, British statesmen had come to recognize its incompatibility with their larger purposes at Washington. The problem was to find some way to transmute the Alliance into an understanding that would include the United States. It will be recalled that they had attempted unsuccessfully to stage a preliminary meeting in London mainly for that purpose. And the possibility of some such entente was the first subject which Balfour took up with Hughes on his arrival in Washington.

On November 11, the day before the Conference formally opened, Mr. Balfour approached Mr. Hughes with the draft of an "arrangement" to supersede the Anglo-Japanese Alliance. Later in the month, the Japanese delegation, on learning of this move, submitted a proposal of their own. Both of these drafts envisaged a tripartite entente not essentially unlike the alliance which they were intended to supersede. Both dealt with rights and interests in eastern Asia as well as in the Pacific Ocean. Both contained mutual guarantees of non-aggression as to the other contracting Powers, guarantees which would virtually estop the United States from continuing its opposition to Japan's encroaching advance in the Far East.[33]

These projects underwent two vital changes after delivery into American hands. Their base was broadened to include a fourth Power, France. And their scope was narrowed to the island possessions of the contracting Powers in the Pacific Ocean.[34]

Various theories have been advanced to explain Hughes's inclusion of France, without much direct evidence available to support any theory. We now know, however, that one motive was to avoid offense to French leaders who regarded their country as an important Far Eastern Power; and that another consideration was to "disarm criticism in this country." With

[33] *For. Rels. 1922.* Vol. 1, pp. 1*ff.*

[34] On Nov. 20, Senator Lodge, Mr. Root, and Mr. Chandler P. Anderson of the American legal staff, discussed the problem of drafting something to supersede the Anglo-Japanese Alliance. Two days later, Lodge and Anderson prepared the draft of a non-aggression treaty covering island possessions in the Pacific. This draft was revised on the 26th, and apparently provided the basis for the Big Three negotiations which led to conclusion of the Four Power Treaty. Diary of Chandler P. Anderson

France in, there would be "four votes and not three, and no one could say that England and Japan could combine against us."[35]

Unwillingness to fit American diplomacy into the mold of Japanese imperialism was clearly implicit in the narrowed geographical scope of the counter-proposal offered by the United States. By restricting that scope to island possessions in the Pacific, THE PROJECT WAS TRANSFORMED, IN PRACTICAL EFFECT, FROM AN AMERICAN RECOGNITION OF JAPAN'S CONQUESTS IN ASIA, INTO A JAPANESE PLEDGE TO RESPECT UNITED STATES SOVEREIGNTY OVER THE PHILIPPINES. No such statement, of course, is to be found in the American draft or in available accounts of the ensuing negotiations. Everything was stated in general terms. But such was certainly the purport of the American draft, and also of the resulting treaty which was publicly announced on December 10 at the fourth plenary session.[36]

This treaty (printed in full at the end of this volume) pledged the four contracting Powers to respect the rights of the others in their "insular possessions and insular dominions in the region of the Pacific Ocean." It obligated them to hold a conference of all four on any dispute "arising out of any Pacific question and involving their said rights. . . ." And it further provided for mutual consultation in case of threatened aggression from any outside quarter.

This Four Power Treaty contained no military pledge or commitment. It did not obligate the contracting Powers to take any kind of coercive action. It was possible to contend that it was little more than a mere gesture. Even if this was so, it was a gesture of considerable symbolic value, at least for the moment. For it temporarily eased the diplomatic tension; it afforded a graceful means of terminating the Anglo-Japanese Alliance without politically isolating Japan; it enhanced the security of American possessions in the western Pacific; and as a result, it cleared the way immediately for a virtual demilitarization of

[35] Mr. Hughes to the authors, Aug. 5, 1940; and as told by Mr. Hughes to Colonel Roosevelt and recorded in the latter's diary, Dec. 29, 1921.

[36] There are only two first-hand accounts of these negotiations. There is a brief account in Ichihashi, *Washington Conference,* Chap. 10; and a more detailed account in the memoranda of Sir Maurice Hankey, secretary to Mr. Balfour, in *For. Rels. 1922,* Vol. 1, pp. 5*ff*.

that area, which in turn made possible Japanese assent to the 5 to 3 ratio proposed by the United States.[37]

Meanwhile, the American delegation had come to a decision on the Japanese proposal to maintain the status quo as to insular fortifications and naval bases in the Pacific. When Mr. Hughes put this proposal to his colleagues, Senators Lodge and Underwood had replied immediately. As to Guam and the Philippines "there should be no hesitation in making the agreement," they said in effect, "since Congress would never consent to spend the vast sums required in adequately fortifying these islands." And in this view, Mr. Root, the fourth American delegate, fully concurred.[38]

On December 12, with the Four Power Treaty agreed upon and ready for signature, the Big Three met again. Kato had now received specific instructions from Tokio, authorizing an agreement along the lines previously discussed. Mr. Hughes was likewise prepared to renounce the further development of American bases in the western Pacific. As to Hawaii, he reiterated, he could make no promises. "The American Government would never consent to, and the Senate would never approve, any restriction on the defenses and naval bases at Hawaii. . . . When he came to the Philippine Islands and Guam, there was a different situation. While . . . many influential people in the United States" regarded naval bases in those islands "as a rational part of the defenses" of this country, and as having "no offensive function, he could understand that others did not comprehend the fundamentally peaceful attitude of the American people." He was accordingly prepared, as part of a "general agreement among the four Powers included in the Quadruple Treaty," to agree "to the maintenance of the status quo in the Philippines and Guam."[39]

While we must postpone until later a final appraisal of this major concession, we may note here in passing that it ran contrary to the main current of professional naval opinion in the

[37] For indications that the Four Power Treaty was so regarded by its chief negotiators, see *For. Rels. 1922*, Vol. 1, pp. 77, 81, 82, 91, 92. Senator Lodge voiced a similar view in the senatorial debate on the treaty, 67 Cong. 2 Sess., *Cong. Rec.* (Vol. 62), pp. 3551-2.

[38] Chief Justice Hughes to the authors, Aug. 5, 1940.

[39] *For. Rels. 1922*, Vol. 1, pp. 90*ff*.

United States. American naval authorities, with very few exceptions, would have resolutely opposed the fortifications agreement, had they been consulted. But they were not consulted.[39] Political strategy prevailed over naval strategy. Mr. Hughes's paramount objectives were improvement of international relations and limitation of fleets. And to this end, the American delegation formally relinquished a sovereign right, whose practical value was at least debatable in view of Japan's occupation of the former German islands, and in view also of recent developments in war technology.

The Big Three Compromise on Capital Ships

The Japanese Government's insistence on keeping the new battleship *Mutsu* developed into one of the knottiest technical problems with which the Conference had to deal. Retention of this ship, it will be recalled, was one of the two conditions exacted for Japanese acquiescence in a ratio lower than 70 per cent. Admission of this claim would upset the tonnage allowances and scrapping schedule so carefully and laboriously worked out in the American plan. An offer to scrap an older battleship, the *Settsu*, did not solve the problem, since the latter was by no means the equivalent of the *Mutsu* in size, in speed, in gun power, or in any other essential feature. To maintain a 10 to 6 ratio under these altered conditions, the United States would have to complete, and Great Britain would have to build, additional capital ships. Any such solution, as Hughes warmly protested, plainly

[39] In 1930, Admiral R. E. Coontz, Chief of Naval Operations in 1921, and one of the naval advisers of the American delegation at the Washington Conference, testified as follows before the Senate Naval Committee:

Chairman: "One thing that we gave up at the time of the Washington treaty was our right to fortify and develop our island bases in the Pacific?"

Coontz: "Yes, sir."

Chairman: "Do you consider that a disadvantage?"

Coontz: "I consider that a very great disadvantage."

Chairman: "Was the Navy Department or the General Board consulted about that at the time?"

Coontz: "To the best of my knowledge, Senator, it was not."

Chairman: "Were you consulted about that agreement?"

Coontz: "No, sir; I heard of it first by rumor. . . . "

Hearings on the London Naval Treaty, p. 436. It is also significant in this connection that Colonel Roosevelt's diary contains no reference to the fortifications agreement prior to its public announcement on Dec. 15, although Roosevelt, as chief technical adviser, was in close touch with the American delegates.

violated the principle and spirit of his original proposal which aimed not merely at stabilizing naval relations but also at securing the greatest possible reduction of armament by scrapping all capital ships under construction.

No argument seemed to have any effect on Baron Kato. Direct pressure on Tokio likewise proved unavailing.[40] The Japanese Government, it appeared, simply would not scrap the *Mutsu*. And to prevent the negotiations from breaking down completely, Mr. Hughes and Mr. Balfour at last consented, on December 12, to consult their experts as to the possibility of rearranging the tonnage allowances and scrapping schedules to preserve the 5:5:3 ratio.[41]

After this meeting of the Big Three, Hughes consulted with Colonel Roosevelt, his technical adviser. Roosevelt had anticipated this very contingency, and had a plan ready to meet it. The Japanese total after completing the *Mutsu* and scrapping the *Settsu* would be 315,000 tons. ". . . Our alternate proposal . . . was to retain the *Colorado* and *Washington*, the two ships farthest advanced.[42] It would take but $7,000,000 to finish these on which $47,000,000 had already been spent. In their place, the United States could scrap the two oldest dreadnoughts, *Delaware* and *North Dakota*. This would "bring our tonnage allotment to 525,000 tons," thus restoring the ratio of 5 to 3.

To preserve parity with the United States under this plan, Great Britain would have to lay down two ships. This prospect disturbed Lord Lee, head of the British Admiralty. Lee told Roosevelt that it "placed them in a very difficult position," for they did "not want to build two additional ships" in the immediate future.[43] But if they must go ahead with such a program, British experts insisted that they build ships that conformed to the strategic requirements of Great Britain.

This led to another difficulty. The American ships nearing completion were battleships of 32,600 tons displacement. The original American proposal had set 35,000 tons as the maximum size for future capital ships, with the exception that Great Britain was to retain the already completed battle cruiser *Hood*

[40] *For. Rels. 1922*, Vol. 1, pp. 84*ff*. [41] *ibid.*, p. 98.

[42] The *West Virginia*, another ship of the same class, was afterward substituted for the *Washington*.

[43] Colonel Roosevelt's diary, Dec. 12.

which displaced over 41,000 tons. The British Admiralty had also drawn plans for four so-called super-*Hoods* of still greater size and power. And the technical advisers of the British delegation now insisted that they be allowed to go ahead with two of these larger ships.

The argument first advanced in support of this counter-proposal was that the loss of a year or more in drafting new plans would place Great Britain at a serious strategic disadvantage. But a long and involved discussion brought out the further point that the British experts were dissatisfied with the proposed 35,000-ton limit, claiming that it was impossible to design a capital ship on that displacement with sufficient speed and gun power and, at the same time, adequate protection against submarine and air attack.[44]

A word of explanation will help perhaps to clarify this point. In designing a warship, the naval architect has always to strike a compromise among several factors. Given a certain displacement, say 35,000 tons, he must decide what proportion of that weight to assign respectively to propelling machinery, fuel capacity, armament, and armor plate. If a very swift vessel is desired, it will be necessary to give more weight to the propelling machinery, with consequent deductions from one or more of the other factors. If the greatest possible protection is desired, it will have to be at the expense of speed, cruising range, or fire power, or perhaps all three. By increasing the displacement, it is possible to combine all these qualities in higher degree. But increasing a ship's weight, and hence its size, also affects its maneuverability. And the cost of construction rises at a rate out of all proportion to the increase in displacement. Thus the prevailing doctrines as to displacement, speed, cruising radius, gun power, and defensive protection vary from one admiralty to another depending on funds available as well as on the strategic and tactical conditions likely to be encountered.

The problem as envisaged by the British Admiralty in 1921 was to design capital ships equal or superior in speed and armament to those of Japan and the United States, and to combine these qualities with the added defensive strength needed to withstand the growing danger of submarine and air attack in such

[44] *ibid.*, Dec. 14; *For. Rels. 1922*, Vol. 1, pp. 99*ff*.

narrow seas as the Mediterranean and the waters surrounding the British Isles. These requirements, contended the British experts, could not be satisfactorily met in a ship of much less than 50,000 tons.

Their plea raised further complications. To increase the maximum from 35,000 to 50,000 tons would enormously add to the cost of construction, and thereby defeat one of the main purposes in calling the Conference. To leave the limit at 35,000 tons, and then make an exception in favor of Great Britain, would necessitate radical revision of the scrapping schedule to avoid upsetting the agreed ratio of British naval strength to that of the United States and Japan.

Under the original American proposal, Great Britain was to keep twenty-two capital ships with a total displacement slightly exceeding 600,000 tons, as against eighteen ships and 500,000 tons for the United States. Owing to the greater age and inferior fighting qualities of the British ships, the framers of the American proposal had allowed this differential in order to give substantial equality to the existing fleets of the two countries. This differential, however, was gradually to disappear through a process of progressive scrapping and replacement. And the capital-ship tonnage of the two fleets was ultimately to be stabilized at 500,000, raised to 525,000 as a result of the *Mutsu* compromise.

The two ships which Great Britain was entitled to build under that compromise would presumably represent considerably greater power, ton for ton, than any ships in either the Japanese or the American fleets. The British Admiralty would therefore have to scrap more than a numerical equivalent in older ships. How much more would depend of course upon the size and fighting qualities of the new ships. According to American calculations, England's four oldest battleships would no more than balance two new ships of 35,000 tons each, and it would take five ships at least to compensate for two super-*Hoods* of 45,000 tons or more displacement. And on this the Japanese were fully in accord with the United States.

These terms led to further discussion in which much was said of the special needs and circumstances of Great Britain. To admit such arguments was contrary to the principle and spirit of the original American proposal, and would open the door to endless debate and hopeless disagreement. One primary aim of the Conference was to reduce, not to increase, the burden of naval armaments, and to this line Mr. Hughes adhered with remarkable singleness of purpose. The total tonnage allowances must not be raised. The limits on individual ships should not be materially increased. If the British Government insisted on completing two super-*Hoods*, they must scrap five older ships in compensation.

On this issue Kato stood firmly behind Hughes. Balfour, after a show of resistance, overruled his experts and, without awaiting instructions from London, accepted a compromise that was virtually a surrender to the American position. Great Britain would build two new ships within the prescribed limit of 35,000 tons; but the displacement of these and of all future replacements was to be calculated on a standard which gave a slightly larger ship than did the formula hitherto used by the United States.[45]

The way was at last clear for a provisional agreement. In a statement released to the press on December 15, it was announced that the Big Three were in accord: (1) that the 5:5:3 ratio be accepted; (2) that the status quo as to fortifications and naval bases be maintained "in the Pacific region" which was defined to include the British colony of Hongkong; (3) that this limitation was not to apply to the "Hawaiian Islands, Australia, New Zealand, and the Islands composing Japan proper, or, of course, to the coasts of the United States and Canada, as to which the respective Powers retain their entire freedom"; (4) that Japan was to retain the *Mutsu*; (5) that the United States was to complete two more battleships of the *Maryland* type, scrapping two older ships on their completion;[46] (6) that Great Britain was to build two new capital ships not exceeding 35,000 British tons (equivalent to about 37,000 American tons) each, and scrap four older ships; (7) that the ten-year naval holiday was to be observed with the exceptions just stated; and (8) that this agreement was contingent on the outcome of negotiations then pending with France and Italy.[47]

[45] *For. Rels. 1922,* Vol. 1, pp. 115*ff.*; Colonel Roosevelt's diary, Dec. 14, 15.

[46] The *Maryland* was the first capital ship completed under the 1916 building program. This ship, commissioned in July 1921, displaced 32,600 tons, and mounted a main battery of eight 16-inch guns.

[47] *For. Rels. 1922,* Vol. 1, pp. 128*ff.*

Courtesy of the Office of Naval Records & Library

U. S. S. *Maryland*, newest and most powerful American battleship in commission at the time of the Washington Conference. Sister ship of the *West Virginia* and *Colorado*.

Europe's Shadow Over Washington

Extension of the provisional Big Three agreement to France and Italy presented formidable difficulties. The British delegates, strongly supported by their technical advisers, had reiterated from the outset that their adherence to any naval limitation treaty depended on conclusion of a satisfactory arrangement with these countries. It was generally assumed that this meant simply French and Italian acquiescence in a British two-power standard in European waters. But actually it meant a good deal more.

Early in the Conference, the American technical staff learned that Admiral Earl Beatty, First Sea Lord of the Admiralty, "could never agree to any plan which did not give England a larger navy than the navies of Japan and France combined"; and that the British delegates were unanimously supporting him in this stand.[48] With the British delegation also committed from the first day of the Conference to recognition of Japan's existing strength which stood to that of Great Britain in approximately the ratio of 3 to 5, the problem became one of inducing France to accept a ratio somewhat less than 2 to 5.

Italy presented no serious problem. The pre-Fascist Italian Government then in power was ready to reduce its naval force to almost any level, as long as such reduction was on the basis of equality with France. But the French Government from the outset took a position and followed a course which seemed in British eyes not only intransigent and unreasonable but designed to alarm English opinion and to bend British policy to the will of France.

In actual fact, the French delegation had come to Washington without any positive naval program. Historically, France had ranked as one of the great naval Powers. The defeat of Germany left the French Navy, despite war losses and neglect resulting from pressure on the land front, second only to Great Britain's in European waters. But France in 1921 had no settled naval policy. Bending to the imperative need for retrenchment, the French Admiralty had marked time following the armistice, laying up ships, retiring personnel, studying the post-war situation, but delaying from month to month the announcement of a definite program for the future.

[48] Colonel Roosevelt's diary, Nov. 16.

Whatever the technical views of French naval authorities, French statesmen in 1921 were concerned far less with naval policy *per se* than with its bearing on their political and diplomatic situation. At the Peace Conference of 1919, the French Government had accepted a strategically unsatisfactory boundary with Germany, in return for military guarantees from Great Britain and from the United States. The failure of the Senate to make good the American pledge had destroyed the whole arrangement. And the Senate's rejection of the League of Nations had cast doubt on the future efficacy of that experiment in collective security.

Furthermore, the French quest for safety against a resurgent and vengeful Germany clashed with British desires for prompt economic rehabilitation in Central Europe. Recurring disputes as to European reconstruction in general, and as to the treatment of the defeated countries in particular, drove the wartime allies apart, leaving France politically isolated and French statesmen embarrassed, apprehensive, and at least temporarily inclined to intransigence.

Under these conditions it was natural that they should view the Washington Conference from the standpoint of their own special European position. Starting with the assumption that Great Britain and the United States would reach an early impasse on the question of relative naval strength, they came prepared to play the rôle of mediator, hoping thereby to win back the support of one or both of the great English-speaking nations. In the supposed desire of the United States to limit land as well as naval armaments, they perceived an opportunity to enter a public plea for guarantees to France, and possibly to offer a nominal reduction of the French Army in return for revival in some form of the unperfected military pledges which England and America had given to France at the Peace Conference.[49]

Events quickly frustrated these hopes and expectations. Mr. Hughes submitted no proposal with regard to land armaments. His naval proposal postponed consideration of French and

[49] See, for example, x.x.x., "Les Etats-Unis et la Paix," *La Revue de Paris*, 28, pt. 4, Aug. 1, 1921, pp. 666*ff*.; x.x.x., "La Conférence de Washington," *ibid*., 28, pt. 6, Nov. 15, 1921, pp. 439*ff*.; Georges Batault, "Le Pacifisme et le Problème du Pacifique," *Mercure de France*, Vol. 152, Dec. 1, 1921, pp. 309*ff*.; Léon Archimbaud, *La Conférence de Washington* (1923), pp. 66*ff*.

Italian strength until a provisional understanding was reached as to the fleets of Great Britain, the United States, and Japan. Contrary to French expectations, the British delegation promptly accepted the American scheme in principle, and established cordial working relations which immediately aroused a natural if quite unfounded suspicion that the two English-speaking Powers had come to a secret agreement before the Conference. An impassioned plea for support in Europe, which Premier Briand delivered on November 21 at the third plenary session devoted to land armaments, evoked sympathetic response, but little enthusiasm, and no specific proposal whatever to renew either British or American commitments to France.[50]

In an executive session two days later, the isolation of France as well as a dangerous tendency to use the arms conference as a sounding board for European politics, was reemphasized in a bitter debate on land armaments in which British and Italian representatives insinuated aggressive motives behind the military policy of France.[51] This trend was accentuated the following day when Lord Curzon, British Foreign Minister, made a public speech in London, warning the French Government to change its present course which, he intimated, was blocking the recovery of Europe and endangering the outlook for world peace.[52]

Briand's departure for France at this juncture happily prevented the Conference from sinking deeper into the morass of European politics. But what was done could not be undone. And the consequent embarrassment, resentment, and apprehension of the French Government and its delegation in Washington unquestionably strengthened their resistance to naval terms which seemed in their eyes to jeopardize the prestige and security of France.

Numerous signs and portents pointed to an eventual crisis over the strength and composition of the French Navy. Briand, it will be recalled, had given notice at the second plenary session, that his navy as a result of the war was already "reduced to proportions quite inadequate for the defense of [French] national interests and geographical position."[53] On the same day it was reported that the experts attached to the French delegation

[50] *Conference*, pp. 114*ff*.; and comment in the newspapers of Nov. 22.
[51] *Conference*, pp. 422*ff*.; and see Sullivan, *Great Adventure*, pp. 89*ff*.
[52] *New York Times*, Nov. 25, p. 1.
[53] *Conference*, p. 110.

favored a substantial increase, rather than any reduction, of their naval establishment.[54] Four days later this view was embodied in an official communication which described the postwar naval retrenchment of France; the present inadequacy of the French Navy to guard the sea approaches and communications of the French Empire; plans already approved for adding cruisers, destroyers, torpedo boats, and submarines; and the necessity of resuming capital-ship construction at a date not later than 1927.[55]

This was followed on November 22 by a newspaper report of still larger demands. According to this report published on the front page of the cautious *New York Times*, under the reliable by-line of Edwin L. James, the French delegation was going to insist on equality with Japan in capital ships, and equality with Great Britain and the United States in submarines. In addition, it was reported, they were demanding complete freedom to build large or small submarines as desired, and to begin replacing their capital ships as early as 1926.

This report, which produced a sensation here and abroad,[56] prepared the way for further inspired stories which threw considerable light on the shape of things to come. The French Government, it was explained, did not intend within the near future to build 300,000 tons of capital ships—the tonnage allowed to Japan under the American proposal. But that figure represented the base upon which French naval authorities were said to be computing their needs as to all subsidiary craft except submarines. And as to these latter, it was reiterated, a still larger force was required, how much larger depending upon the policies of the other Powers.[57]

These and other reports, some of them obviously inspired, grimly foreshadowed the trouble with France that was brewing while Hughes, Balfour, and Kato labored behind closed doors to reconcile their own differences and to reach the provisional accord described in the preceding section. And the outlook was not improved by a growing suspicion among the French delegates that the Big Three were secretly discussing not only the

[54] *New York Times*, Nov. 16, p. 4. [55] *For. Rels. 1922,* Vol. 1, pp. 62-3.
[56] See, for example, *New York Times*, Nov. 23, p. 3; *New York Herald*, Nov. 24, p. 3.
[57] *New York Herald*, Nov. 23, p. 1; *New York Times*, Nov. 24, p. 1.

points in disagreement among themselves but the fate of the French Navy as well.[58]

Meanwhile, the American technical staff was struggling with the problem of setting capital-ship quotas for France and Italy, tolerable alike to those Mediterranean Powers and to Great Britain. As early as November 19, they had decided that a "good basis" would be to allow those Powers "to keep their existing tonnage," but eventually through the process of replacement "to come to 175,000 tons of capital ships with a proportionate allotment for auxiliaries." Such a basis was understood to be "satisfactory to Italy," and was known to be "satisfactory to England." But it was feared that this would not "be at all satisfactory to France."[59]

It could be argued, however, that 175,000 tons of capital ships for France and Italy respectively was "not only fair, but . . . generous.[60] That figure took full acount of the ravages of the late war. Great Britain and the United States were contemplating a 40 per cent reduction of their fleets. No such sacrifice was asked of the Mediterranean Powers. They were to retain for the time being all of their capital-ship tonnage. In the case of France, this included twelve ships—seven dreadnoughts displacing somewhat less than 170,000 tons; and five pre-dreadnoughts of some 90,000 tons. In the case of Italy, five serviceable dreadnoughts with a total displacement of about 110,000 tons; and a sixth which, after undergoing reconstruction, would add another 25,000 tons. The quota of 175,000 tons, to which each might build, after the ten-year holiday, represented considerably greater power than either country then possessed, considering the age, design, and inferior armament of existing ships. And it was an allowance far greater than either could claim on the basis of existing strength relative to the fleets of the leading naval Powers.[61]

The storm broke in all its fury on December 15, following presentation of these terms to France and Italy in the form of an addendum to the original American proposal of November 12. There was a "heated debate" with the French delegates in Mr. Hughes's office in the State Department. This was followed by a

[58] *For. Rels. 1922,* Vol. 1, pp. 86*ff.*
[59] Colonel Roosevelt's diary, Nov. 19.
[60] *ibid.,* Dec. 14.
[61] *For. Rels. 1922,* Vol. 1, pp. 126-7.

tumultuous session of the Subcommittee of Fifteen—a mixed group of civilian statesmen and technical advisers created to consider the claims of France and Italy. The afternoon closed with a still more stormy private session in which Colonel Roosevelt, at the request of Mr. Hughes, attempted to explain the American calculations to a little group of indignant Frenchmen. The debate was resumed the following morning in the Subcommittee of Fifteen where it raged for days with unabated fury.[62]

In the eyes of the French delegation, Hughes's proposal to limit their fleet to 175,000 tons of capital ships was an intolerable affront to the honor, prestige, dignity, and security of France. "They had come to the conference, assured . . . that everything would be done openly. They said they had been left out in the cold; that no one had told them anything, and now they suddenly had this situation placed before them. They said it was unspeakable. They said it was unthinkable."

Admiral de Bon was almost overcome with indignation. "He said that France had been a great nation and had fought for liberty; that she had been one of the greatest naval Powers in the world; that [the American] proposal would wipe France off the face of the ocean; that France as a nation could never consent to this; she must go on and build more ships; she must if for no other reason than that her national honor demanded it."[63]

The proposal was just as unacceptable on technical grounds. There was a "minimum tactical unit," argued de Bon, "below which it was impossible to go." The French Admiralty, he stated, was planning to build twelve new capital ships. Ten was the lowest number that would satisfy the requirement of maintaining a full squadron in the Mediterranean and a single division of two ships in the Atlantic. Given the proposed upper limit of 35,000 tons per ship (and de Bon had not the slightest doubt every Power would build the largest ships allowed), the least that France could accept was a total tonnage of 350,000 tons. And finally, since the existing French dreadnoughts (completed between 1913 and 1916) would all become obsolete about the same time, and since the capacity of French shipyards was limited, it would be necessary to begin replacing capital ships by 1926,

[62] Colonel Roosevelt's diary, Dec. 15, 16; *Conference on the Limitation of Armament, Subcommittees*, pp. 4*ff*.

[63] Colonel Roosevelt's diary, Dec. 15.

instead of 1931 as contemplated in the plan offered by the United States.[64]

It is impossible within the limited compass of this discussion to convey an impression of the heated atmosphere and acrid debate which followed the announcement of this startling counter-proposal. Senator Schanzer reiterated the Italian Government's desire for drastic reduction of armament on practically any basis that recognized Italy's claim of naval equality with France. Mr. Balfour picked technical flaws in the French admiral's statements, and warned that persistence in the demands just put forward would wreck the Conference, with France, and France alone responsible. Baron Kato and his colleagues remained discreetly silent. And Mr. Hughes, with consummate skill and untiring patience, labored to persuade and reassure the alarmed and indignant Frenchmen who stubbornly resisted what seemed to them a concerted attack to cripple their navy and to drive it from the sea.[65]

Although strict secrecy was enjoined on all present at the stormy sessions in which these interchanges occurred, accounts of the proceedings immediately appeared in the public prints.[66] This leak was traced to Lord Riddell, a prominent English journalist who enjoyed the confidence of the British delegation.[67] This calculated indiscretion, which cast France in the rôle of wilful obstructionist, not only stirred up a tempest in the press, but also fanned the fires of French resentment and indignation. Frenchmen denounced the episode as a mean British trick deliberately contrived to injure their national reputation and prestige.[68]

It could not be denied that the French delegation, by their tempestuous conduct, had raised the dispute to the proportions of a major crisis. And it was strongly suspected that a desire to wring European concessions from Great Britain was one of the motives underlying French intransigence at this critical juncture.

[64] *Conference, Subcommittees*, pp. 12*ff*., 32*ff*. [65] *ibid*., pp. 4*ff*., 18*ff*., 38*ff*.

[66] See, for example, *New York Times*, Dec. 17, p. 1; *New York Herald*, Dec. 17, p. 1.

[67] Sullivan, *Great Adventure*, pp. 139-41.

[68] In answer to charges of bad faith, it was claimed on behalf of the British delegation, that this leak to the press antedated Hughes's injunction of secrecy; but evidence now available proves conclusively that such was not the case. See *Conference, Subcommittees*, pp. 20, 44; Sullivan, *op. cit.*, Chap. 6; and *New York Times*, Dec. 17, p. 2.

But there was some feeling, nevertheless, that the British delegation might well make a gesture of compromise. The American technical staff "all agreed that it would be a good thing for England to make a 'beau-geste' and allow France six battleships and 210,000 tons." That, however, was "England's affair." We should "stand by our original percentage basis and let suggested modifications come from some other Power."[69] But none was forthcoming, least of all from the British delegation which was now involved with France in an even more acrimonious controversy over abolition of submarines.[70] Once more the shadow of Europe was creeping over Washington.

Meanwhile, Mr. Hughes had commenced a flank movement to circumvent the impasse which was threatening to wreck the Conference. He had received positive assurances of support from Premier Briand, on the eve of the latter's departure from Washington. Briand had invited Hughes, in case of difficulty with the French delegation, to make a personal appeal to him. Accordingly, on the evening of December 16, after two days of fruitless argument, Hughes cabled Briand, now back in Europe, appealing for his personal intervention to prevent a rupture.[71] Two days later Briand replied: "With regard to the tonnage of capital ships—that is to say, ships of offense, which are the most costly—I have instructed our Delegates in the sense you desire. . . . But so far as defensive ships are concerned (light cruisers, torpedo boats, and submarines), it would be impossible for the French Government . . . to accept reductions corresponding to those which we accept for capital ships subject to this formal reservation which you will certainly understand."[72]

This rather involved phraseology immediately gave rise to further disagreement. It seemed obvious to Hughes that Briand had definitely accepted the proposal to limit French capital-ship tonnage to 175,000 in the future, and that the appended reservation merely served notice that his assent did not extend to subsidiary combat craft. The French delegation, however, took a contrary view, insisting that Briand's assent to the capital-ship ratio was contingent on the other Powers recognizing and

[69] Colonel Roosevelt's diary, Dec. 20.

[70] See pp. 196*ff.*, *infra*.

[71] *For. Rels. 1922,* Vol. 1, pp. 130-4; and Chief Justice Hughes to the authors, Aug. 5, 1940.

[72] *ibid.*, pp. 135-6.

acquiescing in French claims as to the various classes of subsidiary craft.[73]

These claims, foreshadowed from the first days of the Conference, were now officially stated to include 330,000 tons of cruisers and destroyers, and 90,000 tons of submarines. The first figure was 60,000 tons greater than that allotted to Japan in the original American proposal. The second was the same as that originally proposed for Great Britain and the United States. Both exceeded by thousands and thousands of tons any cruiser-destroyer and submarine forces France had ever possessed.[74]

In the end, the French Government unconditionally accepted a capital-ship allowance of 175,000 tons. But this concession was wrenched from the French delegation only after a further appeal to Briand. And the price of that concession was the absolute and final refusal of the French Government to set formal limits on its subsidiary combat forces below the levels just indicated, a stand which not only blocked a further extension of the ratio principle, but also turned the spotlight on a question of profound and far-reaching importance—namely, the function, value, and rôle of the submarine and other new weapons in future wars upon the sea.[75]

[73] *ibid.*, pp. 137-41; *Conference, Subcommittees*, pp. 64*ff.*
[74] *For. Rels. 1922*, Vol. 1, pp. 137-42; *Conference*, p. 86.
[75] *For. Rels. 1922*, Vol. 1, pp. 141*ff.*; *Conference*, pp. 568*ff.*

CHAPTER ELEVEN

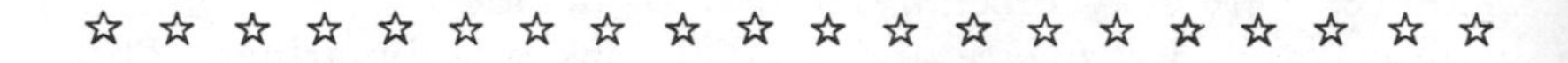

Sea Raiders of the Future

THE submarine problem was a storm center at Washington. No other question intruded itself more persistently. None presented greater difficulties. At one time or another, the Conference considered proposals for outlawing the submarine altogether, for restricting each Power's aggregate tonnage, and for limiting the size of individual ships. But in the end, the most that could be achieved was a pious resolution pledging the signatory Powers in future wars to use their submarines only in accordance with certain specified humanitarian principles.

This failure to limit either the size or the total tonnage of submarines was a contributing cause of further failure, namely, the failure to place any quantitative limitations on so-called auxiliary combatant surface craft. Cruisers and destroyers, the most important classes in this category, were essential components of a fighting fleet, emphatically so since the advent of the submarine. These ships were also the backbone of a country's defenses against submarine attacks on merchant shipping. And cruisers themselves had large potentialities as commerce raiders.

The discussion of submarines and auxiliary surface craft ranged over a broad field. Laymen have frequently, if not generally, brushed aside this discussion of war technology as irrelevant to the larger issues of national defense, national policy, world politics, and world order. Yet the proceedings of the Washington Conference, with respect to submarines, auxiliary surface craft, and air power (to be separately considered in the following chapter), cast a bright light on the shape of things to come. For it was in relation to these so-called, possibly miscalled, auxiliary weapons, that the Conference really, if ineffectually, came to grips with the potentialities and limitations of sea power, and hence with its future rôle and importance as an instrumentality of defense, of national policy, and either of collective security or of world anarchy in the years to come.

Potentialities of the Submarine

War experience with the submarine left disturbing residual effects on naval doctrine and policy. It was clear, in retrospect, that this rapidly developing weapon had profoundly altered the conduct of war upon the sea. Problems of coast defense, commerce protection, commerce destruction, blockade, and oversea invasion had to be reexamined in the light of past achievements and future potentialities of the submarine. And all this led some students of naval strategy and warfare to certain highly unorthodox conclusions.

In February 1921, for example, Admiral W. F. Fullam (U.S.N.), one of the leading exponents of submarine and air power, solemnly asserted that it was "wrong . . . to deceive the people of the United States by the cry that we must have a big surface navy to repel invasion. . . . With an army and navy smaller than in 1914—yes, even without any surface navy at all—no nation could land a large army on the coast of the United States . . . either in the Atlantic or Pacific, if we were supplied with an efficient submarine fleet and a powerful air force."[1]

A considerable group of laymen and a few professionals went so far as to press the heretical view that the capital ship was rapidly becoming as obsolete as the eighteenth century ship-of-the-line. In future wars, argued these heretics, air and underwater attacks would either sink these massive floating forts, drive them from the sea, or at the very least so circumscribe their movements as to render them strategically useless.[2]

Such radical ideas were summarily rejected by the leading admiralties and by a large majority of Service men. The pre-

[1] 66 Cong. 3 Sess. Senate Naval Committee, *Hearings on Naval Appropriation Bill* for 1922, pp. 126-7.

[2] See, in general, our *Rise of American Naval Power*, p. 367, and authorities cited therein.

vailing conservative view was set forth in a report prepared by the General Board, in February 1921, in answer to a senatorial query as to "what constitutes a modern fighting navy." "Concentration of power in attack," was declared to be the "fundamental basis of all warlike operations, ashore and afloat. . . . Types change as advance is made in the mechanical arts and sciences . . . but the general principle of concentration of power in ships . . . that can deliver and receive the heaviest blows and that can overcome the strongest ships that may be brought against them will continue," it was dogmatically and categorically asserted, "as long as navies exist."

"It will be found on analysis," the Board continued, "that the arguments against the expensive capital ship are based upon the old fallacy that war can be cheaply won by hitting, dodging, and running. This belief is usually advanced by the weaker opponent who endeavors to substitute surprise, ruse, and stratagem for powerful, knockout blows. At times it influences stronger nations who see, or hope to see, some short and more economical road to success, due to new inventions, than that afforded by the slower, normal advance in naval methods and material."

"Time and again," it was asserted, "the naval policy of maritime nations has been influenced by these arguments." Commerce raiding had its day. Great things were expected of the early torpedo boats, and greater things of the larger, swifter, and more deadly torpedo boat destroyer. Fast cruisers as commerce destroyers were again tried out in the World War, "but as the German battle fleet could not support them, they eventually succumbed to superior British force which commanded the sea. Speed and dodging again failed.

"Today the opponents of the battleship are basing their arguments upon the present and . . . especially the prospective development of submarines and aircraft." In this, the General Board found "the old battle of words over again—like that of the torpedo against the big ship, the gun against armor, speed against concentrated fighting power. We are asked to accept hopes for accomplishment."

The submarine had undergone "enormous development" during the late war. It had remarkable qualities of "concealment and surprise." Indeed, it had come "very near winning the war for Germany. But as always, necessity and invention combined found means to meet the menace and reduce it to controllable limits." Destroyers and other speedy vessels with their depth bombs, motor boats with listening devices, submarine against submarine, and other expedients, all contributed to the development of an effective anti-submarine defense. "It took a long time, but again surprise and dodging failed." Thus, the Board noted with manifest satisfaction, "the capital ship survived this, perhaps the most serious, danger to which it has yet been exposed."

The submarine menace, moreover, had not driven Great Britain's Grand Fleet from the open sea. Although its "cruising ground" in the North Sea and adjacent waters was "infested by submarines" from beginning to end, "not a single battleship of that fleet was sunk or even very seriously injured by submarine attack." Successful protective measures had enabled the British fleet to perform all the functions for which it had been created. "Throughout the war it was the Grand Fleet at Scapa Flow or thereabouts which controlled the movements of the enemy ships. It was the sea power vested and latent in the battleships which exercised the pressure upon the enemy which kept the sea routes open to the Allies and kept the German High Sea Fleet in its defended harbors until the morale of its personnel was sapped and the offensive power of that fleet was destroyed by inaction."[3]

This achievement, continued the official rejoinder, had secured the British Isles against any serious threat of invasion. It had made the seas comparatively safe for the cruisers, destroyers, and other craft which swept German merchant shipping from the oceans. It had made possible the strangling commercial blockade of the Central Powers, and the transportation of the British and American armies to France.

Last but not least, the British fleet's command of the ocean's surface had covered the operations of the forces mobilized against the submarine blockade. With German battleships and battle cruisers at large, Allied destroyers and other anti-submarine craft could not have kept the sea for twenty-four hours. The commercial convoy system could not have been under-

[3] 66 Cong. 3 Sess. House Naval Committee, *Hearings on Sundry Legislation, 1920-1921*, pp. 925*ff*.

taken. And the unprecedented mining operations, conceived with a view to imprisoning the enemy's U-boats within the North Sea, could not even have been seriously considered.

Everything, concluded the official rejoinder, depended on keeping the enemy's fighting fleet, or detachments of it, off the open sea. In short, to realize either the defensive or the offensive ends of naval strategy, it had now become necessary to control the sub-surface as well as the surface of the sea. But as the ultimately successful anti-submarine campaign had shown, in order to control the sub-surface it was necessary first to exercise indisputable command on the surface. And events had demonstrated to the satisfaction of the principal admiralties that the battleship was still the decisive factor in the exercise of a surface command of the sea.[4]

It was freely admitted that the submarine menace had forced changes in capital-ship design, in fleet organization, and in tactics. These changes already included external bulkheads, a sort of false outer hull, known as a bulge or blister, so constructed as to absorb the shock of torpedo explosions; more extensive internal subdivision of the ship into watertight compartments or cells; stronger escorts of protective destroyers; modified fleet formations; higher speeds in submarine-infested waters; etc. Further changes were in process or in prospect, and the majority of naval experts seemed confident that the submarine could never drive the capital ship from the sea.

At the same time, while the tenor of official opinion varied somewhat from one country to another, there was on the whole very little inclination, even among the most orthodox thinkers, to belittle the past exploits and future potentialities of the submarine as a ruthless commerce destroyer. Despite the ultimately successful defensive measure instituted in 1917 and 1918, Englishmen could not forget their narrow escape from disaster. And with the memory of those dreadful months vividly in mind, they had proposed at the Peace Conference to abolish the submarine altogether.

This proposal had the support of American statesmen and their naval advisers. A Navy Department memorandum prepared just before the armistice favored the total suppression of

[4] See our *Rise of American Naval Power* (1939), pp. 368-9 or (1942), pp. 372-3.

submarines.[5] And this position was elaborated in a further memorandum prepared for President Wilson in Paris. In this document the American naval staff recommended that "all submarines in the world should be destroyed, and their future possession by any Power forbidden. They serve no useful purpose in time of peace," it was contended. "They are inferior to surface craft in time of war except in ability to treacherously attack merchant ships. . . . Civilization demands that naval war be placed on a higher plane and confined to combatant vessels. So long as the submarine exists it will be used in the stress of war to attack neutral trade."[6]

This radical proposal does not appear to have been considered very seriously at Paris. The French were opposed to it. And the question was presently lost to sight in the prolonged wrangle as to whether the victorious Powers should destroy or distribute the ships of the vanquished German Navy.[7]

The outlook for abolishing the submarine dimmed perceptibly following the Peace Conference. French statesmen and naval authorities discovered in this weapon a possible answer to their centuries-old quest for an inexpensive counterpoise to England's overwhelming command of the sea. The admiralties of Japan and Italy found in the submarine promising solutions for certain of their strategic problems. Naval opinion in the United States veered away from the radical proposal supported at Paris. The United States had, in quantity if not in quality, the greatest submarine force in the world. Submarines bulked large in the defensive and offensive plans of the Navy Department, despite widespread popular revulsion against this weapon—a revulsion attributable in considerable degree to World War propaganda. When the Washington Conference assembled in November 1921, all the principal naval Powers—with the possible exception of Great Britain—had plans on foot or work in hand, which envisaged further strengthening of their submarine flotillas.[8]

[5] D. H. Miller, *My Diary at the Conference of Paris, with Documents* (1924), Vol. 2, p. 105.

[6] R. S. Baker, *Woodrow Wilson and World Settlement* (1922), Vol. 3, p. 201.

[7] R. A. Chaput, *Disarmament in British Foreign Policy* (1935), pp. 76-7.

[8] *Navy Yearbook. 1920-1921*, p. 899.

SUBMARINES: OUTLAWRY, LIMITATION, OR HUMANIZATION?

The plans which Mr. Hughes and his associates drafted for the Conference contemplated both the regulation of submarine warfare and the limitation of this species of war craft. The circulated agenda included the item: "rules for control of new agencies of warfare," which was officially interpreted to embrace submarines. And the American proposal, announced at the first plenary session, expressly included submarines in the comprehensive naval limitation plan therein offered.[9]

Briefly, it was proposed to allot 90,000 tons of submarines to Great Britain and the United States, and 54,000 tons to Japan. These quotas contemplated no such drastic limitation as did the provisions relating to capital ships. According to American calculations, the United States had 95,000 tons of submarines built and building in 1921; Great Britain, 82,500 tons; and Japan, only 31,500. The British Admiralty could build 7,500 tons of submarines, and Japan over 20,000, before reaching their respective upper limits. And it was absolutely certain that the French and Italian Governments would demand equally generous treatment for themselves.

The implications of all this did not escape the British delegation. At the second plenary session, it will be recalled, Mr. Balfour gently hinted that the British delegation was not wholly satisfied with this feature of the American proposal. He and his colleagues would like to see the submarine abolished altogether; or, if that were not feasible, they would favor reducing the proposed tonnage quotas, and forbidding the construction of large, long-range cruising submarines whose "whole purpose" was "attack . . . probably . . . by methods which civilized nations would regard with horror."[10]

This suggestion struck a sympathetic chord in American public opinion. The German submarine campaign, dramatized and publicized in American war propaganda, had left the country with a feeling of revulsion against this weapon which struck down noncombatants and innocent neutrals on the high seas. This revulsion made the American public receptive to the British suggestion for abolition, or at least drastic limitation of

[9] *For. Rels. 1921*, Vol. 1, pp. 69, 70; *Conference on Limitation of Armament*, p. 86.
[10] *Conference*, p. 102.

submarines. The *New York Herald* and other metropolitan papers carried on a vigorous agitation for total abolition of those "vipers of the sea." Outstanding leaders in many walks of life joined the crusade. And early in January it was disclosed that the American delegation had received over 400,000 communications urging abolition or drastic limitation, as against only 4,000 for retention of the submarine.[11]

This popular current ran absolutely contrary to the desires and plans of American naval authorities. They had no intention of giving up the submarine. A counter-propaganda in defense of this weapon was started in the press.[12] A special committee, appointed for the declared purpose of analyzing public opinion on this question, prepared instead a detailed statement of the Navy Department's reasons for retaining the submarine.[13] It was publicly predicted that these official arguments would prevail with the Administration, popular pressure to the contrary notwithstanding.[14] And this prediction was presently fulfilled, though under conditions which enabled the American delegation to escape the torrent of popular censure that might otherwise have descended upon them.

It will be recalled from the preceding chapter that the French delegation balked at the terms on which Mr. Hughes proposed to extend to France and Italy the capital-ship ratios embodied in the original American proposal. And it will be further recalled that the French Government accompanied its final reluctant acquiescence in a capital-ship quota of 175,000 tons, with an absolute refusal to consider any submarine quota under 90,000 tons, although France then possessed less than 35,000 tons of submarines built and building.

This stand on submarines, foreshadowed from the outset, both reflected and aggravated the estrangement of France and Great Britain, which marked the work of the Conference from beginning to end. When it was intimated that France desired a submarine force in order to menace Great Britain, Briand countered by asking for what purpose the latter was maintain-

[11] *New York Times*, Jan. 8, 1922, p. 17.

[12] See, for example, *ibid.*, Nov. 16, 1921, p. 4; Nov. 19, p. 1; *New York Herald*, Nov. 17, 1921, p. 1; Nov. 28, p. 2; Nov. 29, p. 2.

[13] Compare the committee's mandate as published in the *New York Herald*, Nov. 26, 1921, with its report, printed in *Conference*, pp. 492*ff*.

[14] *New York Herald*, Nov. 28, p. 2.

ing its fleet of capital ships. With Germany disarmed and Russia virtually so, with England allied to Japan and a friend of America, he assumed the British wanted their capital ships "to fish for sardines." If so, the French needed submarines "to study the flora at the bottom of the sea." Putting sarcasm aside, Briand earnestly insisted that French submarines were no more a menace to Great Britain than were the latter's capital ships to France.[15]

Such rhetoric did not satisfy British statesmen who tended to construe the French submarine program as deliberate blackmail to compel Great Britain to give France stronger support in European politics.[16] And it must be admitted, the execution of that program might well produce just this result. Englishmen harbored vivid memories of the German submarine blockade. A residual effect of that dreadful experience, despite the eventual success of the anti-submarine campaign, was to leave British statesmen abnormally sensitive to any U-boat menace in the future. The formidable submarine force now contemplated would constitute a frightful menace in the hands of a hostile France just across the Channel. By the same token, such a force would give to French statesmen a veritable sword of Damocles with which to coerce Great Britain in time of peace.[17]

Such fears as these preyed constantly upon the minds of the British delegates and technical experts.[18] And on December 22, in anticipation of French demands which for several weeks had been a fertile topic of speculation, rumor, and public comment,[19] the British delegates, contrary to American advice,[20] launched a frontal attack on continued acceptance of the submarine as a lawful weapon of maritime warfare.

[15] *New York Herald*, Nov. 24, p. 1.

[16] See, for example, *New York Herald*, Nov. 27, pp. 1, 2.

[17] Graser Schornstheimer, naval correspondent of the *New York Herald*, contended that France, in possession of the proposed submarine tonnage, could dominate the sea approaches to the British Isles while simultaneously menacing the trade routes in the Mediterranean and eastern Atlantic. Jan. 1, 1922, p. 2.

[18] These fears crept into informal conversations behind the scenes, and into the deliberations of the subcommittee of naval advisers. Colonel Roosevelt's diary, Nov. 16, 17, Dec. 5.

[19] See, for example, *New York Times*, Nov. 22, p. 1; Nov. 24, p. 1; Nov. 27, p. 1; Dec. 17, p. 1.

[20] Colonel Roosevelt's diary, Dec. 19.

In explanation of his plea for the total abolition of submarines, Lord Lee, civilian head of the British Admiralty, "wished to make clear that the British Empire delegation had no unworthy or selfish motives." On the contrary, they were acting on the highest humanitarian principles. Means for combatting the submarine were now so advanced, he contended, that it could no longer be considered an especially valuable weapon either of defense or of legitimate offense. The late war had demonstrated that submarines could not destroy or even immobilize properly defended capital ships and other units of a fighting fleet. German U-boats had failed to prevent the transportation of huge land forces across either the English Channel or the Atlantic Ocean. They had utterly failed to break up the Allied blockade of the Central Powers. They had been really effective only as lawless commerce destroyers.

In that rôle the German U-boats had admittedly achieved a great deal. They had sunk fully 12,000,000 tons of merchant shipping worth over a billion dollars apart from the cargoes lost. They had sunk not only cargo ships, but also passenger and even hospital ships, killing more than 20,000 noncombatants. Events had demonstrated that the submarine was unable, for "technical" reasons, to rescue "even women and children from sinking ships." Lee therefore urged the total abolition of this weapon of "murder and piracy." Great Britain, he concluded, was ready to scrap all its submarines, 100 ships aggregating 80,000 tons, "provided the other Powers would do the same." "'That was the British offer to the world, and he believed it was a greater contribution to the cause of humanity than even the limitation of capital ships."[21]

This radical proposal threw the Conference into a turmoil. Day after day throughout the Christmas season, the strategic value of the submarine and the ethics of its use in war were argued and reargued, with every delegation (including the United States) solidly opposed to Great Britain.

In the first place, it was contended, the submarine was an invaluable adjunct to a country's coast and harbor defenses. In support of this proposition, Admiral de Bon, naval adviser to the French delegation, cited the late war in which the danger of

[21] *Conference*, pp. 476, 484.

torpedo attack kept Allied forces from approaching the German coastline in the North Sea, and also obstructed their operations in the Adriatic, Dardanelles, and eastern Mediterranean.[22] Mr. Hanihara, for the Japanese delegation, insisted that the submarine was a "relatively inexpensive and yet effective" instrumentality of defense for an insular country like Japan.[23] Senator Schanzer held that it was an "indispensable weapon for the defense of the Italian coasts."[24] That was likewise the attitude of the special advisory committee which had studied the problem for the American delegation.

"It will be impossible," the committee reported, "for our fleet to protect our two long coast lines properly at all times. Submarines located at bases along both coasts will be useful as scouts and to attack any enemy who should desire to make raids on exposed positions." Submarines were held to be even more essential to the defense of American oversea possessions. Flotillas stationed in these territories could "harass and greatly disturb an enemy attempting operations against them." They might even prevent their conquest "until our fleet could assemble and commence major operations." Indeed, the committee believed, "a large submarine force" might one day be the decisive factor in the United States "holding its outlying possessions."[25]

The submarine was also defended as a valuable adjunct to larger operations. De Bon recalled the long list of fighting ships which the U-boats had sunk in the late war, and insisted that the underwater torpedo menace, contrary to British assertions, had been a constant threat to the capital ships and other units of the fleets engaged.[26] This danger had compelled every admiralty to surround its large ships with strong forces of destroyers whose high fuel consumption and limited fuel capacity cut down a fleet's operating radius by hundreds if not by thousands of miles.[27] Furthermore, as the American advisory committee pointed out, a fleet operating in submarine infested waters must exercise "eternal vigilance" and steam at "high speed," with consequent "added fatigue to the personnel and greater wear to the ma-

[22] *ibid.*, pp. 506*ff.*
[23] *ibid.*, p. 490.
[24] *ibid.*, p. 488.
[25] *ibid.*, pp. 492*ff.*, 500.
[26] *ibid.*, p. 506.
[27] This point, while implicit, was not fully developed as it might well have been in the report of the American advisory committee.

chinery." "The continued menace of submarines in the vicinity" might in itself "so wear down" and "exhaust" a fleet as to render its ultimate "defeat a simple matter."[28]

Submarines, moreover, provided a fleet with all but invisible "observation posts" from which to watch the enemy's movements. It was the "one type of vessel able to proceed unsupported into distant enemy waters and maintain itself there. And with the further development of radio communication, this function would assume still greater importance.[29]

Finally, it was contended, the submarine could play a legitimate, yet effective rôle as commerce destroyer. Here it was peculiarly the weapon of the weaker naval Power. Only with submarines could such a Power strike in any large way at the enemy's oversea commerce. Even if U-boats operated strictly within the limitations of existing international law (and it was repeatedly iterated that no Government here represented would ever think of using them otherwise), they could seriously interrupt the flow of contraband into the enemy country. Germany was repeatedly denounced for its ruthless war on neutral as well as belligerent shipping, although it was admitted that disregard of existing law had, in that instance, greatly increased the U-boat's efficacy as a commerce destroyer. And the American advisory committee at least was realistic enough to acknowledge that war experience had showed "the general tendency of submarine warfare against commerce, even though starting according to accepted rules" to descend "sharply toward warfare unlimited by international law or any humanitarian rules."[30]

The submarine, in short, appealed to all but the British delegation as a highly promising weapon with a variety of uses. It was admittedly susceptible of abuse, but so was every other weapon. In the words of M. Sarraut of the French delegation: the "inhuman and barbarous use" which one belligerent had made of this particular weapon in the last war was not a valid reason for condemning the submarine, but rather for condemning the belligerent who had so used it.[31]

With the British delegation alone advocating abolition or drastic reduction of submarine forces, and with the French hold-

[28] *Conference*, p. 498.

[29] De Bon, *ibid.*, p. 508; American advisory committee, p. 498.

[30] *ibid.*, p. 494.

[31] *ibid.*, p. 486.

ing out for a quota of 90,000 tons, the outlook even for moderate limitation was by no means favorable. As early as December 19, Mr. Hughes was privately discussing with his naval advisers the possibility of the Conference reaching an unbreakable deadlock on submarines, and hence on anti-submarine craft as well.[32]

As a possible compromise, Hughes proposed, at Roosevelt's suggestion, that the British and American quotas be reduced to 60,000 tons each, and that the other Powers keep what they had. This compromise, which worked out to approximately 43,000 tons for France, 31,500 for Japan, and 20,000 for Italy, was unacceptable to France and Japan.[33] Another suggestion that all five Powers stay within a common upper limit of 60,000 tons was objectionable to Great Britain.[34] And as previously stated, all hope of any tonnage limitation at all vanished when the French Government, on December 28, coupled its acquiescence in a capital-ship allowance of 175,000 tons, with an absolute refusal to consider any submarine quota under 90,000 tons.[35]

This impasse placed the United States delegation in a decidedly embarrassing predicament. They could not expediently allow the submarine question to go completely by default. A swelling chorus within the United States was demanding some kind of restrictive action, and that demand could not prudently be ignored altogether. Under the circumstances the best that could be done was to contrive some sort of agreement which would formally bind the Powers to use their submarines in future wars in as lawful and humanitarian a manner as possible.

Anticipating this particular contingency, Mr. Elihu Root and the legal advisers of the American delegation had prepared a series of resolutions on the use of submarines as commerce destroyers.[36] These resolutions restated the existing legal requirements as to the detention, capture, and destruction of merchant shipping in war. A merchant vessel must be stopped for visit and search before capture. Such a vessel must not be attacked unless it refused to stop after warning. And it must not be destroyed until after provision was made for the safety of passengers and crew. Under no circumstances could a belligerent submarine

[32] Roosevelt diary.

[33] *Conference*, pp. 556, 558, 562; Colonel Roosevelt's diary, Dec. 24.

[34] *For. Rels. 1922*, Vol. 1, pp. 143-4.

[35] *Conference*, pp. 568*ff*.

[36] Diary of Chandler P. Anderson, Dec. 5, 21, 22, 1921.

claim exemption from these rules. If it could not conform thereto, it must "permit the merchant vessel to proceed unmolested."

It was recognized to be a "practical impossibility" to use submarines "as commerce destroyers without violating the requirements universally accepted by civilized nations for the protection of . . . neutrals and noncombatants." It was therefore resolved that the Powers here represented agree to prohibit such use of submarines, and that they invite all other nations to adhere to such an agreement. And to make this prohibition effective, it was further resolved that any person who violated the rules herein adopted should "be liable to trial and punishment as if for an act of piracy. . . ."[37]

The Root Resolutions encountered almost as much opposition as the British proposal to abolish submarines altogether. Admiral de Bon (France), with the support of Senator Schanzer (Italy) and Mr. Hanihara (Japan), tried to kill the Resolutions by having them referred to a "committee of jurists." This stratagem drew a cutting reply from Mr. Root who observed that it was "far from his thought to say anything derogatory of the members of the profession of which he had been a humble member for more years than he cared to remember." Lawyers, he conceded, were the "salt of the earth . . . the noblest work of God . . . superior in intellect and authority to all other people whatsoever. But both this Conference and his own life were approaching their termination." The delegations had all had time to consult their legal experts. Were there technical objections to the language used? If not, what hindered adoption of his proposal? "This was no perfunctory business for a committee of lawyers. It was a statement of action and of undisputed principles universally known and not open to discussion, put in such a form that it might crystallize the public opinion of the world, that there might be no doubt in any future war whether the kind of action that sent down the *Lusitania* was legitimate war or piracy."[38]

Actually the question was by no means as simple as Root's acid rejoinder seemed to imply. The so-called laws of maritime warfare had taken form long before the rise of submarines and aircraft. A surface man-of-war could stop, visit, and search a

[37] *Conference*, p. 596; and see P. H. Jessup, *Elihu Root* (1938), Vol. 2, pp. 453*ff*.
[38] *Conference*, pp. 606, 610, 614.

merchant vessel attempting to run a blockade or suspected of carrying contraband. If the merchantman had sufficient speed, it might escape. If it were armed, it might possibly beat off its assailant. And if the man-of-war captured its prize, but was unable to take it into port, it was usually possible to make some provision for the safety of passengers and crew before destroying the prize at sea.

The advent of the submarine fundamentally altered the conditions of maritime warfare. Submarines were comparatively small craft, filled with machinery. They had scarcely room for their operating personnel, and none at all for the crews and passengers of torpedoed merchantmen. Submarines were fragile ships, with thin plates and little surplus buoyancy, highly vulnerable to ramming and to gunfire when upon the surface. These technical facts, rather than finespun legal theories, conditioned the practice of submarine warfare.

Under the most favorable conditions, the submarine commander could usually do little more than to set the personnel of captured merchantmen adrift in small boats to save themselves as best they might. And when belligerents resorted to the ancient practice of arming their merchant vessels, to flying neutral flags on them, and to fitting out auxiliary warships disguised as innocent merchantmen, the submarine had no recourse but to sink its victims at sight and without warning—or else to abandon the rôle of commerce destroyer altogether.

The Root Resolutions were frankly intended to bring about precisely this latter result. But as the previous debate on total abolition of the submarine had shown, several naval Powers, France in particular, attached high value to the submarine, in large part because of its demonstrated potency as a commerce destroyer. It was obvious that their naval authorities would oppose binding their submarines to observe the traditional rules governing visit, search, and capture at sea, as long as their potential enemies retained the right to arm their merchant shipping.

On January 1, following preliminary skirmishes over the submarine resolutions, the Associated Press reported from Washington that there was a growing disposition in certain quarters "to raise the question whether a commerce carrier remains a merchant ship if it arms in wartime, and to suggest that if the proposed prohibition is to be adopted it would naturally follow that merchant ships be not permitted to mount guns."[39] The next day, "naval people" were said to be asking for a clear definition of the rules governing merchant shipping in war. Were merchant vessels "free to run down or attack submarines?" Was it to remain lawful for a belligerent to convert such vessels into "auxiliary naval craft having all the appearance of merchant ships although really armed?"[40]

These and similar questions raised and discussed in the public prints were but echoes of a heated debate which was going on behind the scenes. It had already raged for two whole days in the main committee on limitation of armaments. It repeatedly intruded upon the deliberations of the subcommittee of naval experts which was meeting almost daily to iron out questions of technical detail. Admiral (not Baron) Kato read before this latter body a paper on armed merchantmen. This stimulated endless discussion but no agreement, for the British experts would entertain no proposal to prohibit arming merchant vessels in wartime.[41]

Meanwhile, the British delegation had executed a devastating flank attack on the French position. This was a speech before the main committee, in which Lord Lee had countered French efforts to block the Root Resolutions, by quoting from a recent article by Captain Castex, a well known French naval officer. From the passages quoted it appeared that Castex justified the unrestricted use of the submarine as a ruthless commerce destroyer. If that was also the position of the French Government, Lee contended, British anxieties were more than warranted. If not, then the French delegation should instantly repudiate the views of their distinguished countryman.[42]

This stratagem left the French only one thing to do. They indignantly repudiated the article in general, and the British interpretation of it in particular. The ground was cut from under them. And they were forced to acquiesce sullenly in a proposal which patently favored Great Britain, the country most vulnerable to submarine war on commerce.[43] But that did not

[39] *New York Times*, Jan. 2, 1922, p. 2.
[40] *ibid.*, Jan. 4, p. 2.
[41] Colonel Roosevelt's diary, Jan. 4, 5, 6.
[42] *Conference*, pp. 650*ff*.
[43] *ibid.*, pp. 652*ff*., 656*ff*., 710, 820*ff*. Dr. R. L. Buell, after a careful analysis of all evidence available, concluded that Lord Lee did misquote Castex, or at least quoted him out of context, but that "his general interpretation of the article was sound." *The Washington Conference* (1922), pp. 221-32.

prevent them from fighting a stubborn rear-guard action with sporadic assistance from the Japanese and Italian delegations.

These guerilla tactics led up to a momentary head-on collision in the main committee which met on January 5 to approve a revised draft of the submarine resolutions. Senator Schanzer said the Italian delegation "understood the term 'merchant vessel' in the Resolution to refer to unarmed merchant vessels." Lord Lee in reply could not believe that Schanzer really intended to propose a "drastic change in international law" which would "destroy the privilege allowed the merchantmen to defend themselves"—a change "which the British Empire delegation could not possibly accept."[44]

For a minute it looked as if the "fat was in the fire." Colonel Roosevelt "slipped Hughes a note reading 'Here comes Banquo's ghost.' " But it proved to be only a ghost. "Both sides realized they were on a highly controversial matter." And with mutual agreement that the armament of merchantmen should be held to the limits set for surface cruisers, it was ruled that the Resolution left the rights of merchant vessels exactly where they were under previously accepted international law.[45]

A few minutes later the danger signals were flying again. In one clause the contracting Powers were asked to "recognize the practical impossibility of using submarines as commerce destroyers without violating" the accepted rules for the protection of neutrals and noncombatants. This phraseology suited no one —it was either too weak or too strong. Amendment after amendment was offered. Controversy centered on the phrase "commerce destroyer." Lord Lee suggested prohibiting use of submarines "for seizure or attacks on commerce." Sir Auckland Geddes, another British delegate, suggested changing it to "operations against commerce." And Mr. Root, who strongly sympathized with the British viewpoint, put in the chairman's hands a still stronger version which would prohibit "the use of submarines in operations against merchant vessels."[46]

This immediately precipitated the issue which had lurked beneath the surface throughout the debate. There was a well established legal distinction between commerce raiding and blockade. But the operations of both sides in the World War had

[44] *Conference,* pp. 688, 690, 692. [45] Colonel Roosevelt's diary, Jan. 5.
[46] *Conference,* pp. 694*ff.*, 700, 702.

gone far toward obliterating that distinction in practice. This had been especially true of the German submarine campaign in which furtive commerce raiding had assumed the dimensions of a blockade in fact if not in law. To prohibit the use of submarines as "commerce destroyers" might be strictly interpreted to include only sporadic raiding. To prohibit their use "against merchant vessels" altogether seemed to exclude them from even a strict blockade—a result highly advantageous to Great Britain.

Mr. Hanihara of the Japanese delegation promptly asked for an opinion on this point. To this Mr. Root replied that he thought "the prohibition would apply to submarines attacking or seizing or capturing or destroying merchant vessels under any circumstances, so long as the vessel remained a merchant vessel." This immediately drew the fire of the Italian delegates who warmly defended the use of submarines for legitimate blockade. And the French, though taking no active part in the discussion, listened with manifest approval while the Italians and Japanese fought "France's battles."[47]

Some skilful maneuvering again saved the day. The objectional words were deleted. The original phraseology was restored despite its now patent ambiguity. And the meeting closed with the five delegations ostensibly in accord as to the language in which to clothe a virtual prohibition of the sort of submarine warfare employed by Germany in the late war.[48]

This phraseology was embodied in a treaty, duly signed, and presented to the contracting Powers for ratification. But this treaty (the text of which is printed in the appendix) was a costly and fruitless victory. There is no denying that it did save the Harding Administration from the popular charge of utterly disregarding an imperative public demand.[49] But as we have seen, each stage in the evolution of this treaty was marked by criminations and recriminations which embittered still further the already strained relations of France and Great Britain. And the Conference, in order to secure an outward appearance of agreement, studiedly evaded the real crux of the submarine

[47] *ibid.*, pp. 702-4; Colonel Roosevelt's diary, Jan. 5.

[48] *Conference*, pp. 704*ff.*

[49] See, for example, *New York Times*, Jan. 7, 1922, p. 12; *New York Herald*, Jan. 8, sec. 2, p. 2.

problem; namely, the denial of merchant-ship privileges and immunities to armed merchant vessels.[50]

Whether this attempt to immobilize what was then regarded as the greatest potential menace to the wartime commerce of Great Britain would stand the strain of future armed conflict, no one could say. It is undeniable that the American delegation sincerely believed that it was the most that could be accomplished.[51] Indeed, as events were to demonstrate, it was really more than could be accomplished. The submarine treaty was duly ratified by the United States, Great Britain, Italy, and Japan. But the French Government, whose spokesmen had led the fight against the Root Resolutions, had not yet ratified this treaty when it was finally superseded by a still milder agreement concluded at the London Naval Conference of 1930.[52]

Auxiliary Surface Craft

The deadlock over submarine tonnage, as stated at the beginning of this chapter, contributed to the failure of the Washington Conference to reach any agreement on tonnage quotas for so-called auxiliary combatant surface craft. Warships falling within this designation included cruisers (other than battle cruisers which were classed as capital ships), destroyers, and smaller combatant craft of various types. Cruisers, in turn, divided into several sub-types, ranging from ships of nearly 10,000 tons displacement, 7- to 8-inch guns, and thirty knots speed, down to ships of 3,500 to 4,000 tons, 5- to 6-inch guns, and of even higher speed. Destroyers likewise embraced sub-types, ranging downward from the flotilla leader of 1,500 to 2,000 tons, thirty-five knots or more speed, 4- to 5-inch guns, and armed in addition with torpedo tubes and anti-submarine depth bombs.

The different classes of cruisers had evolved in response to several distinct functional needs. The original cruiser functions, performed in earlier times mainly by frigates and sloops-of-war, were commerce raiding and commerce protection. The latter function sometimes involved the convoy of merchantmen through zones of special danger, sometimes the pursuit of enemy raiders. All these operations required ships sufficiently large to

[50] See P. H. Jessup, *Elihu Root* (1938), Vol. 2, p. 456.
[51] Colonel Roosevelt's diary, Jan. 4, 5, 6.
[52] Information from Treaty Division, Dept. of State.

keep the sea in any kind of weather, tolerably comfortable accommodations for officers and crew, fuel capacity for long voyages, sufficient speed to overtake merchant vessels and to escape hostile battle cruisers, some armor protection against gunfire, and batteries that could outshoot the enemy's commerce-raiding cruisers.

The ideal cruiser for service in a fighting fleet needed somewhat different characteristics. The speed of modern capital ships and the length of modern gun ranges, gave rise to organized scouting. The battle cruiser, with its fairly high speed and tremendous gun power, was widely regarded as the scout *par excellence*. But these huge ships, enormously expensive to build and to maintain, could not be provided in sufficient numbers to satisfy the scouting requirements of a large fleet; and besides there were scouting operations which called for much greater speed and dexterity than these ships possessed. To meet this additional need, there had evolved several types of extremely fast cruisers, the exact specifications varying from one navy to another depending on the doctrinal ideas in vogue and on the funds available.

The smallest light cruisers tended to merge as a type into the flotilla leader designed both to carry on scouting operations and to lead divisions of destroyers. These latter—long, narrow, ultra-speedy craft—had likewise evolved in response to several needs. Before the advent of the submarine, the destroyer's chief functions had been to launch torpedo attacks against the enemy fleet, and to guard one's own capital ships from attacks by hostile torpedo craft. During the World War, the destroyer had become the spearhead of the anti-submarine campaign. Armed with a load of deadly depth bombs, these craft became the U-boat's mortal enemy. Once located, the fugitive submarine was virtually at the mercy of these swift and relentless pursuers.

The destroyer's success in this rôle enhanced its value as the protective escort of capital ships, aircraft carriers, and heavy cruisers of the fighting fleet. And this same capacity made the destroyer, and numerous smaller types built on somewhat similar lines, indispensable for patrolling submarine infested waters and for convoying merchant shipping through such zones of danger.

From this brief and necessarily general explanation, it is clear that every admiralty would compute its cruiser and destroyer needs in terms not merely of its fighting fleet but also of the volume and importance of its oversea commerce as well as of the location and length of its vital sea communications. It was only natural that American naval authorities, thoroughly indoctrinated with the ideas of Mahan, and responsible for the defense of a compact isolated country of continental dimensions, immense and varied internal resources, and highly diversified industry, should view this problem primarily in terms of fleet requirements. And it is not surprising, therefore, that the American proposal of November 12 should have rested on the tacit assumption that it was feasible to limit the auxiliary surface craft of all Powers in a fixed proportion to the capital-ship tonnage allotted to each.

This assumption, however, necessarily looked very different to British naval authorities, responsible for the security of a scattered empire. Their problem was not merely to command the immediate sea approaches to the British Isles and to their oversea colonies and dominions, but also, in time of war, to guard the intervening stretches of sea and ocean, thousands of miles in extent, over which passed the foodstuffs and raw materials vital not only to the power but even to the life of Great Britain. To patrol those vital lines of communication and to convoy merchant shipping through zones of special danger had required in the late war dozens of cruisers, hundreds of destroyers, and thousands of smaller anti-submarine craft. And all these were in addition to the cruisers and destroyers assigned to the battle fleet.

Under conceivable future circumstances, comparable numbers of these craft might again be required to save the British Empire from economic strangulation and consequent disaster. It all depended on the political and naval policies of those Powers whose geographical position enabled them to threaten the oversea communications of Great Britain. Specifically, under conditions existing in 1921, British cruiser and destroyer policy depended to a large extent on the cruiser and submarine policy of France and to a lesser extent of Italy as well. As previously noted, the salient features of their policies at this juncture were: Italy's claim of full naval parity with France; the latter's refusal to consider any submarine quota under 90,000 tons; and the growing estrangement of France and Great Britain arising from conflicting interests and objectives with regard to the post-war reconstruction of Europe.

Under these conditions, the British Government's policy was perfectly clear and admitted of no compromise. There could be no limitation of subsidiary surface craft as long as France and Italy were free to build submarines. As Prime Minister Lloyd George explicitly instructed Mr. Balfour, head of the British delegation: "We cannot, in the face of French freedom to construct a great submarine fleet, to say nothing of the submarine and cruiser construction of other Powers, enter into any agreement fettering our liberty to build whatever number and classes of cruisers and anti-submarine craft we may consider necessary to the maintenance of national and Imperial life. . . . Even at the cost of complete rupture, we feel certain you will not agree to any restriction in this sphere without previous consultation with the Cabinet."[53]

Every British move at the Conference was in keeping with this position. At the second plenary session, it will be recalled, Balfour accompanied his acceptance of the American proposal "in principle" with a qualification, among others, as to "cruisers which are not connected with or required for fleet action."[54] When it was definitely announced that the French Government would not recede from its extreme stand on submarines, Balfour again left no doubt as to the effect on British policy. "It was perfectly obvious [to him] that the proposed 90,000 tons of submarines were intended to destroy commerce. They could not be intended for any other purpose. . . . It was perfectly clear that if at Britain's very gates a fleet of 90,000 tons of submarines (60,000 tons of which were to be of the newest type) was to be constructed, no limitation of any kind on auxiliary vessels capable of dealing with submarines could be admitted by the Government which he represented. Public notice had now been given in the most formal manner that this great fleet was to be built on the shores nearest to Britain, and it would necessarily be a very great menace to her." Great Britain accordingly

[53] *House of Commons, Parliamentary Debates,* Vol. 238, col. 2099.
[54] *Conference,* pp. 100, 102.

"reserved the full right to build any auxiliary craft which she considered necessary to deal with the situation."[55]

This impasse, reached on December 28, seemed to close the door to any agreement on auxiliary surface craft, but Mr. Hughes did not drop the matter there. He had faced this contingency at least ten days earlier. And when it arose he was prepared with an alternative proposal.[56] He recognized that quantitative limitation was "not deemed practicable" under existing circumstances. He assumed that Mr. Balfour in reserving "entire liberty of action" for Great Britain "did not intend to include capital ships, nor did he understand that it was intended to build, under the guise of auxiliary ships, vessels which might possibly come within the category of capital ships." He therefore hoped that it might still prove possible to limit at least the size and armament of individual ships of this class. And to that end he proposed a qualitative limitation of 10,000 tons and 8-inch guns.[57]

It is impossible with the evidence thus far available to trace in precise and final detail the genealogy of this proposal which was to have world-wide effects on naval development in the ensuing years. But we do know that it originated in the United States, and that it expressed the predominant, though by no means unanimous, opinion in American naval circles.

For reasons analyzed in our earlier work, *The Rise of American Naval Power*,[58] the United States Government after the turn of the century, concentrated mainly on armored ships, to the serious neglect of smaller combatant types. There was an especially acute shortage of light cruisers, none of which were authorized after 1904. Finally, in 1916, Congress took steps to remedy this deficiency, authorizing ten ships originally designed for 7,100 tons displacement, thirty-five knots speed, and a main battery of eight 6-inch guns. But the war intervened, delaying their construction; and when the great conflict drew to a close in 1918, the United States had no cruiser in service that could maintain a speed of even twenty-four knots.

Meanwhile, the British Admiralty had laid down a group of considerably larger and more powerful cruisers. These—the so-

[55] *ibid.*, p. 576.

[56] Colonel Roosevelt's diary, Dec. 19, 21, 28.

[57] *Conference*, pp. 576, 578.

[58] p. 269, and Chaps. 15-16, *passim*.

called "*Hawkins* class"[59]—were ships of nearly 10,000 tons, 7.5-inch guns, thirty knots, and large fuel capacity which gave them an exceptionally long cruising radius.[60] They were purely a war product, designed for the specific purpose of running down German surface raiders that might slip through the North Sea blockade.

But these ships were just as well suited to commerce destruction as to commerce protection. In the state of feeling that rapidly developed after the armistice, American naval authorities felt compelled to envisage the possibility, however remote, of England and America one day coming into armed conflict upon the sea. To cope with these British raiders would require ships of comparable or superior fighting qualities. Desire for such ships was forcefully expressed at the congressional hearings of 1918-1919. And this desire seems to have been one of the factors in the Navy Department's conversion, some months later, to the larger 8-inch gun type of cruiser.[61]

Another factor was unquestionably the developing crisis in the Pacific. During 1920, it will be recalled, there was widespread talk of war with Japan.[62] The main theater of such a conflict would necessarily lie in the western Pacific, far removed from the main fleet bases of the United States. In addition to a battle line of capital ships which might well prove strong enough to drive our fighting fleet from Far Eastern waters, Japan also possessed a rapidly growing force of swift light cruisers—ships under 6,000 tons, with 5.5-inch guns, and speeds exceeding thirty knots.

These ships, which had large fuel capacity for their size, were equipped to carry on a *guerre de course* throughout the western, southwestern, and even west-central Pacific. Only faster ships with heavier batteries could run down and destroy them. And as long as the United States possessed no fortified naval bases west of Hawaii, such ships would have to carry fuel enough for long

[59] The other ships in this class were named the *Raleigh*, *Frobisher*, *Effingham*, and *Cavendish* (the last renamed *Vindictive*).

[60] For technical descriptions of these ships, see *Brassey's Naval Annual*, *1919*, p. 185; and *Proc. of U.S. Nav. Inst.*, Vol. 45, July 1919, p. 1247; Vol. 46, March 1920, p. 443 and Dec. 1920, p. 2012.

[61] 65 Cong. 3 Sess. House Naval Committee, *Hearings on Estimates for 1919*, pp. 1128-30; Navy Dept., *Ann. Repts.*, *1919*, p. 150; *Proc. of U.S. Nav. Inst.*, Vol. 46, Dec. 1920, p. 2013; Hector Bywater, *A Searchlight on the Navy* (1934), p. 69.

[62] See pp. 98*ff.*, *supra*.

cruises thousands of miles from their home ports. In view of these requirements, the cruisers authorized back in 1916 were redesigned and given heavier armament. In December 1919, the General Board urged immediate authorization of "increased numbers and improved types" of cruisers. In March 1920, this was translated publicly into a specific recommendation for twenty ships of 8-inch guns and 10,000 tons displacement. And later in the same year, it was announced that the Navy Department desired to lay down thirty ships of this type within the next three years.[63]

The proposed cruisers, it was admitted, were considerably larger than the average abroad. With certain exceptions, the "favorite light cruiser for the British and all other European nations" was a "3,500 to 5,000 ton vessel," with fuel capacity for 2,500 to 4,000 miles depending on the speed maintained. Such ships were well suited to operations in "narrow seas." But in building for the United States, it was argued, "we have to consider distances over two or three times as great as they had to consider on the other side, and in order to get cruising endurance with the high speed necessary for scouting vessels we have to go to greater displacement, which accounts for the 7,500-ton ship and for the ship for the future of say 10,000 tons or thereabouts."[64]

This view was further developed in the General Board's report on the building program for 1921. In that report it was noted that certain "foreign navies"—a tacit reference to Great Britain and Japan—were "supplied with large numbers of cruisers and light cruisers, the latter, vessels of about 5,000 tons displacement and high speed." It was not thought desirable to "imitate the light cruiser abroad." Rather, we should "proceed at once to vessels of about 10,000 tons displacement, high speed, and long cruising endurance in all weathers, together with heavy armament."[65]

This trend of American naval thought was still more clearly revealed in the argument that we could not "conduct a war

[63] *Brassey's Naval Annual, 1921-1922*, p. 39; *Proc. of U.S. Nav. Inst.*, Vol. 47, March 1921, p. 425; Navy Dept., *Ann. Repts., 1919*, pp. 150-1; same, *1920*, pp. 213, 216; 66 Cong. 2 Sess. House Naval Committee, *Hearings on Estimates for 1920*, pp. 2046-7.

[64] Admiral C. J. Badger, March 1, 1920, before House Committee on Naval Affairs. *Hearings on Estimates for 1920*, pp. 2048-9.

[65] Navy Dept., *Ann. Repts., 1920*, p. 213.

on the other side of the Pacific with the long lines of communication which would have to be maintained, unless we had ships of the light [meaning 10,000-ton] cruiser and battle cruiser type, with a battery and speed able to cope with the vessels which Japan would put afloat with the view to cutting our lines of communication."[66]

Such views manifestly conditioned the American position on cruisers at the arms conference. The American proposal submitted on November 12, allowed "auxiliary combatant craft" with batteries up to and including 8-inch guns.[67] And when it became impossible to effect any quantitative limitation on total auxiliary tonnage, the qualitative limits suggested by Mr. Hughes were such as not to disturb the Navy Department's settled and well known plans for the construction of a large number of 10,000-ton, 8-inch gun cruisers.[68]

The Conference adopted this suggestion after a brief debate in which it was revealed that the technical advisers of the different delegations had already discussed and approved the proposed limits. The French Admiralty, it appeared, would have preferred no tonnage restrictions at all. But it was generally recognized that both gun and tonnage limits were necessary to forestall the evolution of the light cruiser into an expensive and formidable warship of 20,000 tons or more, that would be a capital ship in everything but name.[69]

Beyond that, however, the record is silent. In the evidence now available, there is practically nothing to indicate that the statesmen and naval advisers of the several delegations had any real appreciation of the manner and extent to which these qualitative cruiser limitations affected either their respective strategic problems or the future balance of power upon the sea. And the record reveals no premonition at all that the limits thus casually

[66] Captain T. T. Craven, Feb. 19, 1921, before Senate Committee on Naval Affairs. 66 Cong. 3 Sess., *Hearings on Naval Appropriation Bill for 1922*, pp. 148-9.

[67] *Conference*, p. 90. Commenting on this feature of the American proposal, Hector Bywater, British naval critic, observed that "the General Board . . . is known to favor . . . 10,000 ton cruisers, armed with 8-inch batteries, as the most direct method of balancing Japan's numerical superiority in light cruisers. . . ." in "The Limitation of Naval Armament," *Atlantic Monthly*, Vol. 129, Feb. 1922, pp. 259, 266.

[68] *Conference*, p. 578.

[69] *ibid.*, pp. 590*ff.*

imposed would themselves usher in an expensive qualitative competition that was destined not only to have repercussions on strategic doctrine and theory but also to embarrass and embitter the political relations of England and America for nearly a decade to come.

CHAPTER TWELVE

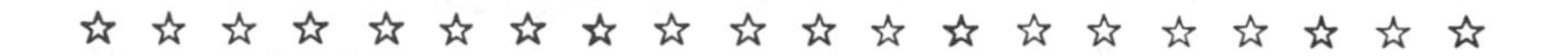

Air Power and Sea Power

NO serious attempt was made at Washington to impose direct limitations on the air components of navies. Statesmen and their technical advisers saw no way of limiting naval aeronautics without throttling at the same time the advance of commercial aviation. Owing to the interchangeability of equipment and personnel, any attempt to restrict naval air power would at once open the question of land armaments, an issue which the French Government was willing to discuss only in terms unacceptable to Great Britain and to the United States. Finally, there was no compelling popular demand for limitation of air power, comparable to that which forced the American delegation to take some action, however innocuous, with respect to submarines.

Indirectly, the Conference did place some restriction on the future use of air power over the sea. This was achieved through limitation of naval aircraft carriers. These limitations, not only on each Power's total tonnage but also on the size and armament of individual carriers, potentially curtailed the use of aircraft beyond reach of land. Just what the ultimate effect might be no one could then foresee. For confusion of thought and doctrinal controversy were still, in 1921, the predominating characteristics of official and popular discussion of the future rôle of air power in the control of the sea.

This confusion and disagreement were inevitable results of the rapid development of aviation during and especially following the World War. At the time of the armistice, men were just beginning to glimpse the naval potentialities of air power. Aviation was cast for a distinctly minor rôle in the Navy Department's

gases; cause shell shock to the persons within a radius of 300 feet; disrupt ammunition hoists, dislodge or jam turrets, dish upper decks at least, kill all persons on upper decks . . . cause fires to break out, and explode all anti-aircraft ammunition."

Detonation of such bombs in the water alongside, Mitchell stated, would produce effects as serious or worse. An explosion forward would cause the ship "to settle by the bow . . . to decrease speed, to steer badly, and consequently to fall out of formation." An explosion aft would cause her "to settle by the stern," and would throw the "main propeller shafts . . . out of line" with consequent damage to the engines; and this, together with probable damage to the rudder, would make the ship unmanageable and a "menace to the ship behind her." Bomb explosions in the water amidships, if they did not sink the ship, would give it a "sharp list, causing difficulties in steering," and seriously affecting the handling and accuracy of the main-battery guns.[5]

Such predictions did not greatly impress the higher naval authorities. Admiral C. B. McVay, Chief of Ordnance, confidently asserted that "airplane development has not reached the stage . . . where there is a serious menace to the modern fighting vessel." Aerial bombs could do no more than "local damage." Indeed, dropping such a bomb upon a "properly protected ship" was, in his judgment, a "good deal like firing a gun at it without a projectile in the gun."[6]

In somewhat more conservative language, the General Board expressed full confidence in the capital ship's ability to hold its established position as the "backbone" of the fighting fleet. Aircraft were unquestionably destined to play an important rôle in the future, but chiefly as "adjuncts of the fleet." It was "confidently asserted that changes of types due to this influence [air power] will be slow and will not seriously affect the value of the ships now built or to be built in the near future." And the Board concluded with the warning that "it would be the height of unwisdom for any nation possessing sea power to pin its faith and

[5] 66 Cong. 3 Sess. House Naval Committee, *Hearings on Sundry Legislation, 1920-1921*, pp. 712, 715.

[6] 66 Cong. 3 Sess. House Appropriations Committee, *Hearings on Naval Appropriation Bill for 1922*, pp. 154-5.

change its practice upon mere theories as to the future development of new and untried weapons."[7]

Extended bombing tests carried on during the spring and summer of 1921 fed the fires of controversy lighted by the devotees of naval aviation. These tests were conducted against old American ships and several ex-German vessels surrendered at the close of the war. These latter included a submarine, a destroyer, a lightly armored cruiser, and a modern battleship. This last was the dreadnought *Ostfriesland*, completed in 1911, and, like all German battleships, notable for its heavy protective armor and for its minute internal subdivision into watertight compartments designed to localize the effects of explosions either inside the ship or in the water alongside.

As was to be expected, the attacking planes made short work of the unarmored submarine and destroyer, sinking them with bombs weighing from 160 to 300 pounds. To the surprise of some observers, the cruiser, after withstanding several direct hits, was sunk by a 600-pound bomb which exploded fairly under her keel. The battleship, however, withstood the hammering of a veritable rain of projectiles, including some weighing half a ton or more. This seemed to vindicate the conservative view that modern battleships were invulnerable to air attack. But that view was rudely shaken when finally two one-ton bombs, each loaded with half a ton of TNT, exploded in the water under the ship's quarter, stove in her armored sides, and sent her to join the others on the botton.[8]

Conservative military observers could scarcely believe their eyes. They had firmly believed and repeatedly asserted that this shocking thing simply could not happen. Yet happen it certainly had, with reverberations "heard around the world."[9]

There were immediate repercussions in America. The earlier prophecies of General Mitchell and others were revived and widely quoted. A vocal section of the press declaimed the doom of the capital ship, and clamored for prompt official recognition to that effect. More conservative press opinion admitted that the

[7] *Hearings on Sundry Legislation, 1920-1921*, pp. 925, 928.

[8] For technical descriptions of these bombing tests, see *Aviation*, Vol. 11, July 4, 1921, pp. 8*ff*.; July 25, pp. 96*ff*.; Aug. 1, pp. 128*ff*.

[9] *New York Times*, July 22, 1921, pp. 1, 2.

theory of the capital ship's invulnerability to air attack had been "knocked sky-high, or, rather, sunk without trace."[10]

There was no escaping this latter conclusion. Experts at the scene all stressed the "grave menace" which confronted the capital ship. The official report frankly admitted that aircraft "carrying high-capacity high-explosive bombs of sufficient size have adequate offensive power to sink or seriously damage any naval vessel at present constructed, provided such projectiles can be placed in the water close alongside the vessel. Furthermore," the report continued, "it will be difficult, if not impossible, to build any type of vessel of sufficient strength to withstand the destructive force that can be obtained from the largest bombs that airplanes may be able to carry from shore bases or sheltered harbors."[11]

This conclusion had far-reaching implications. One in particular, suggested by the passage just quoted, was the implicit admission that shore-based aircraft immeasurably strengthened a country's maritime frontier against attack from overseas. To the chairman of the Senate Naval Committee, the destruction of a modern battleship nearly one hundred miles out to sea by bombs dropped from shore-based planes, conclusively demonstrated the "enormous value of aircraft as auxiliaries of coast defense."[12] General Mitchell, who had predicted the outcome months in advance, asserted positively that "aircraft now in existence or in development, acting from shore bases, can find and destroy all classes of seacraft under war conditions with a negligible loss to the aircraft."[13] Admiral William S. Sims declared that "command of the air" gave "command of the surface, whether it be sea or land"; and that aerial defense absolutely guaranteed our shores against invasion by sea.[14] Admiral William F. Fullam saw in the bombing tests off the Virginia Capes a convincing demonstration of the impossibility in the future of waging intercontinental wars across the oceans.[15] Although comparatively few military experts went so far as Mitchell,

[10] See, for example, the *Literary Digest*, Vol. 70, Aug. 6, 1921, pp. 16-17; and *Aviation*, Vol. 11, Aug. 1, 1921, pp. 133-4.

[11] *Report of the Joint Board on Results of Aviation and Ordnance Tests Held During June and July 1921.* Reprinted in 67 Cong. 1 Sess., *Cong. Rec.* Vol. 61, pp. 8622*ff*.

[12] *New York Times*, July 22, 1921, p. 2. [13] *ibid.*, Sept. 14, 1921, p. 1.

[14] *Aviation*, Vol. 11, Dec. 5, 1921, p. 659. [15] *New York Times*, July 22, 1921, p. 2.

Sims, or Fullam, practically all were now in accord that air power immensely strengthened a country's system of maritime defense against any and all attacks from overseas.

There was less agreement as to the larger lessons deducible from the aerial destruction of the *Ostfriesland*. Shore-based aircraft, together with mines, submarines, fortifications, and mobile land forces, might provide a country with a well-nigh impregnable defense against attack by sea. Such aircraft might even exercise a virtual command of the sea to the limit of their fighting radius—that is to say, to the limit of their round-trip flying radius with a full load of bombs, after deducting the fuel necessary for maneuvering at the scene of action. This fighting radius of bombing planes might come in time to span certain restricted marine areas such as the Mediterranean and the North Sea. But it seemed extremely doubtful at that time whether the fighting radius of land-based bombing planes would ever span the Pacific or even the Atlantic Ocean.[16]

The possibility of using air power, offensively or defensively, over these larger marine areas depended mainly on the potentialities of the naval aircraft carrier. A few planes could be carried on the larger fighting ships, but not enough to exercise a decisive influence on the balance of sea power. Floating airdromes were needed, with large storage space for planes and an immense platform, or flying deck, from which they could take off, and upon which to alight. Given the necessary propelling machinery and sufficient speed and fuel endurance, such vessels could transport all types of planes overseas, either alone or in company with the fleet, to attack an enemy's fighting ships and merchant shipping, and possibly even to deliver surprise blows at their seaports, dockyards, and industrial centers.

Primitive aircraft carriers embodying some of these features had emerged during the World War. Carrier design had evolved rapidly after the war. Several carriers were in service abroad, with others projected or under construction. All these ships were still in the experimental stage. But when the Washington Con-

[16] It was not as clearly appreciated then as it came to be later that the effective fighting radius of a bombing plane really depended in large degree on the fuel endurance of the smaller and faster pursuit planes which must accompany the bomber and fight off counter-attacks by enemy planes. The then extremely limited radius of pursuit planes cut down the bombers' fighting radius by hundreds of miles.

ference met in 1921, there was not the slightest doubt as to the technical feasibility of thus taking the airplane's base to sea.

The possibility that carrier-based planes might be able to duplicate the achievement of shore-based planes in delivering bombs heavy enough to sink modern battleships, shook the foundations of naval doctrine and theory. Carriers with the speed of the fastest cruisers could easily keep beyond range of the enemy's heavy guns. Escorted by equally swift battle cruisers, these carriers could safely approach within striking distance of the enemy fleet.

Even if battleships could withstand the projectiles dropped from the necessarily lighter carrier-based planes, it was probable that light cruisers, and certain that destroyers, could not. If aerial bombardment could disrupt the battle line's protective screen of destroyers, the capital ships would be exposed to torpedo attacks by enemy submarines lurking in the vicinity. Even though the capital ships themselves escaped heavy losses, the destruction or dispersion of the smaller combatant ships would leave unguarded the highly vulnerable train of fuel ships, supply ships, destroyer and submarine tenders, and other auxiliary craft. And the destruction of these indispensable supporting vessels would necessarily compel the surviving combatant units to withdraw in haste to the nearest haven of refuge.[17]

These possibilities gave rise to the heretical doctrine that the aircraft carrier was destined to supplant the conventional battleship as the ultimate foundation of military power at sea. It was now argued that command of the air above gave command on the surface of the sea. Just as shore-based aircraft might destroy or drive off the strongest hostile armada approaching from overseas to attack one's coast, in a similar way might squadrons of swift aircraft carriers with their hundreds of fighting and bombing planes drive any and all enemy forces from vast expanses of open ocean, and thereby establish and maintain effective control of sea communications.[18]

This doctrinal assault on the capital ship focused one of the basic problems confronting naval strategists in 1921. Briefly, they

[17] See, for example, Admiral W. F. Fullam, "Air Menace to the Navy," *New York Times*, Aug. 28, 1921, sec. 7, p. 1.

[18] See, for example, the views of Admiral Sims. *Hearings on Sundry Legislation, 1920-1921*, pp. 669-70; and *Aviation*, Vol. 11, Dec. 5, 1921, p. 659.

had either to develop an effective anti-aircraft defense or to scrap the doctrine of battle fleet supremacy upon which rested the classical theory and practice of command of the sea. Strong considerations militated against the latter choice. Such a course would involve scrapping ships and equipment costing billions of dollars. It would require working out new solutions to virtually all the fundamental problems of naval strategy and tactics. And it would run contrary to the sentiment, training, and experience of the Navy.

Without entering into details, it may be recalled once more that the victory of the World War Allies was almost universally believed attributable in no small degree to their control of the ocean's surface. The ultimate instrument of that control had been the superior battle line of Great Britain's Grand Fleet. That fleet had immobilized the enemy's capital ships and most of their auxiliary surface craft, and had thereby covered the blockade and anti-submarine operations of Allied cruisers, destroyers, and smaller combatant vessels. War experience had demonstrated to the satisfaction of most trained observers that command of the ocean's surface was absolutely essential to all subsidiary operations. In their eyes a superior battle line of first-class battleships was the *sina qua non* of such a surface command. To scrap the capital ship, and with it the time-honored doctrine of battle-fleet supremacy, was simply unthinkable. The problem, as they envisaged it, was rather to contrive ways and means of protecting surface craft from the newly appreciated menace from the air, in order that these might continue to perform their respective, highly integrated, and mutually essential functions in future warfare upon the sea.

Broadly speaking, the experts envisaged three main approaches to this problem. One which could yield results only gradually was to design ships with a view to greater protection against air attack. Another was to improve the quality and use of anti-aircraft artillery, and to equip warships with stronger anti-aircraft batteries. And the third was to provide the surface ships with large escorts of defensive planes especially designed to attack and drive off hostile bombing squadrons.

A few of these defensive aircraft (known variously as "fighter," "combat," or "pursuit" planes) could be carried on the larger fighting ships. But the majority of them would have to be transported in the special aircraft carriers which were also needed to handle the fleet's force of bombing planes. On this need for carriers, naval radicals and conservatives were in accord, the former viewing them as the spearhead of sea power in the future; the latter as necessary adjuncts of the fighting fleet.[19]

Some steps had already been taken toward supplying this need. Beginning in 1918, the General Board annually recommended building aircraft carriers. The post-war reorganization of the fleet in 1919 made definite provision for an air arm. Congressional authorization was secured in June of that year to convert one of the Navy's colliers into an experimental aircraft carrier. And in 1920, the Department came forward with a strong plea for authority to lay down four large high-speed carriers within the next three years.[20]

Congressional response, however, was not encouraging. The House ignored this plea in the annual supply bill. The Senate Naval Committee rectified the omission with an amendment authorizing two carriers. But this legislation was still pending when the short session drew to a close on March 4, 1921.[21]

The outlook was no more favorable in the new Congress which met in special session a few weeks later. The appropriation bill reintroduced in the House embodied no provision for aircraft carriers. Special bills to authorize such vessels languished in the House Naval Committee. Once more the Senate Committee recommended an amendment authorizing two carriers and an appropriation of $15,000,000 toward an estimated total of $52,000,000 needed to build them. This amendment passed the Senate on May 18. On the same day a bill was introduced in the House to authorize one carrier. A week later this House bill was favorably reported from committee. On June 24, a conference committee of the two chambers agreed on one ship and an

[19] For collected comment on the bombing tests, including the official report previously cited, see *Proc. U.S. Nav. Inst.*, Vol. 47, pp. 1451*ff.*, 1635*ff.*, 1640*ff.*, 1824*ff.* For a clear non-technical statement of the issues, see Rep. F. C. Hicks, "Case of the Airplane against the Battleship," *New York Times*, Aug. 28, 1921, sec. 3, p. 4.

[20] *Hearings on Estimates for 1919*, p. 498; Navy Dept., *Ann. Repts., 1919*, pp. 37, 550; same, *1920*, pp. 215-16, 648; *Navy Yearbook, 1920-1921*, pp. 593-4.

[21] 66 Cong. 3 Sess., *H. Repts.* No. 1281; *Sen. Repts.* No. 816; *Cong. Rec.* Vol. 60, pp. 2626, 2828.

initial appropriation of $3,000,000 for it. The Senate accepted this compromise, but the House voted it down on July 7 while the bombing tests were proceeding off the Virginia Capes. On the eleventh Senate leaders publicly acknowledged defeat. Then, ten days later, the bombing tests culminated in the sensational sinking of the supposedly invulnerable dreadnought *Ostfriesland.*[22]

This event reopened the whole question. Official statements pressed the need for aircraft carriers, deemed essential before, but imperative now. Large numbers of defensive pursuit planes were as necessary to protect the capital ships from hostile bombing attack, as was a screen of destroyers for defense against submarines. Without aircraft carriers, the fleet could never hope to perform its mission in future wars. Admiral W. A. Moffat, chief of Naval Aeronautics, publicly reproached Congress for its failure to pass the necessary legislation. And Senator Miles Poindexter, chairman of the Naval Committee, promised a fresh effort and an early victory.[23]

On July 25, the newspapers printed an obviously inspired story dwelling on the newly appreciated menace and on the imperative need for aircraft carriers. The Navy should have at least eight, in the judgment of the authorities. These should be vessels "larger and speedier than any large warship afloat, as fast almost as the fastest destroyer." Specifically, the Department was said to have plans already drawn for carriers of 35,000 tons, 33 knots speed, and storage space for 80 or more reconnaissance, pursuit, and bombing planes. And it was intimated that a legislative measure was then on the way to Congress.[24]

For some reason, the anticipated measure never materialized. The nearest approach to it was a motion, offered by Senator William H. King, Democrat, from Utah, which combined the bitter with the sweet. King, an outspoken sceptic as to the value of capital ships, proposed to "terminate" all work on six of the eight battleships, and on three of the six battle cruisers still under construction; and to convert two of the remaining three battle

[22] 67 Cong. 1 Sess., *H. Repts.* Nos. 12, 100, 229; *Sen. Repts.* No. 35; *Cong. Rec.*, Vol. 61, pp. 1094, 1534*f.*, 1553, 3366, 3375, 3438*f.*, 3444*ff.*, 3520*f.*

[23] *New York Times*, July 22, 1921, p. 2.

[24] *ibid.*, July 25, 1921, p. 13; July 26, p. 2.

cruisers into airplane carriers.[25] This proposal was at that time wholly unacceptable to the Navy Department and likewise to the Republican leadership in the Senate. It was debated briefly and referred to the Naval Committee. There it lay, a warning and a reminder of the congressional impasse on naval policy, and of the futility of seeking further legislation pending the arms conference to which the Administration was now committed, and for which preparations were then in progress.

Aircraft Unlimited

No one can say whether it was because of or in spite of the sensational bombing tests in the summer of 1921, but it is a fact that the American proposal to the Washington Conference offered no plan for limiting aircraft. The agenda, circulated in September, included "rules for the control of new agencies of warfare." But this item, officially construed to embrace aircraft, was strictly interpreted to mean regulation rather than limitation.[26] That position was confirmed at the opening plenary session. And in explanation, it was stated that the possibility of "readily" adapting for military use "special types of commercial aircraft" rendered it impracticable "to prescribe limits for naval aircraft."[27]

The subject was not allowed to rest there, however. France at that time possessed the largest air force in Europe. It was essentially an adjunct of the land armament which the French Government refused to limit without military guarantees which neither Great Britain nor the United States was prepared to give. This great air force was avowedly maintained for the defense of French land frontiers. But in the strained state of Anglo-French relations in 1921, it was not difficult for Englishmen to imagine it becoming a terrible menace to Great Britain whose political economy depended upon sea power, and whose sea power rested ultimately upon security for the British Navy's island base.

Withdrawal of land armaments from the purview of the Conference immediately drew from the British delegation a protest against thereby foreclosing discussion of air power. "It could not be admitted that this was to be barred from future discussion

[25] *Cong. Rec.*, Vol. 61, pp. 4258-9. [26] *For. Rels. 1921*, Vol. 1, pp. 67, 70.
[27] *Conference on the Limitation of Armament*, p. 92.

because France was in a difficult position in regard to her eastern frontier. Great Britain, in spite of her insular position, was exposed to air attack, and could not admit that this question should be set aside."[28]

The British delegation, moreover, was not content to discuss merely the regulation of aerial warfare, as proposed in the American agenda, and as suggested in the Conference. They were utterly sceptical of "trying to limit the use of instruments in the hands of belligerents during the stress of warfare. . . . What the British Empire delegation was interested in was not the question of the use of aircraft in war, but their number in time of peace. Britain and France were neighbors across the Channel and some surprise was felt at the maintenance by France of a number of *cadres* (partially staffed formations) of airplanes far in excess of those maintained by Great Britain."[29]

This thrust secured the appointment of an expert subcommittee to study and report on the question of aircraft, with special reference to their "number, character, and use."[30] General Mitchell, a member of this subcommittee, bluntly proposed a report "that the only practicable limitation as to the numbers of aircraft that could be used for military purposes would be to abolish the use of aircraft for any purpose."[31] And this was substantially the conclusion which the subcommittee reached after proceedings extending through the month of December 1921.

Its report laid great stress on the difficulty of limiting air power without throttling commercial aviation. The latter, "with its attendant development of an aeronautical industry and a personnel skilled in the manufacture, operation, and maintenance of aircraft," was the "basis of air power." Commercial aeronautics and air power were "inseparable." "Granted a flourishing aeronautical industry, the number of the present type of perishable military airplanes active on any given date [was] only one of the elements of air power." The only way to limit that air power was to "limit the science of aeronautics," and to do that at the "present stage" was "to shut the door on progress."

Even if men were willing to pay that price, there were other insuperable obstacles. Any attempt to reduce and limit air

[28] *ibid.*, p. 432. [29] *ibid.*, p. 412.
[30] *ibid.*, p. 414. [31] *Conference on the Limitation of Armaments, Subcommittees*, p. 196.

power on the basis of existing strength—the formula used in determining the 5:5:3 capital-ship ratio—would fail, because of the different stages of development which the air services had reached in the various countries. Any formula based on the size of each country's army and navy would produce results wholly unacceptable to the other Powers. There were also wide differences of opinion as to the amount of air power needed for such particular functions as coast defense, and the policing of uncivilized or semi-civilized colonies. "Geographical position," the "situation and strength of its possible enemies, and the nature of a possible attack," all raised for each country peculiar problems that were not susceptible of negotiation or compromise.

Even if these obstacles were surmounted, there still remained the problem of "devising technical methods" for applying any limitation formula. "Terms of service for personnel differed from country to country, with consequent variations in the "effectiveness of air services and the size of the reserve." There were likewise radical differences in the relative advancement of aeronautical industries, which also had a bearing on the comparative air strength of the Powers. Any attempt to restrict or to regiment aeronautical progress, it was repeatedly stressed, would put commercial aviation in a strait jacket. And besides, the committee knew of no way to enforce any regulations and limitations that might conceivably be devised.[32]

This report which apparently satisfied every delegation except the British, foreclosed all possibility of doing anything with aircraft. Whether or not the conference could have surmounted the formidable difficulties enumerated, had there been any real desire to do so, must remain an unanswered question. The Italian experts insisted that one method would be to "limit the number of pilots in the permanent military establishment" of each country.[33] A leading aeronautical journal expressed doubts as to the extent to which commercial airplanes were actually adaptable for naval use.[34] But these suggestions and others went unheeded. And the civilian delegates, accepting the advice of their technical experts, publicly acknowledged their inability to cope directly with the problem of air power.[35]

[32] *ibid.*, pp. 238*ff*. [33] *Conference*, pp. 782, 792.
[34] "Aircraft and Disarmament," *Aviation*, Vol. 11, Nov. 21, 1921, p. 593.
[35] *Conference*, pp. 790*ff*.

Commenting on this outcome, the conservative *New York Times* observed that "the Conference, after restricting capital ship strength, forbidding submarine warfare upon merchant vessels and placing poison gases on the black list, admits its helplessness to curtail the sinister energies of the most dangerous and destructive instrumentality of modern war, the bombing airplane. The nation that commands the air will be the greatest military Power, first on sea as well as on land, and when the Conference adjourns competition in building commercial planes and dirigibles that may be turned, almost over night, into military aircraft, may and will go on without the slightest hindrance."[36]

Aircraft Carriers Limited

Indirectly, through limitation of naval aircraft carriers, the Conference did impose some restriction on the use of air power over the sea. This limitation originated with the United States. The American proposal, introduced at the opening plenary session, assigned moderate tonnage allowances to the three largest navies in the capital-ship ratio of 5:5:3. Each Power might retain whatever aircraft carriers it had, however, including those under construction. But new construction, including replacements, must be kept within the maximum tonnage allowances which were tentatively set at 80,000 tons for Great Britain and the United States, and 48,000 tons for Japan. Replacements could not be laid down until the ships to be replaced were seventeen years old, and could not be completed for another three years. No replacement carrier could mount larger than 8-inch guns, the rule suggested for all auxiliary combatant ships. And as in the case of capital ships, cruisers, and other types, the tonnage allowances of France and Italy were left for special consideration by the Conference.[37]

Certain implications of this proposal were fairly clear. The trend of aircraft-carrier design in 1921 was toward ships displacing from 25,000 to 35,000 tons. Three ships of 25,000 tons each would almost fill the total tonnage allowance of Great Britain or the United States, and two such ships would exceed the quota of Japan. With all three navies thus limited, three large carriers

[36] Jan. 11, 1922, p. 20.

[37] *Conference*, pp. 88, 90.

might just about meet the minimum requirements of the American fleet concentrated in one ocean. Two carriers might perhaps take care of the simpler needs of Japan's smaller fighting fleet. But three carriers would not adequately provide a mobile air arm for two separate fleets such as Great Britain was then maintaining in the Atlantic and in the Mediterranean. And the proposed tonnage allowances left little or no surplus for detached commands charged with defensive or offensive missions independent of the fighting fleets.[38]

Such independent missions, however, might assume large importance in future wars among maritime Powers. Men had begun before the close of the last war to appreciate the possibility of developing the air arm into a mobile striking force independent of the fighting fleet. Swift aircraft carriers, supported by battle cruisers, it was widely believed, could deliver cut-and-run attacks on an enemy's seaboard, with far more devastating effect than the German battle cruisers alone had been able to achieve in their repeated raids on the English coast during the late conflict. If lucky and not intercepted by hostile planes or other anti-aircraft defenses, the bombers of such a striking force might disrupt naval dockyards, demoralize commercial seaports, and even paralyze industrial centers some distance inland. And there were those who believed that such a force might develop still greater potentialities for commerce destruction on the open sea, where its aircraft could search out and play havoc with merchant convoys unless escorted by capital ships and aircraft carriers of their own.[39]

No one could foresee all the uses and ramifications of mobile air power over the oceans. But certain possibilities were recog-

[38] In 1921 our Navy Department reported the total aircraft carrier tonnage, built and building, of the principal Powers as follows: Great Britain, seven ships, 88,720 tons; Japan, four ships, 32,875 tons; France, one ship, 24,830 tons; United States, one ship, 19,360 tons. Most of these were makeshifts converted from battleships, cruisers, colliers, and passenger liners. Few of them possessed the necessary speed to maneuver with the faster units of a fleet. All were distinctly experimental, and the diversity of specifications reflected the unsettled state of design. The trend was distinctly toward higher speed and greater fuel endurance, which necessitated larger ships. Our own Navy Department was said to favor carriers of about 35,000 tons displacement, 80 planes capacity, 33 knots speed, and 10,000 miles cruising radius. *New York Times*, July 25, 1921, p. 13; *Hearings on Sundry Legislation, 1920-1921*, p. 313; 67 Cong. 1 Sess., *H. Repts.* No. 100, p. 3; *Navy Yearbook, 1920-1921*, pp. 898-9.

[39] See, for example, *Hearings on Sundry Legislation, 1920-1921*, pp. 669-70; *Brassey's Naval Annual, 1921-1922*, p. 109.

nized and certain hypotheses formulated. A large force of aircraft carriers and battle cruisers would give England's future enemies one more deadly weapon with which to assail the vital life lines of the British Empire. Such a force would substantially increase the striking power of the Japanese and American navies in the vast reaches of the Pacific. In short, it could be argued, the potential combination of bombing plane, carrier, and battle cruiser narrowed the oceans, strategically speaking, by opening up new vistas of attack on enemy communications far beyond the very limited radius of major fleet operations.

It could also be argued that aircraft carriers armed with pursuit planes would henceforth be indispensable for the protection not only of the great fighting ships but also of merchant shipping. And despite the universally recognized advantage of shore-based over carrier-based aircraft, the claim was even put forward that aircraft carriers were an essential instrumentality of coast defense.

This latter contention was used by the Japanese delegation at Washington to support a counter-claim for a larger carrier allowance than the 48,000 tons suggested in the American proposal. This counter-claim was advanced at the first meeting of the technical subcommittee of naval experts, on November 16, the Japanese member arguing that the "defense" of Japan, because of "geographical position and special circumstances," required as much tonnage in aircraft carriers as was allotted to Great Britain and to the United States.[40]

This was followed by a cryptic public statement in which Baron Kato intimated that Japan "might desire even to approximate" the tonnage "of the greater navies" in a type of vessel "strictly defensive" in character.[41] A further statement the following day rested Japan's case for special consideration on the argument that "strong aircraft carrier forces" were needed to protect that country's highly inflammable cities from hostile air attack from overseas.[42] The unstated major premise of this argument was inescapable. Aircraft carriers in the hands of Japan's enemies were essentially offensive weapons; but Japan's own

[40] *For. Rels. 1922,* Vol. 1, p. 69n. [41] *New York Times,* Nov. 18, 1921, p. 1.
[42] *ibid.,* Nov. 19, p. 2.

carriers were purely defensive weapons needed to counter the thrusts of hostile carrier-based air power.

This position was obviously untenable. Aircraft carriers might perform both offensive and defensive functions. But their strategic qualities certainly did not depend on the identity of the country possessing them.

As to what those qualities were, expert opinion was divided. According to one view the "sole question" was "one of geography"—whether carriers "were used to ward off an attack in home waters or to carry abroad powerful war engines of the air for use in foreign waters." But there was also expert opinion to the effect that the "aircraft carrier was essentially to be regarded as a vehicle for offensive rather than defensive warfare." Contrary to the Japanese claim, "American tests had shown that defensive operations could be carried on with more freedom and effect from a land base near the coast." And one "naval man of prominence" was quoted as saying at this juncture, that "if it is the dominant thought of the armament conference to make the navies of the future arms of defense rather than of offense, then limitation in the allotment of tonnage for aircraft carriers is quite as essential as limitation for capital ships of the large navies."[43]

The Conference did not formally reach the question of aircraft carriers until late in December. By that time the capital ship quotas had been settled, including those for France and Italy. On the basis of the original American proposal of 80,000 tons of carriers for Great Britain and the United States, and 48,000 tons for Japan, the allowances for France and Italy worked out to 28,000 tons each. And if the Conference accepted a further American proposal to limit the size of individual carriers to 27,000 tons, then only Great Britain and the United States would be able to build more than one ship of the maximum displacement.[44]

This outlook suited none of the visiting delegations. A single aircraft carrier, protested Admiral Acton of Italy, meant no carrier at all during periods of refit, or in case of destruction at sea. Italy's minimum requirement was two ships of the maximum size, or a quota of 54,000 tons, provided that gave parity with France.[45]

[43] *ibid.*, Nov. 20, pp. 1, 3.
[44] *Conference*, p. 600.
[45] *ibid.*, p. 672.

The British delegation was equally dissatisfied with its assigned quota of 80,000 tons. Lord Lee said the British Admiralty viewed the aircraft carriers as "essentially a fleet weapon . . . and it was therefore important that the number of airplane carriers should be adequate and proportionate to the size of the fleet." For this purpose the Admiralty needed five carriers of maximum displacement. Owing to failure to limit submarines, this number could not be reduced, for "airplane carriers were an equally important weapon of antisubmarine defense. . . ."[46]

The French Government was likewise dissatisfied. France, in the words of Admiral de Bon, must have three aircraft carriers —two for the fleet, and one for "use in their colonial possessions." The French Admiralty favored a ship of about 25,000 tons, which would require a quota of 75,000 tons. But for the sake of harmony, he would "voluntarily agree that 60,000 tons might be sufficient for the present. . . ."[47]

Baron Kato then arose to present Japan's claim, foreshadowed from the early days of the Conference. The figure set in the American proposal, 48,000 tons, would give Japan "only one and a half airplane carriers." He begged his colleagues to remember the "insular character of his country, the extensive line of her coast, the location of her harbors, and the susceptibility of her cities, built of frame houses, to easy destruction by fire if attacked by air bombs." Japan, moreover, was a poor country, "economically incapable" of maintaining the "enormous number of airplanes" that would be required to provide permanent defenses at all points on the coast. Their only feasible solution was to have facilities for transporting planes from place to place as needed. And for this purpose, Japan must have at least three large carriers, or a total of 81,000 tons.[48]

After some further bargaining an agreement was reached. The British and American quotas were raised from 80,000 to 135,000 tons; Japan's, from 48,000 to 81,000; and those of France and Italy, from 28,000 to 60,000. It was further agreed, at British

[46] *ibid.*, p. 674. [47] *ibid.*, p. 676.

[48] *ibid.*, pp. 676, 678. This argument may have been entirely sincere, but its soundness was certainly debatable, considering the indisputable superiority of land-based over carrier-based planes, and also the ease with which land planes could fly to any threatened point on the coast, especially in a country no larger than Japan.

insistence, that all existing aircraft carriers be considered experimental, and be therefore replaceable without reference to age. The 8-inch gun limit was confirmed, as was the limitation of individual ships to 27,000 tons displacement. And with this, the question of aircraft carriers was referred to the subcommittee of naval experts for consideration of technical details.[49]

At this point the American experts decided, contrary to their earlier views, that they could advantageously convert into aircraft carriers two of the partially built battle cruisers destined for the junk heap under the capital-ship scrapping schedule. This decision reflected the growing fear in American naval circles that Congress might refuse to authorize any new construction in the near future, leaving the United States with a large treaty quota but no carriers. But the execution of this plan required the consent of the other naval Powers, since it was practically impossible to reduce the battle cruisers (ships of 43,500 tons) below 33,000 tons which was 6,000 tons larger than the maximum originally proposed by the United States and already adopted by the Conference.[50]

The problem of obtaining this consent was simplified by the fact that all the other Powers were pressing special claims of their own. The British desired to install anti-torpedo bulges on "certain of their existing ships, thereby increasing their tonnage some two or three thousand tons apiece." The Japanese wanted to convert two of their unfinished battle cruisers into carriers, though "within the tonnage limit for this type." And the French and Italians desired the right to rearm their existing battleships with 16-inch guns.

Colonel Roosevelt, as chairman of the expert subcommittee, summarized the British, Japanese, French, and Italian claims. The United States, he said, "had no objection to any of them." But the American Government did desire, for reasons of economy, to convert the battle cruisers *Lexington* and *Saratoga* into aircraft carriers of 33,000 tons each. There was no desire, however, "to increase the tonnage limits for future airplane carriers beyond 27,000 tons," nor to "increase our own tonnage limitation after permission to do this." We would simply "build smaller carriers in the future to take up the slack." Put in this way there was

[49] *ibid.*, pp. 678, 680.

[50] Colonel Roosevelt's diary, Jan. 3.

Courtesy of the Office of Naval Records & Library

U. S. S. *Saratoga*, designed as a battle cruiser but converted into an aircraft carrier as provided in the Naval Limitation Treaty. Sister ship of the *Lexington*.

"very little question." The British intimated "that they would like to have permission to build equivalent ships if such turned out to be desirable." And with an understanding to this effect, the subcommittee passed on to other matters.[51]

The American conversion proposal, thus maneuvered through the expert subcommittee, struck a snag in the meeting of delegation chiefs who sat as an executive committee to discuss and amend the treaty draft prepared by a group within the American delegation. The first draft laid before this committee provided several ways in which the Powers might dispose of capital ships named in the scrapping schedule. A ship might be sunk or broken up. It might be demilitarized for use as a gunnery target, or for use as a training ship. It might be converted "to commercial use," or "to harbor use exclusively or to naval auxiliary use." And each Power might rebuild as aircraft carriers not more than two unfinished capital ships, provided these when completed did not exceed 33,000 tons and otherwise conformed to the limitations placed on carriers.

The provisions for converting capital ships to commercial, harbor, or auxiliary naval use, were of British origin. They had been drawn for the ostensible purposes of conserving as much equipment as possible, and of preventing the consequences that would follow the sudden dumping of vast quantities of scrap iron on an already depressed market. But these provisions were peculiarly susceptible of popular misconstruction. "It was of vital importance," Mr. Hughes insisted, "that nothing should be done which would tend to impair the moral value of the whole treaty. No petty economies or fancied saving would compensate the destruction of the moral value. . . . The world looked for something comparable to the destruction of the German fleet at Scapa Flow and would brook nothing which enabled these ships to be kept alive." The provisions in question would actually permit each Power to keep all its ships scheduled for scrapping. "The treaty would be judged by this one fact alone." The average man would say "the treaty was a sham"; that no ships "would be scrapped; and that in this manner they were in reality being saved to be made available immediately in case of war."[52]

[51] *ibid.*, Jan. 4.

[52] *For. Rels. 1922*, Vol. 1, pp. 168, 189*ff*.

This drew a vigorous protest from Mr. Balfour. The same argument, he held, applied with equal relevance to the American proposal to convert two battle cruisers into aircraft carriers. The British delegation had originally favored limiting this type to 25,000 tons. The Americans had raised it to 27,000 tons. Now, "on grounds of economy," they desired to build ships of 33,000 tons. If economy was a relevant argument for one country, surely it was for another.[53]

The main issue, Hughes replied, was not so much economy as the moral effect on world opinion.[54] "The American delegation was opposed to having the treaty seem to say one thing when meaning another." If necessary to accomplish this, he would favor eliminating the aircraft-carrier conversion clause along with the rest. "He would not for the sake of ten or twenty millions of dollars spoil this Treaty." And as for equality of treatment, the treaty draft left Great Britain as free as the United States to convert two of its capital ships into aircraft carriers.[55]

Theoretically, yes; but actually, no, it was held in rejoinder. Great Britain had no ships suitable for that purpose. But the British delegation would consider dropping the provisions to which the Americans objected. And they would like the latter to consider an amendment which would allow "any of the contracting Powers" within its "total tonnage" quota to build two new carriers of 33,000 tons.[56]

This led to a strenuous discussion among the American delegates, with Colonel Roosevelt sitting in as technical adviser. Hughes seemed disposed at first to strike out all the contested sections, including the paragraph on aircraft carriers. "Root and Underwood sided at once with what they believed to be his wishes, namely, to throw out the paragraph and give us no opportunity to convert any of our battle cruisers into airplane carriers." As to this, Roosevelt pointed out that it might be possible to secure funds to complete two partially built ships, but that Congress was in no mood to finance two entirely new ships. Therefore, "if we did not convert our [battle] cruisers into airplane carriers, we might just as well make up our minds that we

[53] *ibid.*, pp. 192-3.

[54] Hughes did answer Balfour on technical grounds as well. For these points, see *ibid.*, pp. 194-5.

[55] *ibid.*, pp. 196-8.

[56] *ibid.*, pp. 199-200.

would be without these all-important craft for the next decade." This argument carried the day, and it was the "sense of the meeting" that provision for conversion of these ships should be included in the treaty.[57]

From this meeting Hughes went to the committee of chief delegates to resume discussion of the treaty. "In short order," he won "assent to all our propositions to exclude conversion features with the exception of airplane carriers." As to the latter, it was agreed to draft a revised article embodying the British desire to build two new carriers comparable to the ones which the United States would secure by conversion, and to put this article in another part of the treaty separated from sections relating to the scrapping of ships.[58]

With very few exceptions, commentaries on the Washington Conference are strangely silent on this phase of the proceedings. Yet the very moderate limitations on aircraft carriers, to say nothing of the total failure to place any direct limitations on aircraft themselves, had a purport and significance as fundamental as the widely acclaimed limitation of capital ships.

The air menace potentially weakened the strategic, and hence the diplomatic position of Great Britain. As the British delegation clearly appreciated, hostile air power constituted a grave, if still inchoate, threat to the island base upon which ultimately depended the sea power of Great Britain.

Air power presented a further threat to the crowded shipping lanes in the North Sea, English Channel, Mediterranean, and eastern Atlantic. Since these sea routes all lay within reach of land-based planes, the limitation of aircraft carriers in no way protected Great Britain against the menace of future attack by air. And the possibility, however remote, of Continental air power paralyzing British sea power was a contingency which American statesmen and naval authorities could never with safety thereafter ignore.

The American people had a still more direct concern with the future of air power in the Pacific. The price paid for the ratio of 5 to 3 in capital ships, it will be recalled, was an agreement to

[57] Colonel Roosevelt's diary, Jan. 11, 12.

[58] *ibid.*, Jan. 12; *For. Rels. 1922*, Vol. 1, pp. 202*ff*.

maintain the status quo with respect to fortifications and naval bases in the western Pacific. Without modern fortified bases west of Hawaii, it would be impossible to maintain our fighting fleet in Asiatic waters. With aircraft unlimited, and with Japan in possession of the former German islands north of the equator, it would be hazardous, in case of war with Japan, for the American battle fleet even to venture into the western Pacific. Only by a *guerre de course* could either the United States or Japan strike at the sea communications of the other. Carrier-based aircraft, it was widely believed, had both defensive and offensive potentialities for such a raiding war on commerce. And it was arguable at least that the future balance of sea power in the Pacific would depend less upon capital ships than upon the relative strength of Japan and the United States in the newer weapons peculiarly adapted to a long-range cut-and-run war on commerce.

CHAPTER THIRTEEN

☆ ☆ ☆ ☆ ☆ ☆ ☆ ☆ ☆ ☆ ☆ ☆ ☆ ☆ ☆ ☆ ☆ ☆ ☆ ☆

Adventures in Treaty Drafting: Zoning the Pacific

ONE evening early in January, Senator Lodge stopped Colonel Roosevelt in the lobby of the Pan American Building where the Conference committees generally held their meetings. Lodge was considerably perturbed. He had learned that "some legal experts were shouldering their way in to consider the question of drafting the [naval] treaty." He felt that "he and the other delegates were the proper people to do this, and that no legal experts should be trusted to try their hand at it."[1]

One can only imagine what the venerable Senator from Massachusetts might have said had he known or even suspected the whole truth. For nearly a month Mr. Hughes had had a group of American experts quietly working on a draft of the naval treaty. The man with whom Lodge was conversing was the chairman of that group. And their completed first draft had been presented that very day to the legal and technical advisers of the other delegations.[2]

These events were but a phase of the unceasing struggle that went on backstage for control of the Washington Conference. That struggle had opened the preceding summer with the British Government's attempt to maneuver the United States into a preliminary meeting at London. It had continued through the pre-conference efforts of Japanese statesmen to exclude certain matters from the agenda. It had been reflected in British efforts to discover in advance the terms of the American proposal. And

[1] Colonel Roosevelt's diary, Jan. 7, 1922.
[2] *ibid.*, Dec. 21, 22, 23, 28, 29, 30, 31; Jan. 2, 3, 4, 5, 6, 7.

it was further manifest in the secret maneuvers of the various delegations to control the language of the treaties which embodied the decisions of the Conference.

As the host in charge of arrangements, the American delegation had a distinct tactical advantage. This tactical position was improved as a result of Mr. Hughes's skilful and firm management of Conference preparations and proceedings. And the advantage was held by the timely, and more or less secret formulation of a draft which became the basis of the Five Power Treaty for the Limitation of Naval Armament.

The preparation of this American draft was mainly the work of Colonel Roosevelt, Admiral Pratt, and Dr. George Grafton Wilson, professor of international law at Harvard University. This group had made considerable progress by the third week in December. When the technical staff of the British delegation proffered their own treaty project a few days later, the American draft was well along toward completion. And as a result, the Americans were in a position to reply that if the British desired "any amendments let their amendments be made to our treaty, not our amendments to their treaty."[3]

Refusal to surrender the initiative did not imply unwillingness to cooperate. Members of the American drafting group frequently consulted with the experts of the other delegations. A meeting was also arranged to give the legal and naval advisers of all five naval Powers an opportunity to state their views on the details still unsettled. Only thus, it was felt, could the Americans protect their work when it should go before the Conference for approval. Unless the treaty draft was "formulated to the last detail, everyone would take a hack at it." For, as Roosevelt trenchantly noted in his diary, "there are flocks of lawyers among the plenipotentiaries who will insert 'whereas' and 'wherefore' until it is almost impossible to tell what any article means."[4]

By January 7, the day on which the American draft was submitted to the subcommittee of experts, only a few articles remained in dispute. Most of the unsettled points were comparatively unimportant. A few, however, presented issues not of detail but of fundamental policy. And of these latter none was

[3] *ibid.*, Dec. 29.

[4] Jan. 6.

more important than the phraseology of the article limiting the development of fortifications and naval bases in the Pacific region.

The original statement, as publicly announced on December 15, had not precisely defined the "Pacific region." The British colony of Hongkong was expressly included. It was stipulated that the limitation was not to apply to the Hawaiian Islands, Australia, New Zealand, "the islands composing Japan proper, or, of course, to the coast of the United States and Canada, as to which the respective Powers retain their entire freedom."

This phraseology, while precise enough for a press release, left something to be desired as a formal statement of legal rights and obligations. What islands, for example, were to be understood as "composing Japan proper?" What were the exact geographical boundaries of the "Pacific region?" Did that region embrace the British naval base at Singapore? Did the exemption of Australia, New Zealand, and the "coasts of the United States and Canada," extend to nearby island possessions? And if so, what was the status of the Aleutian Islands which, though an integral part of Alaska, reached westward more than a thousand miles toward Japan? On the answers to these and similar questions, as much as upon the limitation of tons and guns, depended the outcome of this attempt to establish a stable relationship of sea power in the Pacific.[5]

In mid-December the Big Three—Hughes, Balfour, and Kato—seemed to be in substantial agreement as to what was intended. But the possibility of later divergent interpretations was recognized as soon as the American drafting group attempted a restatement of the verbal understanding. As early as December 21, Colonel Roosevelt was seeking instructions from Mr. Hughes. And on January 2, it was decided to let the "definite proposition . . . come from the other side." The American group would "put into the treaty [draft] an article simply repeating the verbal terms of the agreement." This would compel the others "to come forward with interpretations" and would "leave us in a stronger position."[6]

These tactics were used at the meeting on January 7, attended by the legal and naval experts of the five Powers. Colonel Roose-

[5] *For. Rels. 1922*, Vol. 1, p. 128. [6] Colonel Roosevelt's diary, Dec. 21, Jan. 2.

velt, as chairman, "simply presided," leaving the Japanese and then the British to state their respective views as to the geographical scope of the fortifications agreement.

The Japanese entered a claim to exclude from the agreement certain islands, especially the Bonins which, though distant several hundred miles from the main Japanese coast, were governed not as colonies but as an integral part of "Japan proper." The British, in their turn, claimed exemption for all islands outside a parallelogram bounded on the east by the 180th meridian (International Date Line), on the north by the thirtieth degree of latitude, on the west by the 110th meridian, and on the south by the equator—an area embracing practically all of the Japanese, most of the American, and very few of the British islands.

These two claims—the Japanese to exempt certain islands north of the equator; and the British, to exclude all islands south of the equator—stirred up a forensic tempest in the subcommittee. The British insisted that the Japanese interpretation contradicted the plain import of the previous understanding. The Japanese replied that they could not formally abridge the sovereign right to fortify any part of their homeland without involving their national honor and prestige. They would, however, give an informal promise not to fortify the particular islands thus reserved. To this the American group retorted "that we never could defend a treaty wherein we bound ourselves to obligations and left them unbound except by a gentlemen's agreement." And the meeting broke up with the issues drawn, but no acceptable compromise in sight.[7]

The subject was pursued the following day in a conversation between Colonel Roosevelt and Vice-Admiral (not Baron) Kato, chief naval adviser of the Japanese delegation. Kato reiterated that it mattered little whether his Government fortified the Bonin Islands or not. What really mattered was the prestige of Japan. He then suggested that if the American delegation "would draft a supplementary clause to the original statement, giving an explanation, it would be agreeable to them."[8]

On January 9, Mr. Balfour called on Baron Kato to solicit support for the parallelogram scheme. This had the advantage, from the Japanese point of view, of including the controverted

[7] *ibid.*, Jan. 7. [8] *ibid.*, Jan. 8.

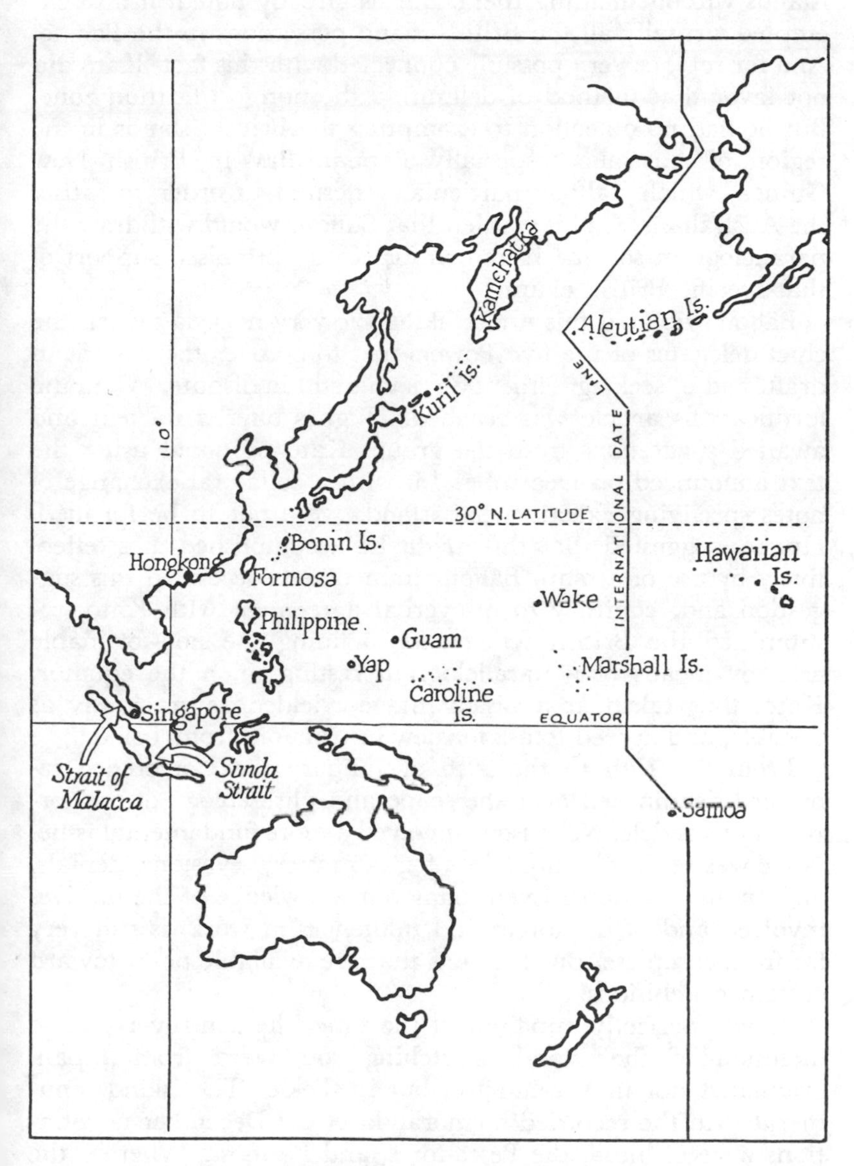

Naval Geography of the Pacific, 1922

islands without naming them. But as already noted, it also exempted virtually all the British island possessions in the Pacific. And for reasons very possibly connected with this fact, Kato did not favor that method of delimiting the non-fortification zone. But he had no objection to exempting the British islands in the region of Australia, especially Papuan Bay in British New Guinea, which Balfour particularly desired in order to satisfy the Australians. And it was left that Balfour would withdraw the parallelogram scheme in return for Kato's promised support of that specific British claim.[9]

Balfour violated this undertaking the very next day when the chief delegates of the five Powers met to go over the American draft, and to seek agreement on details still in dispute. When the fortifications article was reached, Hughes offered no text and awaited suggestions from the group. Kato proposed using the text announced on December 15, with a collateral exchange of notes specifying exactly what islands were not to be fortified. Hughes suggested that this might be accomplished most effectively by use of a map. Balfour immediately seconded this suggestion and, contrary to his verbal agreement with Kato, resubmitted the British scheme for defining the non-fortifiable area by means of a parallelogram resting upon the equator. Kato, thus taken at a disadvantage, yielded as graciously as possible, and agreed to ask for new instructions from Tokio.[10]

From the 10th to the 29th of January the Conference remained deadlocked over the scope and phraseology of the fortifications article. No episode involved a more fundamental issue. None was more obscured in a fog of mystery, evasions, denials, and circumlocutions. Even today our knowledge of the motives involved and of the forces and influences at work, is still very far from complete. But the facts that are available point toward certain conclusions.

As was perfectly apparent at the time, the controversy as to inclusion of the islands stretching southward from Japan, originated not in Washington but in Tokio. The islands enumerated in the recorded memoranda of the December negotiations were Oshima, the Pescadores, and Formosa. Whether the

[9] Yamato Ichihashi, *Washington Conference and After* (1928), p. 86. Ichihashi was present during this conversation in the rôle of interpreter.

[10] *For. Rels. 1922*, Vol. 1, pp. 150*ff.*; Ichihashi, *op. cit.*, p. 88.

Bonins were mentioned as well, no one was afterwards able to say. But Kato in January positively affirmed that "he had originally made it clear that Japan would observe the status quo" as to fortifications and naval bases in these latter as well.[11]

Whatever was expressly included in December, the purpose of the agreement was perfectly obvious. By removing the threat of large-scale naval developments in the American islands of Guam and the Philippines, the Japanese Government felt safe in accepting a capital-ship ratio of 6 to 10 instead of 7 to 10. But this concession from the United States expressly and necessarily assumed a comparable sacrifice on the part of Japan. Fortification of the island screen stretching southward from Japan would give that country's Navy an even tighter grip on the sea communications of the far western Pacific. It would move the strategic frontier of Japan several hundred miles nearer to the Philippines, rendering these islands still more vulnerable to attack, especially to attack by air.[12]

All this was as obvious in Tokio as it was in Washington. It was perfectly clear that the American Government would never have agreed to the status quo in the Philippines, with Japan left free to build military works in the islands lying between. It was everywhere understood that the announcement of December 15 included those islands. The Tokio Cabinet had approved that agreement, or at least tacitly acquiesced in it. Then, over two weeks later, the Japanese delegation received instructions that Oshima and the Bonins were outside the agreement since these were among the "islands composing Japan proper," and hence exempt from the limitation.[13]

The reasons for this move are not altogether clear, for the Japanese Government has never published its side of the story. Baron Kato regarded it as a personal attack on himself instituted by his political enemies with a view to embarrassing him in his relations at Washington.[14] This was undoubtedly a factor, for it was well known that an influential group in Japan was opposed to the Conference and all its works. But there is some reason to believe that dissatisfaction in Tokio arose in part from certain supplementary motives.

[11] *For. Rels. 1922*, Vol. 1, pp. 74, 76, 77, 78, 91, 93, 150, 246-7.
[12] For the views of the General Board, see *New York Times*, Jan. 12, 1922, p. 3.
[13] See Ichihashi, *Washington Conference*, pp. 84-5. [14] *ibid.*, pp. 85-6.

The announcement of December 15 left in doubt the status of the Aleutian Islands off the coast of Alaska. These islands contained sites for naval and air bases well within 2,000 miles of the industrial heart of Japan. Yet there was some disposition in the United States to regard them "as part of the American mainland," and hence susceptible of no limitation.[15]

The December negotiations and announcement were likewise silent as to Singapore. This port in the Malacca Strait dominated not only the East Indies but also the main passage into the Indian Ocean. It had long been a subsidiary naval base of Great Britain. There were reports that the British Government was contemplating a much larger future development there. And in November 1921, while the Washington Conference was in session, Lord Northcliffe, British newspaper magnate, widely regarded as an unofficial spokesman for the Government, had publicly intimated that Singapore should "be available" for the American Navy "if the United States is ever menaced in the Far East. . . ."[16]

Development of a military stronghold at Singapore, it is true, would not constitute a serious strategic threat to the main islands of Japan. The distance from Singapore to those islands was over 3,000 miles. But that was not the only aspect. In case of war with the United States, Japan would become absolutely dependent upon East Indian fuel and raw materials. And the Sunda and Malacca Straits would in such an emergency become Japan's only commercial exits from the Pacific.[17]

British attempts to escape the limitations of the fortifications agreement seem likewise to have arisen from strategic as well as from political considerations. As noted in an earlier chapter,[18] the World War weakened or destroyed the sea power of every European country except Great Britain. The British fleet was no longer chained to the North Sea. British statesmen and naval authorities could now reexamine the problem of empire defense, and redispose their naval forces in accord with the conclusions reached.

Studies to this end were instituted almost immediately following the armistice of November 1918. In February 1919 Admiral Lord Jellicoe, British commander in chief at the Battle of Jutland,

[15] See, for example, *New York Herald*, Jan. 17, 1922, p. 2.

[16] *New York Times*, Nov. 20, 1921, p. 9.

[17] See, for example, *New York Herald*, Jan. 14, 1922, p. 2.

[18] See pp. 38*ff.*, *supra*.

toured the Empire to consult with Dominion authorities and to formulate a plan of imperial defense. His report recommended stationing in the Pacific a fighting fleet of eight battleships, eight battle cruisers, and the necessary auxiliary craft. It also contained the further recommendation that Singapore be developed into a first-class base fully adequate for the needs of such a fleet in war as well as in peace.

The Washington Conference intervened while the British Government was still awaiting final action by the Dominions. But the Imperial Conference in June 1921 had ratified the decision to go ahead at Singapore. And this decision, strongly supported in the Pacific Dominions, was known to the other naval Powers when the subject of fortifications and naval bases arose at Washington.[19]

The Singapore project, however, did not enter into the negotiations leading up to the verbal agreement of December 15. Balfour expressly excepted Australia and New Zealand, but included Hongkong and "other [British] islands in the Pacific." And neither Singapore nor certain nebulous projects centering in the islands north of Australia and New Zealand were even mentioned until questions arose as to the definitive text of the fortifications article.[20]

Then, apparently in compliance with Dominion views, the British delegation offered the novel interpretation that the agreement announced on December 15 was not intended to apply to islands lying south of the equator or west of the 110th meridian. And the parallelogram of latitude and longitude, first introduced on January 7 in the meeting of the expert subcommittee, was the artistic package in which this interpretation was wrapped.

The British claim was supported on several grounds. Singapore, it was contended with some justification, lay in the Indian Ocean quite outside the "Pacific region." The fortifications agreement, it was recalled, had grown out of a peculiarly Japanese-American difficulty, in which Great Britain had been little more than a casually interested bystander. On January 17 the British delegation went so far as to issue a public statement

[19] R. A. Chaput, *Disarmament in British Foreign Policy* (1935), pp. 91, 151.
[20] *For. Rels. 1922*, Vol. 1, pp. 74, 76, 77, 78, 91, 93.

in which it was asserted, absolutely contrary to fact, that they had made no commitment whatever respecting any British possession other than Hongkong. And in any case, it was further contended, "Australia and New Zealand were never in the agreement" and could no more be bound without their consent than could any other "sovereign nation."[21]

Meanwhile, on the 17th, Kato had brought Hughes the answer from Tokio. The Japanese Government "would not agree to the British proposal with regard to the fortifications in the Pacific." But Kato hoped he could secure a reconsideration, and to that end he asked that Hughes postpone further meetings on the naval treaty for a few days.[22]

On January 22, Kato had to acknowledge failure. The question, he told Hughes, "had taken a political turn in Japan." As things now stood, acceptance of the British proposal would cause the Tokio Cabinet to fall. And if that occurred, no treaty whatever could be ratified. The problem was to devise some new formula which would embody the substance of the December agreement in language acceptable to the Japanese Government. As a possible means of resolving the difficulty, Kato suggested simply naming the Japanese islands in which there was to be no increase of fortifications, and the British and American islands in which the limitation was not to apply.[23]

Kato's "circumlocution" was submitted to the American technical staff who approved the idea in principle, but suggested a number of changes which were submitted in turn to the four American delegates. These latter promptly ratified a qualifying phrase which would prohibit Japan from fortifying any islands thereafter acquired. They also approved a verbal change designed to forestall any possible objection to the opening of purely commercial ship-repair yards in the Philippines. But the American delegates overruled the proposal of their experts to exclude Samoa from the limitation on fortifications and naval bases.[24]

The British delegation likewise accepted Kato's counterproposal with qualifications. The parallelogram formula was dropped, as was the claim to exclude all islands south of the equator. But they claimed specific exemption for islands "adja-

[21] *New York Times*, Jan. 18, 1922, p. 2.
[22] *For. Rels. 1922*, Vol. 1, pp. 245-6.
[23] Colonel Roosevelt's diary, Jan. 22.
[24] *ibid.*, Jan. 22, 23.

cent" to Canada, Australia, and New Zealand. And Singapore was tacitly excluded by restricting the limitation on Great Britain to islands east of the 110th meridian. These changes gave the British a large part of what they had previously demanded, though not enough to suit the naval experts of the British delegation. But Balfour overruled his experts; the revised article was redrafted to embody the British and American exceptions; and Kato cabled it to Tokio for approval.[25]

After further delay, aggravated by a breakdown of the trans-Pacific cable, the reply came back from Tokio, and was communicated to Hughes about noon on Sunday, January 29. The Japanese Government acquiesced in the exceptions and qualifications proposed, with one condition. They were willing to extend the fortifications agreement to their Kurile Islands, extending northward from Japan proper toward the Kamchatka Peninsula. And in return they desired also to include the Aleutian Islands of the United States.

This caused further discussion. American experts envisaged the possibility of undertaking naval developments in the Aleutians, especially at Dutch Harbor. But the pressure for agreement was strong. The concession was granted. The Conference cleared the last hurdle that stood in the way of delimiting national zones of strategic dominance in the Pacific, and Colonel Roosevelt, looking back over the negotiations, recorded in his diary:

The fortifications agreement, "leaves us, in my opinion, in a slightly better position than Japan. We trade certain fortifications which we would never have completed, for fortifications which they [the Japanese] would have unquestionably completed. We retain one outpost in the Pacific of great importance [i.e. Hawaii] and they give up all but their mainland."[26]

Naval Limitation and a New Order in Asia

We come finally to the political questions which had a vital bearing on the later stages of the naval negotiations. The Far Eastern crisis which was part of the World War, and which had continued afterward has been described in previous chapters. It is sufficient to recall here that the United States from 1918 to 1921 was pressing Japan to withdraw from Siberia, to restore

[25] *ibid.*, Jan. 23.

[26] Jan. 29, 30.

Shantung to China, to relax its grip on Manchuria, to renounce ambitions incompatible with the open door and with the integrity of China, and to recognize American claims as to cable privileges in the Island of Yap.

The almost total frustration of these efforts had progressively embittered the relations of Japan and the United States. Various journalists and other observers openly predicted war between the two in the near future. American naval authorities framed their plans with that contingency ever in view. And it was widely believed that the Washington Conference could make little headway toward arms limitation unless it could simultaneously bring about marked improvement in political relations throughout the Pacific.

As previously shown, the Four Power Treaty, which superseded the Anglo-Japanese Alliance, made possible the fortifications agreement which in turn cleared the way for Japan's acquiescence in the capital-ship ratio of 3 to 5. The teapot tempest over the Island of Yap was also quieted in December by an agreement, later embodied in a formal treaty, in which the United States at last recognized Japan's mandate over the former German islands north of the equator, in return for commercial rights in those islands, and for special cable-landing rights in Yap.

The problems of eastern Asia, however, presented greater difficulties. Weeks passed with little perceptible progress. Early in January it was rumored that the United States Government welcomed the delay over the fortifications article, since it gave further time for the Far Eastern negotiations. According to another rumor, the American delegation intended to "withhold their final promise not to build the world's biggest fleet until" Japan came to terms on Shantung, Siberia, and Manchuria. Still another rumor accredited the Japanese Government itself with procrastinating on the fortifications article until assured that the Western Powers would not encroach too seriously on Japan's asserted interests in eastern Asia. And under the headline, "NAVAL TREATY AWAITS AGREEMENT ON EAST," the Washington correspondent of the *New York Times* stated on January 20, that there was "good reason to believe" that both sides were acting in accord with a "tacit agreement . . . to let the naval treaty rest" until they had made "further progress on the Far Eastern negotiations."[27]

Where there is much smoke there is likely to be some fire. And so it was in this instance. At a meeting of the American delegation on January 13, one of those present urged "what has been said by so many . . . namely, the advisability of delaying the signing of the naval treaty until the Far Eastern questions have been decided." Though doubt was expressed as to the possibility of doing this, it was informally agreed to "delay all final action as long as possible."

Meanwhile, it was disclosed, the Administration was attempting indirectly to expedite the Far Eastern negotiations. For this purpose the good offices of Mr. Balfour had again been utilized. On behalf of the United States, he had informed the Japanese that failure to reach "an agreement . . . on a number of these important questions" would have disquieting repercussions in America. Such failure, indeed, might even jeopardize the naval treaty's chance of ratification.[28]

A week later, the Senate sounded an unexpected warning to much the same effect. This warning was in the form of a quite spontaneous debate on a resolution, introduced by Senator Walsh of Montana, which requested information as to the progress of negotiations on Shantung. This move took the Conference Senators, Lodge and Underwood, by surprise. And before they could get the situation under control, enough had been said to show what lay in store for the Administration in case they presented the Senate with a naval treaty unaccompanied by a settlement of Far Eastern questions.[29]

This incident, as well as accumulating indications that it would be impossible to hold the Conference together much longer, seem to have provided the stimulus necessary to bring the Japanese and American Governments together in a series of compromises on the Far East. The atmosphere was somewhat cleared by a Japanese declaration promising early withdrawal from Siberia. Some progress was made toward redefining foreign rights and interests in China, and toward freeing that disunited country from the strait jacket of extraterritoriality and a fixed

[27] *New York Times*, Jan. 11, 1922, pp. 1, 2; Jan. 21, p. 4; Jan. 25, p. 1.
[28] Colonel Roosevelt's diary, Jan. 13.
[29] 67 Cong. 2 Sess., *Cong. Rec.*, Vol. 62, pp. 1432*ff*.

customs tariff. The long-standing Shantung controversy which had so agitated American opinion, was finally compromised in a manner fairly acceptable to Japan and to the Western Powers if not to China. And in the closing days of the Conference, all the countries there represented came to an agreement, embodied in the so-called Nine Power Treaty, in which they solemnly engaged to observe the principle of the open door and to respect the territorial integrity of China.

Whether the American delegation actually held up the naval treaty for a single day in order to bring about these results, it is impossible conclusively to say. But we do know that it was Japanese, and to some extent British, procrastination, not American, which delayed final action on the fortifications article for nearly a month. And we know also that the naval treaty was whipped into shape and formally announced in plenary session less than three days after the final word from Tokio was communicated to Mr. Hughes in Washington.[30]

Whether breakdown of the Far Eastern negotiations would have blocked American adherence to the naval treaty, one can only conjecture. That an appearance of success in these negotiations had a vital bearing on popular and senatorial reception of the naval treaty was certainly believed in American official circles. And as events had shown, and were further to show, the members of the American delegation just as certainly regarded the treaties, resolutions, and declarations relating to eastern Asia, no less than the Four Power Treaty covering island possessions, as foundation stones of the new order of sea power in the Pacific.

[30] Colonel Roosevelt's diary, Jan. 29, Feb. 1.

CHAPTER FOURTEEN

Nationalism with a Difference: Contemporary Verdicts on the Washington Conference

"THE NEW CHARTER OF PEACE"

ON Wednesday morning, February 1, 1922, the Washington Conference met in plenary session, the fifth since that memorable opening day nearly three months before. Like that opening session, this too was a colorful occasion. The various delegations once more arrived in automobiles escorted with military pomp and circumstance through cheering crowds of curious onlookers. As before, the auditorium of Memorial Continental Hall was filled to capacity with men and women of official or social prominence.

But there were also points of difference and contrast. Prince Tokugawa, Premier Briand, Admiral Earl Beatty, and other notables had returned to their respective countries. The principal delegates showed signs of the strain they had been undergoing for almost twelve weeks.[1] The audience was "lackadaisical" in marked contrast to the alertness and expectancy of the opening session. Everyone knew substantially what was going to happen, and before the end "50 per cent of the crowd had melted away."[2]

But this occasion, if somewhat less dramatic than the opening session of the Conference, was none the less historic. It began with the formal reading and adoption of resolutions affirming, in general and in particular, the open door and the territorial integrity of China. The Shantung compromise was announced and well received. And Mr. Balfour made a graceful gesture of pro-

[1] Louis Siebold, in *New York Herald*, Feb. 2, 1922, pp. 1-2.
[2] Colonel Roosevelt's diary, Feb. 1.

posing to surrender the British leased naval base at Weihaiwei, also in Shantung, on the same terms as those on which the Japanese had agreed to give up their holdings in that province.[3]

All this, however, was preliminary to the formal public announcement of the Naval Limitation Treaty which Mr. Hughes characterized as an extraordinary and significant agreement. Indeed, he declared, "no more extraordinary or significant Treaty has ever been made." We no longer merely "talk of the desirability of diminishing the burdens of naval armaments, but actually diminish them. . . . This Treaty ends, absolutely ends, the race in competition of naval armament. At the same time it leaves the relative security of the great naval Powers unimpaired. . . . We are taking perhaps the greatest forward step in history to establish the reign of peace."[4]

Three days later the Conference met again in plenary session, this time to approve the final draft of the Nine Power Treaty and other acts relating to China. On this occasion, exactly twelve weeks to the hour from the memorable opening session, Mr. Balfour arose to give his estimate of what had been achieved. He recalled the "spirit of deep anxiety" which "only a few months ago . . . overshadowed the mind of every man who contemplated the state of public feeling in the great Pacific area."

You will remember, he continued, "that . . . although the world was still bleeding from recent wounds, although every nation was groaning under the pressure of taxation, nevertheless men claiming the gift of foresight talked glibly about inevitable wars to come, while the great maritime Powers felt that they were almost committed to that fatal rivalry of shipbuilding which meant not only ruin to the finances of the world, but was a standing menace to its peace. I am not talking about ancient history. I am talking about a state of things which was prevalent within the last twelve months, and indeed on the very eve of the Conference itself."

Since then a miraculous change had occurred. "Confidence has taken the place of mistrust." The Conference, Balfour believed, had inaugurated a "new era . . . for the whole world, but more than anywhere else for that part of the world in which

[3] "The gesture was graceful, but all of us knew that England did not desire to keep it any longer and had no use of it." Colonel Roosevelt's diary.

[4] *Conference on Limitation of Armament*, pp. 228, 248.

the great maritime Powers are most intimately and deeply concerned." This change he attributed to three achievements. The first was the new charter of non-aggression in the Far East. The second was the Four Power Treaty of non-aggression covering island possessions in the Pacific. The third was the reduction of fighting fleets and the "cessation of rival building between the great maritime Powers."

These three, Balfour held, were all interrelated. One could not be judged without taking the others into account. Together they constituted a result "unique in history"—"the diminution of armaments, and with the diminution of armaments a corresponding diminution in the likelihood of armaments being ever required."[5]

Baron Shidehara expressed a similar sentiment on behalf of Japan. He rejoiced that "competition in naval armament, ruinous to national welfare and harmful to international peace, is now a matter of the past." The naval limitation treaty, the submarine treaty "for the suppression of the brutal practices of warfare," the agreements "relating to China" in general and to Shantung in particular, the adjustment of the "difficult question of the Pacific mandates," and the Four Power Treaty—all contributed to relieving the tension. "Freed from suspicion by frankness, assured of peace by good will, we may devoutly give thanks," he concluded, "for the opportunity given by the Washington Conference which, we believe, ushers into a troubled world a new spirit of international friendship and good understanding."[6]

The Italian delegation likewise joined in the chorus of thanksgiving. "We welcome these agreements, and especially the Naval Treaty, with the greatest satisfaction," declared Senator Schanzer. In these he saw the "first decisive step . . . toward eliminating the danger of future wars and creating more solid foundations for the financial policy of the great nations." And though the Conference had not succeeded in limiting all weapons, especially the newer ones, he felt confident that no country would wish to assume the moral responsibility for instituting competition in these legally unlimited weapons.[7]

[5] *ibid.*, pp. 362*ff.*
[6] *ibid.*, p. 380.
[7] *ibid.*, p. 274.

The French delegation alone voiced doubts as to the future. The French Government, M. Sarraut announced, sincerely and confidently joined in the reduction and limitation of naval armament. Recent imputations and insinuations did France a grave injustice. No country had suffered more in the late war; none had a greater desire for peace. But lasting peace would prevail and the peril of war would vanish "only when those who may still feel tempted to unleash the horrors of conflict know that they can no longer do so with impunity. . . . It might even be feared that the mere example set to the world by the reduction of armament would not have in itself sufficient virtue and force to bring peace to mankind." But even if the Conference had not positively assured a "lasting world peace, it has evoked on the horizon a dawn which already promises to mankind a more radiant hope." And with this thought, France took her "place with all her friends at the side of America, whose splendid initiative will have made it possible to give to the universe that great peace of right" in which the nations could "live in liberty, love, and prosperity."[8]

Few if any seemed to take very seriously the anxieties and misgivings of France. The dominant note was one of confidence and optimism. And with his remarkable faculty for putting a mass emotional experience into words, President Harding eloquently summed up the sense of the moment when he told the Conference at its closing session on February 6, "that the faith plighted here today, kept in national honor, will mark the beginning of a new and better epoch in human affairs." For the first time, representatives of the Great Powers had positively declared the "utter futility" of war "and challenged the sanity of competitive preparation for each other's destruction. . . . It is all so fine, so gratifying, so full of promise," he concluded, "that above the murmurings of a world sorrow not yet silenced; above the groans which come of excessive burdens not yet lifted but soon to be lightened; above the discouragements of a world yet struggling to find itself after surpassing upheaval, there is the note of rejoicing which is not alone ours or yours, or of all of us, but comes from the hearts of men of all the world."[9]

[8] *ibid.*, pp. 248-58.

[9] *ibid.*, pp. 396*ff*.

THE ADMINISTRATION'S VERDICT ON THE CONFERENCE

A few days after the close of the Conference, President Harding submitted the Washington Treaties to the Senate. The formal report of the American delegation accompanied them. And it is in the final pages of this document that one finds the Administration's deliberate and carefully phrased judgment on the politico-naval results of the Conference.

The Administration's case for ratification rested on the proposition that the treaties, resolutions, and declarations of the Conference "should be considered as a whole." Each contributed "in combination with the others towards the establishment of conditions in which peaceful security will take the place of competitive preparation for war." The Conference had met for the "declared object" of stopping a competition in building warships "distressingly like the competition that immediately preceded the war of 1914." That competition had arisen from a state of mind in which "expectation of attack" stimulated "preparations to meet the attack." To break the vicious circle of armament competition, it was first necessary "to deal with the state of mind" from which it sprang. "A belief in the pacific intentions of other Powers must be substituted for suspicion and apprehension."

The Four Power Treaty was the means of creating "that new state of mind" in relation to the Pacific region. "It terminated the Anglo-Japanese Alliance and substituted friendly conference in place of war as the first reaction from any controversies which might arise" in that area. "It would not have been possible except as part of a plan including a limitation and a reduction of naval armaments; but that limitation and reduction would not have been possible without the new relations established by the Four Power Treaty or something equivalent to it."

But the "new relations declared in the Four Power Treaty could not . . . inspire confidence or be reasonably assured of continuance without a specific understanding as to the relations of the Powers to China." This had been achieved through the Nine Power Treaty and through supplementary treaties, resolutions, and declarations. "The sum total" of these justified the assumption of "confidence and good will expressed in the Four

Power Treaty and upon which the reduction of armament in the Naval Treaty may be contemplated with a sense of security."[10]

The valedictory orations delivered in the closing plenary sessions and the formal report of the American delegation stimulated widespread comment and discussion on the results of the Washington Conference. What had actually been accomplished? What benefits, if any, had each country derived? What liabilities had each incurred? And what did it all signify as to the future bearing of sea power on world politics and world order?

Any comprehensive survey of public opinion on these and similar questions would itself require a sizable volume. Statesmen, journalists, publicists, clergymen, historians, political scientists, civilian and professional military experts, and many others contributed to the flood of critical literature which poured from the printing presses during the ensuing months. Although it is manifestly impracticable to deal comprehensively with this literature in the limited space here available, it would be impossible to judge the politico-naval results of the Conference wholly apart from the storm of controversy which raged around the Washington Treaties both in this country and abroad.

The Reaction in France

Broadly speaking, Frenchmen viewed the Washington Conference with disappointment and a sense of frustration. The French delegation had gone to Washington, hoping to play the rôle of mediator between England and America, and thereby to revive the defunct military guarantees which Lloyd George and Wilson had offered France at the Paris Peace Conference. They had found no desire for their good offices, and no inclination even to take very seriously the apprehensions of France over the danger of German revenge.

French commentators paid high verbal tribute to Mr. Hughes and his associates for skilful management of the Conference, and for renunciation, in the interest of world peace, of a naval primacy almost within their grasp. Some at least were frank to admit that France had been poorly represented after the first week

[10] 67 Cong. 2 Sess., *Sen. Docs.* No. 126, pp. 865-7. The texts of the principal treaties are printed in Appendix B, *infra.*

of the Conference, and that the French delegation had made serious tactical blunders. But such thoughts did not relieve their disappointment over the total failure of the "present directors of the United States" to appreciate that the security of France was the cornerstone of a durable peace in Europe.[11]

On the naval side, French experts and publicists deeply resented their relegation to the rank of a secondary Power. The points which Sarraut and De Bon had argued in the Conference, were iterated and reiterated. With rising indignation, Frenchmen repudiated British insinuations that France desired a strong navy to support a program of aggression and imperialism. France was not an imperialistic country, though France like England possessed a world-wide empire whose security depended upon sea power. France indeed was more vulnerable than England, for France had land frontiers the defense of which depended on secure water communications with northern Africa whence came a substantial portion of the French army. Since France could never concentrate its entire naval strength in the Mediterranean, mathematical parity with Italy would give the latter actual superiority over the vital line of communications from Europe to northern Africa, a result intolerable to France. And with capital-ship and aircraft-carrier tonnage rigidly limited on the basis of parity with Italy, France had no alternative but to seek security by means of cruisers, destroyers, submarines, shore-based aircraft, and other instruments of power still available.[12]

The Reaction in Japan

Japanese comment ranged all the way from moderate praise to bitter denunciation. Professional naval opinion was hostile in the extreme. The Japanese delegates, it was argued, had sacrificed the Anglo-Japanese Alliance, tied Japan's hands in the western Pacific and Far East, and accepted a dangerously inferior ratio of naval strength. Japan was henceforth vulnerable

[11] From a survey of French press opinion made immediately after the Conference adjourned. *New York Times*, Feb. 8, 1922, p. 2.

[12] See, for example, "L'Accord Naval," *Le Temps*, Feb. 4, 1922, p. 1; Admiral Degouy, "Après Washington et Après Gènes," *Revue des Deux Mondes*, June 1922, pp. 639-66; René La Bruyère, "French Naval Ideas," *Atlantic Monthly*, Vol. 129, June 1922, pp. 826-33.

to Anglo-American attack. And owing to an asserted superiority of American capital ships, the ratio of three to five failed to express the full measure of Japan's inferiority of fighting strength.[13]

Nationalistic editors gave wide currency to these views. Japan, they asserted, had sustained a loss comparable to military defeat in war. Japan, it was alleged, had acquiesced in peaceful conquest, while Great Britain and the United States had won smashing diplomatic victories. About all Japan had gained was a "breathing space in naval competition," and that only at the cost of renouncing Japan's destiny in the Far East.[14]

In marked contrast stood the forthright opinion of Prime Minister Takahashi who publicly endorsed the Washington Treaties as a step toward "lasting peace" and toward the "total abolition of defensive equipments." Prince Tokugawa believed that the radical improvement of Japanese-American relations more than offset the sacrifices made. Japanese "commercial circles" were reported to be enthusiastic over the results achieved, which promised improved trade relations with China and the United States.[15]

Contending that hostile critics represented only a small section of Japanese opinion, Professor Toyokichi Iyenaga declared that "the large majority of the Japanese people" rejoiced in the prospective diversion of capital from armaments to "educational and productive purposes," as well as in the promise of peace and friendly relations with other nations.[16] And Professor Yamato Ichihashi concluded, after thorough investigation, that lay opinion in Japan, as in England and America, tended on the whole to view the results achieved as a "step toward progress, national and international," promising relief from the fiscal burden of uncontrolled navalism, and a probable stimulus to "productive enterprise. . . ."[17]

[13] Yamato Ichihashi, *The Washington Conference and After* (1928), pp. 144-5.

[14] Summarized from Japanese press opinion quoted in *Literary Digest*, Vol. 72. March 25, 1922, pp. 19-20; and Toyokichi Iyenaga, "How Japan Views the Arms Conference," *Current History*, Vol. 16, April 1922, pp. 22-5.

[15] *New York Times*, Feb. 9, 1922, p. 2; March 1, p. 2.

[16] "How Japan Views the Arms Conference," p. 23.

[17] *Washington Conference*, p. 146.

"HANDS ACROSS THE SEA"

British comment presented similar contrasts, though with civilian opinion somewhat more solidly aligned in support of the Washington Treaties. The semiofficial *Times* of London printed columns of almost lyrical praise. February 1, the day on which the Conference met in plenary session to approve the Naval Treaty, promised "to be a great day for all time in the history of the world." The results achieved at Washington showed "what sincerity and good-will can accomplish when they are directed by sound judgment within a strictly limited field and with perfectly clear and definite objects of a concrete kind which are in harmony with the common principles and the common interests of all who assemble to debate them."[18]

The *Daily Telegraph*, Conservative London paper, found cause for great satisfaction in the psychological and material results of the Conference. One might question whether armaments produced wars. But there could be no doubt that "an atmosphere in which [arms] competition is engendered is politically unhealthy and makes for financial and commercial instability. Humanity urgently needs a rest from the alarms of the past if the problems of economic reconstruction are to be attacked in the right spirit and with full energy."[19]

The *Daily Chronicle*, Liberal London daily, was also generous in its praise. The *Manchester Guardian Weekly*, another organ of English Liberal opinion, declared that "the Conference has made a unique contribution to world peace . . . drawn close the English-speaking peoples and . . . given America more confidence in Europe."[20] The London *Outlook* found the "news from Washington . . . magnificent."[21] And so did many, perhaps the vast majority of articulate Englishmen.[22] But not all!

Some, recognizing the futility of naval competition with the United States, bowed to the inevitable, though with manifest

[18] Feb. 2, p. 11; and to the same effect, *ibid.*, Feb. 8, p. 11.

[19] Quoted in *New York Times*, Feb. 5, p. 2.

[20] Feb. 10, p. 101; and *New York Times*, Feb. 6, p. 2.

[21] Vol. 49, Feb. 4, 1922, p. 83.

[22] For examples of Dominion opinion, see F. W. Eggleston, "Washington and After, an Australian View," in *Nineteenth Century*, Vol. 92, Sept. 1922, pp. 455, 461-3; E. E. Braithwaite, "The Dawn of a New Era," *Canadian Magazine*, Vol. 58, pp. 325*ff*., 328.

misgivings. Typical of these was Archibald Hurd, coeditor of *Brassey's Naval Annual.* "After hundreds of years," he noted with regretful resignation, "we have dipped our flag as the one supreme sea Power, having supplied [in the late war] a vindication of the benevolent purpose of the British fleet, which formed a fitting end to a glorious chapter of our history." As a result of the Washington Conference, "the trident of Neptune passes into the joint guardianship of the English-speaking peoples. . . ." And while Englishmen might view this result with misgiving, it was preferable to the expenditure of vast sums in a vain effort to outbuild Japan and the United States.[23]

Others were not so resigned. England's "flabby, fluid, fluctuating" Cabinet was roundly rebuked by one journal for its humiliating acquiescence in the arms proposals of the United States.[24] The Conference was denounced in another as a long step toward the universal hegemony of Washington and Wall Street. President Harding was cynically congratulated on having achieved "the bloodless surrender of the world's greatest Empire, and its deletion as an effective voice at other than parochial conferences."[25]

However, for the concentrated essence of reactionary British dissatisfaction with the Treaties, one must go to Admiral Sir Rosslyn Wester-Wemyss, former First Sea Lord, and Admiral Benson's chief antagonist at the so-called "naval battle of Paris" described in an earlier chapter.[26] In a polemical essay, published simultaneously in England and in France, this hard-hitting advocate of the old order of sea power bitterly criticized the British Government's course at Washington.[27]

The outstanding result of the Conference he declared to be England's voluntary surrender of that naval supremacy which had constituted the cornerstone of British statecraft for "more than three hundred years." This was "an act of renunciation unparalleled . . . in history." Whatever the arguments for

[23] "The British Fleet 'Dips Its Ensign,'" *Fortnightly Review,* Vol. 117, March 1922, pp. 396*ff*.

[24] *Saturday Review* (London), Vol. 133, Feb. 11, 1922, p. 137.

[25] C. H. Douglas, "The World after Washington," *English Review,* Vol. 34, March 1922, pp. 260*ff*.

[26] pp. 62*ff*., *supra.*

[27] "Washington: and After," *Nineteenth Century,* Vol. 91, March 1922, pp. 405*ff*.; *La Revue de Paris,* 29 pt. 2, March 1, 1922, pp. 143*ff*.

taking such a step, it could "only fill with regret and even dismay those who realize its potentialities." British policy had lost its "strongest driving power." England's voice would "no longer carry the same weight as heretofore" in the "councils of the nations." With the loss of authority went a corresponding loss of prestige. Great Britain, in short, had won the late war on the sea only to lose it at the conference table—"truly a paradoxical result of the greatest victory" in history.

France too had suffered at Washington. French insistence on military guarantees as the price of reducing land armaments, and on large submarine and other auxiliary naval forces, had "drawn down upon her head much undeserved abuse." Owing in no small degree to the conduct of the British delegation, "France comes away from Washington with an unmerited reputation of being unreasonable and reactionary."

"The check to Japan's rising naval power" was another "striking feature of the Conference." Japan's insular position, over-population, exclusion from the United States and the British Empire, and growing interests on the Asiatic mainland, all tended to foster naval expansion. Japanese statesmen could not "have assented to the American proposals without considerable misgivings. . . ."

Wemyss also had doubts regarding the Pacific and Far Eastern Treaties. "If events should prove that [Japan's] limited navy is insufficient for the purpose for which it was created, there will arise in Japan a spirit of bitterness which may prove a serious peril to the future of the Four Power Pact." Furthermore, the agreements respecting China ignored the "intolerable state" into which that country was "rapidly falling." The time did not seem distant "when foreign intervention may become inevitable." And if outside intervention should become necessary to restore "law and order in China," Japan was the country "to which, by racial propinquity and geographical position, the task would seem naturally to fall."

The United States, in contrast to Great Britain, France, and Japan, "emerged from the Conference conscious of having gained the substance of all they desire. They have rid themselves of a vast and ruinous ship-building program without giving up the object for which it was projected; they have secured a general ratio of naval strength which leaves them free from anxiety in all quarters; and they have attained an equality with the first naval Power with a minimum of effort."

For all this, Wemyss could discover no political or strategic justification. That American statesmen would use their power "for the preservation of peace is an ideal which they surely aspire to, but circumstances change, ideas alter, and generations differ from one another; the blessing of today may be the curse of tomorrow. . . . Time alone will show."

The United States Navy's Verdict on the Conference

The conclusions of Admiral Wester-Wemyss are absolutely irreconcilable with the trend of American naval opinion on the Washington Conference. The Naval Treaty, as shown in several previous connections, departed in various important respects from the recommendations of American naval authorities. The General Board, as we have seen, considered a two-Power standard—naval strength equal to that of Great Britain and Japan combined—the irreducible minimum if the Anglo-Japanese Alliance continued in force. In case that military partnership was dissolved, the Board was ready to accept a ratio of 10:10:6, provided the battle line of the United States approximated 1,000,000 tons of capital ships. The Board was further prepared to reduce that figure to 800,000 tons, provided Japan's ratio was lowered from 60 to 50 per cent. And what was most important of all, every one of these recommendations was made expressly contingent on complete freedom to develop naval bases anywhere in the world.[28]

As finally concluded, the Naval Treaty disregarded all these recommendations. Total capital-ship tonnage was cut far below the minimum set by the General Board. The Treaty established the 10:10:6 ratio at this lower level. And it relinquished the right to increase fortifications and naval bases in the western Pacific.

Largely, though not exclusively, for these reasons, the Navy followed the Conference negotiations with growing dismay and alarm. The undercurrent of professional apprehension became perceptible in mid-November. It grew in volume and especially

[28] 71 Cong. 2 Sess. Senate Naval Committee, *Hearings on the London Naval Treaty of 1930*, pp. 436-7, 464-5, 469.

in intensity, following upon rumors and then announcement of the agreement as to fortifications and naval bases in the Pacific. And it gave rise to outspoken criticism of the Naval Treaty as finally concluded late in January 1922.[29]

A public address which Admiral H. S. Knapp delivered before the American Society of International Law in April following the Conference, was typical of the trend of naval opinion. The Service, he insisted, was not opposed to the idea of limitation—"quite the reverse." But the concessions offered in the American proposal "went further than accorded with the general sentiment of experienced officers. . . ." Asserting that he voiced an opinion generally prevailing in the Service, Knapp took exception in particular to the fortifications article. All three countries restricted by that article held territories in the western Pacific. Japan and Great Britain already possessed well equipped naval stations either within or near the restricted area. We alone had none, though he believed our need to be the greatest of all.

"Naval opinion, in accepting the 5 to 3 ratio of floating strength between the United States and Japan," Knapp held, had done so "on the basis of the status quo of sovereign right—not the status quo of insular fortifications, naval bases, and naval facilities." Navy men "had no idea that the latter, if proposed, would be entertained, or the former be yielded. . . . For the defense of our Pacific islands, and with no idea of aggression whatever, secure and well provided naval bases are necessary. To surrender the right to go beyond the status quo is to make the defense of our western possessions . . . well-nigh hopeless in case of need. . . ."

Article 19, Knapp continued, "fatally impairs for the United States the 5 to 3 ratio of floating strength with Japan in so far as the western Pacific is concerned. The United States has yielded the possibility of naval equality in that region. . . . Our military prestige has received a blow; and with the waning of military prestige political prestige is likely to wane also. The Treaty may very well mark the beginning of a decreased influence in the Far East, with attendant loss to our proper, if selfish, trade

[29] See, for example, *New York Herald*, Nov. 14, 1921, pp. 1, 2, 3; Nov. 15, p. 2; Nov. 16, p. 5; Dec. 13, p. 17; Dec. 19, p. 2; *New York Times*, Nov. 19, pp. 1, 2; Nov. 30, p. 2; *Army and Navy Journal*, Vol. 59, Dec. 17, p. 371; Dec. 31, p. 419; Feb. 11, 1922, p. 563; Feb. 25, p. 611; March 18, p. 683.

interests, and to our altruistic purposes for China and Siberia." In short, from a purely military standpoint (and he did not deny that there were "other considerations"), the United States in Knapp's opinion, sacrificed much and gained little from the Naval Treaty.[30]

Admiral B. A. Fiske supported and elaborated this conclusion in an article written in reply to Admiral Wemyss. The Naval Treaty failed, in Fiske's judgment, to give the United States parity with Great Britain. The latter still ranked ahead. Capital-ship tonnage was not the only index of sea power. British naval personnel was superior and more numerous. British naval material was greater in quantity and better in quality. And the restrictions imposed on the use of submarines would distinctly benefit England and impede the United States in any future conflict upon the sea.

Japan also, in Fiske's judgment, came off better than the United States. For us to attempt "to make war on Japan with the relative naval forces allotted by the Treaty would be an act of folly." The theater of such a war would have to lie in the western Pacific, since Japan could not attack in the eastern Pacific. The Japanese, if they so desired, could keep their capital ships safe behind mine fields, and "attack with submarines and airplanes any ships that we might send near" their coast. In short, the situation "would be much like that of Great Britain and Germany" in the late war, "but with one paramount difference." The British fleet was never more than 300 miles from its nearest base, "while we should have no bases less than 6,000 miles away, except a most inadequate one in Hawaii, 4,000 miles away."[31]

These views were most thoroughly developed by Captain D. W. Knox whose candid little book, *The Eclipse of American Sea Power*, is perhaps the classic statement of American Service opinion on the Washington Conference.[32] Knox recognized that we had derived some benefit from cancellation of the Anglo-Japanese Alliance, though he found it difficult to envisage Great Britain siding with Japan in a war on the United States. The Conference,

[30] *Proc. Amer. Soc. Int. Law, 1922*, pp. 12, 15*ff*.

[31] "The Strongest Navy," *Current History*, Vol. 16, July 1922, pp. 557, 560-1.

[32] Captain Knox's little book was published in 1922 by the *Army and Navy Journal*. It is now out of print. But a few copies were recently still available through the courtesy of the Navy League of the United States.

he further granted, had probably checked naval rivalry for the time being, but no one could deny that the "elements of competition" were still present. It seemed wholly probable that "expensive competitive building" would be resumed as soon as time should "have restored financial stability and the normal psychological attitude of rivalry between nations." And should this resumption take place in the near future, the slight fiscal saving gained from scrapping the ships under construction would be more than wiped out by the cost of instituting another large building program.

This, Knox declared, was "not the only big price" paid for the "necessarily doubtful and unstable international accord upon which our sacrifices are predicated." We had abandoned a policy "which insured our ability to safeguard American interests the world over." We had relinquished our claim to real naval parity with Great Britain. We had fatally weakened our strategic position in the western Pacific without receiving any commensurate naval concessions in return. In consequence, we no longer possessed "the power to defend the Philippines or to support any other American Far Eastern policy."

In contrast, Knox contended that Great Britain was the gainer "on every count." England was the chief beneficiary of the new code of submarine warfare. The special provision which allowed immediate construction of two new British battleships safeguarded that country's "industrial preparedness." The Treaty removed the threat of American naval supremacy. England's "preponderance in cruisers, merchant marine, and a world-wide system of naval bases and cables" gave that country a total effective naval power far exceeding our own, despite the "ratio of equality with us" in capital ships and aircraft carriers.

Japan, according to Knox, was the "greatest gainer of all." Prior to the Conference, that country was spending more than one-half of its total revenue on armaments mainly designed to prevent American interference with Japan's Oriental policies. The Naval Treaty halted that ruinous effort, leaving Japan "relatively much stronger on the sea than she has ever been before." Relieved of the "burden of building more battleships and battle cruisers," the Japanese Government could now proceed with the "construction of submarines, cruisers, destroyers, aircraft, and other naval auxiliaries . . . with increased vigor, and incidentally with greater secrecy than is possible with large ships."

The limitation on fortifications and naval bases gave this prospective diversion of effort a double significance. Japan held a great number of islands in the western Pacific. These islands, "located well in advance of her home frontiers," were well suited for the use of auxiliary naval craft. Promptly defended following the outbreak of war, they "would serve admirably as points of support for auxiliary operations against a hostile advance." And an American force undertaking such an advance would have to reckon with Japan's immediate seizure of our exposed and virtually undefended islands in the western Pacific.

Japan was also a beneficiary of the submarine agreement. That country's vital sea communications were those with eastern Asia. By prohibiting unrestricted submarine attacks on commerce, the Conference had outlawed the most effective means of disrupting those lines of communication. And conversely, the failure to limit submarine tonnage left Japan in the strongest possible position to repel hostile forces attempting to penetrate into Asiatic waters. In short, from a purely naval standpoint, Knox concluded, the Treaty so increased the relative power of Japan as to render that country henceforth "entirely free from the possibility of interference by America in the Orient."[33]

Almost the only Service voice raised publicly in defense of the Treaty was that of Admiral W. V. Pratt who more than any other American officer had actively participated in the work of the Conference. Pratt found no fault with the strategic and technical objections raised by professional critics. But he considered it a mistake to judge the Treaty on purely technical grounds. The work of the Conference should be viewed as a whole. Stabilization of naval armaments and improved political relations in the Pacific and Far East—the two main purposes for calling the Conference—had been at least partially realized.

In return, it was true, the United States had made concessions and sacrifices. In particular, we had relinquished prospective primacy in capital ships, and the right to fortify and develop

[33] *Eclipse of American Sea Power*, pp. 129*ff*.

naval bases in our far western islands. As to the second, he reminded the critics, "we had held these islands for many years, and never had fortified them." Whether we would actually have done so in the future was a matter for conjecture. As to the sacrifice of naval tonnage, the thirteen unfinished battleships and battle cruisers scrapped under the Treaty had "more than justified their brief existence by the weight they gave to American diplomacy." He found it "difficult to see what would have induced Great Britain and Japan to accept the invitation to this Conference had it not been for the leading position America had taken as a naval Power." And he was convinced "they would not have accepted the 5:5:3 ratios had it not been for our naval preponderance." In other words, "it was the power of our Navy that put the American proposal through."

Viewed in this way, Pratt felt that the United States, while unquestionably making the greatest sacrifice, came out rather well on the whole; and that the decisions reached at the Conference gave promise of an era of more friendly and more stable relations among the great naval Powers.[34]

Popular Reactions in America

The popular response in America was one of enthusiastic though by no means unanimous applause. A large section of the press searched the dictionary for superlatives with which to praise the Administration's achievement. Papers that rarely agreed on any public issue joined in acclaiming the Washington Treaties. The *New York Herald* characterized the Conference as "much the greatest . . . of all time," and declared that the "achievements that optimism hoped for, prayed for, vast as they are in actualities, and vaster yet in potentialities, are today embedded in history."[35]

The *New York Tribune* interpreted the Four Power and Naval Limitation Treaties as the cornerstone of a new "international concert" which delivered "one region of the globe . . . from

[34] "Naval Policy and the Naval Treaty," *North American Review*, Vol. 215, May 1922, pp. 590*ff*.; and "The Case for the Naval Treaty," *Current History*, Vol. 18, April 1923, pp. 1*ff*.

[35] Feb. 2, 1922, p. 10.

the menace of a major war." This was "a monumental contribution to international understanding and human progress."[36]

The *New York Times* was confident that "a reconstructed world will not permit the resumption of competitive warship building." It was doubtful if fleets would be maintained even "at their present strength. . . ." Sea power was destined to "decline in importance." It was the "hope and belief of practical men" that the world's business would henceforth "be carried on without great navies to guard it. . . ."[37]

The *New York World* reminded its readers that "the way to measure the importance of the naval treaty is to remember what would have happened had there been no agitation for disarmament, no Washington Conference, no Hughes proposals, and no agreement." Vividly recalling the vicious circle of armament competition into which the great naval Powers were slipping after the late war, the *World* asserted that "the end of all that distrust and all that taxation would have been war and bankruptcy and unspeakable devastation." The Washington Conference had removed one of the prime causes of war. That cause was "not battleships or guns or armor-plate" *per se*, but the race to produce bigger and better "battleships, guns, and armorplate," which stimulated "fear and suspicion and hatred, subsidized by special interests and carried forward by the mischiefmakers of the world."[38]

In America as elsewhere there were dissenting editorial voices. The ultra-nationalistic Hearst papers attacked the Conference and all its works. The United States, declared one of these dailies, found itself "tied hand and foot to the war machine of foreign imperialism." Another characterized those who hailed the outcome as an unprecedented victory for peace, as the victims of a "pathetic delusion." Not only had the Conference done nothing for peace; it had actually brought "the danger of new wars to the threshold of the most pacific great Power on earth." And the Socialist *New York Call* cynically remarked that the net result which the nations derived from the Conference was merely to "reduce the cost of blowing each other up."

[36] Feb. 2, p. 10.
[37] Feb. 3, p. 14.
[38] Feb. 2, p. 10.

Such utterances, however, were definitely in the minority. The predominant editorial note in the East, in the Middle West, and in the Far West seemed to be one of optimism and confidence. While some were more restrained in their praise than others, a survey of American newspapers following the Conference yielded the general verdict that the results achieved "exceeded all reasonable hopes."[39]

This was likewise the verdict of other important groups in America. Speaking for the American Federation of Labor, Mr. Samuel Gompers found cause for "worldwide rejoicing." Much was still left to be done. The possibility of war still existed. But the danger of war had been reduced, and the fiscal burden lightened. The armament race had been stopped, and the moral force of public opinion successfully demonstrated.[40]

This optimism was shared by the conservative spokesmen of American business and finance. The *Wall Street Journal* printed a highly favorable estimate of the Naval Treaty.[41] The *Bankers Magazine* applauded the "solid achievements of the Washington Conference." Statesmen had there "settled controversial questions that had in them the possibilities of war." The results represented a triumph of common sense over "impractical idealism."[42] The *Commercial and Financial Chronicle* believed the Conference had set a precedent of incalculable importance. We could even envisage a "future when there will no more be armaments in all the world by which peoples that are in heart friendly shall be able to make war upon each other."[43]

Other organized groups were equally outspoken in their approval. A special citizens' committee was organized to conduct a campaign for prompt ratification of the Treaties. This committee included nationally recognized leaders of business, finance, journalism, law, education, and religion. A country-wide survey carried out under the auspices of this group, yielded an impressive picture of public support. "The church forces of the nation"—Protestant, Catholic, and Jewish—were found "to be practically a unit in support of the treaties. . . ." Civic organizations—"commercial, economic, social, and political"—had "expressed themselves with similar unity." The country's

[39] *Literary Digest*, Vol. 72, Feb. 18, p. 7.
[40] *American Federationist*, Vol. 29, March 1922, pp. 195*ff*. [41] Feb. 2, p. 11.
[42] Vol. 104, March 1922, pp. 435-6. [43] Vol. 114-1, Feb. 11, pp. 559-60.

educational institutions were supporting the treaties without a known "dissenting voice." Various "outstanding and representative bodies of women" were on record to the same effect. "The reports of opposition," the committee reported, "are so negligible as to make it clear to us that the people are more significantly united on the proposals of the Conference on Limitation of Armament than they have ever been on any similar issue."[44]

The Senate's Verdict on the Conference

Despite impressive indications of overwhelming popular support, senatorial consent to ratification of the Washington Treaties was by no means a foregone conclusion. There was never much doubt as to the Administration's ability to align a majority. But treaties require more than a simple majority. And there was more than negligible possibility that some combination of Democrats and intransigent Republicans might control enough senatorial votes to block ratification.

Comparatively few Senators, it is true, were willing to brave the public censure almost certain to descend upon the head of anyone who made a frontal assault on the popular Naval Limitation Treaty. The logical point of senatorial attack was the Four Power Pacific Treaty. This substitute for the Anglo-Japanese Alliance was somewhat less popular in America. It could be construed rather plausibly as a quasi-military alliance. So construed, it would involve in an embarrassing dilemma the Republican leadership who had fought Wilson and the League of Nations. And if the Four Power Treaty could be defeated, or at least radically altered, that result might shake public confidence in the other Conference treaties, with disastrous effect on the political fortunes of the Harding Administration.

Rumbles of senatorial thunder portended the gathering storm. The treaty (concluded outside the Conference) in which the United States recognized Japan's Pacific Mandate in return for cable rights in the Island of Yap and for commercial rights throughout the mandated islands, was savagely attacked in the upper chamber by a small but determined minority who ex-

[44] Quoted in 67 Cong. 2 Sess., *Cong. Rec.*, Vol. 62, p. 4227.

ploited all the tricks of parliamentary procedure to delay action and embarrass the Administration.[45]

On February 15 Senator Hitchcock, Democratic leader, moved a request for information regarding the secret negotiations which had resulted in the Four Power Treaty. This request, voted over the protests of the Conference Senators, Lodge and Underwood, was promptly turned down by the Administration. Simultaneously, the Administration leaders in the Senate were resisting pressure to hold public hearings on the Washington Treaties, which would provide a sounding board for the minority opposition. On February 27, the Foreign Relations Committee reported the Four Power Treaty with but a single reservation designed to quiet the apprehensions of the isolationists. Then on March 8, after a week of preliminary skirmishing, the storm broke in full fury, as the parliamentary opposition poured one broadside after another into the Treaty which the Administration consistently held to be an indispensable foundation stone of the new Pacific order.[46]

The opposition concentrated on the proposition that the Four Power Treaty was an alliance in disguise. It was repeatedly declared to be so regarded overseas. If this construction was correct, the United States would be the loser on all counts. Such an alliance, it was contended, would foster counter alliances, involving the American people in all the complications, entanglements, and enmities of Europe and Asia. Ratification of this compact, it was asserted, would link our destinies with two "island empires" whose "only political principle" was to "conquer and exploit weaker peoples. . . ."

Such an act of ratification would place the final stamp of American approval on Japan's unjustifiable retention of the former German islands which interposed a vast strategic barrier between Hawaii and the Philippines. That result, in conjunction with the Naval Treaty's limitation of tonnage and restriction on fortifications, would give Japan indisputable command throughout the western Pacific. In short, the opposition contended, the

[45] For a guide to these proceedings, see *Cong. Rec.*, Vol. 62, index, title: treaties.
[46] *ibid.*, pp. 2587, 2637, 2771, 3107, 3232*ff.*, 3408*ff.*

Four Power Treaty tied our hands in return for nothing more substantial than dubious promises of non-aggression.[47]

At the height of the parliamentary battle, Senator Borah created a sensation by reading excerpts from the transcript of a recent meeting of the Council on Foreign Relations in New York City. At this meeting, Mr. Paul D. Cravath, a lawyer of international eminence, defended the Washington Treaties in general, and the Four Power Treaty in particular, on the ground that they substituted an Anglo-American entente for the Anglo-Japanese Alliance. This, Cravath admitted, was "not recorded at all in black and white. . . ." But he had been "told by every member of the American delegation" that the Conference had established "such a degree of understanding and such a basis of sympathy" between Great Britain and the United States "that both assume that in all future emergencies they can both count on having the very closest cooperation." Cravath knew "definitely" that Balfour shared this view. He understood that the other members of the British delegation did also. Furthermore, while the Treaties left the United States powerless to act alone against Japan, he was "informed that our technical advisers are satisfied that if the United States and Great Britain are on one side, and Japan on the other, that the Anglo-American fleet and the entire Anglo-American naval position would dominate that of Japan in Japanese waters." Thus, without the "expense and temptations" involved in building the world's greatest fleet, "our naval position, as against Japan," was actually "improved rather than weakened" as a result of the Washington Conference.[48]

This disclosure, which seemed to confirm the opposition's darkest suspicions of an alliance with Great Britain, was immediately repudiated. Cravath wired Lodge that he had never said what the written record undeniably attributed to him. Mr. Hughes denied positively and in writing the existence of any secret understanding with Great Britain "with respect to Pacific matters." And it was emphatically reiterated that the Four

[47] See, for example, the leading speeches of Senators Reed (D., Mo.), Robinson (D., Ark.), Johnson (R., Calif.), Borah (R., Ida.), LaFollette (R., Wis.), *Cong. Rec.*, Vol. 62, pp. 3555*ff.*, 3606*ff.*, 3776*ff.*, 3787*ff.*, 4227*ff.*

[48] *ibid.*, pp. 4119, 4160*ff.*

Power Treaty was simply a mutual non-aggression pact, and nothing more.[49]

Despite such positive and absolutely unqualified assurances, the parliamentary battle continued unabated, with frontal assaults, flanking movements, and counter-attacks following one another in bewildering succession. Altogether, the debate on the Four Power Treaty fills more than 200 large and closely printed pages of the *Congressional Record.* From beginning to end there were some fifty roll calls, thirty-three on the final day alone. Thirty reservations were offered, chiefly for purposes of delay and obstruction. In the end, all were defeated save the one originally reported by the Foreign Relations Committee, which simply affirmed that the Treaty involved "no commitment to armed force, no alliance, no obligation to join in any defense." And with this sole reservation, the Senate on March 24 consented to the ratification of the Four Power Treaty by a vote of sixty-seven to twenty-seven, with fifty-five Republicans and twelve Democrats standing in the affirmative, and with four Republicans and twenty-three Democrats in the negative.[50]

This disposition of the Four Power Treaty assured ratification of the considerably more popular Naval Limitation Treaty. There was a desultory debate on the latter, continuing through parts of two days. Democratic Senators complained that the

[49] *ibid.*, pp. 4120, 4157-8. Senators Lodge and Underwood both denied having had any conversation with Mr. Cravath. But Mr. Root refused to make any statement. R. L. Buell, *The Washington Conference* (1922), p. 185.

[50] *Cong. Rec.*, p. 4496. The Senate next turned to the Supplementary Four Power Treaty. This agreement was the result of discussion as to whether the main islands of Japan were included in the "insular possessions and insular dominions" covered by the non-aggression pledge of the principal Treaty. The Supplementary Treaty, which definitely excluded the main island of Japan, was approved unanimously, but with a reservation. This reservation incorporated an interpretative declaration signed back in December in connection with the principal Four Power Treaty. This declaration had dealt with two matters. First, it had excluded from the consultative provision of the Treaty all questions "exclusively within the domestic jurisdiction of the respective Powers"—specifically, immigration so far as the United States was concerned. Second, it had declared that conclusion of the Treaty did not constitute United States recognition of the Japanese mandate over the former German islands, as to which Japanese-American negotiations were then in progress. The second clause automatically became inoperative following conclusion, in February 1922, of the Yap Treaty. The Senate's insistence on including this provision in the reservation to the Supplementary Four Power Treaty late in March, was both meaningless and absurd. For the proceedings on this Treaty, see *Cong. Rec.*, Vol. 62, pp. 4497, 4539*ff.*, 4588*ff.*

Administration was claiming too much credit for an achievement which Senator Borah had initiated, largely with Democratic support, in the face of Administration opposition and hostility. Borah himself reminded the country that only the first step had been taken, and that much still remained to be done if militarism was to be uprooted and destroyed. Senator Johnson of California had doubts as to the wisdom of the non-fortification pledge which looked to him like an "abandonment of the Philippines and a retreat in the Pacific."[51]

Senators Walsh of Montana and Hitchcock of Nebraska, pro-League Wilsonian Democrats, especially deplored the Administration policy which had made it impossible to do anything about limiting land armaments. The continued diversion of productive capital into these, more than into naval armaments, was undermining recovery and economic reconstruction in Europe. The steady drain of productive effort into unproductive capital goods impoverished a country, reduced its living standard and hence its purchasing power, and consequently diminished the real value of its foreign trade. All this had unfavorable repercussions on our own internal economy. European land armaments might involve no direct menace to the United States. But the American people could not escape the indirect economic consequences of militarism overseas.

There could be no real recovery, these Senators asserted, so long as Europe in general, and France in particular, was obsessed with a sense of insecurity against armed aggression. This condition, it was insisted, could be alleviated only when the United States assumed its full share of responsibility for peace and stability in Europe. And the Republican Administration was severely criticized for its alleged hostility to the League of Nations, and for its refusal to resurrect Wilson's defunct military guarantee to France, both of which attitudes had prevented the Conference from dealing constructively with the problem of land armaments.[52]

Only one member, Senator France of Maryland, made a direct attack on the Naval Treaty. He knew that the American people believed "that this Republic should have the most powerful Navy in the world as a first wall of defense for the protection of our own

[51] *ibid.*, pp. 4671-93, 4698-9, 4704-6, 4708-19. [52] *ibid.*, pp. 4689, 4692*f*.

liberties and as the great benevolent right arm to be always extended for conciliation, for propitiation, for mercy, for humanity, for liberty, and for justice over all the peoples of the world." Therefore, he would vote against the Treaty.[53]

No one imagined for a minute, however, that the Naval Treaty could now be defeated. And on March 29, the Senate consented to its ratification, with Senator France casting the only dissenting vote.[54]

The remaining treaties went through in a rush. The submarine agreement was unanimously approved after only a few minutes of discussion.[55] The Nine Power (Open Door) Treaty pertaining to China occupied the Senate less than one day. Members who had displayed the greatest agitation over imagined dangers lurking in the Four Power Pacific Pact, voted unanimously for the China Treaty with little or no perceptible concern over possibilities of future Japanese aggression in eastern Asia.[56] And with the unopposed passage of the closely related Chinese Customs Tariff Treaty, the Senate of the United States placed its final stamp of approval on what was euphoniously hailed and widely believed in as a "new charter of peace."

Viewed in the large, these diverse and antithetical contemporary verdicts on the politico-naval results of the Washington Conference assume a clearly discernible though somewhat blurred pattern. Broadly speaking, while comment nowhere approached unanimity, lay opinion in the principal countries showed a marked and natural tendency to follow the lead of national official pronouncements on the Conference. Thus, for example, the popular verdict was least favorable in France, most favorable in the United States.

A large part, perhaps most, of the public applause, especially in the United States, manifestly represented not so much a reasoned judgment as the release of pent up emotion. Americans had watched their country, still suffering the after-effects of the last war, drifting in a vicious downward spiral of armament competition, toward bankruptcy and more war. The Conference in some miraculous fashion had checked their fateful glide toward

[53] *ibid.*, pp. 4708, 4709*f*.
[54] *ibid.*, pp. 4718-19.
[55] *ibid.*, pp. 4723*ff*.
[56] *ibid.*, pp. 4760*ff*.

disaster, and started them in a new direction. They saw a brighter landscape ahead. And they desperately wanted to believe it was real, and not merely another mirage which would vanish as they struggled to approach it.

On the other hand, the more nationalistic elements in each country tended to deplore the sacrifices and concessions made, and either to minimize or to ignore altogether the advantages gained. Opposition parties, as was to be expected, disparaged the handiwork of their parliamentary adversaries, and indulged in captious criticism. Spokesmen of socialist and other radical groups showed some tendency to belittle the significance of what had been achieved. A large minority drawn from all political faiths lamented the failure of the Conference to take a longer forward stride toward disarmament. And everywhere, except perhaps in Italy, naval officers and civilian naval experts were all but unanimous in viewing the outcome as a diplomatic and strategic defeat for their own particular country.

The all but unanimous distrust with which the Washington Treaties were viewed by the armed Services in every country directly concerned, undoubtedly sprang from a number of causes. But not the least of these, it would appear, was the prevailing scepticism with which army and navy men tended to view the political results of the Conference. With certain notable exceptions, they simply could not believe that pledges of non-aggression could be an effective substitute for armed force in the international struggle for power and profit. For this reason, among others, it seemed to the military mind incredible folly to surrender strategic advantages previously derived from geographic position or from actual or prospective superiority in ships and other elements of military power.

This reasoning was the very antithesis of that which supported the statesman's case for the Washington Treaties. Armament competition had fostered a universal sense of insecurity. This was inexorably developing into a vicious circle of hysterical fear and rampant militarism, trending toward the paralysis and eventual destruction of capitalistic society, immediately through ever rising taxes, ultimately through war and devastation. It had become imperative to break this vicious circle. And this the Conference had gone far toward achieving: first, by checking the rate of armament expansion; second, by delimiting and separating the strategic zones of the leading naval Powers; and third, by pledges of non-aggression which substituted mutual confidence and good will in place of corroding fear and suspicion throughout the vast region of the Pacific and Far East.

CHAPTER FIFTEEN

☆ ☆ ☆ ☆ ☆ ☆ ☆ ☆ ☆ ☆ ☆ ☆ ☆ ☆ ☆ ☆ ☆ ☆ ☆ ☆

Toward a New Order of Sea Power

THE Washington Conference wrote the concluding page of a revolutionary chapter in the annals of sea power and world politics. Broadly speaking, that chapter may be said to have begun with the publication, in 1890, of Captain Alfred Thayer Mahan's famous work, *The Influence of Sea Power upon History*. Mahan traced the steps by which Great Britain in the seventeenth and eighteenth centuries had established a virtually world-wide command of the sea. Under the shelter of dominant naval power, British genius had erected an empire upon which it could be truly said that the sun never set. In the nineteenth century this empire had become the nucleus of a world economic community which, as a result of the combined power of British fleets and finance, had acquired some at least of the attributes of universal sovereignty and a political world order.

The naval sanction of this quasi-world order rested upon a unique combination of geographical, political, and technological conditions. The British Isles lay athwart the ocean portals of northern Europe. Gibraltar, which passed into British hands early in the eighteenth century, dominated sea-borne commerce to and from the Mediterranean. By closing these commercial bottlenecks, the British could blockade or sink most of the naval forces of their Continental enemies, cut them off from their over-sea colonies, destroy their maritime commerce root and branch. Before the advent of submarines and aircraft, control of the water's surface in the North Sea and English Channel insured the British Isles against counter attacks or blockade. And as long as there were no important naval Powers in the Western Hemisphere or in the Far East, local dominance over the North Sea,

English Channel, Mediterranean, and adjacent waters, automatically resulted in a virtually world-wide command of the sea.

It seems obvious, in retrospect, that the surest way for England to achieve this result was to concentrate superior naval forces in or near these bottlenecks of European commerce, sending to more distant seas only such detachments as were needed to cope with the scattered enemy forces which could not be prevented from slipping through the closely guarded waters surrounding Continental Europe. After generations of trial and error, this finally became the policy and the more or less consistent practice of the British Admiralty. And it was largely upon this record of British experience that Mahan built his sea-power interpretation of history and his strategical doctrine of command of the sea.

Mahan spoke at a critical juncture. In 1890 an explosive compound of resurgent mercantilism, rampant nationalism, rising militarism, and missionary evangelism was brewing in the Old World and in the New. Mahan's sea-power interpretation of history—a strange synthesis of brilliant strategical analysis and expansionist propaganda—became a flaming standard for this new imperialism, and gave impetus and direction to navalism the world over.

Mahan's doctrines were hailed in many lands as the key which would open for others, as it had previously for Great Britain, the door to world dominion and empire. All that was needed was a powerful fleet of capital ships, surrounded by various kinds of subsidiary craft, and supported by a system of naval bases at home and overseas. Mahan's followers often ignored or belittled the unique geographical and political conditions which had enabled England to reap global dividends from a local concentration of naval power in European waters. They failed in the main to appreciate that about all any other country could hope to achieve with any attainable fleet of capital ships was a purely local or regional command of the sea.

Such regional dominance might very well be the most effective means of insuring certain countries—the United States, for example—against blockade or invasion. But for obvious geographical reasons, fully analyzed earlier in this volume, no local command of the sea could endow the United States or any other country with a system of colonial defense or with a leverage on world politics even approaching that which British statesmen had long derived from their naval ascendancy in Europe's narrow seas.

Nor could Great Britain herself maintain this historic Pax Britannica in the face of changing conditions and circumstances. The rapid rise of Japanese and American naval Power, attributable in no small degree to the influence of Mahan, undermined British sea power at the periphery. The British Admiralty could thereafter have maintained its global naval dominance only by establishing local superiority, both in the Western Hemisphere and in the Far East, over the steadily growing fleets of the United States and Japan. Any such dispersion of force was contrary in principle to the teachings of Mahan. But it was England's only alternative to surrendering control of those distant seas. And it might well have been seriously attempted, but for the simultaneous and more serious threat to British power at its source, resulting from the accelerating naval pace in Europe, especially in Germany, during the early years of the twentieth century.

Confronted with this new problem for which there was no purely naval solution, British statesmen elected to maintain their historic dominance in European waters, and to seek political substitutes overseas. For this and other reasons, Great Britain entered into a military alliance with Japan, cultivated close relations with the United States, and tacitly recognized America's naval claims in the Western Hemisphere—developments which appear in historical perspective as an important stage in the transition from Pax Britannica toward some new order of sea power.

By and large, however, the broader significance of these events was not recognized at the time. Great Britain was habitually regarded as the senior member of the Anglo-Japanese partnership in the Pacific. With few exceptions, Americans complacently continued to accept England as the world's foremost naval power. And Englishmen themselves still talked as if Britannia actually ruled the waves not only of the North Sea, the English Channel, and the Empire's Mediterranean-Suez life line to India and Australasia, but also of the broad Atlantic and the far broader Pacific as well.

The war of 1914-1918 accentuated this habit of British thought. The British Navy emerged from that conflict stronger in tons and guns than ever before. The war had destroyed or weakened the sea power of every possible European rival. And with the consequent strategic emancipation of British sea power, British discussion of naval matters showed a marked tendency to revert to the historic concept of Pax Britannica.

This trend, however, showed a surprising lack of realism. German air raids and submarine blockade had provided England a foretaste of future perils which threatened the very life of Great Britain. Spread of the European conflict into the Far East had given impetus and opportunity to imperialistic forces within Japan, which were bent on hegemony in eastern Asia and on naval dominance in the western Pacific. And all this coincided with a portentous increase in the military power of the United States.

These events destroyed the last vestiges of world strategic unity, so long symbolized by the dominant sea power of England. With sentiment, territorial possessions, and established policies at stake in the Far East, the United States in 1918 was driving toward a head-on collision with Japan. After the defeat of Germany, America's wartime association with Great Britain cooled almost overnight into growing suspicion and distrust. And there were ominous signs and portents that the two English-speaking Powers were in grave danger of drifting into a costly and dangerous struggle for world power and dominion.

Against this background of potential anarchy and future conflict, President Wilson projected his famous program of world reconstruction. The cornerstone of his new world order was to be a league of nations, involving arrangements for concerted economic and military coercion to enforce the terms of a just and universal peace. Sea blockade would necessarily bulk large in any system of military sanctions. And there was not the slightest doubt in the minds of American statesmen and their naval advisers that Anglo-American equality of sea power was the most effective, and indeed the only acceptable, basis for American collaboration in the proposed world order.

An Anglo-American command of the seas was at that time both geographically and technically feasible. Despite the rise of submarine and air power, Great Britain still dominated the sea approaches to Continental Europe as well as the Mediterranean-Suez route to India and the Far East. The United States wielded a comparable authority in the Western Hemisphere.

And between them, the British and American Navies held the keys to all navigable exits from the Pacific.

Such a Pax Anglo-Americana presented formidable difficulties. To make it effective would require fundamental changes in the British and American thought patterns. There is no denying that British and American interests, while parallel in certain regions and on certain issues, were elsewhere in sharp and seemingly irreconcilable conflict. Whether these and other difficulties could have been overcome, no one can say. For two conditions prevented any attempt even formally to institute in 1919 an Anglo-American command of the seas. One was the utter unwillingness of the British naval class, supported at that time by British statesmanship, to accept the principle of naval parity with the United States. The other was the American Senate's rejection of the League of Nations which, in the view of the Wilson Administration, was the necessary cornerstone of the whole enterprise.

The Administration's alternative to the League of Nations was repeatedly declared to be armed force sufficient, without outside assistance, to defend American territories, interests, and policies throughout the world against any and all possible aggressors. As to what this alternative might ultimately involve, no one could clearly foresee. It all depended on what was to be defended, on the location and strength of potential enemies, and on future developments in naval technology and doctrine.

Characteristically, there is no comprehensive official statement of the political objectives of American naval policy at this critical juncture. Security of the continental United States, of the Panama Canal, and of the sea approaches to North America and the Caribbean, was taken for granted. Defense of our island possessions in the western Pacific was generally accepted as unavoidable. Resistance to Japanese imperialism in eastern Asia was frequently mentioned. And a great deal was said about providing world-wide protection for the American merchant marine which had undergone tremendous expansion during the war, and which was then expected to assume still greater dimensions in the future.

With these objects and others less tangible in view, statesmen and naval experts publicly advocated a "navy second to none." This could be, and was frequently, construed to mean a navy greater than any other—even one "incomparably the greatest" in the world. And we have seen that it was the sense of the General Board, in 1921, that the only safe standard for the United States, as long at least as the Anglo-Japanese Alliance continued in force, was a navy equal to any two others combined.

Such comparisons, it should be remembered, were always made in terms of the relative strength of fighting fleets. The battleship was considered the index of naval power. The fighting fleet, built around a nucleus of capital ships—battleships and battle cruisers—was the supreme embodiment of military power upon the sea. The fleet's "mission" was to destroy or blockade the enemy fleet. Execution of this mission, according to the accepted doctrine, gave command of the sea which afforded security to one's own coast and commerce, while opening the way for devastating attacks on the seaboard and merchant shipping of the enemy country.

Cruisers, destroyers, submarines, and aircraft, according to the accepted doctrine, were "auxiliaries" to be used primarily, though not exclusively, to protect and assist the capital ships in carrying out their appointed mission. Commerce raiding, even on the grand scale practised by the German submarines in the late war, was officially considered a useful but purely secondary operation. The spirit of Mahan still hovered over the Navy Department. And Mahan's fundamental precept—command of the sea through battle-fleet supremacy—was still the cornerstone of American naval doctrine and policy.[1]

The teachings of Mahan, however, had become after the World War a storm center of doctrinal controversy. It was all but universally conceded that the phenomenal rise of submarine and air power had a bearing on future naval operations. There was respectable opinion to the effect that battle fleets were destined to lose much of their former potency in narrow seas menaced by hostile shore based aircraft. Critics of the Mahan school expressed further doubts as to the feasibility of

[1] This point has been repeatedly stated and illustrated in the preceding chapters, but it will do no harm to cite here two unimpeachable statements of American naval doctrine, as of 1920-1921. See War and Navy Departments, *Joint Army and Navy Action in Coast Defense* (1920); and special report of the General Board, Feb. 2, 1921, in 66 Cong. 3 Sess. House Naval Committee, *Hearings on Sundry Legislation, 1920-1921*, pp. 925*ff*.

even attempting, in case of war, to send the American fleet into the western Pacific, where Japan's mandated islands afforded scores of anchorages and lagoons from which submarines and aircraft might operate, possibly with devastating effect, against battleships, and above all against the fleet's extremely vulnerable train of supply and service vessels.

It was generally recognized, moreover, that a fighting fleet of capital ships surrounded by auxiliaries was an instrument of invincible power only so long as it remained within supporting distance of fortified naval bases provided with dry docks, machine shops, stores of fuel and ammunition, and innumerable items of equipment and supply. The American Navy possessed neither bases nor sites for bases anywhere in European waters. In the western Pacific, the United States had sites, but no bases worthy of the name. And the strategic value of those sites had been considerably impaired if not all but destroyed by Japan's wartime occupation of the former German islands north of the equator.

All this pointed toward two general conclusions. The first: that, under conditions prevailing in 1921, the minimum naval standard officially proposed—battle-fleet parity with Great Britain—was certainly adequate to keep any probable combination of future enemies at a safe distance from the continental United States and from the Panama Canal.[2] The second: that, by the same token, the maximum standard publicly discussed—a two-power standard—was just as certainly inadequate to give the United States effective naval dominance in either the eastern Atlantic or the far western Pacific.[3]

Much was said about a Pax Americana; about the destiny of the United States to assume England's historic rôle as mistress of the seas. But such talk ignored the plain facts of political and military geography. It overlooked the total absence of any com-

[2] A recognized English authority estimated in 1921, "that the British Navy could not be a menace to the United States unless its battle-fleet strength—and naturally all the auxiliary forces necessary for making that strength effective—were in the ratio of from three to four to one." A. H. Pollen, "Some Principles of Attack and Defense," *International Conciliation*, pamphlet no. 161, April 1921, p. 143.

[3] The English authority just quoted estimated that the American Navy would have to attain a superiority of three or four to one before it could become a "conceivable menace to Great Britain." And it must be remembered that in making such an estimate, no English expert would err on the side of underestimating the naval power of the United States or the naval needs of Great Britain.

mercial bottlenecks in the Western Hemisphere that were in any way comparable to Europe's narrow seas. The Panama Canal was a vital waterway for no major Power except the United States. An American fleet based in this hemisphere could never hope to dominate the sea communications of Europe and the Far East, unless overwhelmingly superior to the navies of England and Japan combined.

Any determined attempt on the part of the United States to acquire a position of such commanding advantage would inevitably provoke vigorous counter-measures, especially in the two countries most vulnerable to the pressure of hostile sea power. Such counter-measures would tend to neutralize American efforts, thus stimulating demands for still greater efforts in reply. If earlier experience was any guide, the result would be another cycle of armament competition, with recurring war scares and crises accompanying ever increasing demands for more tons and guns and men to man them.

In the end, the American people, with their immeasurably greater resources, might conceivably succeed in establishing a virtually global dominance. But history offered no precedent for assuming, or even for hoping, that the United States could thus impose a Pax Americana without desperate armed conflict leading to the military defeat of Great Britain and Japan. Whatever the outcome of such a struggle, the appalling costs and world-shaking consequences were fearful to contemplate.

The American people, moreover, were then in no mood for any such enterprise. The idea of war with Great Britain was utterly abhorrent to the vast majority of Americans. A spontaneous reaction against wartime militarism had evolved swiftly into an organized movement for reduction and limitation of armament. There was a spreading conviction that armament competition led inexorably toward universal bankruptcy, ruin, war, and revolution. And as the country slid downhill into the unplumbed depths of the post-war economic depression, this conviction stimulated a rising public demand for relief from the fiscal burden and from the seeming political dangers of the impending struggle for command of the seas.

This growing public demand stiffened congressional resistance to all requests for expanding the Navy. It was impossible to secure appropriations for shore developments desired in Guam and the Philippines. Every proposal to authorize additional ships was rejected or ignored. And there were accumulating indications, in the winter and spring of 1920-1921, that Congress might even order work suspended on the numerous capital ships then in varying stages of construction.

American statesmen were thus confronted with the necessity of making a fundamental choice. They might accept the risks and consequences of an armament race, and strive to whip public opinion into supporting the naval increases which the authorities deemed necessary for the realization of the Government's virtually global objectives. They might conceivably abandon certain of these larger objectives—for example, resistance to Japan's advance in eastern Asia—and thereby bring the ends in view more nearly into line with the military means at hand. Or they might attempt collaboration in an international effort to stabilize the relations of the principal maritime Powers on some basis which included mutual reduction and limitation of naval armaments. For reasons previously analyzed, the Harding Administration chose this third course, and advanced along the road leading to the Washington Conference.

From that body there issued the blueprint of a new order of sea power. The essential feature of this new order was the stabilization of political and naval relations by limitations on the strength and indirectly on the use of battle fleets. To this end the total capital-ship tonnage of the principal naval Powers was reduced, and fixed in approximately the ratio of relative existing strength. Limits were placed on the size and armament of individual ships. And there was to be no further development of insular naval bases and fortifications in the western Pacific.

The practical result was to delimit the areas within which each of the leading naval Powers could individually assert an effective surface command of the seas. For Great Britain, the narrow seas of Europe, the eastern Atlantic, and the Mediterranean-Suez route to India and Australasia were put beyond reach of the Japanese and American battle fleets. The United States was assured uninterrupted sway over the sea approaches to North America and the Panama Canal. And Japan was left in virtually indisputable control of the ocean surface in the far western Pacific as far south perhaps as the equator.

All this was but the recognition and attempted perpetuation of existing facts. Britannia had long since ceased to rule the American seas. British naval experts had worked out plans for reestablishing a fleet in the Pacific, but they had yet to take the first steps toward putting those plans into execution. No one seriously contended that the threat of Japanese naval power yet extended beyond the western Pacific. The United States had never possessed a fighting fleet strong enough to challenge British sea power in the Old World or Japanese sea power in the Far East. After more than thirty years, the American Navy's shore facilities in the western Pacific still remained substantially as they were when conquered from Spain in 1898. The Navy Department had plans for strengthening the fleet and for building modern naval bases overseas, but political leaders despaired of winning congressional and popular support for efforts in these directions.[4] And there was respectable opinion to the effect that such efforts would be not only politically dangerous but strategically futile as well, in view of Japan's occupation of the former German islands north of the equator.

This freezing of the status quo as to fighting fleets and insular bases, evoked criticism as well as applause. British critics lamented their delegation's bloodless surrender of first rank upon the sea, ignoring both the existing limitations of British sea power and the consequences of a naval race with the United States. Japanese intransigents saw their country condemned to a permanent naval inferiority prejudicial to realization of their asserted destiny in eastern Asia. American critics deplored the limitation of Pacific bases and fortifications which they viewed as tantamount to abandonment of the Philippines and to a general retreat from the Far East.

Actually, there is little or no evidence that the Harding Administration intended any such withdrawal. The Wood-Forbes Report, released in November 1921, envisaged indefinite continuance of American administration in the Philippines. And all available evidence points to the conclusion that the treaties, resolutions, and declarations relating to eastern Asia were officially regarded as a solemn affirmation of long established American principles.

[4] See, for example, the speech of Senator Lodge on the Naval Treaty, 67 Cong. 2 Sess., *Cong. Rec.* Vol. 62, p. 4683.

What underwent revision were not so much views of national interest and policy overseas as the methods of supporting them. British statesmen, a generation earlier, had sought political substitutes, under the pressure of necessity, for their previous naval dominance in the Western Hemisphere and in the Far East. Somewhat similarly, American statesmen at the Washington Conference abandoned the struggle for a contested and dubious naval primacy in distant seas, in return for cancellation of the Anglo-Japanese Alliance and for mutual pledges of non-aggression covering island possessions in the Pacific as well as the historic American objectives in eastern Asia.

Whether the gain should be regarded as having balanced the sacrifice depends upon many factors and considerations. If national prestige, diplomatic bargaining power, and the security of far-flung national interests depended solely, or even mainly, on the American Navy's ability to defeat the fighting fleets of Great Britain or of Japan in virtually their home waters, then there was undeniably a strong case against the Washington Treaties. But as we have repeatedly emphasized, formidable obstacles—geographical and technological as well as political—stood between the United States and any such global dominance as that formerly exercised by Great Britain.

Surface battle fleets, however, were by no means the only instruments of national policy overseas. The American arsenal fairly bristled with economic weapons which could be used alone or in combination with military measures. Recognition of British naval dominance in the Old World in no way lessened England's dependence on America for indispensable strategic materials in wartime. Presumptive battle-fleet supremacy in the western Pacific did not free Japan from a still more crucial dependence upon American markets and raw materials.

Furthermore, the Washington Treaties placed no building restrictions on submarines and aircraft. War experience and post-war experimentation with these newer weapons had given some hint of their immense potentialities for local coast defense. A strong shore-based air force could be stationed in the Philippines without violating either the letter or the spirit of the Treaties. And there were competent experts who believed, even at that early date, that properly constituted submarine and air forces would render America's distant island possessions all but proof against hostile attack by sea.

The Washington Treaties also left open the possibility of a far ranging *guerre de course*. American naval authorities, while concentrating on their fighting fleet of capital ships, had not lost sight of the potentialities of commerce raiding. The Navy Department in 1922 was designing submarines, cruisers, and aircraft carriers with high speed, formidable armament, and great fuel endurance. And the Treaties in no way interfered with these developments.[5]

Thus while the Washington Treaties rendered the main islands of Japan and Japanese communications with eastern Asia secure against an American attack in force, they did not place America's Far Eastern possessions quite at the mercy of Japan or place that country's sea-borne commerce entirely beyond the reach of American naval Power.

The British Empire's post-Conference position in the Far East was somewhat comparable to, though considerably weaker than, the position of the United States. The British stake in eastern Asia was far greater than the American. British possessions and dominions stretched all the way from the China coast to New Zealand and beyond. The positive military guarantees of the Anglo-Japanese Alliance had been transmuted into the passive non-aggression pledges of the Four Power Treaty. The reduction of naval tonnage had left England with scarcely enough capital ships for the Home and Mediterranean Fleets, with none whatever for the third fleet which the Admiralty had planned to station in the Far East.

At the same time, Great Britain possessed in that region a number of commanding sites and one partially developed naval base of immense potentialities. This was the base at Singapore, carefully excluded from the fortifications article of the Naval Treaty. Cruiser, submarine, and air forces operating from that base in the Malacca Strait might be sufficient, even without the support of a battle fleet, to disrupt hostile sea-borne commerce

[5] The submarine Treaty, it is true, placed restrictions on the use of submarines as commerce raiders, but practically no one really believed that these restrictions would survive the stress and strain of actual war. And as it turned out, this treaty was never ratified.

and to break up attacks aimed at British and other European possessions in the East Indies.

Even though by no means negligible, the naval power which Great Britain and the United States could bring locally to bear in the far western Pacific was potentially far less important than the foundation laid at Washington for Anglo-American cooperation on a much larger scale. Cancellation of the Anglo-Japanese Alliance cleared the way for concentration of American naval forces in the Pacific. A common interest in maintaining peace and the status quo in the Far East seemingly provided the basis for parallel action in that region. And between them, the English-speaking countries held a combination of economic and military weapons, against which Japan's local dominance in the western Pacific lost much of its political significance.

One main artery of Japanese commerce spanned the North Pacific to Canada and the United States. Along this sea route there passed, in 1922, approximately 40 per cent of the merchandise imports and exports of the Island Empire. Another main artery, running southward to the East Indies and beyond, carried an additional 30 per cent of Japan's vital imports. Over these two marine highways moved a large part of the cotton, petroleum, and ores which supported the industry and military power of Japan. Both of these vital trunk lines extended far beyond the zone of Japanese naval control into areas under the indisputable sway of Great Britain or the United States.

The long shadow of Europe, however, fell across this blueprint of Anglo-American cooperation to enforce peace and order in the Pacific. On the balance of power in the Old World depended not only the future security of the British Empire, but also the extent to which Great Britain and the United States could safely divert their naval efforts from the Atlantic to the Pacific. Specifically, the continuance of British naval dominance in the North Sea, English Channel, eastern Atlantic, and Mediterranean-Suez route to India was an essential condition of a Pax Anglo-Americana in the Pacific. And this in turn depended on future developments in war technology and on England's relations with Europe as well as with the United States.

As repeatedly stressed in this volume, the rise of submarine and air power played havoc with the accepted postulates of British naval policy. By 1921 it was at least debatable whether surface fleets organized around a nucleus of capital ships could henceforth execute their historic mission in narrow seas within easy reach of hostile shore-based aircraft. It was still more dubious whether merchant shipping, even under strong naval escort, could successfully weather the perils of aerial and underwater attacks in narrow seas. And Englishmen even then were beginning to voice uneasy forebodings lest Continental air power might ultimately develop into a veritable sword of Damocles threatening destruction to English dockyards, arsenals, and factories—the heart and source of British sea power.

Drastic curtailment of these newer weapons naturally became one of the primary aims of British statesmanship. We have described British efforts at the Washington Conference to secure abolition of submarines and limitation of military aircraft. But there was no separating air power from the problem of land armaments. Until Great Britain was prepared to assume positive responsibility for maintaining European frontiers, French statesmen would entertain no proposals for limiting land armaments. Until such time, moreover, it was quite futile to expect French consent to any limitation of submarines and other auxiliary naval craft, the possession of which gave France some political leverage on Great Britain, as well as added assurance of uninterrupted passage of French troops and supplies from Africa in the event of war in Europe.

British statesmen, however, were unwilling to pay any such price. Instead, they strove to wring what they wanted from France without giving anything substantial in return. The result, as we have seen, was an impasse which prevented any limitation either of military aircraft or of auxiliary naval tonnage. With France, and Italy too, free to build submarines and other torpedo craft without limit, British statesmen and naval authorities would consider no proposal for restricting anti-submarine forces. Cruisers and destroyers were thereby added to the list of unrestricted naval weapons.

This unwillingness, or psychological inability perhaps, of British political and naval leaders to readjust their scheme of statecraft to fit the altered conditions of England's post-war situation, had far reaching implications and consequences. British insistence on all but complete freedom of action with respect to European conditions and crises, helped to undermine the shaky foundations of the League of Nations. The failure to limit auxiliary naval tonnage foreshadowed early resumption of competitive building in the unrestricted classes, a result that could scarcely fail to have unsettling repercussions on Anglo-American relations, and on the new balance of power in the Pacific.

The tragedy of all this is clearer in retrospect than it was in prospect. Renewed naval competition was presently to open a deep fissure in the recently cemented Anglo-American accord, and into this was to be driven the ancient feud over freedom of the seas in war. The future of Occidental interests in the Far East might one day depend in no small degree on Anglo-American cooperation in the Pacific. But the possibility of such a Pax Anglo-Americana would depend not only on the cordiality of British-American relations but also on the security of the British Isles and of the sea routes radiating therefrom. The new order in the Pacific was therefore bound up with the future of British sea power in the Old World. This in turn was inextricably entangled with the balance of land power in Europe, and with the quest for political stability in that war-shattered Continent. Thus in 1922 the problem of sea power was merging with the larger problem of armaments as a whole, which was but one aspect of a gigantic problem of world order and reconstruction. The Washington Conference had taken a step toward a constructive solution of this problem. But much still remained to be done, and some things undone, if the new order of sea power envisaged by Mr. Hughes and his associates was yet to be realized.

APPENDIX A

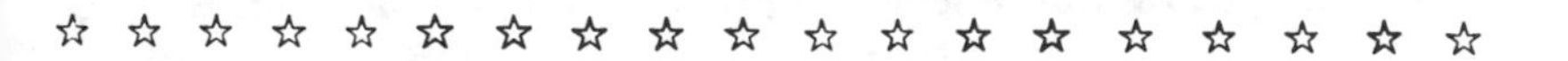

Notes on Methods and Materials

A LIST of the sources used in the preparation of this book would include interviews, letters, diaries, memoirs, biographies, government documents published and unpublished, general histories, monographs on special subjects, newspapers and magazines, and other items. Such a list would virtually duplicate the footnotes of the foregoing chapters. This documentation is readily accessible through the analytical index at the end of the volume. We have therefore dispensed with the conventional bibliography, and offer instead the following notes on basic sources used in dealing with the principal topics covered in this study.

The running critique of Mahan, which extends through the first three chapters, is based upon Mahan's own voluminous writings, reread in the light of changing world conditions down to the close of the World War of 1914-1918. The list of those writings used was that contained in Captain W. D. Puleston's *Life and Works of Captain Alfred Thayer Mahan* (1939), pp. 359*ff*.

For the strategic ideas and doctrines underlying American naval thinking and planning after 1918, we have relied solely upon authorized official statements both published and unpublished. Among these the following are typical of many quoted or cited in the foregoing pages: (1) War & Navy Departments, *Joint Army and Navy Action in Coast Defense* (1920); and (2) special report of the Navy General Board on the function and utility of capital ships, Feb. 2, 1921, in 66 Cong. 3 Sess. House Naval Committee, *Hearings on Sundry Legislation, 1920-1921*, pp. 925*ff*.

For Navy Department policy after 1918, we have likewise depended exclusively upon official statements. These include the reports of the Secretary of the Navy and other papers published in the annual reports of the Navy Department, as well as testimony of responsible naval officials before congressional committees, and Departmental statements released to the press.

The sources for the attitude and maneuvering of the Wilson Administration before and during the Peace Conference and during the long-drawn-out struggle over the League of Nations, as well as for the growing estrangement between Great Britain and the United States during 1919 and 1920, are fully covered by the documentation which accompanies chapters IV and V. But special mention should perhaps be made of the materials used in reconstructing the so-called "Naval Battle of Paris." The principal sources of information regarding that important, and much too neglected, episode are specifically enumerated in footnote 25 of chapter IV.

For materials on the post-war naval crisis in the Pacific, the reader is referred in general to the documentation accompanying chapter VI. This chapter includes, we believe, the first systematic attempt to assemble the extremely fugitive data so far available on America's response to Japan's wartime seizure of the former German islands in the western Pacific. In dealing with this vitally important topic we were fortunately able to supplement available published materials by research in the archives of the Department of State. There we were allowed to examine, for background purposes, still unpublished papers bearing on this crucial issue down through the year 1918.

We have attempted to piece together an accurate picture of the congressional and popular revolt against the Government's naval plans from the armistice of 1918 to the Washington Conference on the Limitation of Armament, chiefly from the following sources: (1) congressional hearings, debates, and votes; (2) relevant news and editorial comment in the daily and weekly press; and (3) an assortment of materials on the activities of widely different interested groups and organizations. Detailed references thereto are contained in the footnotes of chapters IV, V, VII, VIII.

For the diplomatic steps and maneuvers culminating in the Washington Conference, we have had to rely mainly on the annual volumes of *Foreign Relations.* For the preparation of the naval limitation proposal which the American delegation offered at the opening session of the Conference, we have used two principal sources: (1) statements by Admirals R. S. Coontz, W. L. Rodgers, and W. V. Pratt, before the Senate Naval Committee, in *Hearings on the London Naval Treaty of 1930;* and (2) the manuscript diary of Colonel Theodore Roosevelt. In the dual capacity of Assistant Secretary of the Navy and chief technical adviser of the American delegation, Colonel Roosevelt had exceptional opportunities to observe and to participate in the naval phase of the Conference, and his day-by-day diary is a comprehensive record of enduring historical value. As previously noted in our Introduction, we have been able, through the good offices of President Dodds of Princeton University, to use without restriction this source hitherto unavailable to students of American naval policy.

The formal records of the Washington Conference are contained in two volumes published by the Department of State in 1922. The first is entitled *Conference on the Limitation of Armament* (text in English and French), reprinted with certain omissions as Senate Document No. 126 of the 67th Congress, 1st session. The second: *Conference on the Limitation of Armament, Subcommittees* (English and French text). In addition, the 1922 volume of *Foreign Relations,* not published until 1938, contains a large amount of new material on the more intimate negotiations which went on both inside and outside of the Conference.

We have also had access to two important unpublished sources relating to the Washington Conference. These are (1) the diary of the late Honorable Chandler P. Anderson, in the Manuscript Division of the Library of Congress, and (2) the already mentioned diary of Colonel Roosevelt.

The armament problem at the Washington Conference was handled in the plenary sessions and in a number of committees, subcommittees, and other more informal groups. The records of the plenary sessions are contained in *Conference on the Limitation of Armament.* This volume also contains the minutes of the Committee on Program and Procedure with Respect to Limitation of Armament, a sort of steering committee consisting of the heads of the five principal delegations. In this same volume are likewise found the minutes of the important Committee on Limitation of Armament which in effect was a committee of the whole. A mixed committee of delegates and technical experts, the Subcommittee of Fifteen on Naval Limitation, was set up to consider the French and Italian claims, in mid-December 1921, and the minutes of this body which met in closed session are published in the supplementary volume entitled *Subcommittees*, to which reference has already been made.

Much of the Conference business was transacted by an inner group of delegation chiefs, at times only Hughes, Balfour, and Kato. Until the publication in 1938 of *Foreign Relations, 1922*, the sole available first-hand account of the proceedings of this inner group was that in Professor Yamato Ichihashi's *Washington Conference and After* (1928). Ichihashi was Baron Kato's secretary and interpreter. The memoranda of Sir Maurice Hankey, secretary of the British delegation, now available in *Foreign Relations, 1922*, supplement and in the main corroborate Ichihashi's account. There is still additional information in the diary of Colonel Roosevelt who attended several of these inner group meetings as Mr. Hughes's technical adviser.

The Roosevelt diary also describes the functioning of another important body, the Subcommittee of Naval Advisers, composed of technical experts from the five principal delegations. Hitherto almost nothing has been publicly known of the discussions which went on within this subcommittee whose deliberations influenced several major decisions of the Conference. As chief technical adviser of the American delegation, Colonel Roosevelt presided over this body, and his diary contains the only known account of its proceedings.

Roosevelt's diary likewise illuminates for the first time the almost daily meetings of the naval advisers of the American delegation itself, a group virtually ignored in previous studies of the Conference. From the Roosevelt and Anderson diaries one can gain glimpses of the day-by-day activities of those who worked on the successive American drafts of the naval limitation and submarine treaties. And again in the Roosevelt diary there is an eye-witness impression of the meetings of the Advisory Committee which was set up as a sort of liaison between the United States delegation and the American public.

In chapter XIV we have attempted what was probably an impossible undertaking: namely, a comprehensive analysis and summary of contemporary opinion as to the politico-naval results of the Washington Conference. Our conclusions in that chapter are based on: (1) the records of the later plenary sessions of the Conference itself; (2) the senatorial debates and votes on ratification of the Washington Treaties; (3) an intensive study of the New York press; (4) a more extensive survey of the press in other sections of the country; and (5) the opinions of other important groups in the United States, in Europe, and in the Far East, as reflected in articles, pamphlets, petitions, memorials, and numerous other media of individual and group expression. For obvious reasons only a small part of this material, which runs into thousands of items, could be cited in the footnotes. It should also be remarked that because of the language difficulty we have had to rely mainly on the findings of recognized Japanese scholars for our conclusions as to the contemporary verdict in Japan.

These, in conclusion, are the principal sources and materials used in the preparation of this study, in which we have attempted to fill a serious gap in the literature of our national defense. Students of sea power and world politics have long lamented the lack of any comprehensive critique of Mahan in the light of changing world conditions, political and technological. There has hitherto been comparable lack of any detailed treatment of American naval policy and thought from the armistice of 1918 to the Washington Conference. Finally, there is compelling need today for systematic reappraisal of the naval phase and results of that Conference, from the standpoint of longer historical perspective, and in the light of new information unavailable to earlier writers. It is with the hope that we contribute something toward satisfying these needs that we offer this second volume in our series on the naval power and policy of the United States.

The Washington Treaties

I. TREATY FOR THE LIMITATION OF ARMAMENT

[*Signed at Washington, Feb. 6, 1922; ratification advised by the Senate, March 29, 1922; ratified by the President, June 9, 1923; ratifications deposited with the United States Government, Aug. 17, 1923; proclaimed, Aug. 21, 1923*]

The United States of America, the British Empire, France, Italy and Japan;

Desiring to contribute to the maintenance of the general peace, and to reduce the burdens of competition in armament;

Have resolved, with a view to accomplishing these purposes, to conclude a treaty to limit their respective naval armament, and to that end have appointed as their Plenipotentiaries:

[etc., etc.,]

Who, having communicated to each other their respective full powers, found to be in good and due form, have agreed as follows:

CHAPTER I

General Provisions Relating to the Limitation of Naval Armament

Article I

The contracting Powers agree to limit their respective naval armament as provided in the present Treaty.

Article II

The Contracting Powers may retain respectively the capital ships which are specified in Chapter II, Part 1. On the coming into force of the present Treaty, but subject to the following provisions of this Article, all other capital ships, built or building, of the United States, the British Empire and Japan shall be disposed of as prescribed in Chapter II, Part 2.

In addition to the capital ships specified in Chapter II, Part 1, the United States may complete and retain two ships of the *West Virginia* class now under construction. On the completion of these two ships the *North Dakota* and *Delaware* shall be disposed of as prescribed in Chapter II, Part 2.

The British Empire may, in accordance with the replacement table in Chapter II, Part 3, construct two new capital ships not exceeding 35,000 tons (35,560 metric tons) standard displacement each. On the completion of the said two ships the *Thunderer*, *King George V*, *Ajax* and *Centurion* shall be disposed of as prescribed in Chapter II, Part 2.

Article III

Subject to the provisions of Article II, the Contracting Powers shall abandon their respective capital-ship building programs, and no new capital ships shall be constructed or acquired by any of the Contracting Powers except replacement tonnage which may be constructed or acquired as specified in Chapter II, Part 3.

Ships which are replaced in accordance with Chapter II, Part 3, shall be disposed of as prescribed in Part 2 of that Chapter.

ARTICLE IV

The total capital-ship replacement tonnage of each of the Contracting Powers shall not exceed in standard displacement, for the United States 525,000 tons (533,400 metric tons); for the British Empire 525,000 tons (533,400 metric tons); for France 175,000 tons (177,800 metric tons); for Italy 175,000 tons (177,800 metric tons); for Japan 315,000 tons (320,040 metric tons).

ARTICLE V

No capital ship exceeding 35,000 tons (35,560 metric tons) standard displacement shall be acquired by, or constructed by, for, or within the jurisdiction of, any of the Contracting Powers.

ARTICLE VI

No capital ship of any of the Contracting Powers shall carry a gun with a calibre in excess of 16 inches (406 millimetres).

ARTICLE VII

The total tonnage for aircraft carriers of each of the Contracting Powers shall not exceed in standard displacement, for the United States 135,000 tons (137,160 metric tons); for the British Empire 135,000 tons (137,160 metric tons); for France 60,000 tons (60,960 metric tons); for Italy 60,000 tons (60,960 metric tons); for Japan 81,000 tons (82,296 metric tons).

ARTICLE VIII

The replacement of aircraft carriers shall be effected only as prescribed in Chapter II, Part 3, provided, however, that all aircraft carrier tonnage in existence or building on November 12, 1921, shall be considered experimental, and may be replaced, within the total tonnage limit prescribed in Article VII, without regard to its age.

ARTICLE IX

No aircraft carrier exceeding 27,000 tons (27,432 metric tons) standard displacement shall be acquired by, or constructed by, for or within the jurisdiction of, any of the Contracting Powers.

However, any of the Contracting Powers may, provided that its total tonnage allowance of aircraft carriers is not thereby exceeded, build not more than two aircraft carriers, each of a tonnage of not more than 33,000 tons (33,528 metric tons) standard displacement, and in order to effect economy any of the Contracting Powers may use for this purpose any two of their ships, whether constructed or in course of construction, which would otherwise be scrapped under the provisions of Article II. The armament of any aircraft carriers exceeding 27,000 tons (27,432 metric tons) standard displacement shall be in accordance with the requirements of Article X, except that the total number of guns to be carried in case any of such guns be of a calibre exceeding 6 inches (152 millimetres), except anti-aircraft guns and guns not exceeding 5 inches (127 millimetres), shall not exceed eight.

ARTICLE X

No aircraft carrier of any of the Contracting Powers shall carry a gun with a calibre in excess of 8 inches (203 millimetres). Without prejudice to the provisions of Article IX, if the armament carried includes guns exceeding 6 inches (152 millimetres) in calibre the total number of guns carried, except anti-aircraft guns and guns not exceeding 5 inches (127 millimetres), shall not exceed ten. If alternatively the armament contains no guns exceeding 6 inches (152 millimetres) in calibre, the number of guns is not limited. In either case the number of anti-aircraft guns and of guns not exceeding 5 inches (127 millimetres) is not limited.

ARTICLE XI

No vessel of war exceeding 10,000 tons (10,160 metric tons) standard displacement, other than a capital ship or aircraft carrier, shall be acquired by, or constructed by, for, or within the jurisdiction of, any of the Contracting Powers. Vessels not specifically built as fighting ships nor taken in time of peace under government control for fighting purposes, which are employed on fleet duties or as troop transports or in some other way for the purpose of assisting in the prosecution of hostilities otherwise than as fighting ships, shall not be within the limitations of this Article.

Article XII

No vessel of war of any of the Contracting Powers, hereafter laid down, other than a capital ship, shall carry a gun with a calibre in excess of 8 inches (203 millimetres).

Article XIII

Except as provided in Article IX, no ship designated in the present Treaty to be scrapped may be reconverted into a vessel of war.

Article XIV

No preparations shall be made in merchant ships in time of peace for the installation of warlike armaments for the purpose of converting such ships into vessels of war, other than the necessary stiffening of decks for the mounting of guns not exceeding 6 inch (152 millimetres) calibre.

Article XV

No vessel of war constructed within the jurisdiction of any of the Contracting Powers for a non-Contracting Power shall exceed the limitations as to displacement and armament prescribed by the present Treaty for vessels of a similar type which may be constructed by or for any of the Contracting Powers; provided, however, that the displacement for aircraft carriers constructed for a non-Contracting Power shall in no case exceed 27,000 tons (27,432 metric tons) standard displacement.

Article XVI

If the construction of any vessel of war for a non-Contracting Power is undertaken within the jurisdiction of any of the Contracting Powers, such Power shall promptly inform the other Contracting Powers of the date of the signing of the contract and the date on which the keel of the ship is laid; and shall also communicate to them the particulars relating to the ship prescribed in Chapter II, Part 3, Section I (b), (4) and (5).

Article XVII

In the event of a Contracting Power being engaged in war, such Power shall not use as a vessel of war any vessel of war which may be under construction within its jurisdiction for any other Power, or which may have been constructed within its jurisdiction for another Power and not delivered.

Article XVIII

Each of the Contracting Powers undertakes not to dispose by gift, sale or any mode of transfer of any vessel of war in such manner that such vessel may become a vessel of war in the Navy of any foreign Power.

Article XIX

The United States, the British Empire and Japan agree that the status quo at the time of the signing of the present Treaty, with regard to fortifications and naval bases, shall be maintained in their respective territories and possessions specified hereunder:

(1) The insular possessions which the United States now holds or may hereafter acquire in the Pacific Ocean, except (a) those adjacent to the coast of the United States, Alaska and the Panama Canal Zone, not including the Aleutian Islands, and (b) the Hawaiian Islands;

(2) Hongkong and the insular possessions which the British Empire now holds or may hereafter acquire in the Pacific Ocean, east of the meridian of 110° east longitude, except (a) those adjacent to the coast of Canada, (b) the Commonwealth of Australia and its Territories, and (c) New Zealand;

(3) The following insular territories and possessions of Japan in the Pacific Ocean, to wit: the Kurile Islands, the

Bonin Islands, Amami-Oshima, the Loochoo Islands, Formosa and the Pescadores, and any insular territories or possessions in the Pacific Ocean which Japan may hereafter acquire.

The maintenance of the status quo under the foregoing provisions implies that no new fortifications or naval bases shall be established in the territories and possessions specified, that no measures shall be taken to increase the existing naval facilities for the repair and maintenance of naval forces, and that no increase shall be made in the coast defences of the territories and possessions above specified. This restriction, however, does not preclude such repair and replacement of worn-out weapons and equipment as is customary in naval and military establishments in time of peace.

Article XX

The rules for determining tonnage displacement prescribed in Chapter II, Part 4, shall apply to the ships of each of the Contracting Powers.

CHAPTER II

Rules Relating to the Execution of the Treaty—Definition of Terms

Part 1

Capital Ships which may be Retained by the Contracting Powers

In accordance with Article II ships may be retained by each of the Contracting Powers as specified in this Part.

Ships which may be retained by the United States.

Name:	*Tonnage*
Maryland	32,600
California	32,300
Tennessee	32,300
Idaho	32,000
New Mexico	32,000
Mississippi	32,000
Arizona	31,400
Pennsylvania	31,400
Oklahoma	27,500
Nevada	27,500
New York	27,000
Texas	27,000
Arkansas	26,000
Wyoming	26,000
Florida	21,825
Utah	21,825
North Dakota	20,000
Delaware	20,000
Total tonnage	500,650

On the completion of the two ships of the *West Virginia* class and the scrapping of the *North Dakota* and *Delaware*, as provided in Article II, the total tonnage to be retained by the United States will be 525,850 tons.

Ships which may be retained by the British Empire.

Name:	*Tonnage*
Royal Sovereign	25,750
Royal Oak	25,750
Revenge	25,750
Resolution	25,750
Ramillies	25,750
Malaya	27,500
Valiant	27,500
Barham	27,500
Queen Elizabeth	27,500
Warspite	27,500
Benbow	25,000
Emperor of India	25,000
Iron Duke	25,000
Marlborough	25,000
Hood	41,200
Renown	26,500
Repulse	26,500
Tiger	28,500
Thunderer	22,500
King George V	23,000
Ajax	23,000
Centurion	23,000
Total tonnage	580,450

On the completion of the two new ships to be constructed and the scrapping of the *Thunderer*, *King George V*, *Ajax* and *Centurion*, as provided in Article II, the total tonnage to be retained by the British Empire will be 558,950 tons.

Ships which may be retained by France.

Name:	*Tonnage (metric tons)*
Bretagne	23,500
Lorraine	23,500
Provence	23,500
Paris	23,500
France	23,500
Jean Bart	23,500
Courbet	23,500
Condorcet	18,890
Diderot	18,890
Voltaire	18,890
Total tonnage	221,170

France may lay down new tonnage in the years 1927, 1929, and 1931, as provided in Part 3, Section II.

Ships which may be retained by Italy.

Name:	*Tonnage (metric tons)*
Andrea Doria	22,700
Caio Duilio	22,700
Conte Di Cavour	22,500
Giulio Cesare	22,500
Leonardo Da Vinci	22,500
Dante Alighieri	19,500
Roma	12,600
Napoli	12,600
Vittorio Emanuele	12,600
Regina Elena	12,600
Total tonnage	182,800

Italy may lay down new tonnage in the years 1927, 1929, and 1931, as provided in Part 3, Section II.

Ships which may be retained by Japan.

Name:	*Tonnage*
Mutsu	33,800
Nagato	33,800
Hiuga	31,260
Ise	31,260
Yamashiro	30,600
Fu-So	30,600
Kirishima	27,500
Haruna	27,500
Hiyei	27,500
Kongo	27,500
Total tonnage	301,320

Part 2

Rules for Scrapping Vessels of War

The following rules shall be observed for the scrapping of vessels of war which are to be disposed of in accordance with Articles II and III.

I. A vessel to be scrapped must be placed in such condition that it cannot be put to combatant use.

II. This result must be finally effected in any one of the following ways:

(a) Permanent sinking of the vessel;

(b) Breaking the vessel up. This shall always involve the destruction or removal of all machinery, boilers and armor, and all deck, side and bottom plating;

(c) Converting the vessel to target use exclusively. In such case all the provisions of paragraph III of this Part, except sub-paragraph (6), in so far as may be necessary to enable the ship to be used as a mobile target, and except sub-paragraph (7), must be previously complied with. Not more than one capital ship may be retained for this purpose at one time by any of the Contracting Powers.

(d) Of the capital ships which would otherwise be scrapped under the present Treaty in or after the year 1931, France and Italy may each retain two seagoing vessels for training purposes exclusively, that is, as gunnery or torpedo schools. The two vessels retained by France shall be of the *Jean Bart* class, and of those retained by Italy one shall be the *Dante Alighieri*, the other of the *Giulio Cesare* class. On retaining these ships for the purpose above stated, France and Italy respectively undertake to remove and destroy their conning towers, and not to use the said ships as vessels of war.

III. (a) Subject to the special exceptions contained in Article IX, when a vessel is due for scrapping, the first stage of scrapping, which consists in rendering a ship incapable of further warlike service, shall be immediately undertaken.

(b) A vessel shall be considered incapable of further warlike service when there shall have been removed and landed, or else destroyed in the ship:

(1) All guns and essential portions of guns, fire-control tops and revolving parts of all barbettes and turrets;
(2) All machinery for working hydraulic or electric mountings;
(3) All fire-control instruments and range-finders;
(4) All ammunition, explosives and mines;
(5) All torpedoes, war-heads and torpedo tubes;
(6) All wireless telegraphy installations;
(7) The conning tower and all side armor, or alternately all main propelling machinery; and
(8) All landing and flying-off platforms and all other aviation accessories.

IV. The periods in which scrapping of vessels is to be effected are as follows:

(a) In the case of vessels to be scrapped under the first paragraph of Article II, the work of rendering the vessels incapable of further warlike service, in accordance with paragraph III of this Part, shall be completed within six months from the coming into force of the present Treaty, and the scrapping shall be finally effected within eighteen months from such coming into force.

(b) In the case of vessels to be scrapped under the second and third paragraphs of Article II, or under Article III, the work of rendering the vessel incapable of further warlike service in accordance with paragraph III of this Part shall be commenced not later than the date of completion of its successor, and shall be finished within six months from the date of such completion. The vessel shall be finally scrapped, in accordance with paragraph II of this Part, within eighteen months from the date of completion of its successor. If, however, the completion of the new vessel be delayed, then the work of rendering the old vessel incapable of further warlike service in accordance with paragraph III of this Part shall be commenced within four years from the laying of the keel of the new vessel, and shall be finished within six months from the date on which such work was commenced, and the old vessel shall be finally scrapped in accordance with paragraph II of this Part within eighteen months from the date when the work of rendering it incapable of further warlike service was commenced.

Part 3

Replacement

The replacement of capital ships and aircraft carriers shall take place according to the rules in Section I and the tables in Section II of this Part.

Section I

Rules for Replacement

(a) Capital ships and aircraft carriers twenty years after the date of their completion may, except as otherwise provided in Article VIII and in the tables in Section II of this Part, be replaced by new construction, but within the limits prescribed in Article IV and Article VII. The keels of such new construction may, except as otherwise provided in Article VIII and in the tables in Section II of this Part, be laid down not earlier than seventeen years from the date of completion of the tonnage to be replaced, provided, however, that no capital ship tonnage, with the exception of the ships referred to in the third paragraph of Article II, and the replacement tonnage specifically mentioned in Section II of this Part, shall be laid down until ten years from November 12, 1921.

(b) Each of the Contracting Powers shall communicate promptly to each of the other Contracting Powers the following information:

(1) The names of the capital ships and aircraft carriers to be replaced by new construction;
(2) The date of governmental authorization of replacement tonnage;
(3) The date of laying the keels of replacement tonnage.
(4) The standard displacement in tons and metric tons of each new ship to be laid down, and the principal dimensions, namely, length at waterline, extreme beam at or below waterline, mean draft at standard displacement;
(5) The date of completion of each new ship and its standard displacement in tons and metric tons, and the principal dimensions, namely, length at waterline, extreme beam at or below waterline, mean draft at standard displacement, at the time of completion.

(c) In case of loss or accidental destruction of capital ships or aircraft carriers, they may immediately be replaced by new construction subject to the tonnage limits prescribed in Articles IV and VII and in conformity with the other provisions of the present Treaty, the regular replacement program being deemed to be advanced to that extent.

(d) No retained capital ships or aircraft carriers shall be reconstructed except for the purpose of providing means of defense against air and submarine attack, and subject to the following rules: The Contracting Powers may, for that purpose, equip existing tonnage with bulge or blister or anti-air attack deck protection, providing the increase of displacement thus effected does not exceed 3,000 tons (3,048 metric tons) displacement for each ship. No alterations in side armor, in calibre, number or general type of mounting of main armament shall be permitted except:

(1) in the case of France and Italy, which countries within the limits allowed for bulge may increase their armor protection and the calibre of the guns now carried on their existing capital ships so as not to exceed 16 inches (406 millimetres) and
(2) the British Empire shall be permitted to complete, in the case of the *Renown*, the alterations to armor that have already been commenced but temporarily suspended.

Section II

Replacement and Scrapping of Capital Ships

UNITED STATES

[The table is summarized as follows:

The United States was
to scrap: 15 pre-Jutland ships
totalling 227,740 tons,
11 uncompleted ships
totalling 465,800 tons,
to convert 2 uncompleted battle
cruisers of 87,000 tons
into aircraft carriers,

to retain 2 pre-Jutland ships
totalling 21,840 tons
for non-combatant purposes;
Regular replacement was to begin in 1931;
The number of ships was to be stabilized by 1936 at 15.]

THE BRITISH EMPIRE

[The table is summarized as follows:
The British Empire was
to scrap: 20 pre-Jutland ships
totalling 408,500 tons,
4 uncompleted ships
of about 180,000 tons,
to retain 2 pre-Jutland ships
totalling 39,250 tons
for non-combatant purposes;
Regular replacement was to begin in 1931;
The number of ships was to be stabilized by 1936 at 15.]

FRANCE

[The table is summarized as follows:
No ships were to be scrapped;
Replacement was to begin in 1927;
The number of ships was not fixed except that displacement of individual ships should not exceed 35,000 tons, nor total tonnage the limits imposed above.]

ITALY

[The table is summarized as follows:
No ships were to be scrapped;
Replacement was to begin in 1927;
The number of ships was not fixed except that displacement of individual ships should not exceed 35,000 tons, nor total tonnage the limits imposed above.]

JAPAN

[The table is summarized as follows:
Japan was
to scrap: 10 pre-Jutland ships
totalling 163,312 tons,
6 uncompleted ships
totalling 264,000 tons,
to abandon program for 8 ships not yet laid down;
to retain 2 pre-Jutland ships
totalling 29,530 tons
for non-combatant purposes;
Regular replacement was to begin in 1931;
The number of ships was to be stabilized by 1935 at 9.]

Note Applicable to All the Tables in Section II

The order above prescribed in which ships are to be scrapped is in accordance with their age. It is understood that when replacement begins according to the above tables the order of scrapping in the case of the ships of each of the Contracting Powers may be varied at its option; provided, however, that such Power shall scrap in each year the number of ships above stated.

Part 4

Definitions

For the purposes of the present Treaty, the following expressions are to be understood in the sense defined in this Part.

CAPITAL SHIP

A capital ship, in the case of ships hereafter built, is defined as a vessel of war, not an aircraft carrier, whose displacement exceeds 10,000 tons (10,160 metric tons) standard displacement, or which carries a gun with a calibre exceeding 8 inches (203 millimetres).

AIRCRAFT CARRIER

An aircraft carrier is defined as a vessel of war with a displacement in excess of 10,000 tons (10,160 metric tons) standard displacement designed for the specific and exclusive purpose of carrying aircraft. It must be so constructed that aircraft can be launched therefrom and landed thereon, and not designed and constructed for carrying a more powerful armament than that allowed to it under Article IX or Article X as the case may be.

STANDARD DISPLACEMENT

The standard displacement of a ship is the displacement of the ship complete, fully manned, engined, and equipped ready for sea, including all armament and ammunition, equipment, outfit, provisions and fresh water for crew, miscellaneous stores and implements of every description that are intended to be carried in war, but without fuel or reserve feed water on board.

The word "ton" in the present Treaty, except in the expression "metric tons," shall be understood to mean the ton of 2240 pounds (1016 kilos).

Vessels now completed shall retain their present rating of displacement tonnage in accordance with their national system of measurement. However, a Power expressing displacement in metric tons shall be considered for the application of the present Treaty as owning only the equivalent displacement in tons of 2240 pounds.

A vessel completed hereafter shall be rated at its displacement tonnage when in the standard condition defined herein.

CHAPTER III

MISCELLANEOUS PROVISIONS

Article XXI

If during the term of the present Treaty the requirements of the national security of any Contracting Power in respect of naval defense are, in the opinion of that Power, materially affected by any change of circumstances, the Contracting Powers will, at the request of such Power, meet in conference with a view to the reconsideration of the provisions of the Treaty and its amendment by mutual agreement.

In view of possible technical and scientific developments, the United States, after consultation with the other Contracting Powers, shall arrange for a conference of all the Contracting Powers which shall convene as soon as possible after the expiration of eight years from the coming into force of the present Treaty to consider what changes, if any, in the Treaty may be necessary to meet such developments.

Article XXII

Whenever any Contracting Power shall become engaged in a war which in its opinion affects the naval defense of its national security, such Power may after notice to the other Contracting Powers suspend for the period of hostilities its obligations under the present Treaty other than those under Articles XIII and XVII, provided that such Power shall notify the other Contracting Powers that the emergency is of such a character as to require such suspension.

The remaining Contracting Powers shall in such case consult together with a view to agreement as to what temporary modifications if any should be made in the Treaty as between themselves. Should such consultation not produce agreement, duly made in accordance with the constitutional methods of the respective Powers, any one of said Contracting Powers may, by giving notice to the other Contracting Powers, suspend for the period of hostilities its obligations under the present Treaty, other than those under Articles XIII and XVII.

On the cessation of hostilities the Contracting Powers will meet in conference to consider what modifications, if any, should be made in the provisions of the present Treaty.

Article XXIII

The present Treaty shall remain in force until December 31, 1936, and in case none of the Contracting Powers shall have given notice two years before that date of its intention to terminate the Treaty, it shall continue in force until the expiration of two years from the date on which notice of termination shall be given by one of the Contracting Powers, whereupon the Treaty shall terminate as regards all the Contracting Powers. Such notice shall be communicated in writing to the Government of the United States, which shall immediately transmit a certified copy of the notification to the other Powers and inform them of the date on which it was received. The notice shall be deemed to have been given and shall take effect on that date. In the event of notice of termination being given by the Government of the United States, such notice shall be given to the diplomatic representatives at Washington of the other Contracting Powers, and the notice shall be deemed to have been given and shall take effect on the date of the communication made to the said diplomatic representatives.

Within one year of the date on which a notice of termination by any Power has taken effect, all the Contracting Powers shall meet in conference.

ARTICLE XXIV

The present Treaty shall be ratified by the Contracting Powers in accordance with their respective constitutional methods and shall take effect on the date of the deposit of all the ratifications, which shall take place at Washington as soon as possible. The Government of the United States will transmit to the other Contracting Powers a certified copy of the procès-verbal of the deposit of ratifications.

The present Treaty, of which the French and English texts are both authentic, shall remain deposited in the archives of the Government of the United States, and duly certified copies thereof shall be transmitted by that Government to the other Contracting Powers.

In faith whereof the above-named Plenipotentiaries have signed the present Treaty.

II. TREATY RELATING TO THE USE OF SUBMARINES AND NOXIOUS GASES IN WARFARE

[*Signed at Washington, Feb. 6, 1922; ratification advised by the Senate, March 29, 1922; ratifications subsequently received from the British Empire, Italy, and Japan, but none from France; so the Treaty never went into force*]

The United States of America, the British Empire, France, Italy and Japan, hereinafter referred to as the Signatory Powers, desiring to make more effective the rules adopted by civilized nations for the protection of the lives of neutrals and noncombatants at sea in time of war, and to prevent the use in war of noxious gases and chemicals, have determined to conclude a Treaty to this effect, and have appointed as their Plenipotentiaries:

[etc., etc.]

Who, having communicated their Full Powers, found in good and due form, have agreed as follows:

ARTICLE I

The Signatory Powers declare that among the rules adopted by civilized nations for the protection of the lives of neutrals and noncombatants at sea in time of war, the following are to be deemed an established part of international law;

(1) A merchant vessel must be ordered to submit to visit and search to determine its character before it can be seized.

A merchant vessel must not be attacked unless it refuse to submit to visit and search after warning, or to proceed as directed after seizure.

A merchant vessel must not be destroyed unless the crew and passengers have been first placed in safety.

(2) Belligerent submarines are not under any circumstances exempt from the universal rules above stated; and if a submarine can not capture a merchant vessel in conformity with these rules the existing law of nations requires it to desist from attack and from seizure and to permit the merchant vessel to proceed unmolested.

Article II

The Signatory Powers invite all other civilized Powers to express their assent to the foregoing statement of established law so that there may be a clear public understanding throughout the world of the standards of conduct by which the public opinion of the world is to pass judgment upon future belligerents.

Article III

The Signatory Powers, desiring to insure the enforcement of the humane rules of existing law declared by them with respect to attacks upon and the seizure and destruction of merchant ships, further declare that any person in the service of any Power who shall violate any of those rules, whether or not such person is under orders of a governmental superior, shall be deemed to have violated the laws of war and shall be liable to trial and punishment as if for an act of piracy and may be brought to trial before the civil or military authorities of any Power within the jurisdiction of which he may be found.

Article IV

The Signatory Powers recognize the practical impossibility of using submarines as commerce destroyers without violating, as they were violated in the recent war of 1914-1918, the requirements universally accepted by civilized nations for the protection of the lives of neutrals and noncombatants, and to the end that the prohibition of the use of submarines as commerce destroyers shall be universally accepted as a part of the law of nations, they now accept that prohibition as henceforth binding as between themselves and they invite all other nations to adhere thereto.

Article V

The use in war of asphyxiating, poisonous or other gases, and all analogous liquids, materials or devices, having been justly condemned by the general opinion of the civilized world and a prohibition of such use having been declared in treaties to which a majority of the civilized Powers are parties,

The Signatory Powers, to the end that this prohibition shall be universally accepted as a part of international law binding alike the conscience and practice of nations, declare their assent to such prohibition, agree to be bound thereby as between themselves and invite all other civilized nations to adhere thereto.

Article VI

The present Treaty shall be ratified as soon as possible in accordance with the constitutional methods of the Signatory Powers and shall take effect on the deposit of all the ratifications, which shall take place at Washington.

The Government of the United States will transmit to all the Signatory Powers a certified copy of the procès-verbal of the deposit of ratifications.

The present Treaty, of which the French and English texts are both authentic, shall remain deposited in the Archives of the Government of the United States, and duly certified copies thereof will be transmitted by that Government to each of the Signatory Powers.

Article VII

The Government of the United States will further transmit to each of the Non-Signatory Powers a duly certified copy of the present Treaty and invite its adherence thereto.

Any Non-Signatory Power may adhere to the present Treaty by communicating an Instrument of Adherence to the Government of the United States, which will thereupon transmit to each of the Signatory and Adhering Powers a certified copy of each Instrument of Adherence.

In faith whereof, the above named Plenipotentiaries have signed the present Treaty. . . .

III. TREATY ["FOUR POWER PACT"] RELATING TO INSULAR POSSESSIONS AND INSULAR DOMINIONS IN THE PACIFIC OCEAN

[*Signed at Washington, Dec. 13, 1921; ratification advised by the Senate, with a reservation and understanding, March 24, 1922; ratified by the President, June 9, 1923; ratifications deposited with the United States Government, Aug. 17, 1923; proclaimed, Aug. 21, 1923*]

The United States of America, the British Empire, France and Japan,

With a view to the preservation of the general peace and the maintenance of their rights in relation to their insular possessions and insular dominions in the region of the Pacific Ocean,

Have determined to conclude a Treaty to this effect and have appointed as their Plenipotentiaries:

[etc., etc.]

Who, having communicated their Full Powers, found in good and due form, have agreed as follows:

I

The High Contracting Parties agree as between themselves to respect their rights in relation to their insular possessions and insular dominions in the region of the Pacific Ocean.

If there should develop between any of the High Contracting Parties a controversy arising out of any Pacific question and involving their said rights which is not satisfactorily settled by diplomacy and is likely to affect the harmonious accord now happily subsisting between them, they shall invite the other High Contracting Parties to a joint conference to which the whole subject will be referred for consideration and adjustment.

II

If the said rights are threatened by the aggressive action of any other Power, the High Contracting Parties shall communicate with one another fully and frankly in order to arrive at an understanding as to the most efficient measures to be taken, jointly or separately, to meet the exigencies of the particular situation.

III

This Treaty shall remain in force for ten years from the time it shall take effect, and after the expiration of said period it shall continue to be in force subject to the right of any of the High Contracting Parties to terminate it upon twelve months' notice.

IV

This Treaty shall be ratified as soon as possible in accordance with the constitutional methods of the High Contracting Parties and shall take effect on the deposit of ratifications, which shall take place at Washington, and thereupon the agreement between Great Britain and Japan, which was concluded at London on July 13, 1911, shall terminate. The Government of the United States will transmit to all the Signatory Powers a certified copy of the *procès-verbal* of the deposit of ratifications.

The present Treaty, in French and in English, shall remain deposited in the Archives of the Government of the United States, and duly certified copies thereof will be transmitted by that Government to each of the Signatory Powers.

In faith whereof, etc.

[signatures]

IV. DECLARATION ACCOMPANYING THE ABOVE FOUR-POWER TREATY

In signing the Treaty this day between The United States of America, The British Empire, France and Japan, it is declared to be the understanding and intent of the Signatory Powers:

1. That the Treaty shall apply to the Mandated Islands in the Pacific Ocean; provided, however, that the making of the Treaty shall not be deemed to be an assent on the part of the United States of America to the mandates and shall not preclude agreements between The United States of America and the Mandatory Powers respectively in relation to the mandated islands.

2. That the controversies to which the second paragraph of Article I refers shall not be taken to embrace questions which according to the principles of international law lie exclusively within the domestic jurisdiction of the respective Powers.

Washington, D.C. December 13, 1921.

[signatures]

V. SENATE RESERVATION TO THE FOUR-POWER PACIFIC TREATY

The United States understands that under the statement in the preamble and under the terms of this Treaty there is no commitment to armed force, no alliance, no obligation to join in any defense.

VI. SUPPLEMENTARY FOUR-POWER TREATY

[*Signed at Washington, Feb. 6, 1922; ratification advised by the Senate, with a reservation and understanding, March 27, 1922; ratified by the President, June 9, 1923; ratifications deposited with the United States Government, Aug. 17, 1923; proclaimed, Aug. 21, 1923*]

The United States of America, the British Empire, France and Japan have, through their respective Plenipotentiaries, agreed upon the following stipulations supplementary to the Quadruple Treaty signed at Washington on December 13, 1921:

The term "insular possessions and insular dominions" used in the aforesaid Treaty shall, in its application to Japan, include only Karafuto (or the Southern portion of the island of Sakhalin), Formosa and the Pescadores, and the islands under the mandate of Japan.

The present agreement shall have the same force and effect as the said Treaty to which it is supplementary.

The provisions of Article IV of the aforesaid Treaty of December 13, 1921, relating to ratification shall be applicable to the present Agreement, which in French and English shall remain deposited in the Archives of the Government of the United States, and duly certified copies thereof shall be transmitted by that Government to each of the other Contracting Powers.

In faith whereof. . . .

[signatures]

VII. SENATE RESERVATION TO THE SUPPLEMENTARY FOUR-POWER TREATY

[repeats verbatim the declaration (number 4 above) signed in connection with the principal Four Power Treaty (number 3 above)]

VIII. TREATY ["NINE-POWER TREATY"] RELATING TO PRINCIPLES AND POLICIES TO BE FOLLOWED IN MATTERS CONCERNING CHINA

[*Signed at Washington, Feb. 6, 1922; ratification advised by the Senate, March 30, 1922; ratified by the President, June 9, 1923; ratifications deposited with the United States Government, Aug. 5, 1925; proclaimed, Aug. 5, 1925*]

The United States of America, Belgium, the British Empire, China, France, Italy, Japan, the Netherlands and Portugal;

Desiring to adopt a policy designed to stabilize conditions in the Far East, to safeguard the rights and interests of China, and to promote intercourse between China and the other Powers upon the basis of equality of opportunity:

Have resolved to conclude a treaty for that purpose and to that end have appointed as their respective Plenipotentiaries;

[etc., etc.]

Who, having communicated to each other their full powers, found to be in good and due form, have agreed as follows:

Article I

The Contracting Powers, other than China, agree:

(1) To respect the sovereignty, the independence, and the territorial and administrative integrity of China;

(2) To provide the fullest and most unembarrassed opportunity to China to develop and maintain for herself an effective and stable government;

(3) To use their influence for the purpose of effectually establishing and maintaining the principle of equal opportunity for the commeroe and industry of all nations throughout the territory of China;

(4) To refrain from taking advantage of conditions in China in order to seek special rights or privileges which would abridge the rights of subjects or citizens of friendly States, and from countenancing action inimical to the security of such States.

Article II

The Contracting Powers agree not to enter into any treaty, agreement, arrangement, or understanding, either with one another, or, individually or collectively, with any Power or Powers, which would infringe or impair the principles stated in Article I.

Article III

With a view to applying more effectually the principles of the Open Door or equality of opportunity in China for the trade and industry of all nations, the Contracting Powers, other than China, agree that they will not seek, nor support their respective nationals in seeking;

(a) any arrangement which might purport to establish in favour of their interests any general superiority of rights with respect to commercial or economic development in any designated region of China;

(b) any such monopoly or preference as would deprive the nationals of any other Power of the right of undertaking any legitimate trade or industry in China, or of participating with the Chinese Government, or with any local authority, in any category of public enterprise, or which by reason of its scope, duration or geographical extent is calculated to frustrate the practical application of the principle of equal opportunity.

It is understood that the foregoing stipulations of this Article are not to be so construed as to prohibit the acquisition of such properties or rights as may be necessary to the conduct of a particular commercial, industrial, or financial undertaking or to the encouragement of invention and research.

China undertakes to be guided by the principles stated in the foregoing stipulations of this Article in dealing with applications for economic rights and privileges from Governments and nationals of all foreign countries, whether parties to the present Treaty or not.

Article IV

The Contracting Powers agree not to support any agreements by their respective nationals with each other designed to create Spheres of Influence or to provide for the enjoyment of mutually exclusive opportunities in designated parts of Chinese territory.

Article V

China agrees that, throughout the whole of the railways in China, she will not exercise or permit unfair discrimination of any kind. In particular there shall be no discrimination whatever, direct or indirect, in respect of charges or of facilities on the ground of the nationality of passengers or the countries from which or to which they are proceeding, or the origin or ownership of goods or the country from which or to which they are consigned, or the nationality or ownership of the ship or other means of conveying such passengers or goods before or after their transport on the Chinese Railways.

The Contracting Powers, other than China, assume a corresponding obligation in respect of any of the aforesaid railways over which they or their nationals are in a position to exercise any control in virtue of any concession, special agreement or otherwise.

Article VI

The Contracting Powers, other than China, agree fully to respect China's rights as a neutral in time of war to which China is not a party; and China declares that when she is a neutral she will observe the obligations of neutrality.

Article VII

The Contracting Powers agree that, whenever a situation arises which in the opinion of any one of them involves the application of the stipulations of the present Treaty, and renders desirable discussion of such application, there shall be full and frank communication between the Contracting Powers concerned.

Article VIII

Powers not signatory to the present Treaty, which have Governments recognized by the Signatory Powers and which have treaty relations with China, shall be invited to adhere to the present Treaty. To this end the Government of the United States will make the necessary communications to Non-Signatory Powers and will inform the Contracting Powers of the replies received. Adherence by any Power shall become effective on receipt of notice thereof by the Government of the United States.

Article IX

The present Treaty shall be ratified by the Contracting Powers in accordance with their respective constitutional methods and shall take effect on the date of the deposit of all the ratifications, which shall take place at Washington as soon as possible. The Government of the United States will transmit to the other Contracting Powers a certified copy of the procès-verbal of the deposit of ratifications.

The present Treaty, of which the French and English texts are both authentic, shall remain deposited in the archives of the Government of the United States, and duly certified copies thereof shall be transmitted by that Government to the other Contracting Powers.

In faith whereof etc.

[signatures]

IX. A TREATY BETWEEN THE NINE POWERS RELATING TO CHINESE CUSTOMS TARIFF

[text omitted]

LIST OF RESOLUTIONS ADOPTED BY THE WASHINGTON CONFERENCE

[text omitted]

No. 1. Resolution for a Commission of Jurists to Consider Amendment of Laws of War.
No. 2. Resolution Limiting Jurisdiction of Commission of Jurists Provided in Resolution No. 1.
No. 3. Resolution Regarding a Board of Reference for Far Eastern Questions.
No. 4. Resolution Regarding Extraterritoriality in China.
No. 5. Resolution Regarding Foreign Postal Agencies in China.
No. 6. Resolution Regarding Armed Forces in China.
No. 7. Resolution Regarding Radio Stations in China and Accompanying Declarations.
No. 8. Resolution Regarding Unification of Railways in China and Accompanying Declaration by China.
No. 9. Resolution Regarding the Reduction of Chinese Military Forces.
No. 10. Resolution Regarding Existing Commitments of China or with Respect to China.
No. 11. Resolution Regarding the Chinese Eastern Railway, Approved by the Powers Including China.
No. 12. Resolution Regarding the Chinese Eastern Railway, Approved by the Powers other than China.

INDEX

Index